CLYMER®
MANUALS

HONDA

TWINSTAR, REBEL 250 & NIGHTHAWK 250
1978-2016

WHAT'S IN YOUR TOOLBOX?

More information available at Clymer.com
Phone: 805-498-6703

Haynes Publishing Group
Sparkford Nr Yeovil
Somerset BA22 7JJ England

Haynes North America, Inc
859 Lawrence Drive
Newbury Park
California 91320 USA

ISBN-10:1-62092-361-0
ISBN-13: 978-1-62092-361-0
Library of Congress: 2018966650

Author: Ed Scott
Cover: Mark Clifford Photography, Los Angeles, California (www.markclifford.com)

Common spark plug conditions

NORMAL
Symptoms: Brown to grayish-tan color and slight electrode wear. Correct heat range for engine and operating conditions.
Recommendation: When new spark plugs are installed, replace with plugs of the same heat range.

WORN
Symptoms: Rounded electrodes with a small amount of deposits on the firing end. Normal color. Causes hard starting in damp or cold weather and poor fuel economy.
Recommendation: Plugs have been left in the engine too long. Replace with new plugs of the same heat range. Follow the recommended maintenance schedule.

TOO HOT
Symptoms: Blistered, white insulator, eroded electrode and absence of deposits. Results in shortened plug life.
Recommendation: Check for the correct plug heat range, over-advanced ignition timing, lean fuel mixture, intake manifold vacuum leaks, sticking valves and insufficient engine cooling.

CARBON DEPOSITS
Symptoms: Dry sooty deposits indicate a rich mixture or weak ignition. Causes misfiring, hard starting and hesitation.
Recommendation: Make sure the plug has the correct heat range. Check for a clogged air filter or problem in the fuel system or engine management system. Also check for ignition system problems.

PREIGNITION
Symptoms: Melted electrodes. Insulators are white, but may be dirty due to misfiring or flying debris in the combustion chamber. Can lead to engine damage.
Recommendation: Check for the correct plug heat range, over-advanced ignition timing, lean fuel mixture, insufficient engine cooling and lack of lubrication.

ASH DEPOSITS
Symptoms: Light brown deposits encrusted on the side or center electrodes or both. Derived from oil and/or fuel additives. Excessive amounts may mask the spark, causing misfiring and hesitation during acceleration.
Recommendation: If excessive deposits accumulate over a short time or low mileage, install new valve guide seals to prevent seepage of oil into the combustion chambers. Also try changing gasoline brands.

HIGH SPEED GLAZING
Symptoms: Insulator has yellowish, glazed appearance. Indicates that combustion chamber temperatures have risen suddenly during hard acceleration. Normal deposits melt to form a conductive coating. Causes misfiring at high speeds.
Recommendation: Install new plugs. Consider using a colder plug if driving habits warrant.

OIL DEPOSITS
Symptoms: Oily coating caused by poor oil control. Oil is leaking past worn valve guides or piston rings into the combustion chamber. Causes hard starting, misfiring and hesitation.
Recommendation: Correct the mechanical condition with necessary repairs and install new plugs.

DETONATION
Symptoms: Insulators may be cracked or chipped. Improper gap setting techniques can also result in a fractured insulator tip. Can lead to piston damage.
Recommendation: Make sure the fuel anti-knock values meet engine requirements. Use care when setting the gaps on new plugs. Avoid lugging the engine.

GAP BRIDGING
Symptoms: Combustion deposits lodge between the electrodes. Heavy deposits accumulate and bridge the electrode gap. The plug ceases to fire, resulting in a dead cylinder.
Recommendation: Locate the faulty plug and remove the deposits from between the electrodes.

MECHANICAL DAMAGE
Symptoms: May be caused by a foreign object in the combustion chamber or the piston striking an incorrect reach (too long) plug. Causes a dead cylinder and could result in piston damage.
Recommendation: Repair the mechanical damage. Remove the foreign object from the engine and/or install the correct reach plug.

CONTENTS

QUICK REFERENCE DATA

TUNE-UP SPECIFICATIONS

Compression pressure (at sea level)	
Rebel 250 and Nighthawk 250 models	
except 1996-on Rebel 250	14 ± 2 kg/cm2 (199 ± 28 psi)
1996-on Rebel 250	1,100 kPa (159 psi) @ 600 rpm
All models except Rebel 250 and Nighthawk 250	12 ± 2 kg/cm2 (170 ± 28 psi)
Spark plug type	
1978 -1981	
Standard heat range	ND U22FS or NGK C7HS
Cold weather*	ND U20FS or NGK C6H
Extended high-speed riding	ND U24FB or NGK C9H
1982-1983	
Standard heat range	ND U22FSR-U or NGK CR7HS
Cold weather*	ND U20FSR-U or NGK CR6HS
Extended high-speed riding	ND U24FSR-U or NGK CR9HS
1985-1986	
Standard heat range	ND U20FSR-U or NGK CR6HS
Extended high-speed riding	ND U22FSR-U or NGK CR7HS
1991-on	
Standard heat range	ND U20FSR-U or NGK CR6HSA
Cold weather*	ND U16FSR-U or NGK CR5HSA
Extended high-speed riding	ND U22FSR-U or NGK CR7HSA
Spark plug gap	0.6-0.7 mm (0.024-0.028 in.)
Contact breaker point gap	0.3-0.4 mm (0.012-0.016 in.)
Ignition timing mark	
CM185T	F-1 @ 1,200 rpm
CM200T	F @ 1,200 rpm
CM250C, 1985-1987 Rebel 250	F @ 1,300 rpm
1996-on Rebel 250	F @ 1,400 rpm
Nighthawk 250	F @ 1,500 rpm
Idle speed	
CM185T, CM200T	1,200 rpm
250C, 1985-1987 Rebel 250	1,300 rpm
1996-on Rebel 250	1,400 rpm ± 100 rpm
Nighthawk 250	1,500 rpm ± 100 rpm

* Cold weather climate – below 5° ± C (41° ± F)

REPLACEMENT BULBS

Item	1978-1980	1981-2000	2001-on
Headlight	6V 25/35W (1978-1979)	12V 50/35W	12V 60/55W
	6V 36.5/35W (1980)		
Tail/brakelight	6V 5.3/25W	12V 8/27W	12V 8/27W
Turn signals			
Front and rear	6V 17W12V 23/23W	12V 23/23W	
Instrument lights	6V 3W12V 3.4W	12V 3.4W	
Indicator lights	6V 1.7W12V 3.4W	12V 3.4W	
License plate lights	--	12V 8W	12V 8W

ENGINE TORQUE SPECIFICATIONS

Item	N m	ft-lb
Engine mounting bolts		
185-200 models		
8 mm flange bolt	20-25	14.5-18
10 mm flange bolt (front)	33-43	45-60
250 models except 1996-on Rebel 250		
8 mm flange bolt	24-30	17-22
10 mm flange bolt (front)	55-70	40-51
10 mm flange bolt (rear)	80-100	59-73
1996-on Rebel 250		
10 mm flange bolt (front)	62	46
10 mm flange bolt (rear)	88	65
Cylinder head		
Rebel 250 and Nighthawk 250 models except 1996-on Rebel 250		
Bolts	10-14	7-10
Nuts	21-25	15-18
1996-on Rebel 250		
Cylinder head bolts	12	106 in.-lb.
Cylinder head bolts/camshaft holder nuts	23	17
All models except Rebel 250 and Nighthawk 250		
Bolts	10-14	7-10
Nuts	16-20	12-15
Cam sprocket bolts		
All models except 1996-on Rebel 250	17-23	12-17
1996-on Rebel 250	20	177 in.-lb.
Alternator rotor bolts		
185 models	45-50	33-36
200-250 models except 1996-on Rebel 250	55-65	40-47
1996-on Rebel 250	59	43
Oil pump and clutch drive locknut (primary drive gear locknut)		
All models except 1996-on Rebel 250	46-60	33-43
1996-on Rebel 250	53	39
Crankshaft center bearing support bolts and nuts		
All models except 1996-on Rebel 250	10-14	7-10
1996-on Rebel 250		
Bolts	23	17
Nut	12	106 in.-lb.
Crankcase bolts		
All models except 1996-on Rebel 250	10-14	7-10
1996-on Rebel 250	Not specified	

TIRE PRESSURE (COLD)*

Load	Pressure
Rebel 250 and Nighthawk 250	
except 1996-on Rebel 250	
Rider only	
Front and rear	2.0 kg/cm2 (29 psi)
Rider and passenger	
Front and rear	2.0 kg/cm2 (29 psi)
1996-on Rebel 250	
Up to 200 lbs (90 kg)	
Front and rear	2.0 kg/cm2 (29 psi)
All models except Rebel 250 and Nighthawk	
Up to 200 lbs (90 kg)	
Front	1.75 kg/cm2 (25 psi)
Rear	2.0 kg/cm2 (29 psi)

TIRE PRESSURE (COLD)* (continued)

Load	Pressure
Maximum load limit**	
Front	1.75 kg/cm2 (25 psi)
Rear	2.25 kg/cm2 (32 psi)

* Recommended air pressure for factory equipped tires. After market tires may require different air pressure.

** Maximum load limit includes total weight of accessories, rider(s) and luggage. Maximum load limit is 156 kg (345 lbs)

FRAME TORQUE SPECIFICATIONS

Item	N m	ft-lb
Front Axle nut		
185	40-50	29-36
200	50-70	36-50
Front axle		
250 models except 1996-on Rebel 250	55-70	40-51
1996-on Rebel 250	62	46
Front axle holder nuts		
Disc brakes		
Caliper mounting bolts		
All models except 1996-on Rebel 250	24-30	17-22
1996-on Rebel 250	30	22
Caliper pad pin bolt		
All models except 1996-on Rebel 250	15-20	10-14
1996-on Rebel 250	18	159 in.-lbs.
Brake system union bolts		
All models except 1996-on Rebel 250	25-30	18-22
1996-on Rebel 250	34	25
Brake disc bolts		
All models except 1996-on Rebel 250	37-43	27-31
1996-on Rebel 250	Not specified	
Handlebar holder bolts		
1978-1983	20-25	14-18
1985-on except 1996 Rebel 250	20-30	14-22
1996-on Rebel 250	Not specified	
Fork bridge bolts		
Upper		
1978-1983	18-23	13-17
1985-on except 1996-on Rebel 250	9-13	80-115 in.-lbs.
1996-on Rebel 250	11	97 in.-lbs
Lower		
1978-1983	18-23	13-17
1985-on except 1996-on Rebel 250	30-40	22-29
1996-on Rebel 250	34	25
Fork cap bolt		
1978-1983	25-30	18-21
1985-on except 1996-on Rebel 250	15-30	11-21
1996-on Rebel 250	22	16
Steering stem nut		
All models except 1996-on Rebel 250	60-70	43-51
1996-on Rebel 250	74	54
Rear axle nut		
1978-1981	40-50	26-36
1982	55-65	40-75
1985-on except 1996-on Rebel 250	80-100	58-72
1996-on Rebel 250	88	65

ENGINE TORQUE SPECIFICATIONS (continued)

Item	N m	ft-lb
Brake torque link nut		
All models except 1996-on Rebel 250	20-25	14-18
1996-on Rebel 250	Not specified	
Shock absorber mounting nuts		
All models except 1996-on Rebel 250	30-40	22-29
1996-on 250 Rebel		
Upper mount	26	20
Lower mount	42	31
Driven sprocket nut		
1978-1983	55-65	40-47
1985-on except 1996-on Rebel 250	60-70	43-51
1996-on Rebel 250	64	48
Swing arm pivot bolt/nut		
1978-1983	50-60	36-43
1985-on except 1996-on Rebel 250	50-70	36-50
1996-on Rebel 250	88	65

DRIVE CHAIN REPLACEMENT NUMBERS

1978-1983	No. 428-HD 112
1985-1987	
Diado	No. 420VC6 108LE
Takasago	No. RK 520MO-Z2X 108LE
Nighthawk 250	
Diado	No. 520VC6 106LE
Takasago	No. RK 520MO-Z9 106LE
Rebel 250 (1996-on)	
Diado	No. 520VC5 106LE
Takasago	No. RK 520MO-Z9 106LE

FLUIDS

Engine oil (at oil change)	
185 cc	1.4 liter (1.5 U.S. qt.)
200 cc	1.3 liter (1.4 U.S. qt.)
250 cc	1.5 liter (1.6 U.S. qt.)
Fork oil	
185 cc	98 cc (3.3 oz.)
200 cc	115 cc (3.9 oz.)
250 cc (1985-on)	238 cc (8.1 oz.)
Fuel	
All models	10.5 liters (2.8 U.S. gal., 2.31 Imp. gal.)

CLYMER®
MANUALS

HONDA

TWINSTAR, REBEL 250 & NIGHTHAWK 250
1978-2016

CHAPTER ONE

GENERAL INFORMATION

This detailed comprehensive manual covers the Honda Twinstar from 1978-1987, and 1996-2016, and the Nighthawk 250 from 1991-2002. There were no models produced within this motorcycle series in 1984 or from 1988-1990.

There are three Rebel 250 models: the CMX250C, CMX250CD (Limited) and the CMX250X. They differ only in appearance (striping, nameplates., etc.). There are no mechanical differences between these models.

The expert text gives complete information on maintenance, tune-up, repair and overhaul. Hundreds of photos and drawings guide you through every step. The book includes all you will need to know to keep your Honda running right.

A shop manual is a reference. You want to be able to find information fast. As in all Clymer books, this one is designed with you in mind. All chapters are thumb tabbed. Important items are extensively indexed at the rear of the book. All procedures, tables, photos, etc., in this manual are for the reader who may be working on the bike for the first time. All the most frequently used specifications and capacities are summarized in the Quick Reference Data pages at the front of the book.

Keep the book handy in your tool box. It will help you better understand how your bike runs, lower repair costs and generally improve your satisfaction with the bike.

Table 1 is at the end of this chapter.

MANUAL ORGANIZATION

All dimensions and capacities are expressed in English units familiar to U.S. mechanics as well as in metric units.

This chapter provides general information and discusses equipment and tools useful both for preventive maintenance and troubleshooting.

Chapter Two provides methods and suggestions for quick and accurate diagnosis and repair of problems. Troubleshooting procedures discuss typical symptoms and logical methods to pinpoint the trouble.

Chapter Three explains all periodic lubrication and routine maintenance necessary to keep the Honda running well. Chapter Three also includes recommended tune-up procedures, eliminating the need to constantly consult chapters on the various assemblies.

Subsequent chapters describe specific systems such as the engine, clutch, transmission, fuel, exhaust, suspension and brakes. Each chapter provides disassembly, repair and assembly procedures in simple step-by-step form.

If a repair is impractical for a home mechanic, it is so indicated. It is usually faster and less expensive to take such repairs to a dealer or competent repair shop. Specifications concerning a particular system are included at the end of the appropriate chapter.

Some of the procedures in this manual specify special tools. In most cases, the tool is illustrated either in actual use or alone. Well equipped mechanics may find they can substitute similar tools already on hand or can fabricate their own.

NOTES, CAUTIONS AND WARNINGS

The terms NOTE, CAUTION and WARNING have specific meanings in this manual. A NOTE provides additional information to make a step or procedure easier or clearer. Disregarding a NOTE could cause inconvenience, but would not cause equipment damage or personal injury.

A CAUTION emphasizes areas where equipment damage could occur. Disregarding a CAUTION could cause permanent mechanical damage; however, personal injury is unlikely.

A WARNING emphasizes areas where personal injury or even death could result from negligence. Mechanical damage may also occur. WARNINGS *are to be taken seriously*. In some cases, serious injury or death has resulted from disregarding similar warnings.

Throughout this manual keep in mind 2 conventions. "Front" refers to the front of the bike. The front of any component, such as the engine, is the end which faces toward the front of the bike. The "left-" and "right-hand" sides refer to the position of the parts as viewed by a rider sitting on the seat facing forward. For example, the throttle control is on the right-hand side and the clutch lever is on the left-hand side. These rules are simple, but even experienced mechanics occasionally become disoriented.

SERVICE HINTS

Most of the service procedures covered are straightforward and can be performed by anyone reasonably handy with tools. However, you should consider your own capabilities carefully before attempting any operation involving major disassembly of the engine.

Some operations, for example, require the use of a press. It would be wiser to have these performed by a shop equipped for such work, rather than trying to do the job yourself with makeshift equipment. Other procedures require precise measurements. Unless you have the skills and equipment required, it would be better to have a qualified repair shop make the measurements for you.

There are many items available that can be used on your hands before and after working on your bike. A little preparation prior to getting "all greased up" will help when cleaning up later.

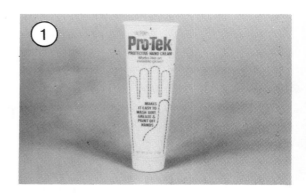

Before starting out, work Vaseline, soap or a product such as Pro-Tek Invisible Glove (**Figure 1**) onto your forearms, into your hands and under your fingernails and cuticles. This will make cleanup a lot easier.

For cleanup, use a waterless hand soap such as Sta-Lube and then finish up with powdered Boraxo and a fingernail brush.

Repairs go much faster and easier if the bike is clean before you begin work. There are special cleaners, such as Gunk or Bel-Ray Degreaser, for washing the engine and related parts. Just spray or brush on the cleaning solution, let it stand, then rinse it away with a garden hose. Clean all oily or greasy parts with cleaning solvent as you remove them.

> *WARNING*
> *Never use gasoline as a cleaning agent. It presents an extreme fire hazard. Be sure to work in a well-ventilated area when using cleaning solvent. Keep a fire extinguisher, rated for gasoline fires, handy in any case.*

Special tools are required for some repair procedures. These may be purchased from a dealer or motorcycle shop, rented from a tool rental dealer o fabricated by a mechanic or machinist (often at considerable savings).

Much of the labor time charged for by mechanics is for the removal and disassembly of other parts to reach the defective unit. It is usually possible to perform the preliminary operations yourself and then take the defective unit to the dealer for repair.

Once you have decided to tackle the job yourself, read the entire section in this manual which pertains to it, making sure you have identified the proper one. Study the illustrations and text until you have a good idea of what is involved in completing the job satisfactorily. If special tools or replacement parts are required, make arrangements to get them before you start. It is frustrating and time-consuming to get partly into a job and then be unable to complete it.

Simple wiring checks can be easily made at home, but knowledge of electronics is almost a necessity for performing tests with complicated electronic testing gear.

During disassembly of parts keep a few general cautions in mind. Force is rarely needed to get things apart. If parts are a tight fit, such as a bearing in a case, there is usually a tool designed to separate them. Never use a screwdriver to pry parts with machined surfaces such as crankcase halves. You will mar the surfaces and end up with leaks.

Make diagrams (or take a Polaroid picture) wherever similar-appearing parts are found. For instance, crankcase bolts are often not the same length. You may think you can remember where everything came from, but mistakes are costly. There is also the possibility you may be sidetracked and not return to work for days or even weeks, in which interval carefully laid out parts may have become disturbed.

Tag all similar internal parts for location and mark all mating parts for position. Record number and thickness of any shims as they are removed. Small parts such as bolts can be identified by placing them in plastic sandwich bags. Seal and label them with masking tape.

Wiring should be tagged with masking tape and marked as each wire is removed. Again, do not rely on memory alone.

Protect finished surfaces from physical damage or corrosion. Keep gasoline and hydraulic brake fluid off plastic parts and painted surfaces.

Frozen or very tight bolts and screws can often be loosened by soaking with penetrating oil, such as WD-40 or Liquid Wrench, then sharply striking the bolt head a few times with a hammer and punch (or screwdriver for screws). Avoid heat unless absolutely necessary, since it may melt, warp or remove the temper from many parts.

No parts, except those assembled with a press fit, require unusual force during assembly. If a part is hard to remove or install, find out why before proceeding.

Cover all openings after removing parts to keep dirt, small tools, etc., from falling in.

When assembling 2 parts, start all fasteners, then tighten evenly.

Wiring connections and brake components should be kept clean and free of grease and oil.

When assembling parts, be sure all shims and washers are installed exactly as they came out.

Whenever a rotating part butts against a stationary part, look for a shim or washer. Use new gaskets if there is any doubt about the condition of the old ones. A thin coat of oil on gaskets may help them seal effectively.

Heavy grease can be used to hold small parts in place if they tend to fall out during assembly. However, keep grease and oil away from electrical and brake components.

High spots may be sanded off a piston with sandpaper, but fine emery cloth and oil will do a much more professional job.

Carbon can be removed from the head, the piston crowns and the exhaust ports with a dull screwdriver. Do *not* scratch machined surfaces. Wipe off the surface with a clean cloth when finished.

The carburetor is best cleaned by disassembling and soaking the parts in a commercial carburetor cleaner. Never soak gaskets and rubber parts in these cleaners. Never use wire to clean out jets and air passages; they are easily damaged. Use compressed air to blow out the carburetor *after* the float has been removed.

A baby bottle makes a good measuring device for adding oil to the front forks. Get one that is graduated in fluid ounces and cubic centimeters. After it has been used for this purpose, do *not* let a small child drink out of it as there will always be an oil residue in it.

Take your time and do the job right. Do not forget that a newly rebuilt engine must be broken in the same as a new one. Keep the rpm within the limits given in your owner's manual when you get back on the road.

TORQUE SPECIFICATIONS

Torque specifications throughout this manual are given in Newton meters (N•m) and foot-pounds (ft.-lb.). Newton meters have been adopted in place of meter kilograms (mkg) in accordance with the International Modernized Metric System. Tool manufacturers offer torque wrenches calibrated in both values.

Torque wrenches calibrated in meter kilograms can be used by performing a simple conversion. All you have to do is move the decimal point one place to the right; for example, 4.7 mkg = 47 N•m. This conversion is accurate enough for mechanical work even though the exact mathematical conversion is 3.5 mkg = 34.3 N•m.

SAFETY FIRST

Professional mechanics can work for years and never sustain a serious injury. If you observe a few rules of common sense and safety, you can enjoy many hours servicing your own machine. If you ignore these rules you can hurt yourself or damage the bike.

1. Never use gasoline as a cleaning solvent

2. Never smoke or use a torch in the vicinity of flammable liquids such as cleaning solvent in open containers.

3. If welding or brazing is required on the machine, remove the fuel tank to a safe distance, at least 50 feet away.

4. Use the proper sized wrenches to avoid damage to nuts and injury to yourself.

5. When loosening a tight or stuck nut, think about what would happen if the wrench should slip. Be careful; protect yourself accordingly.

6. Keep your work area clean and uncluttered.

7. Wear safety goggles during all operations involving drilling, grinding or using a cold chisel.

8. Never use worn tools.

9. Keep a fire extinguisher handy and be sure it is rated for gasoline and electrical fires.

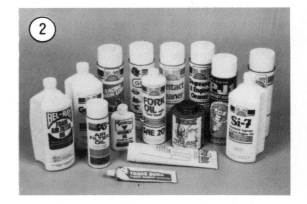

SPECIAL TIPS

Because of the extreme demands placed on a bike, several pints should be kept in mind when performing service and repair. The following items are general suggestions that may improve the overall life of the machine and help to avoid costly failutres.

1. Use a locking compound such as Loctite 242 (blue Loctite) on all bolts and nuts, even if they are secured withh lockwashers. This type of Loctite does not harden completely and allows easy removal of the bolt or nut. A screw or bolt lost from an egine cover or bearing retainer could easily cause serious and expensive damage before its loss is noticed.

When applying Loctite, use a small amount. If too much is used, it can work its way down the threads and enter bearings or seals.

2. Use a hammer-driven impact tool to remove tight fasteners, particularly engine cover screws. These tools help to prevent the rounding off of bolt heads.

3. When replacing missing or broken fasteners (bolts, nuts and screws), especially on the engine or frame components, always use Honda replacement parts. They are specially hardned for each application. The wrong fasteners could easily cause serious and expensive damage, not to mention rider injury.

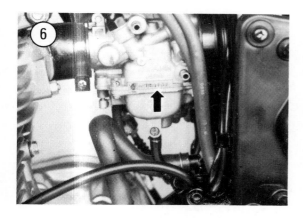

EXPENDABLE SUPPLIES

Certain expendable supplies are required during maintenance and repair work. These include grease, oil, gasket cement, wiping rags and cleaning solvent. Ask your dealer for the special locking compounds, silicone lubricants and other products (**Figure 2**) which make vehicle maintenance simpler and easier. Cleaning solvent or kerosene is available at some service stations or hardware stores.

PARTS REPLACEMENT

Honda makes frequent changes during a model year—some minor, some relatively major. When you order parts from the dealer or other parts distributor, always order by engine and frame number. Write the numbers down and carry them with you. Compare new parts to old before purchasing them. If they are not alike, have the parts manager explain the difference to you.

SERIAL NUMBERS

You must know the model serial number and VIN number for registration purposes and when ordering replacement parts.

The frame serial number is stamped on the right-hand side of the steering head (**Figure 3**). The vehicle identification number (VIN) is on the left-hand side of the steering head (**Figure 4**). The engine serial number is located on the lower left-hand side of the crankcase below the alternator (**Figure 5**). The carburetor identification number is located on the left-hand side of the carburetor body above the float bowl (**Figure 6**).

On Rebel 250 models, the color label is attached to the air filter cover (**Figure 7**) under the left-hand side cover. When ordering color-coded parts always specify the color indicated on this label.

TUNE-UP AND TROUBLESHOOTING TOOLS

Multimeter or Volt-ohm Meter

This instrument (**Figure 8**) is invaluable for electrical system troubleshooting and service. A few of its functions may be duplicated by homemade test equipment, but for the serious mechanic it is a must. Its uses are described in the applicable sections of the book.

Strobe Timing Light

This instrument is necessary for tuning. By flashing a light at the precise instant the spark plug

4. When installing gaskets in the engine, always use Honda replacement gaskets *without* sealer, unless designated. These gaskets are designed to swell when they come in contact with oil. Gasket sealer will prevent the gaskets from swelling as intended, which can result in oil leaks. These Honda gaskets are cut from material of the precise thickness needed. Installation of a too-thick or too-thin gasket in a critical area could cause engine damage.

fires, the position of the timing mark can be seen. Marks on the alternator flywheel line up with the stationary mark on the crankcase while the engine is running.

Suitable lights range from inexpensive neon bulb types to powerful xenon strobe lights (**Figure 9**). Neon timing lights are difficult to see and must be used in dimly lit areas. Xenon strobe timing lights can be used outside in bright sunlight. Both types work on the bike; use according to the manufacturer's instructions.

Portable Tachometer

A portable tachometer is necessary for tuning (**Figure 10**). Ignition timing and carburetor adjustments must be performed at the specified engine speed. The best instrument for this purpose is one with a low range of 0-1,000 or 0-2,000 rpm and a high range of 0-4,000 rpm. Extended range (0-6,000 or 0-8,000 rpm) instruments lack accuracy at lower speeds. The instrument should be capable of detecting changes of 25 rpm on the low range.

Compression Gauge

A compression gauge (**Figure 11**) measures the engine compression. The results, when properly interpreted, can indicate general ring and valve condition. They are available from motorcycle or auto supply stores and mail order outlets.

BASIC HAND TOOLS

A number of tools are required to maintain a bike in top riding condition. You may already have some of these tools for home or car repairs. There are also tools made especially for bike repairs; these you will have to purchase. In any case, a wide variety of quality tools will make bike repairs easier and more effective.

Top quality tools are essential; they are also more economical in the long run. If you are now starting to build your tool collection, stay away from the "advertised specials" featured at some parts houses, discount stores and chain drug stores. These are usually a poor grade tool that can be sold cheaply and that is exactly what they are—*cheap*. They are usually made of inferior material and are thick, heavy and clumsy. Their rough finish makes them difficult to clean and they usually don't last very long.

Quality tools are made of alloy steel and are heat treated for greater strength. They are lighter and better balanced than cheap ones. Their surface is smooth, making them a pleasure to work with and easy to clean. The initial cost of good quality tools may be more but it is cheaper in the long run.

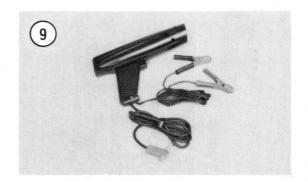

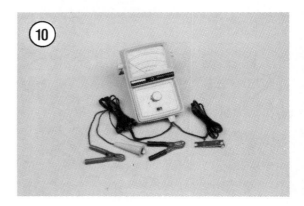

Keep your tools clean and in a tool box. Keep them organized with the sockets and related drives together and the open end and box wrenches together, etc. After using a tool, wipe off dirt and grease with a clean cloth and place the tool in its correct place. Doing this will save a lot of time you would have spent trying to find a socket buried in a bunch of clutch parts. Also be careful when lending tools to so called "friends"—make sure they return them promptly; if not, your collection will soon disappear.

The following tools are required to perform virtually any repair job on a bike. Each tool is described and the recommended size given for

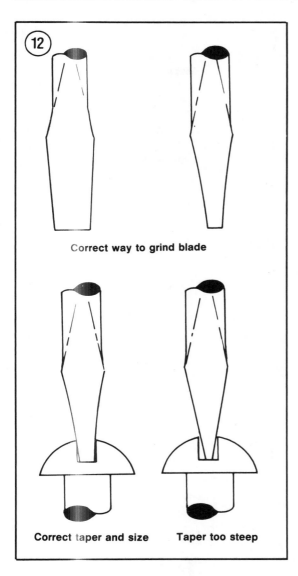

Correct way to grind blade

Correct taper and size   **Taper too steep**

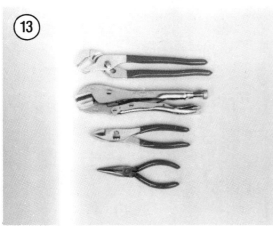

starting a tool collection. Don't try to buy every-thing in all sizes in the beginning; do it a little at a time until you have the necessary tools. This section includes the tools that should be on hand for simple repairs. Additional tools and some duplicate may be added as you become more familiar with the bike. Almost all motorcycles (with the exception of the U.S. built Harley and some English bikes) use met-ric size bolts and nuts. If you are starting your col-lection now, buy metric sizes.

Screwdrivers

The screwdriver is a very basic tool, but if used improperly it will do more damage than good. The slot on a screw has a definite dimension and shape. A screwdriver must be selected to conform with that shape. Use a small screwdriver for small screws and a large one for large screws or the screw head will be damaged.

Two basic types of screwdriver are required to re-pair the bike – the common (flat blade) screwdriver and the Phillips screwdriver.

Screwdrivers are available in sets which often in-clude an assortment of common and Phillips blades. If you buy them individually, buy at least the fol-lowing:

    a. Common screwdriver – 5/16 × 6 in. blade.
    b. Common screwdriver – 3/8 × 12 in. blade.
    c. Phillips screwdriver – size 2 tip, 6 in. blade.

Use screwdrivers only for driving screws. Never use a screwdriver for prying or chiseling. Do not try to remove a Phillips or Allen head screw with a common screwdriver; you can damage the head so that the proper tool will be unable to remove it.

Keep screwdrivers in the proper condition and they will last longer and perform better. Always keep the tip of a common screwdriver in good con-dition. **Figure 12** shows how to grind the tip to the proper shape if it becomes damaged. Note the sym-metrical sides of the tip.

Pliers

Pliers come in a wide range of types and sizes. Pliers are useful for cutting, bending and crimping. They should never be used to cut hardened objects or to turn bolts or nuts. **Figure 13** shows several pli-ers useful in bike repairs.

Each type of pliers has a specialized function. Gas pliers are general purpose pliers and are used mainly for holding things and for bending. Vise Grips are used as pliers or to hold objects very tight like a vise. Needlenose pliers are used to hold or bend small objects. Channel lock pliers can be adjusted to hold various sizes of objects; the jaws remain parallel to grip around objects such as pipe or tubing. There are many more types of pliers. The ones described here are most suitable for bike repairs.

Box and Open-end Wrenches

Box and open-end wrenches are available in sets or separately in a variety of sizes. See **Figure 14** and **Figure 15**. The size number stamped near the end refers to the distance between 2 parallel flats on the hex head bolt or nut.

Box wrenches are usually superior to open-end wrenches. Open-end wrenches grip the nut on only 2 flats. Unless an open-end fits well, it may slip and round off the points on the nut. The box wrench grips all 6 flats. Both 6-point and 12-point openings on box wrenches are available. The 6-point gives superior holding power; the 12-point allows a shorter swing.

Combination wrenches which are open on one side and boxed on the other are also available. Both ends are the same size.

Adjustable (Crescent) Wrenches

An adjustable wrench (also called crescent wrench) can be adjusted to fit nearly any nut or bolt head. See **Figure 16**. However, it can loosen and slip, causing damage to the nut and injury to your knuckles. Use an adjustable wrench only when other wrenches are not available.

Crescent wrenches come in sizes ranging from 4-18 in. overall. A 6 or 8 in. wrench is recommended as an all-purpose wrench.

Socket Wrenches

This type is undoubtedly the fastest, safest and most convenient to use. See **Figure 17**. Sockets which attach to a ratchet handle are available with 6-point or 12-point openings and 1/4, 3/8, 1/2 and 3/4 inch drives. The drive size indicates the size of the square hole which mates with the ratchet handle.

Torque Wrench

A torque wrench is used with a socket to measure how tight a nut or bolt is installed. They come in a wide price range and with either 3/8 or 1/2 in. square drive. The drive size indicates the size of the square drive which mates with the socket. Purchase one that measures 0-140 N•m (0-100 ft.-lb.)

Impact Driver

This tool might have been designed with the bike in mind. See **Figure 18**. It makes removal of

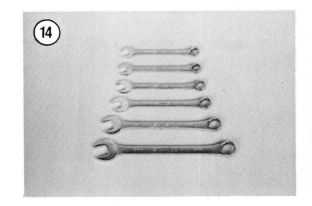

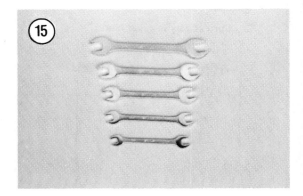

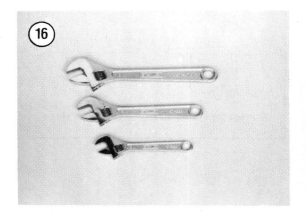

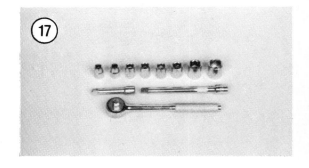

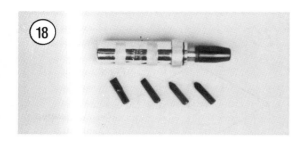

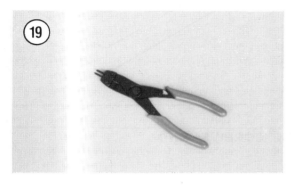

engine and clutch parts easy and eliminates damage to bolts and screw slots. This tool is available at most large hardware, motorcycle or auto parts stores.

Circlip Pliers

Circlip pliers (sometimes referred to as snap-ring pliers) are necessary to remove the circlips used on the transmission shaft assemblies. See **Figure 19**.

Hammers

The correct hammer is necessary for bike repairs. Use only a hammer with a face (or head) of rubber or plastic or the soft-faced type that is filled with buck shot. These are sometimes necessary in engine tear-downs. *Never* use a metal-faced hammer on the bike as severe damage will result in most cases. You can always produce the same amount of force with a soft-faced hammer.

Ignition Gauge

This tool (**Figure 20**) has both flat and wire measuring gauges and is used to measure spark plug gap or breaker point gap (models so equipped). This device is available at most auto or motorcycle supply stores.

Other Special Tools

A few other special tools may be required for major service. These are described in the appropriate chapters and are available either from a Honda dealer or other manufacturers as indicated.

MECHANIC'S TIPS

Removing Frozen Nuts and Screws

When a fastener rusts and cannot be removed, several methods may be used to loosen it. First, apply penetrating oil such as Liquid Wrench or WD-40 (available at any hardware or auto supply store).

Apply it liberally and let it penetrate for 10-15 minutes. Rap the fastener several times with a small hammer; do not hit it hard enough to cause damage. Reapply the penetrating oil if necessary.

For frozen screws, apply penetrating oil as described, then insert a screwdriver in the slot and rap the top of the screwdriver with a hammer. This loosens the rust so the screw can be removed in the normal way. If the screw head is too chewed up to use a screwdriver, grip the head with Vise Grips pliers and twist the screw out.

Remedying Stripped Threads

Occasionally, threads are stripped though carelessness or impact damage. Often the threads can be cleaned up by running a tap (for internal threads on nuts) or die (for external threads on bolts) through threads. See **Figure 21**.

Removing Broken Screws or Bolts

When the head breaks off a screw or bolt, several methods are available for removing the remaining portion.

If a large portion of the remainder projects out, try gripping it with Vise Grips. If the projecting portion is too small, file it to fit a wrench or cut a slot in it to fit a screwdriver. See **Figure 22**.

If the head breaks off flush, use a screw extractor. To do this, centerpunch the remaining portion of the screw or bolt. Drill a small hole in the screw and tap the extractor into the hole. Back the screw out with a wrench on the extractor. See **Figure 23**.

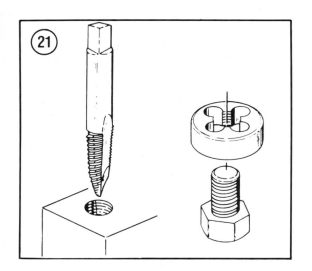

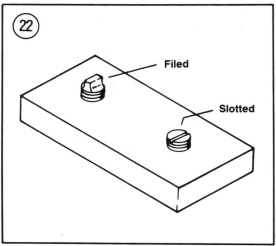

Filed

Slotted

REMOVING BROKEN SCREWS AND BOLTS

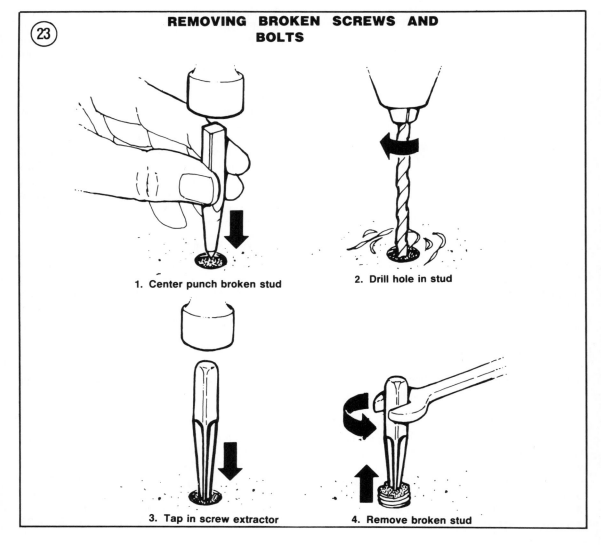

1. Center punch broken stud

2. Drill hole in stud

3. Tap in screw extractor

4. Remove broken stud

Table 1 CONVERSION FORMULAS

Multiply:	By:	To get the equivalent of:
Length		
Inches	25.4	Millimeter
Inches	2.54	Centimeter
Miles	1.609	Kilometer
Feet	0.3048	Meter
Millimeter	0.03937	Inches
Centimeter	0.3937	Inches
Kilometer	0.6214	Mile
Meter	3.281	Mile
Fluid volume		
U.S. quarts	0.9463	Liters
U.S. gallons	3.785	Liters
U.S. ounces	29.573529	Milliliters
Imperial gallons	4.54609	Liters
Imperial quarts	1.1365	Liters
Liters	0.2641721	U.S. gallons
Liters	1.0566882	U.S. quarts
Liters	33.814023	U.S. ounces
Liters	0.22	Imperial gallons
Liters	0.8799	Imperial quarts
Milliliters	0.033814	U.S. ounces
Milliliters	1.0	Cubic centimeters
Milliliters	0.001	Liters
Torque		
Foot-pounds	1.3558	Newton-meters
Foot-pounds	0.138255	Meters-kilograms
Inch-pounds	0.11299	Newton-meters
Newton-meters	0.7375622	Foot-pounds
Newton-meters	8.8507	Inch-pounds
Meters-kilograms	7.2330139	Foot-pounds
Volume		
Cubic inches	16.387064	Cubic centimeters
Cubic centimeters	0.0610237	Cubic inches
Temperature		
Fahrenheit	$(F - 32°) \times 0.556$	Centigrade
Centigrade	$(C \times 1.8) + 32$	Fahrenheit
Weight		
Ounces	28.3495	Grams
Pounds	0.4535924	Kilograms
Grams	0.035274	Ounces
Kilograms	2.2046224	Pounds
Pressure		
Pounds per square inch	0.070307	Kilograms per square centimeter
Kilograms per square centimeter	14.223343	Pounds per square inch
Kilopascals	0.1450	Pounds per square inch
Pounds per square inch	6.895	Kilopascals
Speed		
Miles per hour	1.609344	Kilometers per hour
Kilometers per hour	0.6213712	Miles per hour

CHAPTER TWO

TROUBLESHOOTING

Diagnosing mechanical problems is relatively simple if you use orderly procedures and keep a few basic principles in mind.

The troubleshooting procedures in this chapter analyze typical symptoms and show logical methods of isolating causes. These are not the only methods. There may be several ways to solve a problem, but only a systematic, methodical approach can guarantee success.

Never assume anything. Do not overlook the obvious. If you are riding along and the engine suddenly quits, check the easiest, most accessible problems first. Is there gasoline in the tank? Is the fuel shutoff valve in the ON position? Has a spark plug wire fallen off?

If nothing obvious turns up in a quick check, look a little further. Learning to recognize and describe symptoms will make repairs easier for you or a mechanic at the shop. Describe problems accurately and fully. Saying that "it won't run" isn't the same as saying "it quit at high speed and won't start" or that "it sat in my garage for 3 months and then wouldn't start."

Gather as many symptoms together as possible to aid in diagnosis. Note whether the engine lost power gradually or all at once. Remember that the more complicated a machine is, the easier it is to troubleshoot because symptoms point to specific problems.

After the symptoms are defined, areas which could cause the problems are tested and analyzed. Guessing at the cause of a problem may provide the solution, but it can easily lead to frustration, wasted time and a series of expensive, unnecessary parts replacements.

You do not need fancy equipment or complicated test gear to determine whether repairs can be attempted at home. A few simple checks could save a large repair bill and time lost while the bike sits in a dealer's service department. On the other hand, be realistic and don't attempt repairs beyond your abilities. Service departments tend to charge a lot for putting together a disassembled engine that may have been abused. Some dealers won't even take on such a job—so use common sense and don't get in over your head.

OPERATING REQUIREMENTS

An engine needs 3 basics to run properly: correct fuel-air mixture, compression and a spark at the correct time. If one or more are missing, the engine just won't run. The electrical system is the weakest link of the 3 basics. More problems result from electrical breakdowns than from any other source. Keep that in mind before you begin tampering with carburetor adjustments and the like.

If the bike has been sitting for any length of time and refuses to start, check and clean the spark plugs

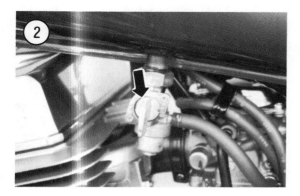

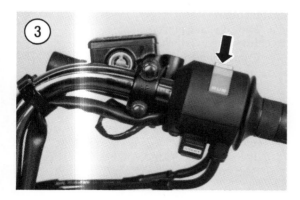

and then look to the gasoline delivery system. This includes the fuel tank, fuel shutoff valve and the fuel line to the carburetor. Gasoline deposits may have formed and gummed up the carburetor's jets and air passages. Gasoline tends to lose its potency after standing for long periods. Condensation may contaminate the fuel with water. Drain the old fuel and try starting with a fresh tankful.

EMERGENCY TROUBLESHOOTING

When the bike is difficult to start or won't start at all, it does not help to wear out your leg on the kickstarter or wear down the battery using the starter. Check for obvious problems even before getting out your tools. Go down the following list step by step. Do each one; you may be embarrassed to find your kill switch is stuck in the OFF position, but that is better than wearing down the battery. If it still will not start, refer to the appropriate troubleshooting procedure which follows in this chapter.

WARNING
Do not use an open flame to check in the tank in Step 1. A serious explosion is certain to result.

1. Is there fuel in the tank? Open the filler cap (**Figure 1**) and rock the bike. Listen for fuel sloshing around.
2. Is the fuel shutoff valve (**Figure 2**) in the ON position?
3. Make sure the kill switch (**Figure 3**) is not stuck in the OFF position.
4. Are all spark plug wires (**Figure 4**) on tight? Push all of them on and slightly rotate them to clean the electrical connection between the plug and the connector.
5A. On Rebel 250 models, is the choke lever (**Figure 5**) in the right position? The lever should be moved *down* for a cold engine and *up* for a warm engine.
5B. On all other models, is the choke knob in the right position? The knob should be pulled *up* for a cold engine and pushed *down* for a warm engine.

ENGINE STARTING

An engine that refuses to start or is difficult to start is very frustrating. More often than not, the problem is very minor and can be found with a simple and logical troubleshooting approach.

The following items show a beginning point from which to isolate engine starting problems.

Engine Fails to Start

Perform the following spark test to determine if the ignition system is operating properly.
1. Remove one of the spark plugs from the cylinder.

2. Connect the spark plug wire and connector to the spark plug and touch the spark plug's base to a good ground such as the engine cylinder head (**Figure 6**). Position the spark plug so you can see the electrodes.

> *WARNING*
> *On models with an electronic ignition system, if it is necessary to hold the high voltage lead, do so with an insulated pair of pliers. The high voltage generated by the ignition pulse generator and CDI unit could produce serious or fatal shocks.*

3. Crank the engine over with the kickstarter or with the starter. A fat blue spark should be evident across the plug's electrodes.

4. If the spark is good, check for one or more of the following possible malfunctions:
   a. Obstructed fuel line.
   b. Low compression.
   c. Leaking head gasket.
   d. Choke not operating properly.
   e. Throttle not operating properly.

5. If spark is not good, check for one or more of the following:
   a. Weak ignition coil(s).
   b. Faulty contact breaker points (models so equipped).
   c. Weak CDI pulse generator (models so equipped).

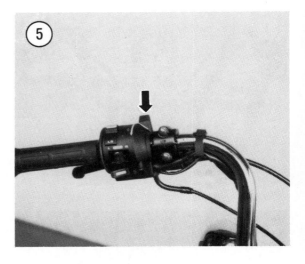

d. Broken or shorted high tension lead to the spark plug(s).
e. Loose electrical connections.
f. Loose or broken ignition coil ground wire.

Engine Is Difficult to Start

Check for one or more of the following possible malfunctions:
   a. Fouled spark plug(s).
   b. Improperly adjusted choke.
   c. Contaminated fuel system.
   d. Improperly adjusted carburetor.
   e. Weak ignition coil(s).
   f. Faulty contact breaker points (models so equipped).
   g. Weak CDI pulse generator (models so equipped).
   h. Incorrect type ignition coil(s).
   i. Poor compression.

Engine Will Not Crank

Check for one or more of the following possible malfunctions:
   a. Discharged battery (models so equipped).
   b. Defective starter motor, starter solenoid or start switch (models so equipped).
   c. Defective or broken kickstarter mechanism (models so equipped).
   d. Seized piston(s).
   e. Seized crankshaft bearings.
   f. Broken connecting rod(s).
   g. Locked-up transmission or clutch assembly.

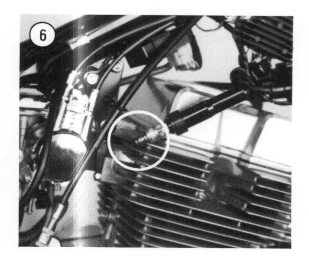

ENGINE PERFORMANCE

In the following checklist, it is assumed that the engine runs, but is not operating at peak performance. This will serve as a starting point from which to isolate a performance malfunction.

The possible causes for each malfunction are listed in a logical sequence and in order of probability.

**Engine Will Not Start
Or Is Hard To Start**

a. Fuel tank empty.
b. Obstructed fuel line or fuel shutoff valve.
c. Sticking float valve in carburetor.
d. Carburetor incorrectly adjusted.
e. Improper choke operation.
f. Fouled or improperly gapped spark plug(s).
g. Improperly adjusted contact breaker points (models so equipped).
h. Weak CDI pulse generator (models so equipped).
i. Ignition timing incorrect (faulty component in system).
j. Broken or shorted ignition coil(s).
k. Weak or faulty spark unit or pulse generator(s).
l. Improper valve timing.
m. Clogged air filter element.
n. Contaminated fuel.

**Engine Will Not Idle or
Idles Erratically**

a. Carburetor incorrectly adjusted.
b. Fouled or improperly gapped spark plug(s).

c. Leaking head gasket or vacuum leak.
d. Improperly adjusted contact breaker points (models so equipped).
e. Weak CDI pulse generator (models so equipped).
f. Ignition timing incorrect (faulty component in system).
g. Improper valve timing.
h. Obstructed fuel line or fuel shutoff valve.

Engine Overheating

a. Obstructed cooling fins on the cylinder and cylinder head.
b. Improper ignition timing (faulty component in system).
c. Improper spark plug heat range.

Engine Misses at High Speed

a. Fouled or improperly gapped spark plugs.
b. Improper ignition timing (faulty component in system).
c. Improper carburetor main jet selection.
d. Clogged jets in the carburetor.
e. Weak ignition coil.
f. Improperly adjusted contact breaker points (models so equipped).
g. Weak CDI pulse generator (models so equipped).
h. Improper valve timing.
i. Obstructed fuel line or fuel shutoff valve.

**Engine Continues to
Run with Ignition OFF**

a. Excessive carbon build-up in engine.
b. Vacuum leak in intake system.
c. Contaminated or incorrect fuel octane rating.

Engine Misses at Idle

a. Fouled or improperly gapped spark plugs.
b. Spark plug caps faulty.
c. Ignition cable insulation deteriroated (shorting out).
d. Dirty or clogged air filter element.
e. Carburetor incorrectly adjusted (too lean or too rich).
f. Choke valve stuck.
g. Cloged jet(s) in the carburetor.
h. Carburetor float height incorrect.

Engine Backfires— Explosions in Mufflers

a. Fouled or improperly gapped spark plugs.
b. Spark plug caps faulty.
c. Ignition cable insulation deteriorated (shorting out).
d. Ignition timing incorrect.
e. Improper valve timing.
f. Contaminated fuel.
g. Burned or damaged intake and/or exhaust valves.
h. Weak or broken intake and/or exhaust valve springs.

Pre-ignition (Fuel Mixture Ignities Before Spark Plug Fires)

a. Hot spot in combustion chamber(s) (piece of carbon).
b. Valve(s) stuck in guide.
c. Overheating engine.

Smoky Exhaust and Engine Runs Roughly

a. Carburetor mixture too rich.
b. Choke not operating correctly.
c. Water or other contaminants in fuel.
d. Clogged fuel line.
e. Clogged air filter element.

Engine Loses Power at Normal Riding Speed

a. Carburetor incorrectly adjusted.
b. Engine overheating.
c. Improper ignition timing (faulty component in system).
d. Improperly adjusted contact breaker points (models so equipped).
e. Weak CDI pulse generator (models so equipped).
f. Incorrectly gapped spark plugs.
g. Weak ignition coil(s).
h. Obstructed mufflers.
i. Dragging brake(s).

Engine Lacks Acceleration

a. Carburetor mixture too lean.
b. Clogged fuel line.
c. Improper ignition timing (faulty component in system).
d. Improper valve clearance.
e. Dragging brake(s).

ENGINE NOISES

1. *Knocking or pinging during acceleration*—Caused by using a lower octane fuel than recommended. May also be caused by poor fuel. Pinging can also be caused by spark plugs of the wrong heat range. Refer to *Spark Plug Selection* in Chapter Three.
2. *Slapping or rattling noises at low speed or during acceleration* —May be caused by piston slap (excessive piston to cylinder wall clearance).
3. *Knocking or rapping while decelerating*—Usually caused by excessive rod bearing clearance.
4. *Persistent knocking and vibration*—Usually caused by excessive main bearing clearance.
5. *Rapid on-off squeal*—Compression leak around cylinder head gasket or spark plugs.

EXCESSIVE VIBRATION

Usually this is caused by loose engine mounting hardware. If not, it can be difficult to find without disassembling the engine.

FRONT SUSPENSION AND STEERING

Poor handling may be caused by improper tire pressure, a damaged or bent frame or front steering components, a worn front fork assembly, worn wheel bearings or dragging brakes.

BRAKE PROBLEMS

Sticking disc brakes may be caused by a stuck piston(s) in a caliper assembly or warped pad shim(s).

A sticking drum brake may be caused by worn or weak return springs, dry pivot and cam bushings or improper adjustment. Grabbing brakes may be caused by greasy linings which must be replaced. Brake grab may also be due to an out-of-round drum. Glazed linings will cause loss of stopping power.

2

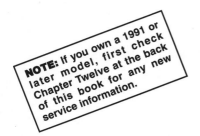
NOTE: If you own a 1991 or later model, first check Chapter Twelve at the back of this book for any new service information.

CHAPTER THREE

LUBRICATION, MAINTENANCE AND TUNE-UP

A motorcycle, even in normal use, is subjected to tremendous heat, stress and vibration. When neglected, any bike becomes unreliable and actually dangerous to ride.

To gain the utmost in safety, performance and useful life from the Honda it is necessary to make periodic inspections and adjustments. Minor problems are often found during these inspections that are simple and inexpensive to correct at the time. If they are not found and corrected at this time they could lead to major and more expensive problems later on.

Start out by doing simple tune-up, lubrication and maintenance. Tackle more involved jobs as you become more acquainted with the bike.

This chapter explains lubrication, maintenance and tune-up procedures required for the Honda Rebel 250 and all Twinstar models.

Tables 1-5 are located at the end of this chapter.

ROUTINE CHECKS

The following simple checks should be performed at each stop at a service station for gas.

Engine Oil Level

Refer to *Engine Oil Level Check* under *Periodic Lubrication* in this chapter.

General Inspection

1. Quickly inspect the engine for signs of oil or fuel leakage.

2. Check the tires for embedded stones. Pry them out with your ignition key.
3. Make sure all lights work.

> *NOTE*
> *At least check the brake light. It can burn out at any time. Motorists cannot stop as quickly as you and need all the warning you can give.*

Tire Pressure

Tire pressure must be checked with the tires cold. Correct tire pressure varies with the load you are carrying. See **Table 1**.

Battery

On Twinstar models, remove the right-hand side cover and check the battery electrolyte level. It is

not necessary to remove the side cover on Rebel 250 models. The level must be between the upper and lower level marks on the case (**Figure 1**).

For complete details see *Battery Removal, Installation and Electrolyte Level Check* in this chapter.

Check the level more frequently in hot weather; electrolyte will evaporate rapidly as heat increases.

Lights and Horn

With the engine running, check the following.
1. Pull the front brake lever on and check that the brake light comes on.
2. Push the rear brake pedal down and check that the brake light comes on soon after you have begun depressing the pedal.
3. Press the headlight dimmer switch to both the HI and LO positions and check to see that both headlight elements are working.
4. Turn the turn signal switch to the left and right positions and check that all 4 turn signals are working.
5. Push the horn button and make sure that the horn blows loudly.
6. If the horn or any of the lights failed to operate properly, refer to Chapter Seven.

PRE-CHECKS

The following checks should be performed prior to the first ride of the day.
1. Inspect all fuel lines and fittings for wetness.
2. Make sure the fuel tank is full of fresh gasoline.

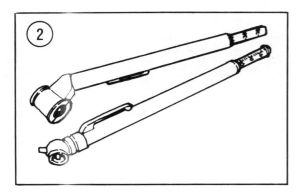

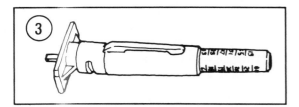

3. Make sure the engine oil level is correct.
4. Check the operation of the front brake. On disc brake models, add hydraulic fluid to the brake master cylinder if necessary.
5. Check the throttle and the rear brake pedal. Make sure they operate properly with no binding.
6. Inspect the front and rear suspension; make sure it has a good solid feel with no looseness.
7. Check tire pressure. Refer to **Table 1**.
8. Check the exhaust system for damage.
9. Check the tightness of all fasteners, especially engine mounting hardware.

SERVICE INTERVALS

The services and intervals shown in **Table 2** are recommended by the factory. Strict adherence to these recommendations will ensure long service from the Honda. If the bike is run in an area of high humidity, the lubrication services must be done more frequently to prevent possible rust damage.

For convenience when maintaining your motorcycle, most of the services shown in the table are described in this chapter. However, some procedures which require more than minor disassembly or adjustment are covered elsewhere in the appropriate chapter.

TIRES AND WHEELS

Tire Pressure

Tire pressure should be checked and adjusted to maintain the smoothness of the tire, good traction and handling and to get the maximum life out of the tire. A simple, accurate gauge (**Figure 2**) can be purchased for a few dollars and should be carried in your motorcycle tool kit. The appropriate tire pressures are shown in **Table 1**.

Tire Inspection

The tires take a lot of punishment so inspect them periodically for excessive wear, cuts, abrasions, etc. If you find a nail or other object in the tire, mark its location with a light crayon prior to removing it. This will help locate the hole for repair. Refer to Chapter Eight for tire changing and repair information.

Check local traffic regulations concerning minimum tread depth. Measure the tread depth at the center of the tire tread using a tread depth gauge (**Figure 3**) or small ruler. Honda recommends that original equipment tires be replaced when the front tire tread depth is 1.5 mm (1/16 in.) or less, when the rear tread depth is 2.0

mm (3/32 in.) or less or when tread wear indicators appear across the tire indicating the minimum tread depth.

Rim Inspection

Frequently inspect the wheel rims. If a rim has been damaged it might have been enough to knock it out of alignment. Improper wheel alignment can cause severe vibration and result in an unsafe riding condition.

Wheel Spoke Tension

1. Tap each spoke with a wrench. The higher the pitch of sound it makes, the tighter the spoke. The lower the sound frequency, the looser the spoke. A "ping" is good; a "clunk" says the spoke is too loose.
2. If one or more of the spokes are loose, tighten them as described under *Wheels* in Chapter Eight.

CRANKCASE BREATHER HOSE
(U.S. MODELS ONLY)

Remove both side covers, seat and fuel tank. Inspect the breather hoses for cracks and deterioration and make sure that all hose clamps are tight.

EVAPORATION EMISSION CONTROL
(CALIFORNIA MODELS ONLY)

Inspect the hoses (**Figure 4**) for cracks, kinks and deterioration. Make sure that all hoses are tight where they attach to the various components. For complete hose routing, refer to Chapter Six.

BATTERY

**Removal, Installation and
Electrolyte Level Check**

The battery is the heart of the electrical system. Check and service the battery at the interval indicated in **Table 2**. Most electrical system troubles can be attributed to neglect of this vital component.

The electrolyte level may be checked with the battery in the frame. However, on all models except the Rebel 250, it is necessary to remove the right-hand side panel. On Rebel 250 models, the electrolyte level is visible through the slot in the battery cover (**Figure 5**). The electrolyte level should be maintained between the 2 marks on the battery case (**Figure 1**). If the electrolyte level is low, it's a good idea to remove the battery from the frame so it can be thoroughly serviced and checked.

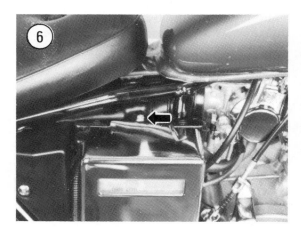

1A. On Rebel 250 models, perform the following:
  a. Remove the bolt (**Figure 6**) securing the battery outer cover and hinge the cover down.
  b. Hinge the inner cover (**Figure 7**) down.
  c. Disconnect the breather tube (A, **Figure 8**).
  d. Disconnect the battery negative lead (C, **Figure 8**) and positive lead (B, **Figure 8**).
  e. Slide the battery out the rest of the way and remove from the bike's frame.

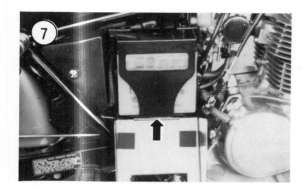

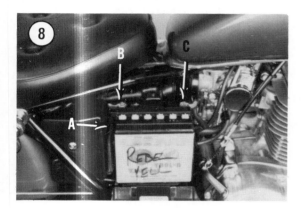

1B. On all other models, perform the following:
a. Remove the right-hand side panel.
b. Disconnect the breather tube (A, **Figure 9**) and remove the rubber retaining strap (B, **Figure 9**).
c. Disconnect the battery negative lead (B, **Figure 10**), slide the battery slightly out and disconnect the battery positive lead (A, **Figure 10**).
d. Slide the battery and tray out the rest of the way and remove from the bike's frame.

WARNING
Protect your eyes, skin and clothing. If electrolyte gets into your eyes, flush your eyes thoroughly with clean water and get immediate medical attention.

CAUTION
Be careful not to spill battery electrolyte on painted or polished surfaces. The liquid is highly corrosive and will damage the finish. If it is spilled, wash it off immediately with soapy water and thoroughly rinse with clean water.

2. Remove the cap from the battery cells and add distilled water to correct the level. Never add electrolyte (acid) to correct the level.

NOTE
If distilled water has been added, reinstall the battery caps and gently shake the battery for several minutes to mix the existing electrolyte with the new water.

3. After the fluid level has been corrected and the battery allowed to stand for a few minutes, remove the battery caps and check the specific gravity of the electrolyte with a hydrometer (**Figure 11**). See *Battery Testing* in this chapter.

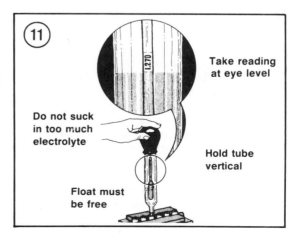

4. After the battery has been refilled, recharged or replaced, install it by reversing these removal steps.

CAUTION
If you removed the breather tube from the frame, be sure to route it so that residue will not drain onto any part of the bike's frame. The tube must be free of bends or twists as any restrictions may pressurize the battery and damage it.

Testing

Hydrometer testing is the best way to check battery condition. Use a hydrometer with numbered graduations from 1.100 to 1.300 rather than one with just color-coded bands. To use the hydrometer, squeeze the rubber ball, insert the tip into the cell and release the pressure on the ball. Draw enough electrolyte to float the weighted float inside the hydrometer. Note the number in line with the surface of the electrolyte, this is the specific gravity for this cell. Squeeze the rubber ball again and return the electrolyte to the cell from which it came.

The specific gravity of the electrolyte in each battery cell is an excellent indication of that cell's condition. A fully charged cell will read from 1.260-1.280, while a cell in good condition reads from 1.230-1.250 and anything below 1.120 is discharged.

Specific gravity varies with temperature. For each 10° the electrolyte temperature exceeds 27° C (80° F), add 0.004 to readings indicated on the hydrometer. Subtract 0.004 for each 10° below 27° C (80° F).

If the cells test in the poor range, the battery requires recharging. The hydrometer is useful for checking the progress of the charging operation. **Table 3** shows approximate state of charge.

Charging

WARNING
During the charging process, highly explosive hydrogen gas is released from the battery. The battery should be charged only in a well-ventilated area away from any open flames (including pilot lights on home gas appliances). Do not allow any smoking in the area. Never check the charge by arcing (connecting pliers or other metal objects) across the terminals; the resulting spark can ignite the hydrogen gas.

CAUTION
Always remove the battery from the bike's frame before connecting the battery charger. Never recharge a battery in the bike's frame; the corrosive mist that is emitted during the charging process will corrode all surrounding surfaces.

1. Connect the positive (+) charger lead to the positive (+) battery terminal and the negative (–) charger lead to the negtive (–) battery terminal.

NOTE
The 1978-1980 models have a 6-volt battery (3 battery vent caps) and electrical system, while models since 1981 have a 12-volt battery (6 battery vent caps) and electrical system.

2. Remove all vent caps from the battery, set the charger to either 6 or 12 volts (depending on the bike's electrical system) and switch the charger ON. If the output of the charger is variable, it is best to select a low setting—1 1/2 to 2 amps.

CAUTION
The electrolyte level must be maintained at the upper level during the charging cycle; check and refill as necessary.

3. After the battery has been charged for about 8 hours, turn the charger OFF, disconnect the leads and check the specific gravity of each cell. It should be within the limits specified in **Table 3**. If it is, and remains stable for 1 hour, the battery is considered charged.

4. Clean the battery terminals, electrical cable connectors and surrounding case and reinstall the battery in the frame, reversing the removal steps.

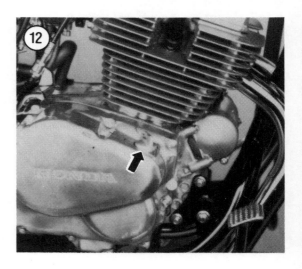

Coat the battery terminals with Vaseline or silicone spray to retard corrosion and decomposition of the terminals.

CAUTION
Route the breather tube (A, Figure 9) so that it does not drain onto any part of the frame. The tube must be free of bends or twists as any restriction may pressurize the battery and damage it.

New Battery Installation

When replacing the old battery with a new one, be sure to charge it completely (specific gravity 1.260-1.280) before installing it in the bike. Failure to do so or using the battery with a low electrolyte level will permanently damage the new battery.

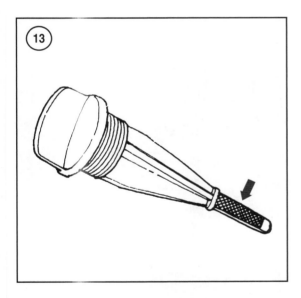

PERIODIC LUBRICATION

Oil

Oil is graded according to its viscosity, which is an indication of how thick it is. The Society of Automotive Engineers (SAE) system distinguishes oil viscosity by numbers. Thick oils have higher viscosity numbers than thin oils. For example, an SAE 5 oil is a thin oil while an SAE 90 oil is relatively thick.

Grease

Where grease is specified, use a good quality (preferably waterproof). Water does not wash grease off parts as easily as it washes oil off. In addition, grease maintains its lubricating qualities better than oil on long and strenuous rides. In a pinch, though, the wrong lubricant is better than none at all. Correct the situation as soon as possible.

Engine Oil Level Check

Engine oil level is checked with the dipstick/oil filler cap, located on the top of the crankcase on the right-hand side (**Figure 12**).
1. Place the bike on level ground.
2. Start the engine and let it idle for 2-3 minutes.
3. Shut off the engine and let the oil settle.
4. Unscrew the dipstick and wipe it clean. Reinsert the dipstick onto the threads in the hole; do not screw it in.
5. Remove the dipstick and check the oil level. The level should be between the 2 lines (**Figure 13**) and not above the upper one. If the level is below the lower line, add the recommended type engine oil to correct the level.

Engine Oil Change

Change the engine oil at the factory-recommended oil change interval indicated in **Table 2**. This assumes that the motorcycle is operated in moderate climates. In extreme climates, oil should be changed every 30 days. The time interval is more important than the mileage interval because acids formed by combustion blowby will contaminate the oil even if the motorcycle is not run for several months. If the motorcycle is operated under dusty conditions, the oil will get dirty more quickly and should be changed more frequently than recommended.

Use only a high-quality detergent motor oil with an API classification of SE or SF. The classification is stamped on top of the can or printed on the label on the plastic bottle (**Figure 14**). Try to use the same brand of oil at each change. Use of oil additives is not recommended as it may cause clutch slippage. Refer to **Figure 15** for correct oil viscosity to use under anticipated ambient temperatures (not engine temperature).

> *NOTE*
> *Never dispose of motor oil in the trash, on the ground, or down a storm drain. Many service stations accept used motor oil and waste haulers provide curbside used motor oil collection. Do not combine other fluids with motor oil to be recycled. To locate a recycler, contact the American Petroleum Institute (API) at www.recycleoil.org.*

To change the engine oil and filter you will need the following:

   a. Drain pan.

   b. Funnel.

   c. Can opener or pour spout.

   d. 2 quarts of oil.

1. Start the engine and let it reach operating temperature; 15-20 minutes of stop-and-go riding is usually sufficient.

2. Turn the engine off and place the bike on level ground.

3. Place a drain pan under the crankcase and remove the drain plug (**Figure 16**). Remove the dipstick/oil filler cap; this will speed up the flow of oil.

> *CAUTION*
> *Do not let the engine start and run without oil in the crankcase.*

4. Let the oil drain for at least 15-20 minutes. During this time, kick the kickstarter a couple of times or push the starter button (models so equipped) a couple of times to help drain any remaining oil.

5. Inspect the sealing washer on the crankcase drain plug. Replace if its condition is in doubt.

6. Install the drain plug and washer and tighten to 25 N•m (18 ft.-lb.).

7. Insert a funnel into the oil fill hole and fill the engine with the correct viscosity and quantity of oil. Refer to **Figure 15** and **Table 4**.

8. Install the dipstick/oil filler cap.

9. Start the engine, let it run at idle speed and check for leaks.

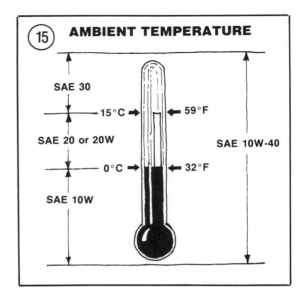

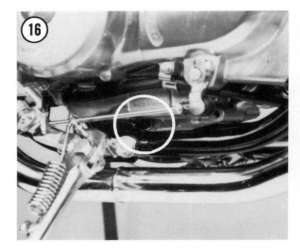

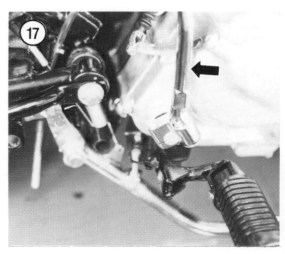

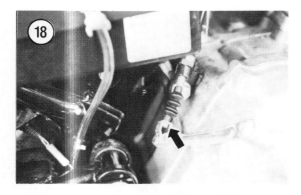

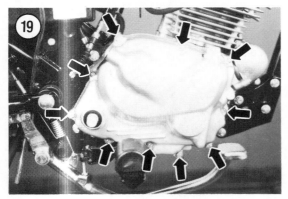

10. Turn the engine off and check for correct oil level; adjust as necessary.

Oil Filter Screen Cleaning

The oil filter screen should be cleaned at the interval indicated in **Table 2**.

1. Drain the engine oil as described in this chapter.
2. On models so equipped, remove the kickstarter pedal (**Figure 17**).
3. Remove the right-hand side of the exhaust system as described in Chapter Six.
4. Disconnect the clutch cable from the lever (**Figure 18**).
5. Remove the bolts securing the right-hand crankcase cover (**Figure 19**) and remove the cover and gasket.
6. Remove the Phillips head screws (A, **Figure 20**) securing the oil pump assembly and remove the assembly.
7. Remove the oil filter screen (B, **Figure 20**) from the oil pump housing. Clean the screen in solvent with a medium soft toothbrush and carefully dry with compressed air.
8. Inspect the screen; replace it if there are any breaks or holes in the screen.

NOTE
*Make sure the O-ring (**Figure 21**) is in place in the crankcase prior to installing the oil pump assembly.*

9. Install the screen onto the oil pump and install the oil pump.
10. Install by reversing these removal steps, noting the following.
11. Fill the crankcase with the recommended type and quantity of engine oil as described in this chapter.

Front Fork Oil Change

NOTE
The following procedure applies to motorcycles equipped with fork drain plugs. On other models, you'll need to remove and partially disassemble the forks to change the oil.

It's a good practice to change the fork oil at the interval indicated in **Table 2**, or when it becomes contaminated.

1. Place wood block(s) under the engine to support it securely with the front wheel off the ground.

NOTE
On some models, it may be necessary to partially remove the front forks or the handlebar assembly to gain access to the upper fork cap bolt. Refer to Chapter Eight.

2. Remove the upper cap bolt (**Figure 22**).

3. On models so equipped, place a drain pan under the fork and remove the drain screw (**Figure 23**). Allow the oil to drain for at least 5 minutes. Never reuse oil.

> *CAUTION*
> *Do not allow the fork oil to come in contact with any of the brake components.*

4. Install the drain screw.

5. Repeat Steps 2-4 for the other fork.

6. Fill each fork tube with DEXRON automatic transmission fluid or 10W fork oil. Refer to **Table 4** for fork oil capacities.

> *NOTE*
> *To measure the correct amount of fluid, use a plastic baby bottle. These have measurements in fluid ounces (oz.) and cubic centimeters (cc) on the side.*

7. Install the fork cap bolts and tighten to the following torque specifications:

   a. Rebel 250: 15-30 N•m (11-22 ft.-lb.).

   b. All other models: 25-30 N•m (18-21 ft.-lb.).

8. If partially removed, install the fork assemblies as described in Chapter Eight.

9. Remove the wood block(s) from under the engine.

10. Road test the bike and check for leaks.

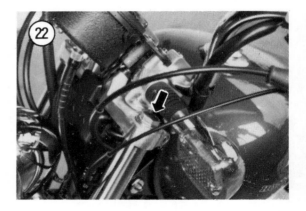

Drive Chain Lubrication (Chain-driven Models)

Oil the drive chain at the interval indicated in **Table 2** or sooner if it becomes dry.

1. Place wood block(s) under the engine or frame to support the bike securely.

2A. *Non-O-ring type chain*—Oil the bottom run of the chain with a good grade of motorcycle chain lubricant. Make sure the lubricant penetrates down between the side plates of the chain links, into the pins, bushings and rollers.

2B. *O-ring type chain*—Oil the bottom run of the chain with SAE 80-90 gear lubricant. Do not apply regulat motorcycle chain lubricant to an O-ring chain. Make sure the lubricant penetrates down between the side plates of the chain links, into the pins, bushings and rollers.

3. Rotate the rear wheel to bring the unoiled portion of the chain within reach. Continue until all the chain is lubricated.

Control Cable Lubrication

The throttle and choke control cables should be lubricated at the interval indicated in **Table 2**. They should also be inspected at this time for fraying and the cable sheath should be checked for chafing. The cables are relatively inexpensive and should be replaced when found to be faulty.

The throttle and choke control cables can be lubricated either with oil or with any of the popular

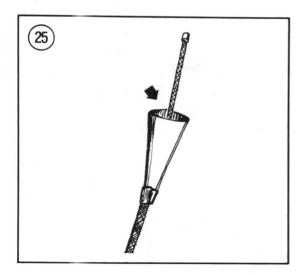

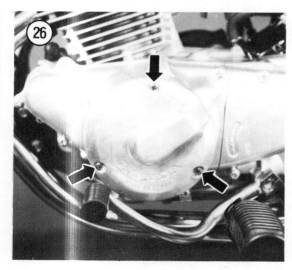

2. Make a cone of stiff paper and tape it to the end of the cable sheath (**Figure 25**).

3. Hold the cable upright and pour a small amount of thin oil (SAE 10W-30) into the cone. Work the cable in and out of the sheath for several minutes to help the oil work its way down to the end of the cable.

> *NOTE*
> *To avoid a mess, place a shop cloth at the end of the cable to catch the oil as it runs out.*

4. Remove the cone, reconnect the cable and adjust the cable(s) as described in this chapter.

> *NOTE*
> *While the throttle cable(s) is removed and the switch assembly disassembled, apply a light coat of grease to the metal surfaces of the throttle grip assembly.*

Lubricator method

1. Disconnect the cable from the lever (**Figure 24**).
2. Attach a lubricator following the manufacturer's instructions.
3. Insert the nozzle of the lubricant can in the lubricator, press the button on the can and hold it down until the lubricant begins to flow out of the other end of the cable.

> *NOTE*
> *Place a shop cloth at the end of the cable(s) to catch all excess lubricant that will flow out.*

4. Remove the lubricator, reconnect the cable(s) and adjust the cable as described in this chapter.

Contact Breaker Points Lubriction (Models so Equipped)

Lubricate the breaker point assembly at the interval indicated in **Table 2** or when the points are inspected, whichever comes first.

1. Remove the screws securing the ignition cover (**Figure 26**) and remove the cover and gasket.
2. Apply a small amount of high-temperature grease onto the felt pad that rides against the breaker point cam (**Figure 27**). If too much grease is appled, the cam will sling the grease onto the points, fouling them.
3. Install the ignition cover and gasket.

Miscellaneous Lubrication Points

Lubricate the clutch lever (**Figure 28**), front brake lever (**Figure 29**), rear brake pedal (**Figure 30**), side stand pivot points and footrest pivot points with SAE 10W/30 engine oil.

cable lubricants and a cable lubricator. The first method requires more time and complete lubrication of the entire cable is less certain.

Examine the exposed end of the inner cable. If it is dirty or the cable feels gritty when moved up and down in its housing, first spray it with a lubricant/solvent such as LPS-25 or WD-40. Let this solvent drain out, then proceed with the following steps.

Oil method

1. Disconnect the cable from the lever (**Figure 24**).

> *NOTE*
> *On the throttle cable(s) it is necessary to remove the screws securing the right-hand switch assembly together to gain access to the throttle cable(s) ends.*

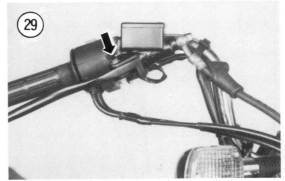

PERIODIC MAINTENANCE

Drive Chain Adjustment
(Chain-driven Models)

Check and adjust, if necessary, the drive chain at the interval indicated in **Table 2**. The drive chain should be removed, cleaned and lubricated at the interval listed in **Table 2**.

1. Place the transmission in NEUTRAL.
2. On models so equipped, remove the rear axle nut cotter pin. Discard the cotter pin.
3A. On Rebel 250 models, perform the following:
   a. Loosen the rear axle nut (A, **Figure 31**) and both axle adjusting locknuts (B, **Figure 31**).
   b. Screw the adjusters (C, **Figure 31**) in or out as required in equal amounts. The free movement of the drive chain, pushed up mid-way between both sprockets, should be 5/8-1 in. (20-30 mm). Refer to **Figure 32**.
3B. On all other models, perform the following:
   a. Loosen the rear axle nut (A, **Figure 33**) and both axle adjusting locknuts (B, **Figure 33**).
   b. Screw the adjusters (C, **Figure 33**) in or out as required in equal amounts. The free

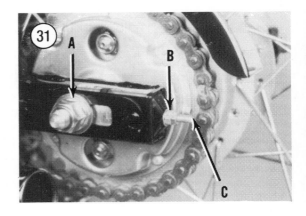

movement of the drive chain, pushed up mid-way between both sprockets, should be 5/8-1 in. (20-30 mm). Refer to **Figure 32**.
4. Rotate the rear wheel to move the chain to another position and recheck the adjustment; chains rarely wear or stretch evenly and as a result, the free play will not remain constant over the entire chain. If the chain cannot be adjusted within these limits, it is excessively worn and stretched

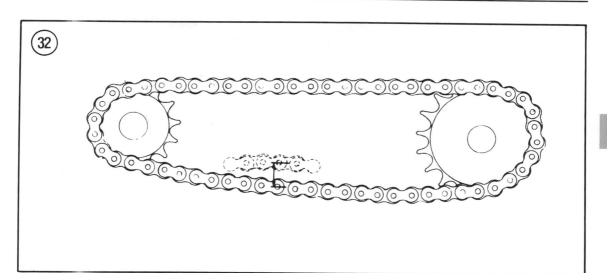

3

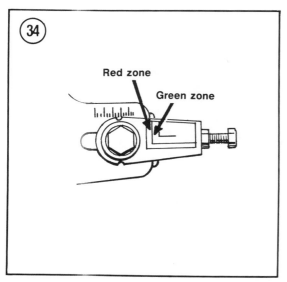

and must be replaced as described in Chapter Nine.

5. When the adjustment is correct, sight along the chain from the rear sprocket to see that it is correctly aligned. It should leave the top of the rear sprocket in a straight line. If it cocked to one side or the other, the rear wheel is incorrectly aligned and must be corrected by turning the adjusters counter to one another until the chain and sprocket are correctly aligned.

6A. On 1982-1983 models, make sure the index mark aligns with the same graduation on the scale on both sides of the swing arm (**Figure 34**). Replace the drive chain when the red zone on the label aligns with the rear of the swing arm.

6B. On 1985-on models, make sure the index marks align with or are the same distance from the rear edge of the adjuster slots (**Figure 35**). Replace the drive chain when the red zone on the label and the index mark on the adjuster align or overlap after adjustment is complete.

7. When alignment is correct, readjust the free play as described in Step 3-5.

8. Tighten the rear axle nut to the following torque specifications:

    a. 1978-1981: 40-50 N•m (26-36 ft.-lb.).

    b. 1982: 55-65 N•m (40-47 ft.-lb.).

    a. 1985-on: 80-100 N•m (58-72 ft.-lb.).

9. On models so equipped, install a new cotter pin and bend the ends over completely.

10. Adjust the rear brake pedal free play as described in this chapter.

Drive Chain Cleaning and Inspection (Chain-driven Models)

Clean and lubricate the drive chain at the interval indicated in **Table 2**.

1. Remove the drive chain as described in Chapter Nine.

2. Immerse the drive chain in a pan of kerosene or non-flammable solvent and allow it to soak for about a half hour. Move it around and flex it during this period so that the dirt between the links, pins and rollers may work its way out.

3. Scrub the rollers and side plates with a stiff brush and rinse away loosened dirt. Rinse it a couple of times to make sure all dirt and grit are washed out. Dry the chain with a shop cloth and hang it up to thoroughly dry.

4. After cleaning the drive chain, examine it carefully for wear or damage. If any signs are visible, replace the drive chain.

5. Lay the drive chain against a ruler (**Figure 36**) and compress the links together. Then stretch them apart. If more than a 6 mm (1/4 in.) of movement is possible, the drive chain is worn and must be replaced.

> *NOTE*
> *Always inspect both sprockets (**Figure 37**) every time the chain is removed. If any wear is visible on the teeth, replace the sprocket(s). Never install a new chain over worn sprockets or a worn chain over new sprocket(s).*

6. Lubricate the drive chain as described in this chapter.

Drive Belt Tension Inspection (Belt-driven Models)

Adjust the drive belt at the interval indicated in **Table 2**. The drive belt should be "cold" (at room

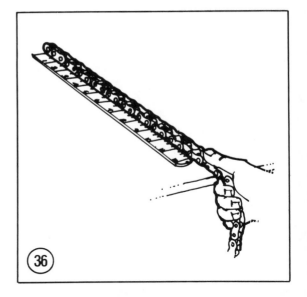

(36)

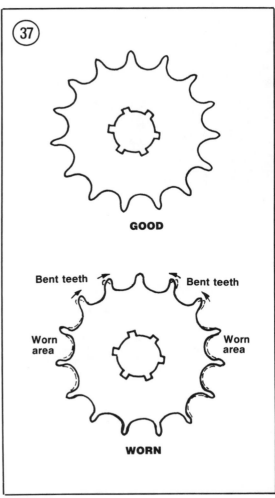

(37)

GOOD

Bent teeth   Bent teeth

Worn area   Worn area

WORN

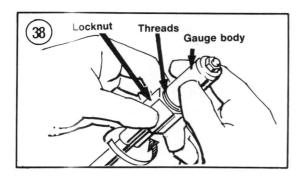

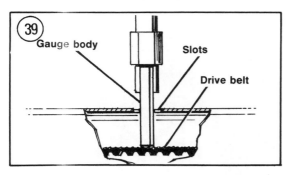

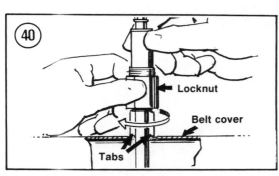

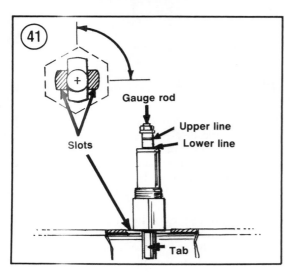

temperature) for this procedure. Do not perform this procedure after riding the bike.

> *CAUTION*
> *The drive belt requires **no** lubrication. Any type of lubrication or solvents applied to the drive belt can cause damage to the drive belt and it must be replaced. If the belt is dirty, clean with water and a clean cloth.*

With special tool

The special tool used in this procedure is furnished in the owner's tool kit.

1. Place the bike on the centerstand.
2. Shift the transmission into NEUTRAL.
3. Remove the rubber inspection cap from the top of the drive belt cover.
4. Turn the gauge locknut in the direction shown in **Figure 38** until the threads on the gauge body are covered by the locknut.
5. Insert the gauge into the hole in the top of the drive belt cover (**Figure 39**) until the gauge rod touches the top surface of the drive belt.
6. Hold onto the gauge body and turn the locknut clockwise or down until the locknut tabs touch on the drive belt cover (**Figure 40**).
7. Turn the locknut so the tabs fit into the slots in the drive belt cover and push down on the locknut and gauge body until the bottom surface of the locknut bottoms out on the drive belt cover. Rotate the locknut 90° in either direction and lock the special tool in place on the drive belt cover.
8. The gauge rod that protrudes above the gauge body (**Figure 41**) has 2 lines. The position of the gauge rod indicates the amount of drive belt tension. If the rod is above the upper limit line, the belt is too loose and if it is below the lower line, the belt is too tight. The correct amount of belt tension is midway between these 2 lines.
9. Rotate the rear wheel and check drive belt tension. The gauge rod is resting on the top surface of the drivebelt and should remain in one position at all times as the drive belt moves past the gauge rod.
10. If the gauge rod moves up and down in Step 9, this indicates that the belt is loose in one position and is tight in another position. If this condition exists, check the drive and driven pulleys for wear or damage. Also, the drive belt may be stretched in one or more places.
11. If adjustment is necessary, adjust the drive belt as described in this chapter.

Without special tool

The drive belt tension can be checked by this method but it is not recommended since it is not very accurate.

1. Place the bike on the centerstand.
2. Shift the transmission into NEUTRAL.

CAUTION
Excessive drive belt slack of 1 3/8 in. (35 mm) or more may cause the drive belt to come in contact with surrounding parts which will shorten belt life.

3. The free movement of the drive belt, pushed up on the bottom run of the drive belt midway between the 2 pulleys (**Figure 42**) should be 5/8-1 in. (15-20 mm).
4. Rotate the rear wheel and check drive belt tension at several locations.
5. If the slack is uneven at various locations, check the drive and driven pulleys for wear or damage. Also, the drive belt may be stretched in one or more places.
6. If adjustment is necessary, adjust the drive belt as described in this chapter.

Drive Belt Adjustment

1. Place the bike on the centerstand.
2. Shift the transmission into NEUTRAL.
3. Completely rotate the rear wheel several times to ensure equal tension on the drive belt.
4. Loosen the rear axle nut and the axle adjusting locknuts.
5. Screw the adjuster in or out as required in equal amounts. The free movement of the drive belt is as indicated in the *Drive Belt Tension Inspection* procedure in this chapter.
6. Rotate the rear wheel to move the drive belt to another position and recheck the adjustment; drive belts rarely wear or stretch evenly and as a result, the free play will not remain constant over the entire drive belt. If the drive belt cannot be adjusted within these limits, it is excessively worn and stretched and must be replaced as described in Chapter Nine.
7. Tighten the rear axle nut to 40-47 ft.-lb. (55-65 N•m).
8. Adjust the rear brake pedal free play as described in this chapter.

Disc Brake Fluid Level

The fluid level in the front brake reservoir should be up to the upper mark within the reservoir. This upper level mark is visible only

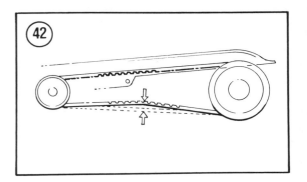

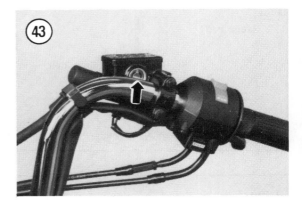

when the master cylinder top cover is removed. If the brake fluid level reaches the lower level mark (**Figure 43**), visible through the viewing port on the side of the master cylinder reservoir, the fluid level must be corrected by adding fresh brake fluid.

1. Place the bike on level ground and position the handlebars so the master cylinder reservoir is level.
2. Clean any dirt from the area around the top cover before removing the cover.
3. Remove the screws securing the top cover (**Figure 44**). Remove the top cover and the

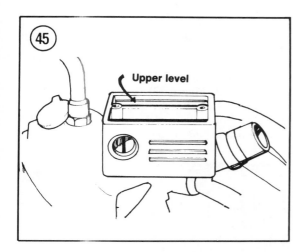

Upper level

diaphragm. Add brake fluid until the level is to the upper level line within the master cylinder body (**Figure 45**). Use fresh brake fluid from a sealed brake fluid container.

> *WARNING*
> *Use brake fluid from a sealed container and clearly marked DOT 3 or DOT 4 only (specified for disc brakes). Others may vaporize and cause brake failure. Do not intermix different brands or types of brake fluid as they may not be compatible. Do not intermix a silicone based (DOT 5) brake fluid as it can cause brake component damage leading to brake system failure.*

> *CAUTION*
> *Be careful when handling brake fluid. Do not spill it on painted or plated surfaces or plastic parts as it will destroy the surface. Wash the area immediately with soapy water and thoroughly rinse it off.*

4. Reinstall the diaphragm and the top cover. Tighten the screws securely.

Disc Brake Lines

Check brake lines between the master cylinder and the brake caliper. If there is any leakage, tighten the connections and bleed the brakes as described in Chapter Ten. If this does not stop the leak or if a brake line is obviously damaged, cracked or chafed, replace the brake line and bleed the system.

Disc Brake Pad Wear

Inspect the brake pads for excessive or uneven wear, scoring and oil or grease on the friction surface. Look at the pads through the slot (**Figure 46**) in the top of the caliper assembly. Replace both pads if the wear line on the pads reaches the brake disc.

If any of these conditions exist, replace the pads as described in Chapter Ten.

Disc Brake Fluid Change

Every time the reservoir cap is removed, a small amount of dirt and moisture enters the brake fluid. The same thing happens if a leak occurs or any part of the hydraulic system is loosened or disconnected. Dirt can clog the system and cause unnecessary wear. Water in the brake fluid vaporizes at high temperature, impairing the hydraulic action and reducing the brake's stopping ability.

To maintain peak performance change the brake fluid as indicated in **Table 2**. To change brake fluid, follow the *Bleeding the Brake System* procedure in Chapter Ten. Continue adding new fluid to the master cylinder and bleeding out at the caliper until the fluid leaving the caliper is clean and free of contaminants.

> *WARNING*
> *Use brake fluid from a sealed container and clearly marked DOT 3 or DOT 4 only (specified for disc brakes). Others may vaporize and cause brake failure. Do not intermix different brands or types of brake fluid as they may not be compatible. Do not intermix a silicone based (DOT 5) brake fluid as it can cause brake component damage leading to brake system failure.*

Front Brake Lever Adjustment (Drum Brake Models)

The front brake cable should be adjusted so there will be 10-20 mm (3/8-3/4 in.) of brake lever movement required to actuate the brake, but it must not be so closely adjusted that the brake shoes contact the brake drum with the lever in the released position.

Minor adjustments should be made at the hand lever, but major adjustments should be made at the brake lever at the brake mechanism on the wheel.

1. Loosen the locknut (A, **Figure 47**) and turn the adjusting barrel (B, **Figure 47**) in order to obtain the correct amount of free play. Tighten the locknut.

2. Because of normal brake wear, this adjustment will eventually be "used up." It is then necessary to loosen the locknut (A) and screw the adjusting barrel (B) all the way in toward the hand grip. Tighten the locknut (A).

3. At the brake mechanism on the wheel, turn the adjustment nut (**Figure 48**), until the brake lever can once again be used for fine adjustment.

4. When the 2 arrows on the brake arm and brake panel align (**Figure 49**) the brake shoes must be replaced as described in Chapter Ten.

Rear Brake Pedal
Height Adjustment

The rear brake pedal height should be adjusted at the interval listed in **Table 2**.

1. Place wood block(s) under the engine or frame to support the bike securely.

2. Make sure the brake pedal is in the at-rest position.

3. The correct height above the front footpeg is as follows:

    a. Rebel 250 models: 3/8-3/4 in. (10-20 mm.) (**Figure 50**).

    b. All other models: 3/4-1 1/4 in. (20-30 mm) (**Figure 51**).

4A. On Rebel 250 models, to adjust the height, loosen the locknut and turn the adjust bolt (**Figure 52**) to achieve the correct height.

4B. On all other models, to adjust the height, loosen the locknut (A, **Figure 53**) and turn the adjust bolt (B, **Figure 53**) to achieve the correct height.

5. Tighten the locknut. Adjust the pedal free play as described in this chapter.

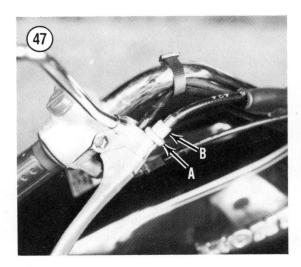

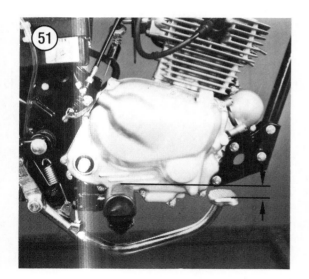

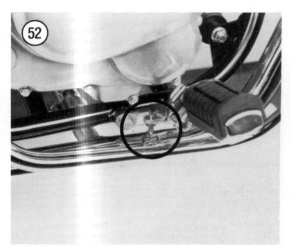

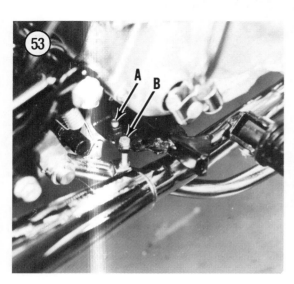

**Rear Brake Pedal
Free Play**

Free play is the distance the rear brake pedal travels from the at-rest position to the applied position when the pedal is depressed by hand.

1. Adjust the rear brake to the correct height as described in this chapter.

2. Turn the adjust nut on the end of the brake rod (**Figure 54**) until the pedal has 20-30 mm (3/4-1 1/4 in.) free play.

3. Rotate the rear wheel and check for brake drag.

4. Operate the brake pedal several times to make sure the pedal returns to the at-rest position immediately after release.

5. Adjust the rear brake light switch as described in Chapter Seven.

Clutch Free Play Adjustment

In order for the clutch to fully engage and disengage, there must be 10-20 mm (3/8-3/4 in.) of free play at the clutch lever end (**Figure 55**).

1. At the clutch lever, loosen the locknut (A, **Figure 56**) and turn the adjuster (B, **Figure 56**) in or out to obtain the correct amount of free play. Tighten the locknut.

CAUTION
Do not screw the adjuster out so that there is more than 8 mm (0.3 in.) of threads exposed between the adjuster and the locknut.

2. Start the engine and pull the clutch lever in and shift into first gear. If shifting is difficult, if the bike creeps when stopped or if the clutch slips when accelerating in high gear, the clutch will have to be adjusted at the clutch housing.

3. At the clutch lever, loosen the locknut (A, **Figure 56**) and turn the adjuster (B, **Figure 56**) in all the way toward the hand grip. Tighten the locknut (A).

4. At the clutch housing, loosen the locknut (C, **Figure 57**) and turn the adjuster (D, **Figure 57**) in or out to obtain the correct amount of free play. Tighten the locknut (C).

5. If necessary, do some final adjusting at the clutch lever as described in Step 1.

6. Road test the bike to make sure the clutch fully disengages when the lever is pulled in; if it does not, the bike will creep in gear when stopped. Also make sure the clutch fully engages; if it does not, the clutch will slip, particularly when accelerating in high gear.

7. If the proper amount of adjustment cannot be achieved using this procedure, the cable has stretched to the point where it needs replacing. Refer to Chapter Five for complete procedure.

Throttle Adjustment and Operation

The throttle grip should have 2-6 mm (1/8-1/4 in.) rotational free play (**Figure 58**). If adjustment is

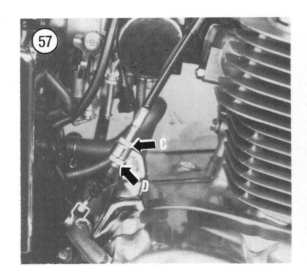

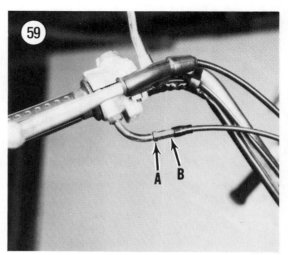

necessary, make minor adjustments at the throttle grip and the major adjustments at the top of the carburetor.

Models since 1985 have a dual-cable or push/pull type of throttle cable assembly. Pre-1985 models are equipped with only a single pull cable.

1A. On single-throttle cable models, loosen the locknut (A, **Figure 59**) and turn the adjuster (B, **Figure 59**) at the throttle grip in or out to achieve proper free play rotation. Tighten the locknut (A).

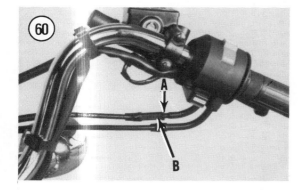

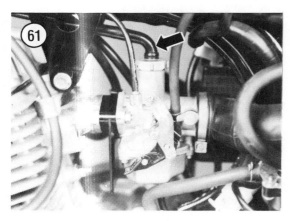

1B. On dual-throttle cable models, loosen the locknut (A, **Figure 60**) and turn the adjuster (B, **Figure 60**) at the throttle grip in or out to achieve proper free play rotation. Tighten the locknut (A).

2. If the proper amount of free play caonnot be achieved, loosen the locknut and turn the adjuster (B) all the way in toward the throttle grip. Tighten the locknut (A).

3A. On single-cable models, slide the rubber cap (**Figure 61**) on the carburetor cap and turn the adjuster until the proper amount of free play is achieved.

3B. On dual-cable models, perform the following:
  a. Remove the screws securing the throttle cable cover (**Figure 62**) and remove the cover.
  b. At the rear cable (the pull cable), loosen the locknut (A, **Figure 63**) and turn the adjuster (B, **Figure 63**) until the proper amount of free play is achieved. Tighten the locknut.
  c. Install the throttle cable cover and tighen the screws securely.

4. Check the throttle cable(s) from the grip to the carburetor. Make sure they are not kinked or chafed. Replace as necessary.

5. Make sure the throttle grip rotates freely from a fully closed to fully open position. Check with the handlebar at center, at full right and at full left. If necessary, remove the throttle grip and apply a lithium base grease to it.

> *WARNING*
> *With the engine idling, move the handlebar from side to side. If idle speed increases during this movement, the throttle cable(s) may need adjusting or may be incorrectly routed through the frame. Correct this problem immediately. Do **not** ride the bike in this unsafe condition.*

Cam Chain Tensioner Adjustment
(185 and 200 Models)

NOTE
On 250 models, the camshaft chain tensioner is completely automatic and does not require any periodic adjustment. There are no provisions for tensioner adjustment on the engine.

In time the camshaft chain and guide will wear and develop slack on 185 and 200 models. This will cause engine noise and if neglected too long will cause engine damage. Adjust the camshaft chain tensioner at the interval indicated in **Table 2**.

1. Remove the right-hand side cover and disconnect the battery negative lead (**Figure 64**).
2. Remove the screws (**Figure 65**) securing the ignition cover and remove the cover and gasket.
3. Turn the crankshaft *counterclockwise* using the bolt on the end of the crankshaft (**Figure 66**). Turn the engine until the ignition timing mark "T-1" (Model CM185T) or "T" mark (Model CM200T) aligns with the index mark (**Figure 67**).
4. Loosen the locknut (**Figure 68**) with a 10 mm wrench. The tensioner will automatically adjust to the correct tension.
5. Hold the adjuster bolt stationary and tighten the locknut. Do not let the adjuster bolt rotate during this procedure.
6. Install the ignition cover and gasket. Tighten the screws securely.
7. Connect the battery negative lead and install the right-hand cover.

Air Filter Element Cleaning

The air filter element should be removed and cleaned at the interval listed in **Table 1**.

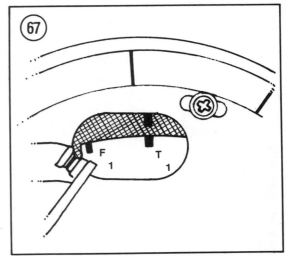

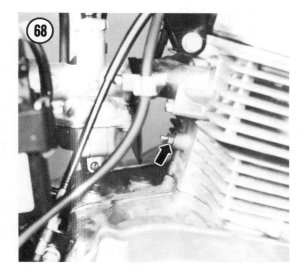

The air filter removes dust and abrasive particles from the air before the air enters the carburetor and engine. Without the air filter, very fine particles could enter into the engine and cause rapid wear of the piston rings, cylinder and bearings and might clog small passages in the carburetors. Never run the bike without the air filter element installed.

Proper air filter servicing can do more to ensure long service from your engine than almost any other single item.

1A. On Rebel 250 models, perform the following:
  a. Remove the screw (**Figure 69**) securing the left-hand side cover and remove the cover.
  b. Remove the screws (**Figure 70**) securing the air filter cover and remove the cover.
  c. Pull the filter set spring out (A, **Figure 71**).
  d. Remove the air filter element (B, **Figure 71**) from the air box.
  e. Disconnect the hose from the element holder (**Figure 72**).

1B. On all other models, perform the following:
  a. Remove the left-hand side cover.
  b. Remove the nuts (**Figure 73**) securing the air filter cover and remove the cover.
  c. Pull the filter set spring out (A, **Figure 74**).
  d. Pull out the element and holder (B, **Figure 74**). On Model CM200T, disconnect the hose from the element holder (**Figure 75**).

2. Remove the air filter element from the holder.

3. Clean the element gently in a non-flammable or high flash point cleaning solvent until all dirt is removed. Thoroughly dry in a clean shop cloth until all residue is removed. Let dry for about one hour.

> *NOTE*
> *Inspect the element; if it is torn or broken in any area it should be replaced. Do not run with a damaged element as it may allow dirt to enter the engine.*

4. Pour a small amount of SAE 80-90 gear oil or foam air filter oil onto the element and work it into the porous foam material. Do not oversaturate as too much oil will restrict air flow. The element should be discolored by the oil and should have an even color indicating that the oil is distributed evenly. If foam air filter oil was used, let the element dry for another hour prior to installation. If installed too soon, the chemical carrier in the foam air filter oil will be drawn into the engine and may cause damage.

5. Wipe out the interior of the air box with a shop rag dampened with cleaning solvent. Remove any foreign matter that may have passed through a broken element.

6. Install by reversing these removal steps, noting the following.

7. On Rebel 250 models, make sure the rubber ring (**Figure 76**) is in place on the element prior to installation. This ring is necessary for proper sealing.

8. Make sure the element is correctly seated into the air box so there is no air leak.

Fuel Shutoff Valve
Strainer Cleaning (1982-on Models)

The fuel strainer is built into the shutoff valve and removes particles which might otherwise enter into the carburetor and may cause the float needle to remain in the open position.

1. Turn the shutoff valve to the OFF position.

2. Unscrew the fuel cup (**Figure 77**), O-ring and screen from the shutoff valve. Dispose of fuel remaining in the fuel cup properly.

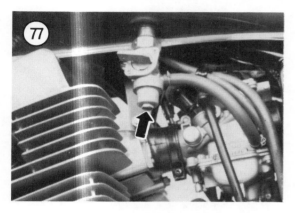

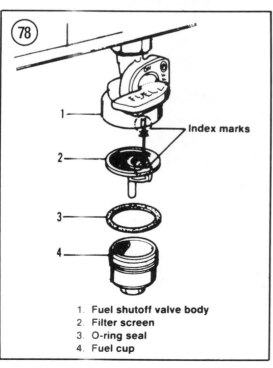

1. Fuel shutoff valve body
2. Filter screen
3. O-ring seal
4. Fuel cup

3. Clean the screen with a medium soft toothbrush and blow out with compressed air. Replace the screen if it is broken in any area.

4. On models so equipped, align the index marks on the filter screen and shutoff valve body (**Figure 78**).

5. Install the O-ring seal and screw on the fuel cup.

6. Hand-tighten the fuel cup and tighten to a final torque of 3-5 N•m (2-4 ft.-lb.). Do not overtighten the fuel cup as it may be damaged.

7. Turn the fuel shutoff valve to the ON position and check for leaks.

Fuel Shutoff Filter and Valve Removal/Installation

The fuel filter is built into the shutoff valve and removes particles which might otherwise enter into the carburetor and may cause the float needle to remain in the open position.

1. Turn the shutoff valve to the OFF position (A, **Figure 79**) and remove the fuel line (B, **Figure 79**) to the carburetor.

2. Place the loose end in a clean, sealable metal container. This fuel can be reused if it is kept clean.

3. Open the valve to the RESERVE position and remove the fuel filler cap. This will allow air to enter the fuel tank and speed up the flow of fuel. Drain the fuel tank completely.

4. Unscrew the locknut securing the fuel shutoff valve to the fuel tank.

5. After removing the valve from the fuel tank, insert a corner of a shop cloth into the opening in the tank to stop the dribbling of fuel onto the engine and frame.

6. Remove the fuel filter from the shutoff valve. Clean the filter with a medium soft toothbrush and blow out with compressed air. Replace the filter if it is broken in any area.

7. Install by reversing these removal steps, noting the following.

8. Be sure to install a gasket between the shutoff valve and the fuel tank.

9. Tighten the locknut to 20-24 N•m (15-18 ft.-lb.).

10. Turn the fuel shutoff valve to the ON position and check for leaks.

Fuel Line Inspection

Inspect the fuel line from the fuel shutoff valve to the carburetor. If it is cracked or starting to deteriorate it must be replaced. Make sure the hose clamps are in place and holding securely.

> *WARNING*
> *A damaged or deteriorated fuel line presents a very dangerous fire hazard to both the rider and the vehicle if fuel should spill onto a hot engine or exhaust pipe.*

Wheel Bearings

There is no factory-recommended mileage interval for cleaning and repacking the wheel bearings. They should be inspected and serviced if necessary every time the wheel is removed or whenever there is a likelihood of water contamination. Service procedures are covered in Chapter Eight and Chapter Nine.

Wheel Hubs, Rims and Spokes

Check the wheel hubs and rims for bends and other signs of damage. Check both wheels for broken or bent spokes. Replace damaged or broken spokes as described in Chapter Eight. Plunk each spoke with your finger like a guitar string or tap each one lightly with a small metal tool. All spokes should emit the same sound. A spoke that is too tight will have a higher pitch than others; one that is too loose will have a lower pitch. If only one or two spokes are slightly out of adjustment, adjust with a spoke wrench made for this purpose. If more are affected, the wheel should be removed and trued as described in Chapter Eight.

Front Suspension Check

1. Apply the front brake and pump the forks up and down as vigorously as possible. Check for smooth operation and check for any oil leaks.

2. Make sure the upper and lower fork bridge bolts are tight (**Figure 80**).

3. On models so equipped, remove the caps from the Allen bolts. Make sure the bolts securing the handlebar holders (**Figure 81**) are tight and that the handlebar is secure.

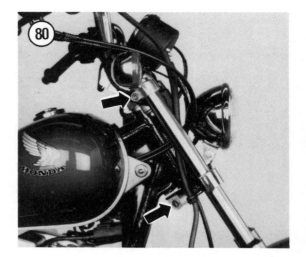

4. Make sure the front axle (**Figure 82**) or axle nut is tight and on models so equipped, make sure the cotter pin (**Figure 83**) is in place.

> *CAUTION*
> *If any of the previously mentioned bolts and nuts are loose, refer to Chapter Eight for tightening procedures and torque specifications.*

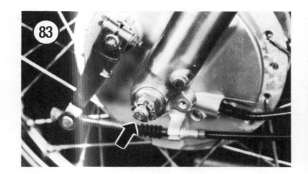

4. Make sure the rear axle nut is tight (**Figure 85**) and on models so equipped, make sure the cotter pin (**Figure 86**) is in place.
5. Check the tightness of the rear brake torque arm bolt (**Figure 87**). Make sure the cotter pin is in place.

CAUTION
If any of the previously mentioned bolts and nuts are loose, refer to Chapter Nine for correct procedures and torque specifications.

Nuts, Bolts and Other Fasteners

Constant vibration can loosen many of the fasteners on the motorcycle. Check the tightness of all fasteners, especially those on:
  a. Engine mounting hardware.
  b. Engine crankcase covers.
  c. Handlebar and front forks.
  d. Gearshift lever.
  e. Brake pedal and lever.
  f. Exhaust system.
  g. Lighting equipment.

Rear Suspension Check

1. Place a wood block(s) under the engine to support it securely with the rear wheel off the ground.
2. Push hard on the rear wheel (sideways) to check for side play in the rear swing arm bushings. Remove the wood block(s).
3. Check the tightness of the upper and lower mounting nuts (**Figure 84**) on each shock absorber.

Sidestand Rubber

The rubber pad on the sidestand kicks the sidestand up if you should forget. If it wears down to the molded line, replace the rubber as it will no longer be effective and must be replaced.

Steering Head Adjustment Check

Check the steering head ball bearings for looseness at the interval listed in **Table 2**.

Place a wood block(s) under the engine to support it securely with the front wheel off the ground.

Hold onto the front fork tube and gently rock the fork assembly back and forth. If you feel looseness, refer to *Steering Head Adjustment* in Chapter Eight.

Crankcase Breather (U.S. Models Only)

The residue in the breather drain tube should be drained at the interval indicated in **Table 2** or sooner if a considerable amount of riding is done at full throttle or in the rain.

Remove the drain plug (**Figure 88**) and drain out all residue. Install the cap; make sure the clamp is tight.

Refer to Chapter Six for complete details on the breather system.

TUNE-UP

Perform a complete tune-up at the interval listed in **Table 2** if the bike is used for normal riding. More frequent tune-ups may be required if the bike is ridden in stop-and-go traffic. The purpose of the tune-up is to restore the performance lost due to normal wear and deterioration of parts.

The spark plugs should be routinely replaced at every other tune-up or if the electrodes show signs of erosion. In addition, this is a good time to clean the air filter element. Have the new parts on hand before you begin.

Because the different systems in an engine interact, the procedures should be done in the following order:

a. Tighten the cylinder head nuts and bolts.
b. Adjust valve clearances.
c. Run a compression test.
d. Check and adjust the ignition components and timing.
e. Set the idle speed.

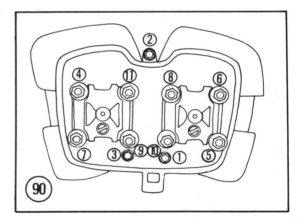

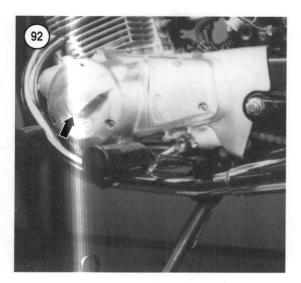

Table 5 summarizes tune-up specifications.

To perform a tune-up on your Honda, you will need the following tools and equipment:

a. 18 mm (5/8 in.) spark plug wrench.

b. Socket wrench and assorted sockets.

c. Flat feeler gauge.

d. Compression gauge.

e. Spark plug feeler gauge and gap adjusting tool.

f. Test light (static timing—contact breaker point ignition.

g. Ignition timing light.

Cylinder Head Nuts and Bolts

The engine must be at room temperature for this procedure.

1. Place wood block(s) under the engine to hold the bike securely.

2. Remove the right-hand side cover and disconnect the battery negative lead.

3. Remove the seat.

4. Remove the fuel tank as described in Chapter Six.

5. Remove the bolts (**Figure 89**) securing the cam cover and remove the cam cover and gasket.

NOTE
In the following steps, use the torque pattern shown in **Figure 90**.

6. Tighten the cylinder head nuts to the following torque specification:

a. Rebel 250: 21-25 N•m (15-18 ft.-lb.).

b. All other models: 16-21 N•m (12-15 ft.-lb.).

7. Tighten the cylinder head bolts to 7-10 N•m (10-14 ft.-lb.).

Valve Clearance Adjustment

Valve clearance measurement and adjustment must be performed with the engine cold (at room temperature). The correct valve clearance for intake and exhaust valves is 0.06-0.10 mm (0.002-0.004 in.).

1. Perform Steps 1-7 of *Cylinder Head Nuts and Bolts* in this chapter.

2A. On 250 cc engines, remove the ignition timing cap (**A, Figure 91**) and the center cap (**B, Figure 91**) on the left-hand crankcase cover.

2B. On all other models, remove the screws securing the ignition cover (**Figure 92**) and remove the cover and gasket.

3. Remove the spark plugs. This will make it easier to rotate the engine.

4. Using the 17 mm bolt (**Figure 93** or **Figure 94**) on the end of the crankshaft, rotate the engine *counterclockwise* until the ignition timing mark "T" (200-250) or "T-1" (185) aligns with the index mark as follows:

a. 185-200 models: **Figure 95**.

b. 250 models: **Figure 96**.

The No. 1 cylinder must be at top dead center (TDC) on the compression stroke. A cylinder at TDC will have both of its rocker arms loose, indicating that both the intake and exhaust valves are closed. If both rocker arms are tight, give the crankshaft one full turn.

5. Check the clearance of both intake and exhaust valves on the No. 1 cylinder (left-hand side) by inserting a flat feeler gauge between the adjusting screw and the valve stem (**Figure 97**). When the clearance is correct, there will be a slight drag on the feeler gauge when it is inserted and withdrawn.

6. To correct the clearance, back off the adjuster locknut and screw the adjuster in or out far enough to insert the feeler gauge without resistance. Screw in the adjuster until a slight resistance can be felt on the gauge. Hold the adjuster to prevent it from turning further and tighten the locknut (**Figure 98**). Then, recheck the clearance to make sure the adjuster did not turn after the correct clearance was achieved.

7. Rotate the crankshaft one full turn (360°) *counterclockwise* until the ignition timing mark "T" (200-250 models) or "T-1" (185 models) aligns with the index mark as follows:

a. 185-200 models: **Figure 95**.

b. 250 models: **Figure 96**.

The No. 2 cylinder must be at top dead center (TDC) on the compression stroke. A cylinder at TDC will have both of its rocker arms loose, indicating that both the intake and exhaust valves are closed.

8. Repeat Step 5 and Step 6 for the No. 2 cylinder.

9. Install all items removed.

10. On 250 models, make sure the O-ring seal (**Figure 99**) is in place and install the ignition timing cap.

Compression Test

Check the cylinder compression at the interval indicated in **Table 2**. Record the results and compare them to the results at the next interval. A running record will show trends in deterioration so that corrective action can be taken before complete failure.

The results, when properly interpreted, can indicate general cylinder, piston ring and valve condition.

1. Warm the engine to normal operating temperature, then shut it off. Make sure the choke valve and throttle valve are completely open.

2. Remove the spark plugs.

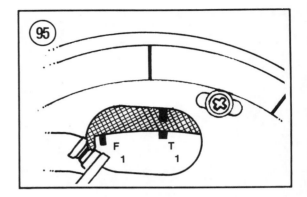

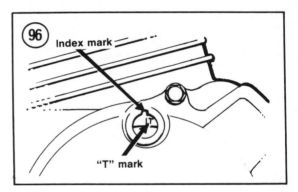

3. Connect the compression tester to one cylinder following the manufacturer's instructions (**Figure 100**).

4. Have an assistant crank the engine over until there is no further rise in pressure.

5. Remove the tester and record the reading. When interpreting the results, actual readings are not as important as the difference between the readings. The recommended cylinder compression pressure and the maximum allowable difference between cylinders are listed in **Table 5**. Greater differences than that listed in **Table 5** indicate broken rings, leaky or sticking valves, a blown head gasket or a combination of all.

If the compression readings do not differ between the cylinders by more than 10%, the rings and valves are in good condition.

If a low reading (10% or more) is obtained on one of the cylinders, it indicates valve or ring trouble. To determine which, pour about a teaspoon of engine oil through the spark plug hole onto the top of the piston. Turn the engine over once to clear the oil, then take another compression test and record the reading. If the compression increases significantly, the valves are good, but the rings are defective on that cylinder. If the compression does not increase, the valves require servicing. A valve could be hanging open or burned or a piece of carbon could be on a valve seat.

Spark Plug Selection

Spark plugs are available in various heat ranges, hotter or colder than plugs originally installed at the factory.

Select plugs of a heat range designed for the loads and temperature conditions under which the bike will be run. The use of incorrect heat ranges can cause seized pistons, scored cylinder walls or damaged piston crowns.

In general, use a hot plug for low speeds, low engine loads and low temperatures. Use a cold plug for high speeds, high engine loads and high temperatures. The plug should operate hot enough to burn off unwanted deposits, but not so hot that it is damaged or causes preignition. A spark plug of the correct heat range will show a light tan color on the portion of the insulator within the cylinder after the plug has been in service.

In areas where seasonal temperature variations are great, the factory recommends a "2-plug system"–cold plugs for hard summer riding and hot plugs for slower winter operation.

The reach (length) of a plug is also important. A longer than normal plug could interfere with the valves and pistons, causing permanent and severe damage. Refer to **Figure 101**. The recommended spark plugs are listed in **Table 5**.

Spark Plug Removal/Cleaning

1. Grasp the spark plug lead (**Figure 102**) as near to the plug as possible and pull it off the plug. If the boot is stuck to the plug, twist it slightly to break it loose.

2. Blow away any dirt that has accumulated in the spark plug wells.

CAUTION
The dirt could fall into the cylinders when the plugs are removed, causing serious engine damage.

3. Remove spark plugs with an 18 mm spark plug wrench.

NOTE
If plugs are difficult to remove, apply penetrating oil around base of plugs and let it soak in for about 10-20 minutes.

4. Inspect each spark plug carefully. Look for a plug with broken center porcelain, excessively eroded electrodes and excessive carbon or oil fouling. Replace such plugs. If deposits are light, the plug may be cleaned in solvent with a wire brush in a special spark plug sandblast cleaner. Regap the plug as explained in this chapter.

Spark Plug Gapping and Installation

New plugs should be carefully gapped to ensure a reliable, consistent spark. You must use a special spark plug gapping tool with a wire feeler gauge.

Be sure to replace both spark plugs at the same time and both plugs must be of the same heat range.

1. Remove the new plugs from the box. Do not screw on the terminal nut (**Figure 103**); it is not used.
2. Insert a round feeler gauge between the center and the side electrode of each plug (**Figure 104**). The correct gap is 0.6-0.7 mm (0.024-0.026 in.). If the gap is correct, you will feel a slight drag as you pull the gauge through. If there is no drag or the gauge won't pass through, bend the side electrode *with the gapping tool* (**Figure 105**) to set the proper gap.
3. Put a *small* amount of aluminum anti-seize compound on the threads of each spark plug.
4. Screw each spark plug in by hand until it seats. Very little effort is required. If force is necessary, you have the plug cross-threaded; unscrew it and try again.
5. Tighten the spark plugs an additional 1/2 turn after the gasket has made contact with the head. If you are reinstalling the original plugs are reusing the old gasket, only tighten an additional 1/4 turn.

CAUTION
Do not overtighten. This will squash the gasket and destroy its sealing ability.

6. Install each spark plug lead; make sure the lead is on tight.

Reading Spark Plugs

Much information about engine and spark plug performance can be determined by careful examination of the spark plugs. This information is more valid after performing the following steps.

1. Ride the bike a short distance at full throttle in any gear.

101

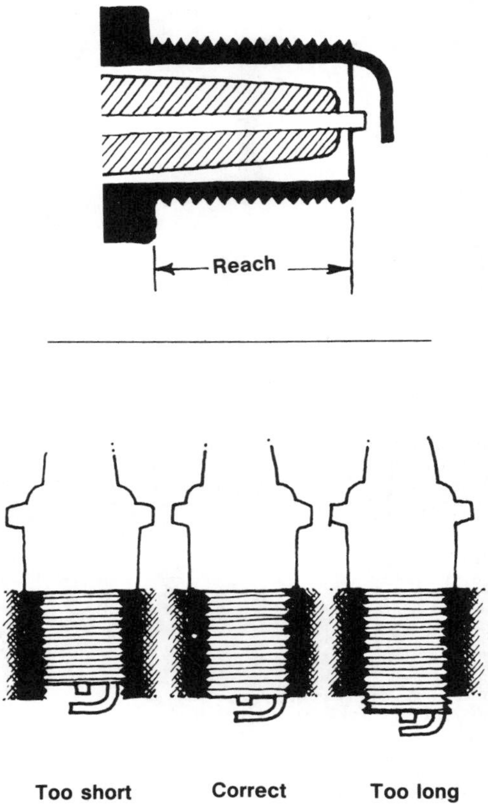
Reach
Too short
Correct
Too long

102

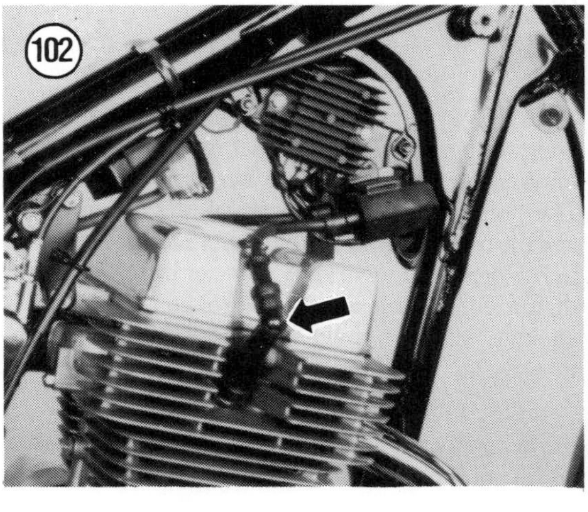

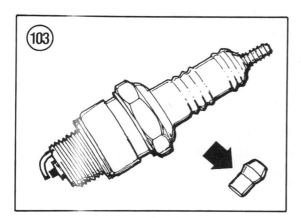

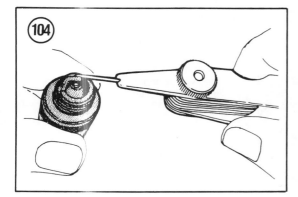

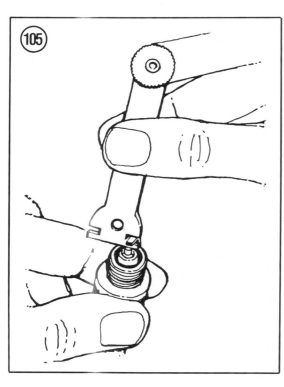

2. Turn the engine kill switch to the OFF position before closing the throttle and simultaneously pull in the clutch or shift to NEUTRAL; coast and brake to a stop.

3. Remove the spark plugs and examine them. Compare them to **Figure 106**. If the insulator is white or burned, the plug is too hot and should be replaced with a colder one.

A too-cold plug will have sooty or oily deposits ranging in color from dark brown to black. Replace with a hotter plug and check for too-rich carburetion or evidence of oil blowby at the piston rings.

If the plug has a light tan or gray colored deposit and no abnormal gap wear or electrode erosion is evident, the plug and the engine are running properly.

If the plug exhibits a black insulator tip, a damp and oily film over the firing end and a carbon layer over the entire nose, it is oil fouled. An oil fouled plug can be cleaned, but it is better to replace it.

If any one plug is found unsatisfactory, discard and replace all plugs.

Breaker Points Inspection and Cleaning (Models So Equipped)

Through normal use, the surfaces of the breaker points pit and burn. If they are not too badly pitted, they can be dressed with a few strokes of a clean point file or Flexstone (available at many auto parts stores). Do not use emery cloth or sandpaper, as particles remain on the points and cause arcing and burning. If a few strokes of the file do not smooth the points completely, replace the breaker point assembly.

If the points are still serviceable after filing, remove all residue with lacquer thinner or contact cleaner. Close the points on a piece of clean white paper such as a business card. Continue to pull the card through the closed points until no particles or discoloration are transferred to the card. Finally, rotate the engine and observe the points as they open and close. If they do not meet squarely (**Figure 107**) replace them as described in Chapter Seven.

Contact Breaker Point Gap (Models So Equipped)

The point gap must be adjusted correctly before adjusting the ignition timing.

1. Remove the screws (**Figure 108**) securing the ignition cover and remove the cover and gasket.

2. Rotate the crankshaft using the 17 mm bolt (**Figure 109**) on the end of the crankshaft. Turn the crankshaft until the points are at their widest gap.

SPARK PLUG CONDITION

(106)

NORMAL
- Identified by light tan or gray deposits on the firing tip.
- Can be cleaned.

GAP BRIDGED
- Identified by deposit buildup closing gap between electrodes.
- Caused by oil or carbon fouling. If deposits are not excessive, the plug can be cleaned.

OIL FOULED
- Identified by wet black deposits on the insulator shell bore and electrodes.
- Caused by excessive oil entering combustion chamber through worn rings and pistons, excessive clearance between valve guides and stems, or worn or loose bearings. Can be cleaned. If engine is not repaired, use a hotter plug.

CARBON FOULED
- Identified by black, dry fluffy carbon deposits on insulator tips, exposed shell surfaces and electrodes.
- Caused by too cold a plug, weak ignition, dirty air cleaner, too rich a fuel mixture or excessive idling. Can be cleaned.

LEAD FOULED
- Identified by dark gray, black, yellow or tan deposits or a fused glazed coating on the insulator tip.
- Caused by highly leaded gasoline. Can be cleaned.

WORN
- Identified by severly eroded or worn electrodes.
- Caused by normal wear. Should be replaced.

FUSED SPOT DEPOSIT
- Identified by melted or spotty deposits resembling bubbles or blisters.
- Caused by sudden acceleration. Can be cleaned.

OVERHEATING
- Identified by a white or light gray insulator with small black or gray brown spots and with bluish-burnt appearance of electrodes.
- Caused by engine overheating, wrong type of fuel, loose spark plugs, too hot a plug or incorrect ignition timing. Replace the plug.

PREIGNITION
- Identified by melted electrodes and possibly blistered insulator. Metallic deposits on insulator indicate engine damage.
- Caused by wrong type of fuel, incorrect ignition timing or advance, too hot a plug, burned valves or engine overheating. Replace the plug.

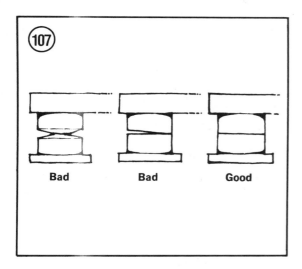

Bad   Bad   Good

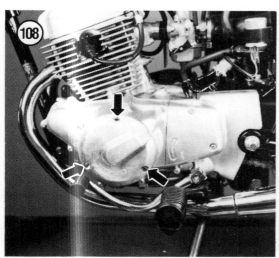

3. Measure the gap between the contacts with a flat feeler gauge (**Figure 110**). The correct gap is 0.3-0.4 mm (0.012-0.016 in.).

4. If the gap measured does not fall within the limits, slightly loosen the mounting screws (**Figure 111**) on the fixed arm of the breaker point assembly.

5. Adjust the gap by moving the fixed arm in either direction until the gap is at the mid-point—0.35 mm (0.014 in.). Tighten the mounting screws and recheck the gap. Readjust if necessary.

6. Adjust the ignition timing as described in this chapter.

Contact Breaker Point
Ignition Timing

Static method

The contact breaker point gap must be correct before checking and adjusting ignition timing. The

one set of points fires both cylinders so it is necessary to check ignition timing on only one cylinder. Use the No. 1 cylinder (left-hand side) as it is on the same side as the breaker points.

This procedure requires the use of a special tool (test light). It can be a homemade unit (**Figure 112**) that consists of 2 "C" or "D" size flashlight batteries and a light bulb, all mounted on a piece of wood, some light gauge electrical wire and 2 alligator clips. These items can be purchased from a hardware store.

1. Remove the screws (**Figure 108**) securing the ignition cover and remove the cover and gasket.
2. Turn the ignition switch to the ON position and the engine kill switch to the RUN posititon.

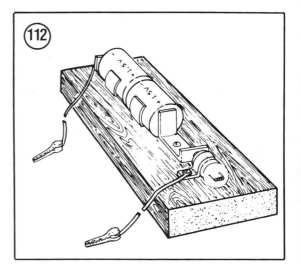

> *NOTE*
> *Before attaching the test light, check the batteries by touching the 2 test leads together. The light should be ON. If not, replace the batteries and/or check all connections on the tester. Be sure the test light operates correctly before using it.*

3. Connect one of the alligator clips to the positive contact breaker point terminal. Do not disconnect the electrical wire going to it.
4. Connect the other alligator clip to a good ground like the base plate (A, **Figure 113**). The light should be ON.
5. Turn the crankshaft *counterclockwise* using the 17 mm bolt (B, **Figure 113**) on the end of the crankshaft. Turn until the ignition timing mark "F-1" (Model CM185T) or "F" (Model CM200T) aligns with the index mark (**Figure 114**). The ignition timing is correct if the light goes OUT when these marks align. If the light does not go out, proceed to Step 6.
6. To adjust timing, loosen the base plate screws (C, **Figure 113**) and slightly rotate the base plate in either direction until timing is correct.

> *NOTE*
> *If timing is too early, rotate the base plate **counterclockwise**, if it is too late rotate it **clockwise**.*

7. Tighten the screws securely and recheck the ignition timing.
8. Disconnect the test light and install the ignition cover and gasket. Tighten the screws securely.

With strobe light

1. Remove the screws (**Figure 115**) securing the ignition cover and remove the cover and gasket.
2. Connect a portable tachometer following the manufacturer's instructions.

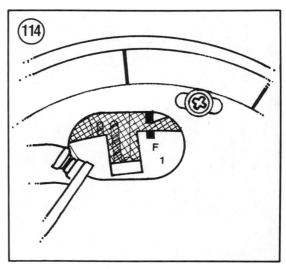

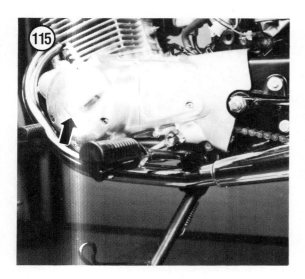

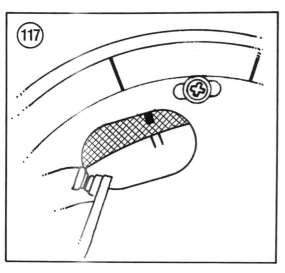

3. Connect a timing light, following the manufacturer's instructions, to the No. 1 cylinder (left-hand side).

4. Start the engine and let it idle at 1,200 ± 100 rpm. Aim the timing light at the timing marks and pull the trigger (**Figure 116**). If the timing mark "F-1" (Model CM185T) or "F" (Model CM200T) aligns with the fixed pointer (**Figure 114**) the timing is correct.

5. If the timing is incorrect, loosen the base plate screws (C, **Figure 113**) and slightly rotate the base plate in either direction until timing is correct.

> *NOTE*
> *If timing is too early, rotate the base plate **counterclockwise**; if it is too late, rotate it **clockwise**.*

6. Tighten the base plate screws securely and recheck ignition timing.

7. Also check the ignition advance alignment. Restart the engine and increase engine speed to 3,100 rpm and check the alignment of the full advance marks and the fixed pointer (**Figure 117**). If idle speed alignment is correct but the full advance is incorrect, inspect the ignition advance mechanism as described in Chapter Seven.

8. Shut the engine OFF and disconnect the portable tachometer and timing light.

9. Install the ignition cover and gasket. Tighten the screws securely.

CDI Ignition Timing

All models since 1981 are equipped with a capacitor discharge ignition (CDI) system. This system uses no breaker points and is non-adjustable. The ignition timing should be checked to make sure all ignition components are operating correctly.

Incorrect ignition timing can cause a drastic loss of engine performance and efficiency. It may also cause overheating.

Before starting on this procedure, check all electrical connections related to the ignition system. Make sure all connections are tight and free of corrosion and that all ground connections are tight.

1. Start the engine and let it reach normal operating temperature. Shut the engine off.

2. Place the bike on the side stand or centerstand.

3A. On CM200T models, remove the screws (**Figure 118**) securing the ignition cover and remove the cover and gasket.

3B. On Rebel 250 models, remove the ignition timing cap (**Figure 119**).

4. Connect a portable tachometer following the manufacturer's instructions.

NOTE
No. 1 cylinder is on the left-hand side and No. 2 is on the right-hand side. The left-hand side refers to a rider sitting on the seat looking forward.

5. Connect a timing light to the No. 1 (left-hand side) cylinder following the manufacturer's instructions.

6. Fill in the timing marks on the pulse generator rotor or alternator rotor with white grease pencil or typewriter white correction fluid. This will make the marks more visible.

7. Start the engine and let it idle at the idle speed listed in **Table 5**. If necessary, readjust the idle speed as described in this chapter.

8A. On CM200T Models, perform the following:
   a. Increase engine speed slightly above 2,800 rpm.
   b. Aim the timing light at the timing hole and pull the trigger. If the fixed pointer aligns between the full advance timing marks (**Figure 117**) the timing is correct. If full advance is not correct, refer to Chapter Seven and check the pulse generator and CDI unit.

8B. On Rebel 250 Models, perform the following:
   a. Let the engine idle at the speed listed in **Table 5**.
   b. Aim the timing light at the timing hole and pull the trigger. If the timing mark "F" aligns with the fixed pointer on the crankcase cover (**Figure 120**), the timing is correct.
   c. Increase engine speed to slightly above 3,500 rpm.
   d. Aim the timing light at the timing hole and pull the trigger. If the fixed pointer aligns between the full advance timing marks (**Figure 121**) the timing is correct.
   e. If timing at either idle or full advance is not correct, refer to Chapter Seven and check the pulse generator and CDI unit. There is no method for adjusting ignition timing.

9. Shut off the engine and disconnect the timing light and portable tachometer.

10. Make sure the O-ring seal (**Figure 99**) is in place and install the ignition timing cap.

Carburetor Idle Speed Adjustment

Before making this adjustment, the air filter element must be clean and the engine must have adequate compression. See *Compression Test* in

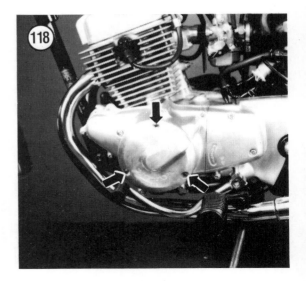

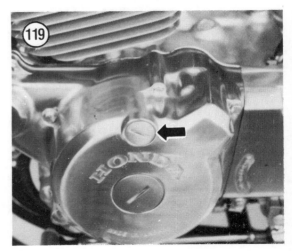

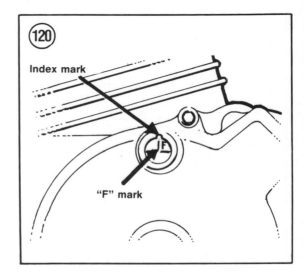

Index mark

"F" mark

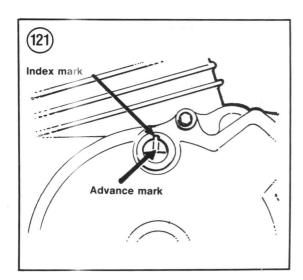

Index mark

Advance mark

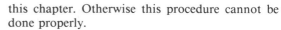

3

this chapter. Otherwise this procedure cannot be done properly.

1. Start the engine and let it reach normal operating temperature. Make sure the choke knob or lever is in the OPEN position.

2. Connect a portable tachometer following the manufacturer's instructions.

3A. On Rebel 250 models, turn the idle adjust knob (**Figure 122**) in or out to adjust idle speed.

3B. On all other models, turn the idle adjust screw (**Figure 123**) in or out to adjust idle speed.

4. The correct idle speed is listed in **Table 5**.

5. Open and close the throttle a couple of times; check for variations in idle speed. Readjust if necessary.

WARNING
*With the engine running at idle speed, move the handlebar from side to side. If the idle speed increases during this movement, the throttle cable may need adjusting or it may be incorrectly routed through the frame. Correct this problem immediately. Do **not** ride the bike in this unsafe condition.*

Carburetor Idle Mixture

The idle mixture (pilot screw) is preset at the factory and *is not to be reset*. Do not adjust the pilot screw (**Figure 124**) unless the carburetor has been overhauled. If so, refer to Chapter Six for service procedures.

Table 1 TIRE PRESSURE (COLD)*

Load	Pressure
Rebel 250	
Rider only	
Front and rear	2.0 kg/cm² (28 psi)
Rider and pasenger	
Front and rear	2.0 kg/cm² (28 psi)
All models except Rebel 250	
Up to 200 lbs. (90 kg)	
Front	1.75 kg/cm² (25 psi)
Rear	2.0 kg/cm² (28 psi)
Maximum load limit**	
Front	1.75 kg/cm² (25 psi)
Rear	2.25 kg/cm² (32 psi)

*Recommended air pressure for factory equipped tires. Aftermarket tires may require different air pressure.
**Maximum load limit incudes total weight of motorcycle with accessories, rider(s) and luggage. Maximum load limit is 135 kg (300 lb.).

Table 2 SERVICE INTERVALS*

Every 500 km (300 miles)	• Inspect and adjust the drive belt (belt-driven models)
Every 1,000 km (600 miles) or 6 months	• Check engine oil level
	• Check battery specific gravity and electrolyte level
	• Check hydraulic fluid level in brake master cylinder (disc brake models)
	• Lubricate rear brake pedal and shift lever
	• Lubricate side and center stand pivot points
	• Inspect front steering for looseness
	• Lubricate drive chain
	• Check wheel bearings for smooth operation
	• Check clutch lever free play
	• Clean fuel shutoff valve and filter.
	• Check wheel spoke condition
	• Check wheel runout
	• Insect brake linings and pads for wear
Every 6,400 km (4,000 miles)	• Change engine oil
	• Clean air filter element
	• Check and clean fuel shutoff valve filter or strainer
	• Inspect spark plug, regap if necessary
	• Check and adjust valve clearance
	• Adjust cam chain tensioner
	• Inspect fuel lines for chafed, cracked or swollen ends
	• Lubricate control cables
	• Remove, clean and lubricate drive chain (chain-driven models)
	• Check and adjust carburetor idle speed
	• Check and adjust throttle operation and free play
	• Inspect crankcase breather hose for cracks or loose hose clamps; drain out all residue
	• Check engine mounting bolts for tightness
	• Check all suspension components
(continued)	• Adjust rear brake pedal height and free play

Table 2 SERVICE INTERVALS* (continued)

Every 12,800 km **(8,000 miles)**	• Complete engine tune-up including a compression test • Check and adjust the choke • Dismantle and clean the carburetor • Change oil in front forks • Remove and clean engine oil filter screen • Inspect fuel lines for wetness or damage • Inspect entire brake system for leaks or damage • Inspect swing arm bushings • Lubricate speedometer housing @ front hub • Inspect wheel bearings • Inspect and repack the steering head bearings • Lubricate the speedometer drive cable • Check and adjust headlight aim • Lubricate drum brake camshafts • Lubricate breaker point cam
Every 19,200 km **(12,000 miles)**	• Inspect the emission control system
Every 24,000 km **(38,000 miles)** **or every 2 years**	• Change hydraulic fluid in brake master cylinder (disc brake models)
Every 4 years	• Replace the hydraulic brake hose (disc brake models)

*This Honda factory maintenance schedule should be considered as a guide to general maintenance and lubrication intervals. Harder than normal use and exposure to mud, water, sand, high humidity, etc. will naturally dictate more frequent attention to most maintenance items.

Table 3 STATE OF CHARGE

Specific gravity	State of charge
1.110-1.130	Discharged
1.140-1.160	Almost discharged
1.170-1.190	One-quarter discharged
1.200-1.220	One-half charged
1.230-1.250	Three-quarter charged
1.260-1.280	Fully charged

Table 4 CAPACITIES

Engine oil		
Model	@ oil change	@ overhaul
185 cc	1.4 liter (1.5 U.S. qt.)	1.5 liter (1.6 U.S. qt.)
200 cc	1.3 liter (1.4 U.S. qt.)	1.5 liter (1.6 U.S. qt.)
250 cc	1.5 liter (1.6 U.S. qt.)	1.8 liter (1.9 U.S. qt.)
Fork oil (per leg)		
185 cc	98 cc (3.3 oz.)	
200 cc	115 cc (3.9 oz.)	
250 cc (1985-on)	238 cc (8.1 oz.)	
Fuel		
All models	10.5 liters (2.8 U.S. gal., 2.31 Imp. gal.)	

Table 5 TUNE-UP SPECIFICATIONS

Cylinder head (Rebel 250)	
Bolts	10-14 N•m (7-10 ft.-lb.)
Nuts	21-25 N•m (15-18 ft.-lb.)
Cylinder head (All models except Rebel 250)	
Bolts	10-14 N•m (7-10 ft.-lb.)
Nuts	16-20 N•m (12-15 ft.-lb.)
Compression pressure (at sea level)	
Rebel 250	14 ±2 kg/cm² (199 ±28 psi)
All models except Rebel 250	12 ±2 kg/cm² (170 ±28 psi)
Spark plug type	
1978-1981	
Standard heat range	ND U22FS or NGK C7HS
Cold weather*	ND U20FS or NGK C6H
Extended high-speed riding	ND U24FB or NGK C9H
1982-1983	
Standard heat range	ND U22FSR-U or NGK CR7HS
Cold weather*	ND U20FSR-U or NGK CR6HS
Extended high-speed riding	ND U24FSR-U or NGK CR8HS
1985-1986	
Standard heat range	ND U20FSR-U or NGK CR6HS
Extended high-speed riding	ND U22FSR-U or NGK CR7HS
Spark plug gap	0.6-0.7 mm (0.024-0.028 in.)
Contact breaker point gap	0.3-0.4 mm (0.012 -0.016 in.)
Ignition timing mark	
CM185T	''F-1'' @ 1,200 rpm
CM200T	''F'' @ 1,200 rpm
CM250C, Rebel 250	''F'' @ 1,300 rpm
Idle speed	
CM185T, CM200T	1,200 rpm
250C, Rebel 250	1,300 rpm

*Cold weather climate—below 5° C (41° F)

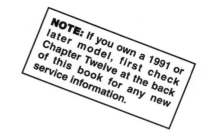
NOTE: If you own a 1991 or later model, first check Chapter Twelve at the back of this book for any new service information.

CHAPTER FOUR

ENGINE

The engine in the Rebel 250 and Twinstar is an air-cooled, 4-stroke twin cylinder engine with a chain-driven single overhead camshaft. Each valve has its own rocker arm with an adjuster.

The crankshaft is supported by a ball bearing at each end with a center bearing plate that is attached to the inner surface of the left-hand crankcase half.

The oil pump supplies oil under pressure throughout the engine and is driven by a gear on the right-hand end of the crankshaft.

This chapter provides complete service and overhaul procedures for the Honda twin engine. The engine used in all models is identical with the exception of displacement, which ranges from 181 cc (185 models) to 234 cc (250 models), and other minor variations. Where differences occur they are identified.

Although the clutch and the transmission are located within the engine, they are covered separately in Chapter Five to simplify the presentation of this material.

Before beginning engine work, reread the service hints in Chapter One. You will do a better job with this information fresh in your mind.

Table 1 provides complete engine specifications. **Table 2** lists all torque specifications and both tables are located at the end of this chapter.

ENGINE PRINCIPLES

Figure 1 explains how the engine works. This will be helpful when troubleshooting or repairing your engine.

SERVICING ENGINE IN FRAME

The following components can be serviced while the engine is mounted in the frame (the bike's frame is a great holding fixture for breaking loose stubborn bolts and nuts):

a. Camshaft and rocker arm assemblies.
b. Clutch assembly.
c. Alternator and ignition system.
d. Carburetor assembly.
e. External shift mechanism.

ENGINE

On 1978-1983 models the engine is a stressed portion of the frame which acts as the lower portion of the frame. On 1985-on models (there was no 1984 model) the frame is a semi-double cradle type and the engine sits within the frame instead of being part of it.

If the engine is not going to be serviced, just removed, then the external components can be left

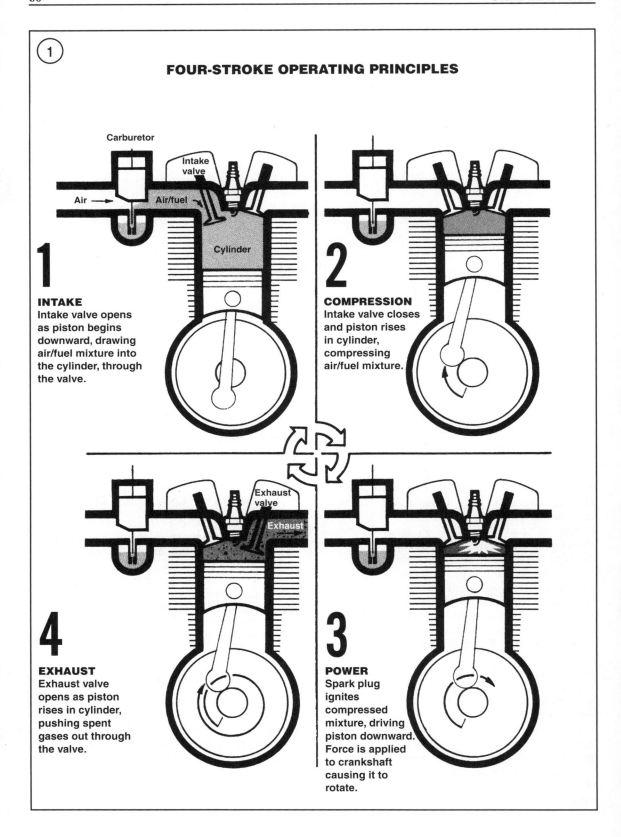

① **FOUR-STROKE OPERATING PRINCIPLES**

1 INTAKE
Intake valve opens as piston begins downward, drawing air/fuel mixture into the cylinder, through the valve.

2 COMPRESSION
Intake valve closes and piston rises in cylinder, compressing air/fuel mixture.

4 EXHAUST
Exhaust valve opens as piston rises in cylinder, pushing spent gases out through the valve.

3 POWER
Spark plug ignites compressed mixture, driving piston downward. Force is applied to crankshaft causing it to rotate.

in place. This will take less time but the weight of the engine is much greater.

Removal/Installation

WARNING
Due to the weight of the complete engine assembly, a minimum of 2, preferably 3, people should be used during the removal and installation procedure.

1. Place wood blocks under the engine or frame to support it securely.

2. Remove both side covers, seat and any accessories (i.e. fairing, crash bars, etc.).

3. Disconnect the battery negative lead (**Figure 2**).

4. Drain the engine oil as described under *Changing Engine Oil* in Chapter Three.

5. Turn the fuel shutoff valve to the OFF position (A, **Figure 3**) and disconnect the fuel line to the carburetor (B, **Figure 3**).

6. Remove the fuel tank as described in Chapter Six.

7. Disconnect the spark plug wires (**Figure 4**) and tie them up out of the way.

8. On all models except the Rebel 250, remove the ignition coil as described in Chapter Seven.

9. Remove the exhaust system as described in Chapter Six.

10. Remove the carburetor assembly as described in Chapter Six.

11. Loosen the bolt and nut (**Figure 5**) clamping the shift lever and remove the lever.

12A. On Rebel 250 models, remove the clamping bolt (**Figure 6**) securing the rear brake pedal to the pivot pin and remove the brake pedal.

12B. On all other models, remove the rear brake light switch (A, **Figure 7**); remove the circlip (B, **Figure 7**) securing the rear brake pedal and remove the brake pedal.

13. Disconnect all electrical connectors (alternator, rectifier, neutral indicator, condensor and wire to the starter).

14. Remove the cam cover and gasket.

15. Remove the drive sprocket as described in Chapter Five or the drive pulley as described in Chapter Nine.

16. Loosen the locknut and unscrew the adjusting nut (**Figure 8**) on the clutch cable at the crankcase cover. Remove the cable from the actuating arm.

17. Remove the clutch as described in Chapter Five.

18. Remove the alternator as described in this chapter.

19. Remove the external shift mechanism as described in Chapter Five.

20. Remove the oil pump assembly as described in this chapter.

21. Remove the starter as described in Chapter Seven.

22A. On 1978-1982 models, perform the following:

   a. Loosen the right-hand bolts securing the foot-rest assembly.

   b. Remove the left-hand through-bolts (**Figure 9**) securing the footrest assembly. Remove the right-hand bolts and remove the footrest assembly.

22B. On 1985-on models, remove the bolts (**Figure 10**) securing the right-hand foot-rest assembly and remove the assembly.

23. Take a final look all over the engine to make sure everything has been disconnected.

24. Place a suitable size jack, with a piece of wood to protect the crankcase, under the engine. Apply a *small amount* of jack pressure up on the engine.

25A. On 1978-1983 models, perform the following:

   a. Loosen, but do not remove, all engine mounting bolts and nuts (**Figure 11**).

   b. Remove the 8 mm bolts and nuts (A, **Figure 11**) securing the engine front hanger plate to the frame and the engine. Remove the hanger plate.

   c. Remove the 10 mm through-bolts and nuts (B, **Figure 11**) securing the engine to the frame at the rear. Note the location of the engine ground strap on the upper bolt at the right-hand side.

   d. Remove the 8 mm bolts and nuts (C, **Figure 11**) securing the engine upper hanger plate to the frame and the cylinder head. Remove the hanger plate.

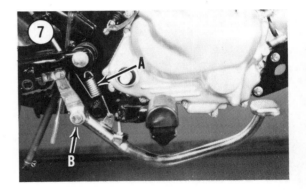

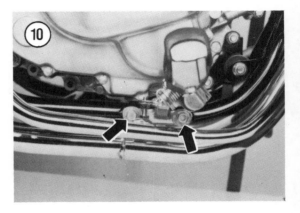

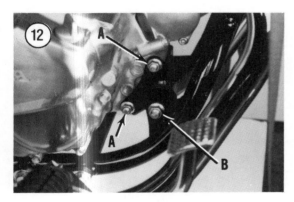

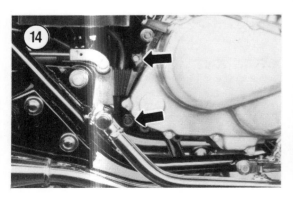

25B. On 1985-on models, perform the following:

  a. Loosen, but do not remove, all engine mounting bolts and nuts.

  b. Remove the 8 mm bolts and nuts (A, **Figure 12**) securing the engine front hanger plate to the engine.

  c. Remove the 10 mm through-bolt and nut (B, **Figure 12**) securing the engine front hanger plate to the frame. Remove the hanger plate. Don't lose the rubber cushion and spacer (**Figure 13**) on each side of the hanger plate where the bolt goes through.

  d. Remove the 10 mm through-bolts and nuts (**Figure 14**) securing the engine to the frame at the rear.

  e. Remove the 8 mm bolts and nuts (**Figure 15**) securing the engine upper hanger plate to the frame and the cylinder head. Remove the hanger plate.

26. Jack the engine up a little more and carefully and slowly pivot the engine toward the right-hand side of the frame. Move it out far enough so that everyone can get a good handhold on the engine.

27. Move the engine out of the frame area on the right-hand side.

28. Place the engine in an engine stand or take it to a work bench for further disassembly.

29. Install by reversing these removal steps, noting the following.

> *WARNING*
> *Due to the weight of the complete engine assembly, it is suggested that all components removed be left off until the engine assembly is reinstalled into the frame. If you choose to install a completed engine assembly, it requires at least 2 people.*

30. On Rebel 250 models, make sure the front mounting bolt rubber cushions and spacers are in place on the mounting bracket prior to installing the 10 mm mounting through-bolt.

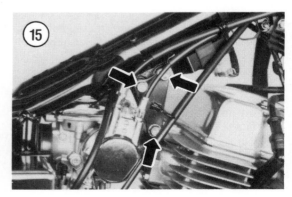

31. Tighten the bolts and nuts to the torque specifications listed in **Table 2**.
32. Fill the crankcase with the recommended type and quantity of engine oil. Refer to Chapter Three.
33. Adjust the drive chain, rear brake pedal and clutch cable as described in Chapter Three.
34. Start the engine and check for leaks.

CYLINDER HEAD AND CAMSHAFT

Removal

CAUTION
To prevent any warpage and damage, remove the cylinder head and camshaft only when the engine is at room temperature.

1. Remove the engine as described in this chapter.
2. Remove the cam cover if not already removed.
3. Loosen the cylinder head bolts and 8 mm nuts in 2-3 stages in the sequence shown in **Figure 16**.
4. Remove the cylinder head nuts securing the camshaft holder assemblies and carefully remove both holder assemblies.

NOTE
Don't lose the the locating dowels on each camshaft holder assembly.

5. Temporarily install the alternator rotor onto the crankshaft and rotate it until one of the cam sprocket bolts is exposed (**Figure 17**). Remove the exposed bolt.
6. Rotate the crankshaft 360° *counterclockwise* and remove the other sprocket bolt.

NOTE
Don't drop the bolts into the cam chain cavity as they will fall into the crankcase.

NOTE
The following step is necessary to allow maximum amount of cam chain slack for ease of cam chain removal from the sprocket.

7A. On 1978-1983 models, perform the following:
  a. Remove the cam chain tensioner upper bolt (A, **Figure 18**). Don't lose the rubber O-ring seal on the bolt.
  b. Loosen the lower locknut (B, **Figure 18**). Pull the tensioner assembly (C, **Figure 18**) all the way up and tighten the locknut.
7B. On 1985-on models, perform the following:
  a. Cut a piece of wire (approximately 0.08 in./2 mm in diameter) and about 1 1/2 in. (38 mm) long. A straightened No. 2 paper clip will work.

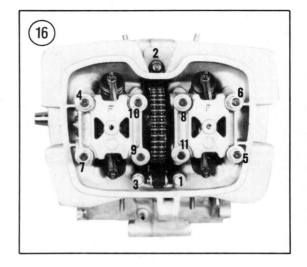
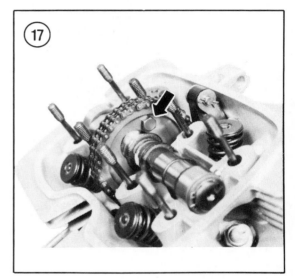
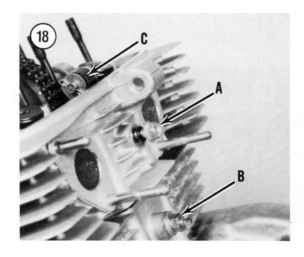

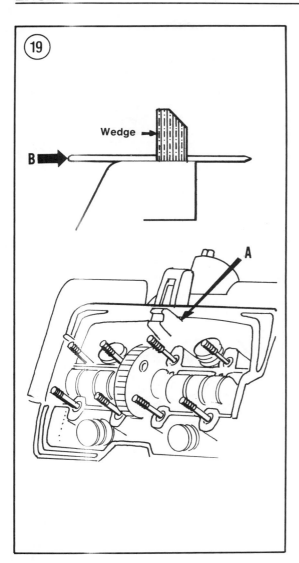

b. Pull the tip of the cam chain tensioner wedge (A, **Figure 19**) up with a pair of pliers until the hole in the wedge is exposed.

c. Hold the wedge up and insert the piece of cut wire into the hole in the tip (B, **Figure 19**).

d. Bend the end of the wire over a little so it will not accidentally fall out during this procedure.

e. Remove the upper bolt and washer securing the cam chain tensioner to the cylinder head.

8. Slide the cam chain and sprocket off of the cam boss to the left-hand side. Pull up on the cam chain and remove it from the sprocket: place the cam chain onto the cam (**Figure 20**).

9. Tie a piece of wire to the cam chain and secure the other end to the exterior of the engine. This will prevent the chain from falling into the crankcase when the cam is removed.

10. Carefully withdraw the camshaft toward the right-hand side of the engine. Don't let the right-hand bearing cap fall off during removal. Remove the cam sprocket also.

NOTE
*Make sure to keep the cam chain secured with a piece of wire (A, **Figure 21**) after the cam is removed.*

11. Remove the cylinder head bolts (B, **Figure 21**).

CAUTION
*Remember that the cooling fins are fragile and may be damaged if tapped or pried too hard. **Never** use a metal hammer.*

12. Loosen the cylinder head by tapping around the perimeter with a rubber or soft-faced mallet. If necessary, *gently* pry the cylinder head loose with a

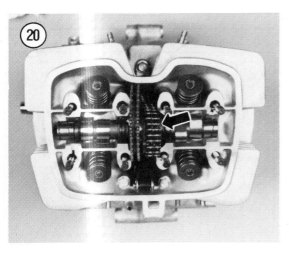

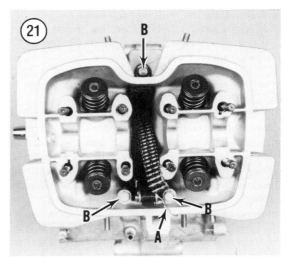

broad-tipped screwdriver only in the ribbed areas of the fins.

NOTE
It is sometimes possible to loosen the cylinder head with the engine compression. If removed, install the spark plugs. Rotate the engine with the kickstarter or starter. As the pistons reach top dead center on the compression stroke they may pop the cylinder head loose.

13. Lift the cylinder head straight up and off the crankcase studs and remove the cylinder head.
14. Remove the nuts securing the intake manifold and remove the manifold.
15. Remove the cylinder head gasket and locating dowels (don't lose the O-ring seals).
16. Place a clean shop cloth into the cam chain opening in the cylinder to prevent the entry of foreign matter.
17. Remove the alternator rotor that was temporarily installed in Step 5.

Cylinder Head Inspection

1. Remove all traces of gasket material from the cylinder head and cylinder mating surfaces.
2. *Without removing the valves*, remove all carbon deposits from the combustion chamber and valve ports with a wire brush. A blunt screwdriver or chisel may be used if care is taken not to damage the head, valves and spark plug threads.
3. After the carbon is removed from the combustion chamber and the valve intake and exhaust ports, clean the entire head in cleaning solvent. Blow dry with compressed air.
4. Clean away all carbon from the piston crowns. Do not remove the carbon ridge at the top of the cylinder bores.
5. Check for cracks in the combustion chambers and exhaust ports. A cracked head must be replaced.
6. After the head has been thoroughly cleaned, place a straightedge across the cylinder head/cylinder gasket surface (**Figure 22**) at several points. Measure the warp by inserting a flat feeler gauge between the straightedge and the cylinder head at each location. There should be no warpage; if a small amount is present, it can be resurfaced by a Honda dealer or qualified machine shop.
7. Check the cam cover mating surface using the procedure in Step 6. There should be no warpage.
8. Inspect the valves as described in this chapter.

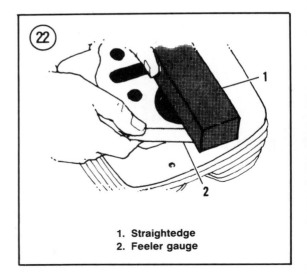

1. Straightedge
2. Feeler gauge

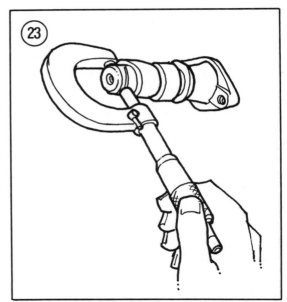

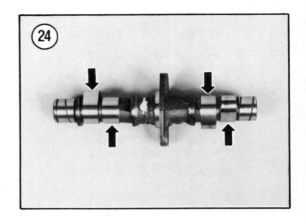

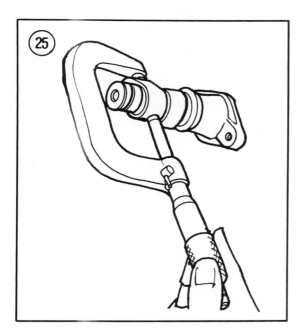

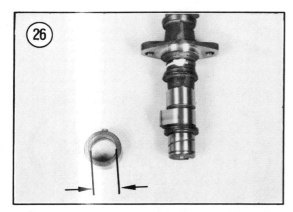

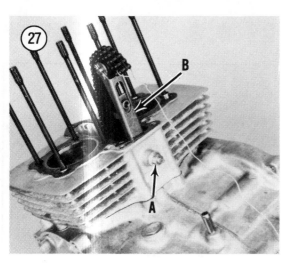

Camshaft Inspection

1. Remove the circlip and remove the thrust washer and the cam bushing from the left-hand side of the cam.
2. Slide the bushing off the right-hand side of the cam.
3. Wash all parts in solvent and thoroughly dry.
4. Measure both the right- and left-hand cam bearing journals (**Figure 23**) with a micrometer. Compare to the dimensions given in **Table 1**. If either is worn to the service limit or greater, the cam must be replaced.
5. Check the cam lobes for wear (**Figure 24**). The lobes should show no signs of scoring and the edges should be square. Slight damage may be removed with a silicon carbide oilstone. Use No. 100-120 grit stone initially, then polish with a No. 280-320 grit stone.

> *NOTE*
> *The cam is dark in color due to the manufacturing hardening process. It is not caused by lack of lubrication or excessive engine heat.*

6. Even though the cam lobe surface appears to be satisfactory, with no visible signs of wear, the cam lobes must be measured with a micrometer (**Figure 25**). Compare to the dimensions given in **Table 1**.
7. Measure the inside diamater of each cam bushing (**Figure 26**). Compare to the dimension listed in **Table 1**. Replace either bushing if worn to the service limit or greater.
8. Inspect the cam sprocket teeth for wear; replace if necessary.

Cylinder Head and
Camshaft Installation

1. On 1978-1983 models, loosen the cam chain tensioner locknut (A, **Figure 27**), pull the tensioner assembly (B, **Figure 27**) all the way up and tighten the locknut.

> *NOTE*
> *This is to allow maximum amount of cam chain slack for ease of cam chain installation onto the sprocket. On 1985-on models this is not necessary since the cam chain tensioner is held in the up position with the piece of wire installed during the removal steps.*

2. Install a new head gasket (A, **Figure 28**), locating dowels (B, **Figure 28**) and O-rings seals. Make sure the front chain guide (C, **Figure 28**) is installed in the cylinder.

3. Install the cylinder head onto the crankcase studs. With your fingers, carefully insert the cam chain into the cam chain cavity on the side of the cylinder head while pushing the cylinder head down into position. Tie the wire attached to the cam chain to the exterior of the engine.

4. Apply oil to the crankcase threads.

5. Install the cam chain tensioner bolt. Make sure the O-ring seal (**Figure 29**) is in place. If the O-ring is left off there will be a guaranteed oil leak.

6. Pull up on the cam chain, making sure it is properly engaged on the crankshaft sprocket. Rotate the crankshaft, using the 17 mm bolt (**Figure 30**) on the end of the crankshaft, *counterclockwise* until the ignition timing mark "T" (200-250 models) or "T-1" (185 models) aligns with the index mark as follows:

   a. 185 models: **Figure 31**.

   b. 200-250 models: **Figure 32**.

If the alternator assembly is removed, refer to Step 7.

> *NOTE*
> *The engine must be at top dead center (TDC) for the following steps for correct valve timing.*

> *CAUTION*
> *When rotating the crankshaft, keep the cam chain taut and engaged with the timing sprocket on the crankshaft.*

7. Rotate the crankshaft until the alternator rotor locating pin (**Figure 33**) is pointing directly up to the cam (12 o'clock position). This will locate one cylinder at the TDC position.

8. Lubricate all cam lobes and bearing journals with molybdenum disulfide grease. Also coat the cam bearing surfaces in the cylinder head and cam holders.

9. Position the cam sprocket with the punch marks facing toward the left-hand side. Install the cam and cam sprocket in from the right-hand side through the cam chain (**Figure 34**).

10. Rotate the cam sprocket until the 2 punch marks (A, **Figure 35**) are parallel with the top surface of the cylinder head.

11. Slide the cam bushing and thrust washer onto the left-hand side of the cam. Install the circlip and make sure the circlip is properly seated in the cam groove.

12. Slide the bushing onto the right-hand side of the cam.

13. Position the cam bushing locating dowels into the grooves in the cylinder head (**Figure 36**).

14. Make sure the cam sprocket punch marks (A, **Figure 35**) are still parallel with the top surface of

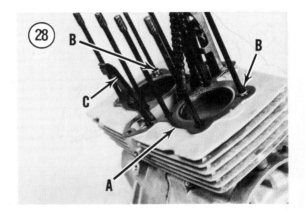

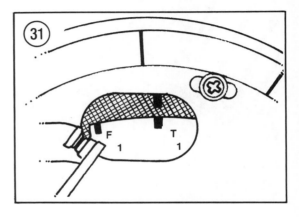

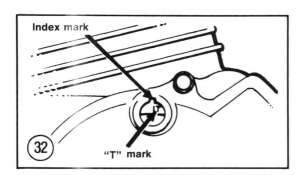

Index mark

"T" mark

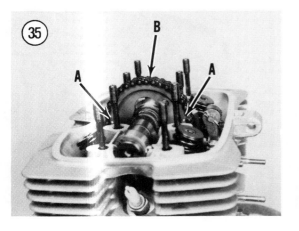

B

A   A

the cylinder head and pull the cam chain up onto the cam sprocket (B, **Figure 35**).

> *CAUTION*
> *Very expensive damage could result from improper cam and cam chain alignment. Recheck your work several times to make sure alignment is correct.*

15. Rotate the cam so that the notch on left-hand end (A, **Figure 37**) is parallel with the top surface of the cylinder head and is pointing toward the rear (intake side) of the engine.

> *NOTE*
> *If the engine is relatively new or a new cam chain or tensioner has been installed, Step 16 may be difficult. Carefully insert a long, broad-tipped screwdriver down into the cam chain cavity and depress the chain tensioner from the inside. This will give you additional chain slack, enabling the cam sprocket and chain to slide up onto the cam boss. Be careful not to damage anything in the cam chain cavity with the screwdriver.*

16. Slide the cam chain and sprocket up onto the boss on the cam. The sprocket bolt holes in the cam and the sprocket should now align (B, **Figure 37**). Make sure alignment is correct (**Figure 38**).

B   A

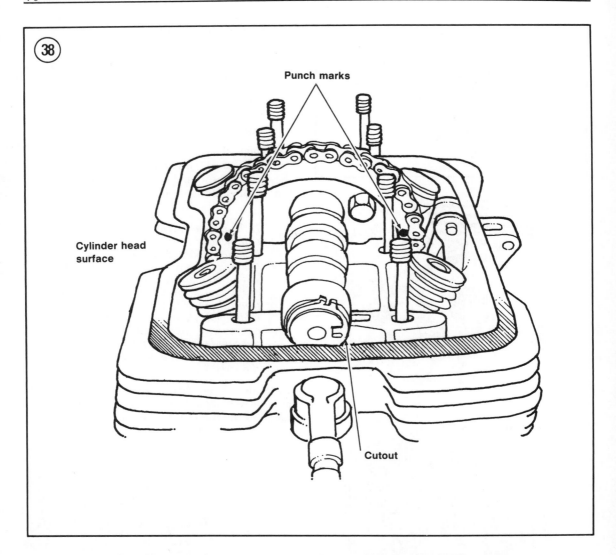

Punch marks

Cylinder head
surface

Cutout

17. If alignment is incorrect, reposition the cam chain on the sprocket and recheck the alignment. Refer to **Figure 31** or **Figure 32**, **Figure 33** and **Figure 37**.

18. After alignment is correct, install one bolt only finger-tight, rotate the crankshaft and install the other bolt. Make sure the sprocket is correctly seated on the cam boss and tighten bolts to the torque specification listed in **Table 2**.

> *CAUTION*
> *If there is any binding while rotating the crankshaft, **stop**. Determine the cause before proceeding.*

19. After installation is complete, rotate the crankshaft several complete revolutions. Make sure all timing marks align. If all marks align, the timing is correct.

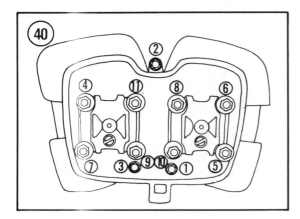

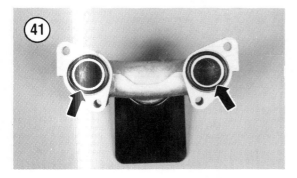

NOTE
Make sure the locating dowels are in place on the bottom of each holder or on the cylinder stud holes in the cylinder head.

20. Install both camshaft holder assemblies with the "F" mark (**Figure 39**) located toward the front (exhaust side) of the engine.

21. On 1985-on models, perform the following:

   a. Straighten the ends of the wire installed in the cam chain tensioner wedge.

   b. Using a pair of pliers, pull up on the wedge of the cam chain tensioner and remove the wire from the tensioner.

   c. Make sure the wedge slides down after the wire is removed. If necessary, *gently* tap on the end of the wedge with a plastic mallet. The wedge must move down to apply the proper tension on the cam chain.

22. Tighten the cylinder head nuts and bolts to the torque specification listed in **Table 2**. Tighten in 2-3 stages using the torque sequence shown in **Figure 40**.

CAUTION
O-ring seals tend to become hardened after prolonged use and heat and therefore lose their ability to seal properly. If these seals allow any air leak, it may cause a burned valve(s). Replace as a pair, even if only one is damaged or deteriorated.

23. Make sure both O-ring seals (**Figure 41**) are in place and in good condition. Install the intake manifold and nuts. Tighten the nuts securely.

24. Make sure the heat shield (**Figure 42**) is installed on the intake manifold.

25. Adjust the valves and cam chain tension as described in Chapter Three.

VALVES AND VALVE COMPONENTS

Removal

Refer to **Figure 43** for this procedure.

1. Remove the cylinder head as described in this chapter.

CAUTION
To avoid loss of spring tension, do not compress the springs any more than necessary to remove the keepers.

2. Compress the valve springs with a valve compressor tool (**Figure 44**). Remove the valve keepers and release the compression. Remove the valve compressor tool.

3. Remove the valve spring collar and valve springs (**Figure 45**).

NOTE
The inner and outer valve seats and valve stem seal will stay in the cylinder head.

4. Prior to removing the valve, remove any burrs from the valve stem (**Figure 46**). Otherwise the valve guide will be damaged.

5. Remove the valve.

6. Mark all parts as they are disassembled so that they will be installed in their original locations.

Inspection

1. Clean the valves with a wire brush and solvent.

2. Inspect the contact surface of each valve for burning or pitting (**Figure 47**). Unevenness of the contact surface is an indication that the valve is not serviceable. On Rebel 250 models, the valve contact surface *cannot be ground* and the valve must be replaced if defective.

3. Inspect the valve stem for wear and roughness and measure the vertical runout of the valve stem as shown in **Figure 48**. The runout should not exceed 0.05 mm (0.002 in.).

4. Measure the valve stem for wear (**Figure 49**). Compare with specifications given in **Table 1**.

5. Remove all carbon and varnish from the valve guide with a stiff spiral wire brush.

6. Insert each valve in its guide. Hold the valve with the head just slightly off the valve seat and rock it sideways. If it rocks more than slightly, the guide is probably worn and should be replaced. As a final check, take the cylinder to a dealer and have the valve guides measured.

7. Measure each valve spring free length with a vernier caliper (**Figure 50**). All should be within the length specified in **Table 1** with no signs of bends or distortion. Replace defective springs in pairs (inner and outer).

8. Check the valve spring retainer and valve keepers. If they are in good condition they may be reused; replace as necessary.

9. Inspect the valve seats. If worn or burned, they must be reconditioned. This should be performed by a dealer or qualified machine shop.

Installation

1. Coat the valve stems with molybdenum disulfide grease. To avoid damage to the valve stem seal, turn the valve slowly while inserting the valve into the cylinder head.

2. Install the bottom spring retainers and new seals.

3. Install the valve springs with their closer wound coils facing the cylinder head and install the valve spring retainer.

> *CAUTION*
> *To avoid loss of spring tension, do not compress the springs any more than necessary to install the keepers.*

4. Compress the valve springs with a compressor tool (**Figure 44**) and install the valve keepers. Remove the compressor tool.

5. After all springs have been installed, gently tap the end of the valve stem (**Figure 51**) with a soft

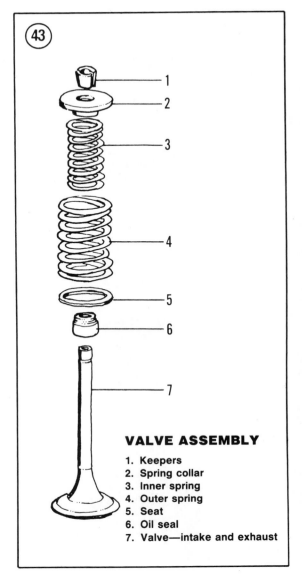

VALVE ASSEMBLY

1. **Keepers**
2. **Spring collar**
3. **Inner spring**
4. **Outer spring**
5. **Seat**
6. **Oil seal**
7. **Valve—intake and exhaust**

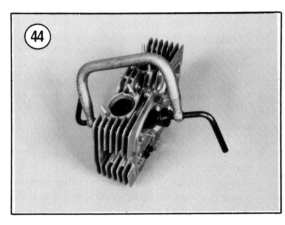

aluminum or brass drift and hammer. This will ensure that the keepers are properly seated.

6. Install the cylinder head as described in this chapter.

Valve Guide Replacement

When valve guides are worn so that there is excessive stem-to-guide clearance or valve tipping, the guides must be replaced. Replace all, even if only one is worn. This job should be done only by a dealer as special tools are required. If the valve guides are replaced, replace the valves also.

4

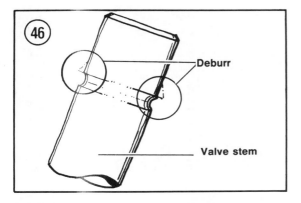

Deburr

Valve stem

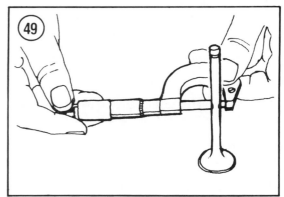

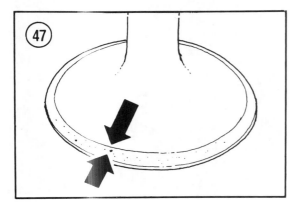

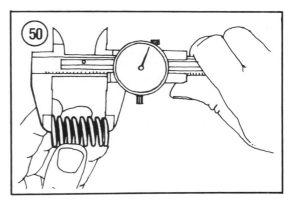

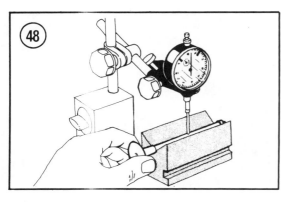

Valve Seat Reconditioning

This job is best left to a dealer or qualified machine shop. They have special equipment and knowledge for this exacting job. You can still save considerable money by removing the cylinder head and taking the head to the shop for repairs.

Valve Lapping

Valve lapping is a simple operation which can restore the valve seal without machining if the amount of wear or distortion is not too great.

NOTE
On Rebel 250 models, valve lapping or grinding the valves is not recommended as the valve face is coated with a special material. Lapping or grinding the valve will remove this surface and will lead to almost instant valve failure. Do not lap or grind the valves.

1. Coat the valve seating area in the cylinder with a lapping compound such as Carborundum or Clove Brand.
2. Insert the valve into the head.
3. Wet the suction cup of the lapping stick (**Figure 52**) and stick it onto the valve head.
4. Lap the valve to the seat by rotating the lapping stick in both directions. Every 5 to 10 seconds, rotate the valve 180° in the seat; continue lapping until the contact surface of the valve and the valve seat are uniform gray. Stop as soon as they are to avoid removing too much material.
5. Thoroughly clean the valves and the cylinder head in cleaning solvent to remove all lapping compound. Any compound left on the valves or the cylinder head will end up in the engine's oil supply and cause damage.

Valve Seat Seal Testing

After the lapping procedure has been completed, install the valve assemblies into the cylinder head and test the valve seat seal.

Pour solvent into each intake and exhaust port in the cylinder head and check the seal of each valve.

There should be no leakage past the valve-to-valve seat seal. If solvent leaks past any of the valve seats, repeat the lapping procedure until there is no leakage at all.

ROCKER ARM/CAMSHAFT HOLDER ASSEMBLIES

Removal

1. Remove the right- and left-hand side covers.
2. Remove the fuel tank as described in Chapter Six.

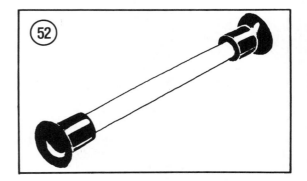

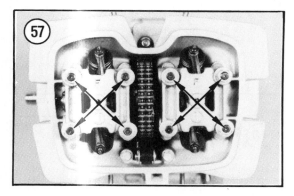

3. Remove the bolts (**Figure 53**) securing the cam cover and remove the cam cover and gasket.

NOTE
The following steps are shown with the engine removed for clarity.

4A. On Rebel 250 models, remove the timing cap (A, **Figure 54**) and the center cap (B, **Figure 54**).
4B. On all other models, remove the screws securing the ignition cover and remove the cover.
5. Rotate the crankshaft using the bolt **Figure 55** or **Figure 56** on the end of the crankshaft, rotate the engine *counterclockwise* until the ignition

timing mark "T" (200-250 models) or "T-1" (185 models) aligns with the index mark as follows:
   a. 185 models: **Figure 31**.
   b. 200-250 models: **Figure 32**.

CAUTION
To avoid undue stress to the camshaft, loosen all nuts even though you may want to remove only one of the camshaft holder assemblies.

6. Loosen all cylinder head nuts evenly in a crisscross pattern, in 2-3 stages (**Figure 57**). After all have been loosened, remove all nuts.
7. Pull the camshaft holder assemblies straight up and off the crankcase studs. Don't lose the locating dowels on the bottom surface of each holder assembly.

Disassembly/Inspection/Assembly

Rocker arm assemblies should be disassembled, inspected and then assembled one at a time to avoid the intermixing of parts. This is especially true with a well run-in engine (high mileage). Once wear patterns are developed on these parts, they should only be installed as they were removed or excessive wear may occur.

NOTE
If the rest of the engine is disassembled, or at least the oil pump, in Step 1 you can use one of the 5 mm bolts that secures the oil pump assembly to the crankcase.

1. Screw in a 5 mm bolt into the rocker arm shaft (**Figure 58**) and withdraw the shaft. Remove the rocker arm and spring.
2. As the parts are disassembled, mark them so they will be reinstalled into their original positions. Mark them in sets with "I" (intake) or "E" (exhaust). The intake valves are at the rear of the engine and the exhaust valves are at the front. Also mark the cylinder numbers with the "L" (left-hand side) or "R" (right-hand side).
3. Wash all parts in cleaning solvent and thoroughly dry. Be sure to clean out the oil passageway in the rocker arm.
4. Inspect the rocker arm pad (**Figure 59**) where it rides on the cam lobe and where the adjuster rides on the valve stem. If the pad is scratched or unevenly worn, inspect the cam lobe for scoring, chipping or flat spots. Replace the rocker arm if defective. If damage is severe, the camshaft may also require replacement.
5. Check the springs for breakage or distortion. Replace as necessary.

6. Measure the inside diameter of the rocker arm bore (A, **Figure 60**) and the outside diameter of the rocker arm shaft (B, **Figure 60**). Compare with dimensions in **Table 1**. Replace if worn to the service limit or beyond.

7. Inspect the rocker arm shaft for signs of wear or scoring.

8. Coat the rocker arm shaft and rocker arm bore with assembly oil or clean engine oil.

9. Assemble the parts in the order shown in **Figure 61** and into their original positions as marked in Step 2.

10. Assemble the spring onto the long end of the rocker arm and place this assembly into position in the camshaft holder.

NOTE
Position the rocker arm shaft with the threaded end facing out (so it can be removed with the 5 mm bolt the next time).

11. Slide in the rocker arm shaft and push the shaft in until it seats. After assembly is complete it should look like **Figure 58** with the exception of the 5 mm bolt (used for removal).

12. Repeat for the other rocker arm assemblies.

Installation

1. If removed, install the locating dowels onto the base of the camshaft holders.

2. Install the camshaft holder assemblies with the "F" mark (**Figure 62**) located toward the front (exhaust side) of the engine.

3. Make sure the timing marks are still correct; refer to Step 5, *Removal*. If incorrect, readjust before tightening the cylinder head nuts.

4. Install the cylinder head nuts (**Figure 57**) and tighten in a crisscross pattern in 2-3 stages to the torque specification listed in **Table 2**.

CAUTION
*If there is any binding while rotating the crankshaft, **stop**. Determine and correct the cause before proceeding.*

5. After installation is complete, rotate the crankshaft several complete revolutions using the bolt on the end of the crankshaft (**Figure 56**).

6. Install all items removed.

7. Adjust the valve clearance as described in Chapter Three.

**CAMSHAFT CHAIN
AND TENSIONER**

In order to gain access to the camshaft chain and tensioner, the engine must be removed and the crankcase split.

The cam chain tensioner on the 1985-on models is slightly different from earlier models shown in this procedure. The removal, inspection and installation procedures are the same for all models.

Removal/Installation

1. Perform Steps 1-10, *Crankcase Disassembly*, in this chapter.

2. Remove the spring pin and flat washer (**Figure 63**) securing the tensioner assembly to the crankshaft center support.

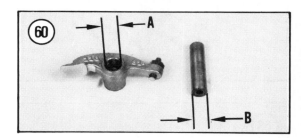

3. Pull the tensioner assembly straight up and off the pin (**Figure 64**) and remove the tensioner assembly.

4. Position the cam chain as shown in **Figure 65**. Then work the loose end of the cam chain up so that the flat portion of the chain will pass over the tensioner pin (**Figure 66**). Remove the cam chain.

5. Install by reversing these removal steps, noting the following.

6. Perform Steps 2-16, *Crankcase Assembly*, in this chapter.

7. On all models except the Rebel 250, adjust the cam chain tensioner as described in Chapter Three.

Inspection

1. Clean all parts in solvent and thoroughly dry with compressed air.

2. Inspect the top surface of the guide (A, **Figure 67**) and the tensioner assembly (B, **Figure 67**). If either is worn or is starting to disintegrate they must be replaced.

3. Inspect the tensioner components (**Figure 68**); if any part is defective, replace the assembly as it cannot be serviced.

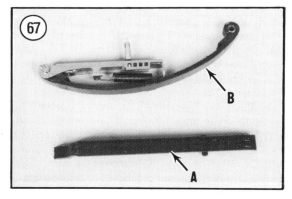

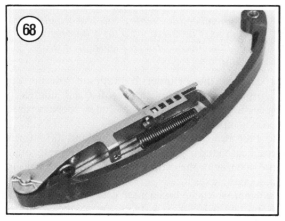

NOTE
On 1978-1983 models, inspect the
O-ring seal on the lower adjuster
(Figure 69). Replace the O-ring if it has
become hard as it will no longer seal
efficiently.

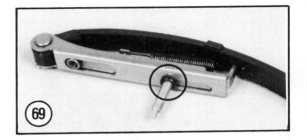

4. Honda does not provide service information for
the service length of the cam chain. As a rule of
thumb, lay the cam chain alongside a ruler (**Figure
70**) and compress the links together. Then stretch
the cam chain apart. If more than 6.3 mm (1/4 in.)
of movement within 304 mm (12 in.) is possible,
replace the cam chain as it is worn and will be
noisy and may cause engine damage.

5. If the cam chain needs to be replaced it is a
good idea to replace the crankshaft and cam
sprocket at the same time and vice-versa. They
may also be defective and should be replaced. If
the sprocket on the crankshaft is faulty, the
crankshaft assembly must be replaced.

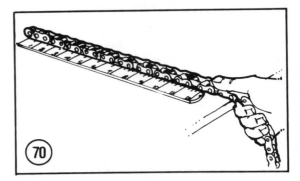

CYLINDER

Removal

1. Remove the cylinder head as described in this
chapter.

2. Remove the cylinder head gasket (A, **Figure 71**),
locating dowels and O-rings (B, **Figure 71**) and the
cam chain guide (C, **Figure 71**).

3A. On 1978-1983 models, perform the following:
   a. Remove the cam chain tensioner lower
      locknut and O-ring from the adjuster bolt (A,
      Figure 72).
   b. Push the adjuster bolt through from the
      outside to move the bolt and tensioner (B,
      Figure 72) out of the hole in the cylinder. The
      tensioner will stay with the crankcase.

3B. On 1985-on models, remove the cam chain
tensioner lower bolt and washer. The tensioner will
stay with the crankcase.

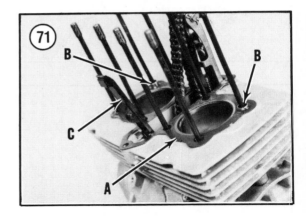

CAUTION
Remember the cooling fins are fragile
and may be damaged if tapped or pried
on too hard. Do not use a metal
hammer.

4. Loosen the cylinder by tapping around the
perimeter with a rubber or soft-faced mallet. If
necessary, *gently* pry the cylinder loose with a
broad-tipped screwdriver.

5. Pull the cylinder straight out and off of the
crankcase studs. Work the cam chain wire through
the opening in the cylinder and tie the loose end to
the engine exterior.

6. Remove the cylinder base gasket and discard it.
Remove the dowel pins from the crankcase studs.

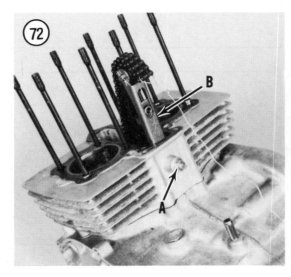

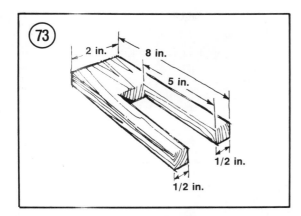

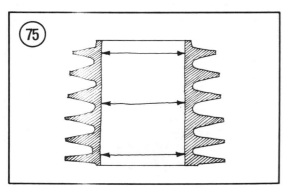

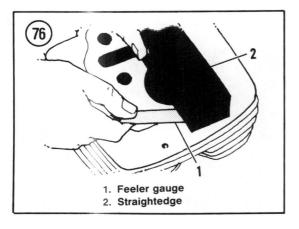

1. Feeler gauge
2. Straightedge

7. Install a piston holding fixture under both pistons. This will protect the piston skirt from damage. This fixture may be purchased or may be a homemade unit of wood. See **Figure 73** for dimensions.

Inspection

The following procedure requires the use of highly specialized and expensive measuring instruments. If such equipment is not readily available, have the measurements performed by a dealer or qualified machine shop.

1. Soak with solvent any old cylinder head gasket material on the cylinder. Use a broad-tipped *dull* chisel and gently scrape off all gasket residue. Do not gouge the sealing surface as oil and air leaks will result.

2. Inspect the cylinder for signs of wear, distortion or damage. If the piston ever seizes, then it will be necessary to have the cylinders honed to remove the minute particles of aluminum from the cylinder walls to prevent further damge when the engine is rebuilt.

3. Measure the cylinder bore with a cylinder gauge or inside micrometer in both directions (**Figure 74**) at the top middle and bottom (**Figure 75**).

4. Measure in 2 axes—in line with the piston pin and at 90° to the pin. If the taper or out-of-round is 0.05 mm (0.002 in.) or greater, the cylinders must be rebored to the next oversize and new pistons installed.

NOTE
The new pistons should be obtained before the cylinders are rebored so that the pistons can be measured; slight manufacturing tolerances must be taken into account to determine the actual size and working clearance.

5. Check the cylinder wall for scratches; if evident, the cylinders should be rebored.

NOTE
*The maximum wear limit for the cylinders is listed in **Table 1**. If the cylinder is worn to this limit, the cylinder block must be replaced. Never rebore a cylinder if the finished rebore diameter will be this dimension or greater.*

6. After the cylinders have been thoroughly cleaned, place a straightedge across the gasket surface at several points (**Figure 76**). Measure the warp by inserting a feeler gauge between the straightedge and cylinder head mating surface at each location. There should be no warpage; if a

small amount is present, it can be resurfaced by a
Honda dealer or machine shop.

Installation

1. Check that the crankcase top surface and the
cylinder bottom surface are clean before installing
a new base gasket.
2. Install a new cylinder base gasket (A, **Figure 77**)
and the locating dowels (B, **Figure 77**).
3. Apply assembly oil or clean engine oil to the
piston rings and the cylinder walls.
4. Install a piston holding fixture (A, **Figure 78**)
under both pistons. This can be a purchased unit or
a home made unit (**Figure 73**).
5. Make sure the end gaps of the piston rings are
not lined up with each other—they must be
staggered.
6. Install the cylinder and slide it down onto the
crankcase studs (B, **Figure 78**).
7. Carefully feed the cam chain and wire up
through the opening in the cylinder and tie it to the
engine.
8. Compress each piston ring as it enters each
cylinder either with your fingers, or by using
aircraft type hose clamps of the appropriate size
(**Figure 79**), as the cylinder starts over each ring.
9. Slide the cylinder down until it bottoms on the
piston holding fixtures.
10. Remove the piston holding fixtures (and hose
clamps if used) and slide the cylinder down into
place on the crankcase.
11A. On 1978-1983 models, perform the
following:
   a. Pull the cam chain tensioner to the rear until
    the stud comes through the hole in the
    cylinder.
   b. Install the O-ring seal (**Figure 80**) and the
    locknut.
11B. On 1985-on models, pull the cam chain
tensioner to the rear and install the bolt and
washer.
12. Install the cylinder head as described in this
chapter.
13. Adjust the valves and the cam chain tensioner
as described in Chapter Three.
14. Follow the *Break-in Procedure* in this chapter
if the cylinder was rebored or honed or new pistons
or piston rings were installed.

PISTON, PISTON PIN AND PISTON RINGS

The pistons are made of an aluminum alloy. The
piston pin is made of steel and is a precision fit.
The piston pin is held in place by a clip at each
end.

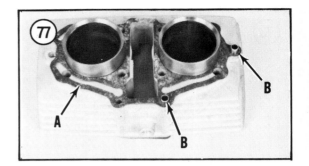

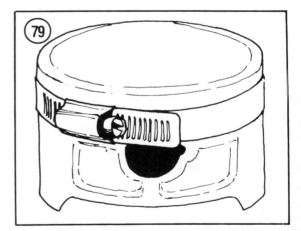

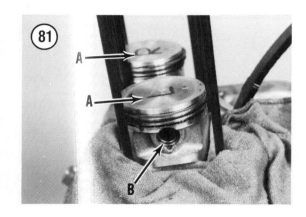

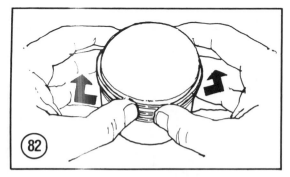

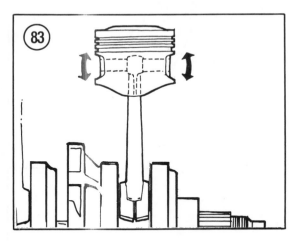

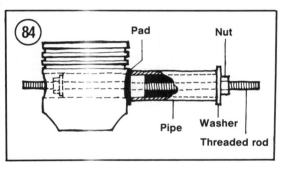

Pad   Nut

Pipe   Washer

Threaded rod

The engine must be removed from the frame to remove the pistons.

Piston Removal

1. Remove the cylinder head and cylinder as described in this chapter.
2. Mark the top of each piston (A, **Figure 81**) with a L (left) or R (right) so they will be installed onto the correct cylinder. Remember that the left-hand side refers to a person sitting in the seat facing foward.

> *WARNING*
> *The edges of all piston rings are very sharp. Be careful when handling them to avoid cutting fingers.*

3. Remove the top ring with a ring expander tool or by spreading the ends with your thumbs just enough to slide the ring up over the piston (**Figure 82**). Repeat for the remaining rings.
4. Before removing the piston, hold the rod tightly and rock the piston as shown in **Figure 83**. Any rocking motion (do not confuse with the normal sliding motion) indicates wear on the piston pin, piston pin bore or connecting rod small-end bore (more likely a combination of these).

> *NOTE*
> *Wrap a clean shop cloth under the piston so that the piston pin clip will not fall into the crankcase.*

5. Remove the clips from each side of the piston pin bore (B, **Figure 81**) with a small screwdriver or scribe. Hold your thumb over one edge of the clip when removing it to prevent the clip from springing out.
6. Use a proper size wooden dowel or socket extension and push out the piston pin. Mark the piston pin to match the piston so they will be reassembled into the same set.

> *CAUTION*
> *Be careful when removing the pin to avoid damaging the connecting rod. If it is necessary to gently tap the pin to remove it, be sure that the piston is properly supported so that lateral shock is not transmitted to the lower connecting rod bearing.*

7. If the piston pin is difficult to remove, heat the piston and pin with a butane torch. The pin will probably push right out. Heat the piston to only about 140° F (60° C), i.e., until it is too warm to touch, but not excessively hot. If the pin is still difficult to push out, use a homemade tool as shown in **Figure 84**.

4

8. Lift the piston off the connecting rod.

9. If the piston is going to be left off for some time, place a piece of foam insulation tube over the end of the rod to protect it.

10. Repeat for the other piston.

Inspection

1. Carefully clean the carbon from the piston crown with a chemical remover or with a soft scraper (**Figure 85**). Do not remove or damage the carbon ridge around the circumference of the piston above the top ring. If the pistons, rings and cylinder are found to be dimensionally correct and can be reused, removal of the carbon ring from the top of the piston or the carbon ridge from the top of the cylinders will promote excessive oil consumption.

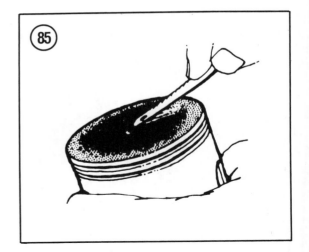

> *CAUTION*
> *Do not wire brush the piston skirts.*

2. Examine each ring groove for burrs, dented edges and wide wear. Pay particular attention to the top compression ring groove as it usually wears more than the others.

3. Measure the piston-to-cylinder clearance as described under *Piston Clearance* in this chapter.

4. If damage or wear indicates piston replacement, select a new piston as described under *Piston Clearance* in this chapter.

5. Measure the inside diameter of the piston pin bore with a snap gauge (**Figure 86**) and measure the outside diameter of the piston pin with a micrometer (**Figure 87**). Compare with dimensions given in **Table 1**. Replace the pistons and piston pins as a set if either or both are worn.

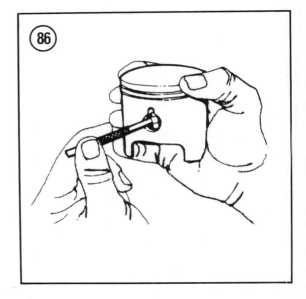

6. Check the piston skirt for galling and abrasion which may have been caused by piston seizure. If light galling is present, smooth the affected area with No. 400 emery paper and oil or a fine oilstone. However, if galling is severe or if the piston is deeply scored, replace it.

Piston Clearance

1. Make sure the piston and cylinder walls are clean and dry.

2. Measure the inside diameter of the cylinder bore at a point 13 mm (1/2 in.) from the upper edge with a bore gauge (**Figure 88**).

3. Measure the outside diameter of the piston across the skirt (**Figure 89**) at right angles to the piston pin. Measure at a distance 10 mm (0.40 in.) up from the bottom of the piston skirt at 90° to the piston pin axes (**Figure 90**). Check against the measurements listed in **Table 1**.

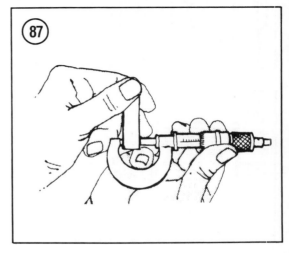

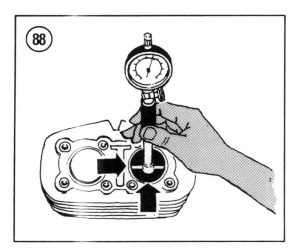

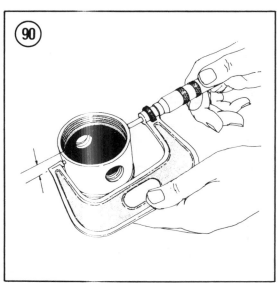

4. Piston clearance is the difference between the maximum piston diameter and the minimum cylinder diameter. Subtract the dimension of the piston from the cylinder dimension. The piston-to-cylinder clearance service limit is listed in **Table 1**. If the clearance is greater than specified, the cylinders should be rebored to the next oversize and new pistons installed.

5. To establish a final overbore dimension with a new piston, add the piston skirt measurement to the specified clearance. This will determine the dimension for the cylinder overbore size. Remember, do not exceed the cylinder maximum service limit inside diameter indicated in **Table 1**.

Piston Installation

1. Apply molybdenum disulfide grease to the inside surface of the connecting rod.

> *CAUTION*
> *Be sure to install the correct piston onto the same rod from which it was removed, "L" or "R" (A, **Figure 81**).*

2. Oil the piston pin with assembly oil and install it in the piston until its end extends slightly beyond the inside of the boss.

3. Place the piston over the connecting rod with the arrow pointing forward (exhaust side) of the engine or the "IN" mark on the piston crown (**Figure 91**) toward the rear (intake side) of the engine.

4. Line up the piston pin with the hole in the connecting rod and push the piston pin through the

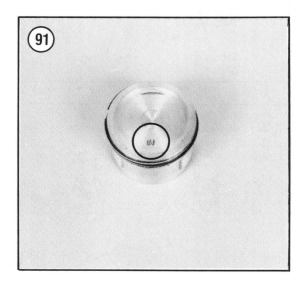

connecting rod and into the other side of the piston until it is even with the piston pin clip grooves.

> *CAUTION*
> *If it is necessary to tap the piston pin into the connecting rod, do so gently with a block of wood or a soft-faced hammer. Make sure you support the piston to prevent the lateral shock from being transmitted to the connecting rod bearing.*

> *NOTE*
> *In the next step, install the clips with the gap away from the cutout in the piston (Figure 92).*

5. Install new piston pin clips in both ends of the pin boss. Make sure they are seated in the grooves in the piston.

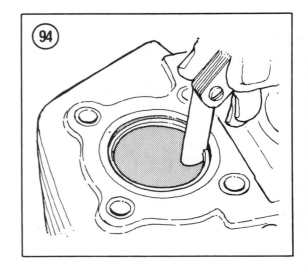

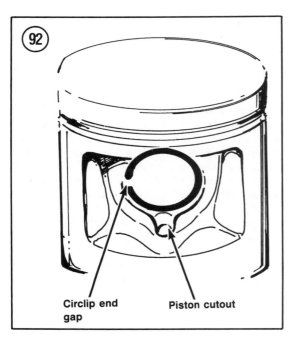

Circlip end gap

Piston cutout

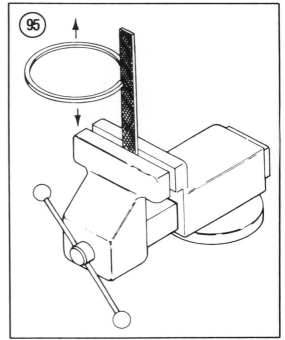

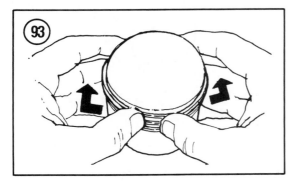

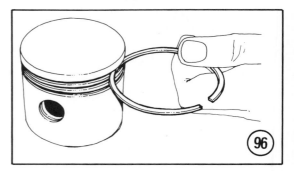

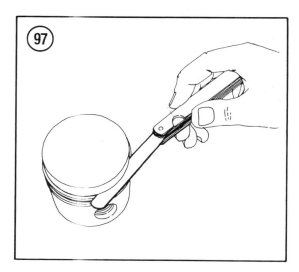

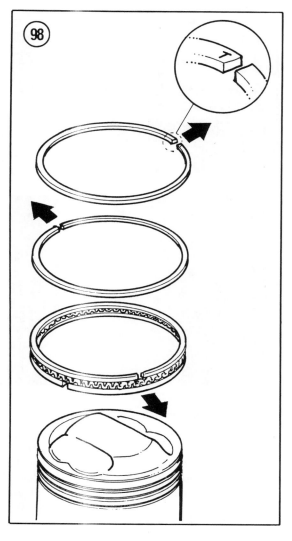

6. Check the installation by rocking the piston back and forth around the pin axis and from side to side along the axis. It should rotate freely back and forth but not from side to side.

7. Install the piston rings as described in this chapter.

8. Install the cylinder and cylinder head as described in this chapter.

Piston Ring
Removal/Installation

> *WARNING*
> *The edges of all piston rings are very sharp. Be careful when handling them to avoid cutting fingers.*

1. If you haven't already done so, remove the top ring with a ring expander tool or by spreading the ends with your thumbs just enough to slide the ring up over the piston (**Figure 93**). Repeat for the remaining rings.

2. Carefully remove all carbon buildup from the ring grooves with a broken piston ring. Inspect the grooves carefully for burrs, nicks or broken and cracked lands. Recondition or replace the piston if necessary.

3. Measure each ring for wear. Place each ring, one at a time, into the cylinder and push it in about 15 mm (5/8 in.) with the crown of the piston to ensure that the ring is square in the cylinder bore. Measure the gap with a flat feeler gauge (**Figure 94**) and compare to dimensions in **Table 1**. If the gap is greater than specified, the rings should be replaced. When installing new rings, measure their end gap in the same manner as for old ones. If the gap is less than specified, carefully file the ends (**Figure 95**) with a fine-cut file until the gap is correct.

4. Roll each ring around its piston groove as shown in **Figure 96** to check for binding. Minor binding may be cleaned up with a fine-cut file.

5. Measure the side clearance of each ring in its groove with a flat feeler gauge (**Figure 97**) and compare to dimensions given in **Table 1**. If the clearance is greater than specified, the rings must be replaced. If the clearance is still excessive with the new rings, the piston must also be replaced.

6. Install the piston rings in the order shown in **Figure 98**.

> *NOTE*
> *Install all rings with their markings facing up. Do not intermix the top and second ring; refer to **Figure 99**.*

7. Install the piston rings—first the bottom one, then the middle one, then the top—by carefully spreading the ends of the ring with your thumbs and slipping the ring over the top of the piston. Remember that the marks on the piston rings are toward the top of the piston.

8. Make sure the rings are seated completely in their grooves all the way around the piston and that the ends are distributed around the piston. The important thing is that the ring gaps are not aligned with each other when installed.

9. If new rings were installed, measure the side clearance of each ring in its groove with a flat feeler gauge (**Figure 97**) and compare to dimensions given in **Table 1**.

10. Follow the *Break-in Procedure* in this chapter if new pistons or piston rings have been installed or the cylinders were rebored or honed.

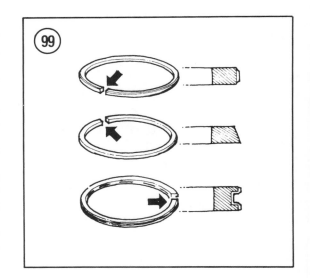

IGNITION ADVANCE MECHANISM (BREAKER POINT IGNITION)

Removal/Installation (CM185T)

1. Remove the right-hand side cover and disconnect the battery negative lead (**Figure 100**).

2. Remove the screws securing the ignition cover and remove the cover and gasket.

3. Remove the screws securing the base plate (A, **Figure 101**). Disconnect the electrical connector and remove the breaker point base plate assembly.

4. Remove the gearshift lever (B, **Figure 101**).

5. Remove the screws securing the rear left-hand crankcase cover (C, **Figure 101**) and left-hand crankcase cover (D, **Figure 101**) and remove both covers.

6. Disconnect the alternator electrical connector (**Figure 102**) and neutral indicator wire.

> *NOTE*
> *If necessary, use a strap wrench (**Figure 103**) to keep the alternator from turning while removing the bolt.*

7. Remove the bolt securing the ignition advance mechanism and the alternator rotor. Remove the ignition advance mechanism.

8. Install by reversing these removal steps, noting the following.

9. Align the pin on the back side of the ignition advance mechanism with the notch in the alternator rotor and install the mechanism.

10. Install and tighten the alternator rotor bolt to the torque specification listed in **Table 2**.

11. Install all items removed and check ignition timing as described in Chapter Three.

Removal/Installation (CM200T)

1. Remove the right-hand side cover and disconnect the battery negative lead (**Figure 100**).

2. Remove the screws (**Figure 104**) securing the ignition cover and remove the cover and gasket.

3. Hold onto the 17 mm indexing nut (A, **Figure 105**) and remove the inner bolt (B, **Figure 105**) securing the ignition advance mechanism.

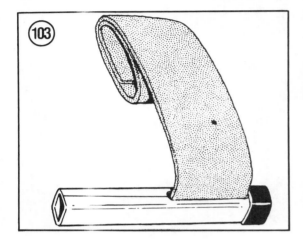

4. Remove the screws securing the base plate (C, **Figure 105**). Disconnect the electrical connector and remove the breaker point base plate assembly.

5. Remove the ignition advance mechanism.

6. Install by reversing these removal steps, noting the following.

7. Align the pin (A, **Figure 106**) on the back side of the ignition advance mechanism with the notch (B, **Figure 106**) in the alternator rotor.

8. Install the mechanism and hold it in place (**Figure 107**) while installing the breaker point base plate assembly.

9. Tighten the inner bolt and the 17 mm indexing nut securely.

10. Install all items removed and check ignition timing as described in Chapter Three.

IGNITION ADVANCE MECHANISM (ELECTRONIC IGNITION SYSTEM)

All models since 1981 are equipped with a capacitor discharge ignition system (CDI). This system uses no mechanical method for advancing and retarding the igniton for the various engine speeds.

The ignition advance mechanism is removed during alternator removal and installation as described in this chapter.

ALTERNATOR

Removal/Installation (CM185T)

1. Remove the right-hand side cover and disconnect the battery negative lead (**Figure 100**).
2. Remove the screws securing the ignition cover and remove the cover and gasket.
3. Remove the screws securing the base plate (A, **Figure 101**). Disconnect the electrical connector and remove the breaker point base plate assembly.
4. Remove the gearshift lever (B, **Figure 101**).
5. Remove the screws securing the rear left-hand crankcase cover (C, **Figure 101**) and left-hand crankcase cover (D, **Figure 101**) and remove both covers and gaskets.
6. Disconnect the alternator electrical connector (**Figure 102**) and neutral indicator wire.

NOTE
*If necessary, use a strap wrench (**Figure 103**) to keep the alternator from turning while removing the bolt.*

7. Remove the bolt securing the ignition advance mechanism and the alternator rotor. Remove the ignition advance mechanism.
8. Screw a flywheel puller all the way in until it stops. Turn the puller with a wrench until the rotor disengages from the crankshaft. Remove the rotor and puller.

NOTE
Don't lose the locating pin on the crankshaft.

9. Inspect all alternator components as described in Chapter Seven.
10. Install by reversing these removal steps, noting the following.
11. Align the pin on the back side of the ignition advance mechanism with the notch in the alternator rotor and install the mechanism.
12. Install and tighten the alternator rotor bolt to the torque specification listed in **Table 2**.
13. Install all items removed and check ignition timing as described in Chapter Three.

Removal/Installation (1980 CM200T)

1. Remove the right-hand side cover and disconnect the battery negative lead (**Figure 100**).
2. Remove the screws (**Figure 104**) securing the ignition cover and remove the cover and gasket.
3. Remove the screws securing the rear left-hand crankcase cover (A, **Figure 108**) and remove the cover and gasket.
4. Remove the gearshift lever (B, **Figure 108**).

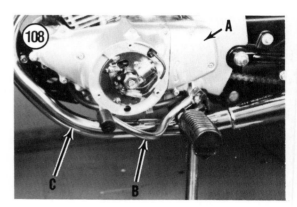

5. Remove the left-hand side of the exhaust system (C. **Figure 108**) as described in Chapter Six.
6. Hold onto the 17 mm indexing nut (A, **Figure 105**) and remove the inner bolt (B, **Figure 105**) securing the ignition advance mechanism.
7. Remove the screws securing the base plate (C, **Figure 105**). Disconnect the electrical connector and remove the breaker point base plate assembly.
8. Remove the ignition advance mechanism.
9. Disconnect the alternator electrical connector (A, **Figure 109**) and neutral indicator wire (B, **Figure 109**).

10. Remove the bolts securing the left-hand crankcase cover and remove the cover and gasket.

NOTE
*If necessary, use a strap wrench (**Figure 103**) to keep the alternator from turning while removing the bolt.*

11. Remove the bolt securing the alternator rotor (**Figure 110**).
12. Screw a flywheel puller all the way in until it stops. Use the Honda flywheel puller (part No. 07733-002000) or K & N puller (part No. 82-0100) or equivalent. Turn the puller with a wrench (**Figure 111**) until the rotor disengages from the crankshaft. Remove the rotor and puller.

NOTE
*Don't lose the locating pin on the crankshaft (**Figure 112**).*

13. Inspect all alternator components as described in Chapter Seven.
14. Install by reversing these removal steps, noting the following.
15. Tighten the alternator bolt to the torque specification listed in **Table 2**.
16. Align the pin (A, **Figure 106**) on the back side of the ignition advance mechanism with the notch (B, **Figure 106**) in the alternator rotor.
17. Install the mechanism and hold it in place (**Figure 107**) while installing the breaker point base plate assembly.
18. Tighten the inner bolt and the 17 mm indexing nut securely.
19. Install all items removed and check ignition timing as described in Chapter Three.

Removal/Installation (1981-1982 CM200T)

1. Remove the right-hand side cover and disconnect the battery negative lead (**Figure 100**).
2. Remove the screws (**Figure 104**) securing the ignition cover and remove the cover and gasket.
3. Remove the screws securing the rear left-hand crankcase cover (A, **Figure 113**) and remove the cover and gasket.
4. Remove the clamping bolt and remove the gearshift lever (B, **Figure 113**).
5. Remove the left-hand side of the exhaust system (C, **Figure 113**) as described in Chapter Six.

6. Hold onto the outer 17 mm indexing nut (A, **Figure 114**) and remove the inner bolt (B, **Figure 114**) securing the ignition pulse generator rotor.

7. Remove the base plate attachment screws (C, **Figure 114**), disconnect the pulse generator connectors and remove the pulse generator plate assembly.

8. Remove the ignition pulse generator rotor assembly.

9. Disconnect the alternator electrical connector (A, **Figure 115**) and neutral indicator wire (B, **Figure 115**).

10. Remove the bolts securing the left-hand crankcase cover (C, **Figure 115**) and remove the cover and gasket.

11. Remove the alternator rotor bolt (**Figure 110**).

NOTE
If necessary, use a strap wrench to keep the alternator rotor from turning while removing the bolt.

12. Screw a flywheel puller all the way in until it stops. Use a Honda puller (part No. 07733-002001) or K & N puller (part No. 82-0100) or equivalent. Turn the puller with a wrench (**Figure 111**) until the rotor disengages from the crankshaft. Remove the rotor and puller.

NOTE
*Don't lose the locating pin on the crankshaft (**Figure 112**).*

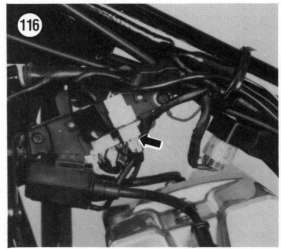

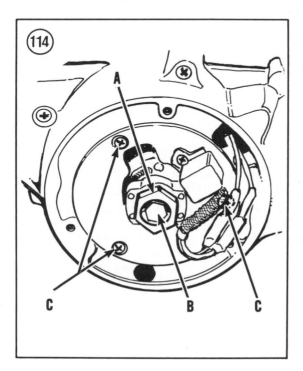

13. Inspect all alternator components as described in Chapter Seven.

14. Install by reversing these removal steps, noting the following.

15. Tighten the alternator rotor bolt to the torque specification listed in **Table 2**.

**Removal/Installation
(1982-1983 CM250C and
1985-on Rebel 250)**

1. Remove the right-hand side cover and disconnect the battery negative lead.

2. Disconnect the electrical connector (**Figure 116**) to the alternator.

3. Remove the clamping bolt and remove the gearshift lever (A, **Figure 117**).

4. Remove the bolts securing the drive sprocket cover (B, **Figure 117**) and remove the cover.

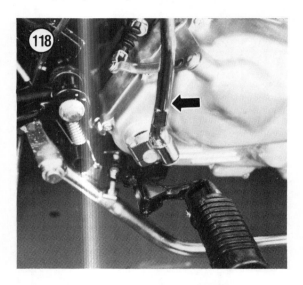

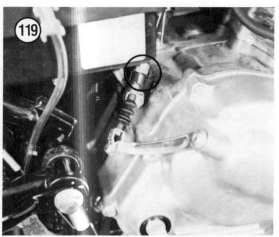

5. Remove the bolts securing the left-hand crankcase cover (C, **Figure 117**) and remove the cover and gasket. Carefully pull the electrical wire grommet from the groove in the crankcase.

6. Remove the alternator rotor bolt and washer (**Figure 110**).

NOTE
If necessary, use a strap wrench to keep the alternator rotor from turning while removing the bolt.

7. Screw a flywheel puller all the way in until it stops. Use a Honda puller (part No. 07733-002001) or K & N puller (part No. 82-0100) or equivalent. Turn the puller with a wrench (**Figure 111**) until the rotor disengages from the crankshaft. Remove the rotor and puller.

NOTE
*Don't lose the locating pin on the crankshaft (**Figure 112**).*

8. Inspect all alternator components as described in Chapter Seven.

9. Install by reversing these removal steps, noting the following.

10. Tighten the alternator rotor bolt to the torque specification listed in **Table 2**.

OIL PUMP

The oil pump is located on the right-hand side of the engine forward of the clutch assembly. The oil pump can be removed with the engine in the frame.

Removal/Installation

NOTE
This procedure is shown with the clutch assembly removed for clarity. It is not necessary to remove the clutch assembly for oil pump removal and installation.

1. Drain the engine oil as described in Chapter Three.

2. Remove the right-hand side of the exhaust sytem as described in Chapter Six.

3. On models so equipped, remove the kickstarter pedal (**Figure 118**).

4. Loosen the locknut and adjusting nut (**Figure 119**) and remove the clutch cable from the actuating lever on the crankcase cover.

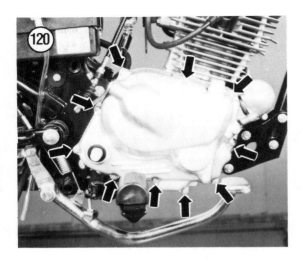

5. Remove the screws (**Figure 120**) securing the right-hand crankcase cover and remove the cover and gasket. Don't lose the locating dowels.

6. Remove the bolts (**Figure 121**) securing the oil pump cover and remove the cover and the rotor shaft.

7. Remove the oil pump drive gear (**Figure 122**).

8. Remove the Phillips head screws (**Figure 123**) securing the oil pump and remove the oil pump assembly.

> NOTE
> *Remove the small O-ring seal (**Figure 124**) from the crankcase and discard it. A new O-ring seal must be installed whenever the oil pump is removed.*

9. Install by reversing these removal steps, noting the following.

10. Install a new O-ring seal (**Figure 124**) in the crankcase.

11. Refill the crankcase with the recommended type and quantity of engine oil. Refer to Chapter Three.

Disassembly/Inspection/Assembly

Refer to **Figure 125** this procedure.

1. Inspect the outer housing for cracks.

2. Remove the Phillips screw (A, **Figure 126**) securing the pump cover (B, **Figure 126**) to the body and remove the cover.

3. Remove the inner and outer rotors. Inspect both parts for scratches and abrasions. Replace both parts if evidence of this is found.

4. If not already removed, remove the rotor shaft.

5. Clean all parts in solvent and thoroughly dry. Coat all parts with fresh engine oil before assembly.

6. Install the rotor shaft (**Figure 127**).

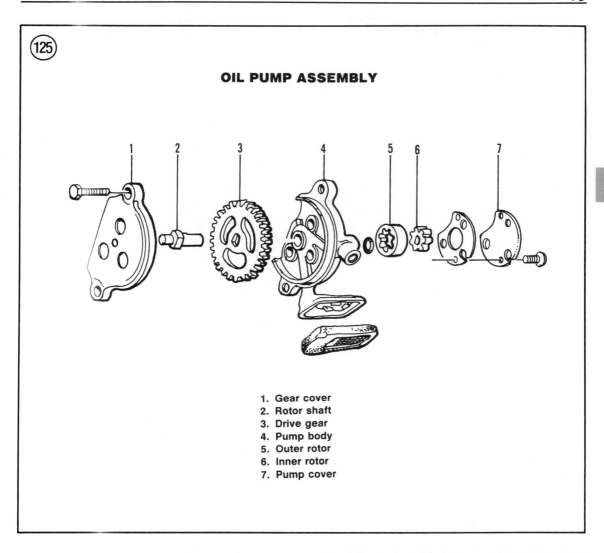

OIL PUMP ASSEMBLY

1. Gear cover
2. Rotor shaft
3. Drive gear
4. Pump body
5. Outer rotor
6. Inner rotor
7. Pump cover

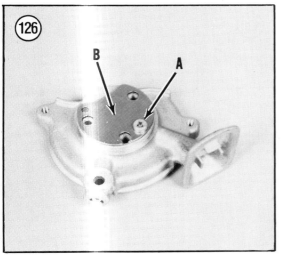

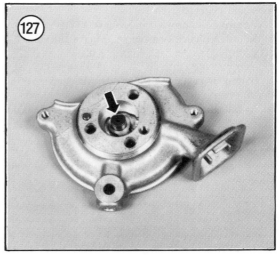

7. Install the outer rotor (**Figure 128**) and inner rotor (**Figure 129**) into the pump body.

8. Measure the clearance between the outer rotor and the oil pump body with a flat feeler gauge (**Figure 130**). If the clearance is 0.25 mm (0.010 in.) or greater, replace the worn part.

9. Measure the clearance between the inner rotor tip and the outer rotor as shown in **Figure 131**. If the clearance is 0.2 mm (0.008 in.) or greater, replace the worn part.

10. Measure the clearance between the rotor end and the pump body with a straightedge and a flat feeler gauge (**Figure 132**). If the clearance is 0.12 mm (0.0048 in.) or greater, replace either the rotors or the oil pump assembly.

11. Install the cover and screws and tighten the screws securely.

OIL PUMP AND CLUTCH DRIVE GEARS

Removal/Installation

NOTE
*Before removing all clutch components, remove the oil pressure pad and spring (A, **Figure 133**) and loosen the 14 mm locknut (B, **Figure 133**). Wedge a soft aluminum wedge between the clutch drive gear and the clutch outer housing (C, **Figure 133**).*

1. Remove the clutch assembly as described in Chapter Five.

2. Remove the bolts (**Figure 134**) securing the oil pump gear cover and remove the cover.

3. Remove the oil pump drive gear (**Figure 135**).

4. Remove the 14 mm locknut (**Figure 136**) loosened prior to Step 1.

5. Remove the dowel pin (**Figure 137**).

6. Remove the lockwasher (A, **Figure 138**) and the oil pump drive gear (B, **Figure 138**).

7. Remove the clutch drive gear (**Figure 139**).

8. Install by reversing these removal steps, noting the following.

9. Install the lockwasher with the "OUTSIDE" mark (A, **Figure 138**) facing toward the outside.

10. Tighten the locknut to the torque specification listed in **Table 2**.

11. Be sure to install the oil pressure pad and spring (A, **Figure 133**).

Inspection

Inspect both gears. Check for excessive wear, burrs, pitting or chipped or missing teeth. Remove

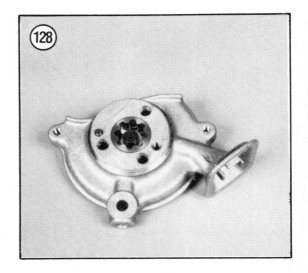
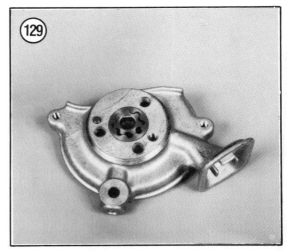
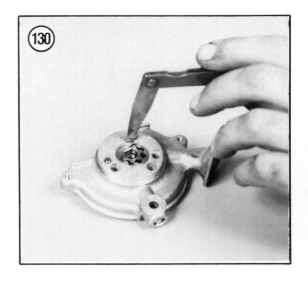

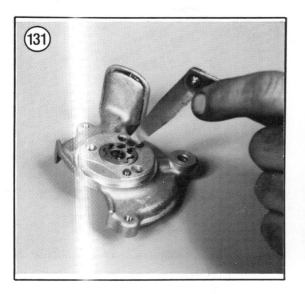

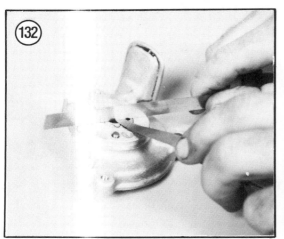

all small nicks with an oilstone. If damage is severe, replace the gear(s).

If either or both gears must be replaced, inspect the mating gear on the clutch outer housing and the oil pump. If they are damaged, they must also be replaced.

CRANKCASE

Disassembly of the crankcase—splitting the cases—and removal of the crankshaft assembly and transmission assemblies require that the engine be removed from the frame.

The crankcase is made in 2 halves of precision diecast aluminum alloy and is of the "thin-walled" type. To avoid damage, do not hammer or pry on any of the interior or exterior projected walls. These areas are easily damaged. The cases are assembled with a gasket between the 2 halves and dowel pins align the halves when they are bolted together.

The procedure which follows is presented as a complete, step-by-step, major lower end rebuild that should be followed if an engine is to be completely reconditioned. However, if you're replacing a part that you know is defective, the disassembly should be carried out only until the failed part is accessible; there is no need to disassemble the engine beyond that point so long as you know the remaining components are in good condition and that they were not affected by the failed part.

Disassembly

1. Remove the engine and remove all exterior engine assemblies as described in this chapter and other related chapters:

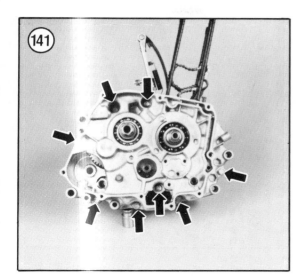

a. Cylinder head.
b. Cylinder and pistons.
c. Clutch assembly.
d. Alternator.
e. External shift mechansim.
f. Oil pump.
g. Starter motor and starter gears (models so equipped).

2. Remove the Phillips screws (**Figure 140**) on the left-hand side of the crankcase.

3. Remove the bolts (**Figure 141**) from the right-hand crankcase side that secure the crankcase halves together. To prevent warpage, loosen the bolts in a crisscross pattern.

4. Place the engine on wood blocks with the right-hand side facing upward.

5. Carefully tap around the perimeter of the crankcase with a plastic or soft-faced mallet—do not use a metal hammer—to separate the crankcase halves.

6. If the crankcase will not separate using this method, check to make sure that all screws and bolts are removed. If you still have a problem, take the crankcase assembly to a dealer and have it separated.

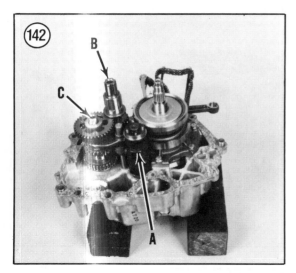

> *CAUTION*
> *Never pry between case halves. Doing so may result in oil leaks, requiring replacement of the case halves.*

> *CAUTION*
> *Do not tap on the left-hand end of the crankshaft to try to separate the crankcase halves. Doing so will disturb the crankshaft-to-support bearing relationship in the left-hand crankcase half.*

7. Remove the right-hand crankcase half. All the internal components should stay in the left-hand half.

8. Don't lose the locating dowels if they came out of the case. They do not have to be removed from the case if they are secure.

9. Remove the gearshift drum and shift forks (A, **Figure 142**) as described in Chapter Five.

10. Remove the transmission main shaft (B, **Figure 142**) and countershaft (C, **Figure 142**) assemblies. Withdraw both assemblies as a unit at the same time, keeping them meshed together to minimize damage.

11. Remove the bolts and nut (**Figure 143**) securing the crankshaft assembly and center bearing support.

12. Carefully remove the crankshaft assembly from the crankcase half. The cam drive chain and chain tensioner assembly will come out with the crankshaft assembly.

13. Inspect the crankcase halves and crankshaft as described in this chapter.

14. Remove the neutral indicator switch (**Figure 144**).

Inspection

1. Clean both crankcase halves inside and out with cleaning solvent. Thoroughly dry with compressed air and wipe off with a clean shop cloth. Be sure to remove all traces of old gasket material from all mating surfaces.

2. Make sure all oil passages are clean (A, **Figure 145** and **Figure 146**). Blow the passages out with compressed air.

3. Carefully inspect the cases for cracks and fractures, especially in the lower areas; they are vulnerable to rock damage. Also check the areas around the stiffening ribs, around bearing bosses and threaded holes.

4. If any cracks are found, have them repaired by a shop specializing in the repair of precision aluminum castings or replace them.

5. Make sure the crankcase studs (B, **Figure 145**) are not bent and the threads are in good condition. Make sure they are screwed in tight in each case half. Retighten if necessary.

6. Check the bearings (crankshaft, transmission, gearshift drum) in the case halves. Check for roughness, pitting, galling and play by rotating them slowly by hand. If any roughness or play can be felt in the bearing it must be replaced as described in this chapter.

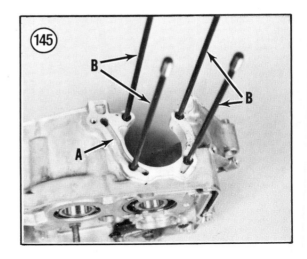

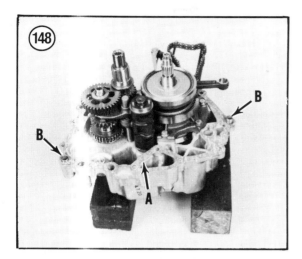

Assembly

Before installing of parts, coat all surfaces with assembly oil or fresh engine oil. Do not get any oil on the sealing surfaces of the case halves.

1. Install the neutral indicator switch and tighten securely.

2. Place the left-hand crankcase on wood blocks.

3. Install the crankshaft assembly into the left-hand crankcase. Be sure to align the threaded stud on the crankcase (**Figure 147**) with the hole in the center bearing support of the crankshaft.

4. Install the bolts and nut (**Figure 143**) securing the crankshaft and center bearing support. Tighten in a crisscross pattern to the torque specification listed in **Table 2**.

5. Install the transmission main shaft (B, **Figure 142**) and countershaft (C, **Figure 142**) assemblies as described in Chapter Five.

6. Install the gearshift drum and shift forks (A, **Figure 142**) as described in Chapter Five.

> *NOTE*
> *Make sure the mating surfaces are clean and free of all old gasket material. Make sure you get a leak-free seal.*

> *NOTE*
> *Apply a light coat of non-hardening gasket sealer (Three Bond 1104 or Gasgacinch or equivalent) to one side of the gasket prior to installation.*

7. Install a new crankcase gasket (A, **Figure 148**) and the locating dowels (B, **Figure 148**) if they were removed.

8. If the crankshaft end was tapped on during disassembly, see *CAUTION* under *Disassembly*, Step 6 then tap on the right-hand end with a plastic mallet until the crankshaft assembly (A, **Figure 149**) is correctly seated in the center bearing support (B, **Figure 149**). It will come to a stop when it is correctly seated.

> *NOTE*
> *If the crankshaft-to-center bearing support relationship has been disturbed, and is not corrected, the crankcase halves will not seat completely.*

9. Position the connecting rod, cam drive chain and tensioner in the position shown in **Figure 150**. This alignment is necessary so that the right-hand crankcase will fit on correctly.

10. Set the right-hand crankcase half over the crankshaft and press the case squarely and fully down onto the left-hand case half.

NOTE
Make sure the connecting rod, cam drive chain and tensioner are correctly positioned through the opening in the crankcase half.

11. Lightly tap the case halves together with a plastic or rubber mallet until they seat—do not use a metal hammer as it will damage the cases.

CAUTION
Crankcase halves should fit together without force. If the crankcase halves do not fit together completely, do not attempt to pull them together with the crankcase screws and bolts. Separate the crankcase halves and investigate the cause of the interference. If the transmission shafts were disassembled, recheck to make sure that a gear is not installed backwards. Do not risk damage by trying to force the cases together.

NOTE
In the following step, install the 2 longer bolts in the locations shown in **Figure 151**.

12. Install the bolts on the right-hand side that secure the crankcase halves together. Tighten the bolts in a crissross pattern to the torque specification listed in **Table 2**.
13. Turn the crankcase over and install the Phillips head screws (**Figure 140**). Tighten the screws securely.

CAUTION
To prevent damage when rotating the crankshaft in the next step, pull up on the cam drive chain making sure it is properly engaged with the sprocket on the crankshaft.

14. After the crankcase halves are completely assembled, rotate the crankshaft. Make sure it rotates freely; if not, tapping the end of the crankshaft with a plastic or soft-faced mallet (**Figure 152**) should free it. If there still is binding and the crankshaft will not rotate freely, disassemble the crankcase and correct the problem.

NOTE
After a new crankcase gasket is installed, it must be trimmed. Carefully trim off all excess crankcase gasket material where the cylinder base gasket

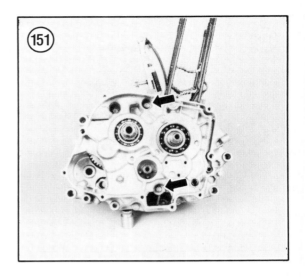

comes in contact with the crankcase. If it is not trimmed, the cylinder base gasket will not seal properly.

15. Install all exterior engine assemblies as described in this chapter and other related chapters:
  a. Cylinder head.
  b. Cylinder and pistons.
  c. Clutch assembly.
  d. Alternator.
  e. External shift mechanism.
  f. Oil pump.
  g. Starter motor and starter gears (models so equipped).
16. Install the engine as described in this chapter.
17. Fill the crankcase with the recommended type and quantity of engine oil as described in Chapter Three.

Bearing Replacement

1. Before removing the bearings, remove the oil seals from the left-hand case half (**Figure 153**). There are no oil seals in the right-hand case half.

Pry out the oil seals with a small screwdriver, taking care not to damage the crankcase bore. If the seals are old and difficult to remove, heat the cases as described in Step 3 and use an awl to punch a small hole in the steel backing of the seal. Install a small sheet metal screw partway into the seal and pull the seal out with a pair of pliers.

CAUTION
Do not install the screw too deep or it may contact and damage the bearing behind it.

2. In the left-hand crankcase half, remove the screws (A, **Figure 154**) securing the oil through plate (B, **Figure 154**) and remove the plate.
3. The bearings are installed with a slight interference fit. The crankcase must be heated in an oven to a temperature of about 100° C (212° F). An easy way to check the proper temperature is to drop tiny drops of water on the case; if they sizzle and evaporate immediately, the temperature is correct. Heat only one case at a time.

CAUTION
Do not heat the cases with a torch (propane or acetylene); never bring a flame into contact with the bearing or case. The direct heat will destroy the case hardening of the bearing and will likely cause warpage of the case.

4. Remove the case from the oven and hold onto the 4 crankcase studs with a kitchen pot holder, heavy gloves or heavy shop cloths—*it is hot.*
5. Hold the crankcase with the bearing side down and tap it squarely on a piece of soft wood. Continue to tap until the bearing(s) fall out. Repeat for the other half.

CAUTION
Be sure to tap the crankcase squarely on the piece of wood. Avoid damaging the sealing surface of the crankcase as it forms an oil-tight seal when the case halves are assembled.

6. If the bearings are difficult to remove, they can be gently tapped out with a socket or piece of pipe the same size as the bearing outer race.

NOTE
If the bearings or seals are difficult to remove or install, don't take a chance on expensive damage. Have the work performed by a dealer or competent machine shop.

7. While heating up the crankcase halves, place the new bearings in a freezer if possible. Chilling them will slightly reduce their overall diameter while the hot crankcase is slightly larger due to heat expansion. This will make bearing installation much easier.

8. While the crankcase is still hot, press each new bearing(s) into place in the crankcase by hand until it seats completely. Do not hammer it in. If the bearing will not seat, remove it and cool it again. Reheat the crankcase and install the bearing again.

9. Bearing identification for the right-hand crankcase half is as follows:

    a. Crankshaft: A, **Figure 155**.

    b. Transmission main shaft: B, **Figure 155**.

    c. Transmission countershaft: C, **Figure 155**.

10. Bearing identification for the left-hand crankcase half is as follows:

    a. Crankshaft: A, **Figure 156**.

    b. Transmission main shaft: B, **Figure 156**.

    c. Transmission countershaft: C, **Figure 156**.

11. Clean the oil through plate in solvent and thoroughly dry with compressed air. Make sure to completely clean the oil path holes as shown in **Figure 157** and **Figure 158**.

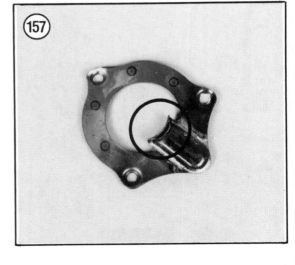

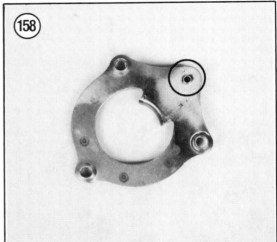

12. Install the oil through plate. Apply Loctite (Lock N' Seal No. 2114) to the screw threads (A, **Figure 154**) before installation. Install a new O-ring seal (**Figure 159**).

CAUTION
*Do not drive in the oil seal for the transmission countershaft (**Figure 160**) below the crankcase surface lip. If driven in too far, it will block the oil passageway in the shaft and cause a loss of oil pressure and component failure.*

CRANKSHAFT AND CONNECTING RODS

Removal/Installation

1. Perform Steps 1-11 of *Crankcase Disassembly* in this chapter and remove the crankshaft assembly (**Figure 161**).
2. Remove the spring pin and flat washer (**Figure 162**) securing the tensioner assembly to the crankshaft center bearing support.
3. Pull the tensioner assembly straight up and off the pin (**Figure 163**) and remove the tensioner assembly.
4. Position the cam drive chain in the crankshaft assembly as shown in **Figure 164**. Then work the

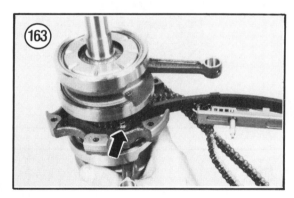

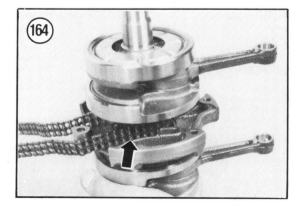

loose end of the chain up so that the flat portion of
the chain will pass over the tensioner pin (**Figure
165**). Remove the cam drive chain.

5. Install by reversing these removal steps, noting
the following.

6. Perform Steps 3-15 of *Crankcase Assembly* in
this chapter.

Inspection

1. Measure the inside diameter of the connecting
rod small end (A, **Figure 166** and **Figure 167**) with
snap gauge and an inside micrometer. Compare to
dimensions given in **Table 1**.

2. Check the connecting rod-to-crankshaft side
clearance with a flat feeler gauge (**Figure 168**).
Compare to dimensions given in **Table 1**.

3. Inspect the center bearing support (B, **Figure
166**). Make sure it rotates smothly with no signs of
wear or damage. If any roughness or play can be
felt in the bearing it must be replaced. This bearing

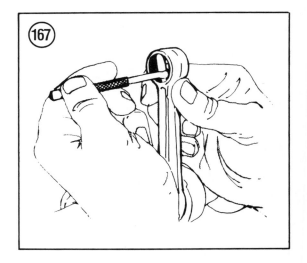

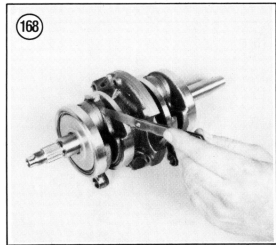

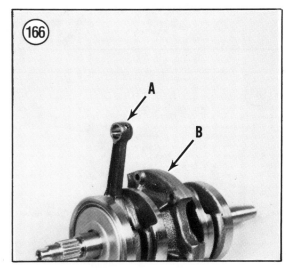

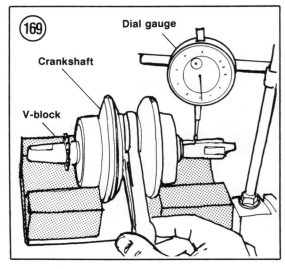

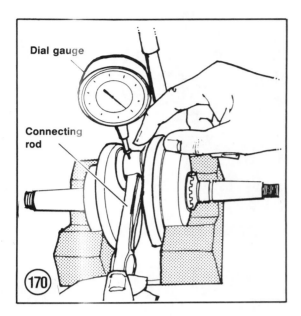

Dial gauge

Connecting rod

(170)

and support assembly is pressed into place and removal and installation must be entrusted to a dealer as special tools are required.

4. Mount the crankshaft assembly in a pair of V-blocks as shown in **Figure 169**. Rotate the crankshaft slowly several complete revolutions. Measure the runout, using a dial indicator, at each end. Replace the crankshaft if the runout exceeds 0.1 mm (0.004 in.) at either end.

5. Mount the crankshaft assembly as in Step 4 and measure the clearance between the connecting rod and the crankpin (**Figure 170**). Compare against dimensions given in **Table 1**.

NOTE
If either connecting rod requires replacement, this is a job for a Honda dealer. It requires a large press to separate and reassemble the crankshaft. In addition the runout (alignment) of the 2 crank halves must be within 0.01 mm (0.0004 in.) of each other.

NOTE
*Other inspections of the crankshaft assembly involve accurate measuring equipment and should be entrusted to a dealer or competent machine shop. The crankshaft assembly operates under severe stress and dimensional tolerances are critical. These dimensions are given in **Table 1**. If any are off by the slightest amount it may cause a considerable amount of damage or destruction of the engine.*

(171)

6. Inspect the splines and threads (**Figure 171**) on the right-hand end of the crankshaft. If severely damaged, the crankshaft assembly must be replaced.

KICKSTARTER
(MODELS SO EQUIPPED)

Removal

1. Place wood block(s) under the engine or frame to support the bike securely.

2. Drain the engine oil as described in Chapter Three.

3. Remove the right-hand side of the exhaust system as described in Chapter Six.

4. Remove the kickstarter pedal (**Figure 172**).

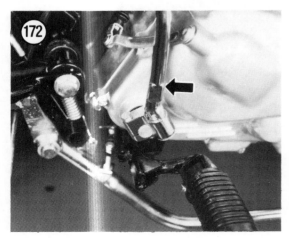

(172)

5. Loosen the locknut and adjusting nut (**Figure 173**) and remove the clutch cable from the activating arm on the crankcase cover.

6. Remove the screws (**Figure 174**) securing the right-hand crankcase cover and remove the cover and gasket. Don't lose the locating dowels.

> *NOTE*
> *The following step is shown with the clutch assembly removed for clarity. It is not necessary to remove it for this procedure.*

7. Carefully unhook the return spring with Vise Grips pliers.

8. Remove the kickstarter assembly (**Figure 175**) from the crankcase.

Disassembly/Inspection

Refer to **Figure 176** for this procedure.

1. Slide off the return spring, collar and thrust washer.

2. Remove the guide plate and the 18 mm circlip.

3A. On CM200T models, remove the large thrust washer, drive ratchet, small thrust washer and the starter gear.

3B. On all other models, remove the drive ratchet and the starter gear.

4. Clean all parts in solvent and thoroughly dry with compressed air.

5. Measure the inside diameter of the kickstarter gear. Compare to the dimension listed in **Table 1**. Replace if worn to the service limit dimension or greater.

6. Measure the outside diameter of the kickstarter shaft where the kickstarter gear rides. Compare to the dimension listed in **Table 1**. Replace if worn to the service limit dimension or less.

7. Inspect the gears for chipped or missing teeth. Replace any gears as necessary.

8. Make sure the ratchet gear operates properly and smoothly on its shaft.

9. Check all parts for uneven wear; replace any that are questionable.

10. Apply assembly oil or fresh engine oil to all sliding surfaces of all parts.

Assembly/Installation

> *NOTE*
> *Align the punch marks on the kickstarter shaft and the drive ratchet as shown in **Figure 176**.*

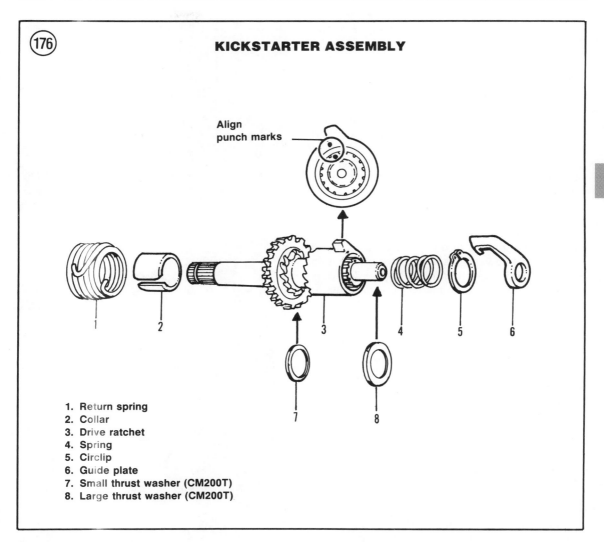

KICKSTARTER ASSEMBLY

Align
punch marks

1
2
3
4
5
6
7
8

1. Return spring
2. Collar
3. Drive ratchet
4. Spring
5. Circlip
6. Guide plate
7. Small thrust washer (CM200T)
8. Large thrust washer (CM200T)

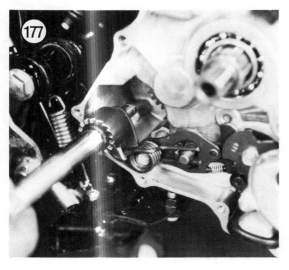

1. Install the drive ratchet, spring, 18 mm circlip and guide plate onto the kickstarter shaft.

2. Install the subassembly into the crankcase (**Figure 177**). The guide plate must index into the notch (**Figure 178**) in the crankcase.

3A. On CM200T models, install the small thrust washer, starter gear and large thrust washer (**Figure 179**) onto the kickstarter shaft.

3B. On all other models, install the starter gear onto the kickstarter shaft.

4. Install the collar and the return spring.

WARNING
In the following step, the spring is under pressure. Protect yourself accordingly.

5. Use a screwdriver (**Figure 180**) or Vise Grips pliers and hook the return spring onto the web on the crankcase (**Figure 181**).

6. Continue installation by reversing *Removal* Steps 1-6.

BREAK-IN PROCEDURE

If the rings were replaced, new pistons installed, the cylinder rebored or honed or major lower end work performed, the engine should be broken in just as though it were new. The performance and service life of the engine depend greatly on a careful and sensible break-in.

For the first 800 km (500 miles) of operation, no more than one-third throttle should be used and speed should be varied as much as possible within the one-third throttle limit. Prolonged steady running at one speed, no matter how moderate, is to be avoided as well as hard acceleration.

Following the first 800 km (500 mile) of operation more throttle can be used but full throttle should not be used until the bike has covered 1,600 km (1,000 miles) and then it should be limited to short bursts of speed until 2,400 km (1,500 miles) have been logged.

The mono-grade oils recommended for break-in and normal use provide a better bedding pattern for rings and cylinders than do multi-grade oils. As a result, piston ring and cylinder bore life are greatly increased. During this period, oil consumption will be higher than normal. It is therefore important to frequently check and correct oil level. At no time, during the break-in or later, should the oil level be allowed to drop below the bottom line on the dipstick; if the oil level is low, the oil will become overheated resulting in insufficient lubrication and increased wear.

800 km (500 mile) Service

It is essential that the oil be changed after the first 800 km (500 miles). In addition, it is a good idea to change the oil and clean the filter screen at the completion of the 2,400 km (1,500 miles) of operation to ensure that all of the particles produced during break-in are removed from the lubrication system. The small added expense may be considered a smart investment that will pay off in increased engine life.

Table 1 ENGINE SPECIFICATIONS

Item	Specification	Wear limit
General		
Engine type	Air-cooled, 4-stroke, SOHC, Twin	
Bore and stroke		
185 models	53×41 mm (2.09×1.61 in.)	
200 models	53×44 mm (2.09×1.73 in.)	
250 models	53×53 mm (2.1×2.1 in.)	
Displacement		
185 models	181 cc (11.02 cu. in.)	
200 models	194.1 cc (11.85 cu. in.)	
250 models	234 cc (14.2 cu. in.)	
Compression ratio		
185 models	9.0 to 1	
200 models	8.8 to 1	
250 models	9.2 to 1	
Cylinder		
Bore		
185-200 models	53.00-53.01 mm (2.086-2.087 in.)	53.1 mm (2.09 in.)
Out of round and taper	—	0.05 mm (0.002 in.)
Warpage across top	—	0.1 mm (0.004 in.)
Piston/cylinder clearance	—	0.1 mm (0.004 in.)
Piston		
Diameter	52.97-52.99 mm (2.085-2.086 in.)	52.87 mm (2.081 in.)
Piston pin bore		
185-200 models	14.002-14.008 mm (0.5513-0.5515 in.)	14.05 mm (0.553 in.)
250 models	15.002-15.008 mm (0.5906-0.5908 in.)	15.05 mm (0.593 in.)
Piston pin outer diameter		
185-200 models	13.994-14.000 mm (0.5509-0.5512 in.)	13.90 mm (0.550 in.)
250 models	14.994-15.000 mm (0.5903-0.5906 in.)	14.98 mm (0.590 in.)
Piston rings		
Number per piston		
Compression	2	
Oil control	1	
Ring end gap		
Top and second	0.15-0.35 mm (0.006-0.014 in.)	0.5mm (0.02 in.)
Oil (side rail)	0.2-0.9 mm (0.008-0.036 in.)	—
Ring side clearance		
Top and second	0.015-0.045 mm (0.0006-0.0018 in.)	0.12 mm (0.0048 in.)
Oil (side rail)	—	—

(continued)

Table 1 ENGINE SPECIFICATIONS (continued)

Item	Specification	Wear limit
Connecting rod		
Small end inner diameter		
185-200 models	14.016-14.034 mm (0.5518-0.5525 in.)	14.08 mm (0.5543 in.)
250 models	15.016-15.034 mm (0.5912-0.5919 in.)	15.08 mm (0.594 in.)
Connecting rod big end side clearance	0.1-0.4 mm (0.0039-0.0158 in.)	0.6 mm (0.0236 in.)
Connecting rod big end radial clearance	0.004-0.012 mm (0.0002-0.0005 in.)	0.05 mm (0.0020 in.)
Camshaft		
Cam lobe height		
Intake		
185-200 models	27.695 mm (1.0904 in.)	26.6 mm (1.0472 in.)
250 models	27.437 mm (1.0801 in.)	27.2 mm (1.07 in.)
Exhaust		
185-200 models	27.522 mm (1.0835 in.)	26.5 mm (1.0433 in.)
250 models	27.263 mm (1.0733 in.)	27.0 mm (1.06 in.)
Runout	—	0.05 mm (0.0020 in.)
Bearing journal OD	19.967-19.980 mm (0.7861-0.7866 in.)	19.92 mm (0.7843 in.)
Bushing ID	20.063-20.083 mm (0.7899-0.7907 in.)	20.20 mm (0.7965 in.)
Valves		
Valve guide inner diameter		
Intake and exhaust	5.475-5.485 mm (0.2156-0.2159 in.)	5.50 mm (0.2165 in.)
Valve stem outer diameter		
Intake	5.450-5.465 mm (0.2146-0.2152 in.)	5.42 mm (0.2134 in.)
Exhaust	5.430-5.445 mm (0.2138-0.2144 in.)	5.40 mm (0.2126 in.)
Stem to guide clearance		
Intake	0.010-0.035 mm (0.0004-0.0014 in.)	0.08 mm (0.003 in.)
Exhaust	0.030-0.055 mm (0.0012-0.0022 in.)	0.10 mm (0.004 in.)
Valve seat width		
Intake and exhaust	1.1-1.5 mm (0.04-0.06 in.)	1.8 mm (0.07 in.)

(continued)

Table 1 ENGINE SPECIFICATIONS (continued)

Item	Specification	Wear limit
Valve springs free length		
Intake and exhaust		
Inner	29.9 mm (1.1772 in.)	29.0 mm (1.1417 in.)
Outer		
185-200 models	36.45 mm (1.4350 in.)	35.3 mm (1.3898 in.)
250 models	38.2 mm (1.50 in.)	37.0 mm (1.46 in.)
Rocker arm assembly		
Rocker arm bore ID	10.000-10.015 mm (0.3937-0.3943 in.)	10.0 mm (0.3976 in.)
Rocker arm shaft OD	9.978-9.987 mm (0.3928-0.3932 in.)	9.17 mm (0.3610 in.)
Oil pump		
Inner rotor tip to outer clearance	0.15 mm (0.059 in.)	0.2 mm (0.0079 in.)
Outer rotor to body clearance	0.15-0.018 mm (0.0059-0.0071 in.)	0.25 mm (0.0098 in.)
End of rotor to body clearance	0.01-0.07 mm (0.0004-0.0028 in.)	0.12 mm (0.0048 in.)
Kickstarter system		
Kickstarter gear ID	18.020-18.041 mm (0.7094-0.7103 in.)	18.07 mm (0.7114 in.)
Kickstarter shaft OD (where gear rides)	17.959-17.980 mm (0.7070-0.7079 in.)	17.93 mm (0.7059 in.)

Table 2 ENGINE TORQUE SPECIFICATIONS

Item	N·m	ft.-lb.
Engine mounting bolts		
185-200 models		
8 mm flange bolts	20-25	14.5-18
10 mm through-bolts	33-43	45-60
250 models		
8 mm flange bolts	24-30	17-22
10 mm flange bolt (front)	55-70	40-51
10 mm through-bolts (rear)	80-100	59-73
Cylinder head (Rebel 250)		
Bolts	10-14	7-10
Nuts	21-25	15-28
Cylinder head		
(All models except Rebel 250)		
Bolts	10-14	7-10
Nuts	17-20	12-15
Cam sprocket bolts	17-23	12-17
Alternator rotor bolt		
185 models	45-50	33-36
200-250 models	55-65	40-47
Oil pump and clutch		
drive locknut	45-60	33-43
Crankshaft center bearing		
support bolts and nut	10-14	7-10
Crankcase bolts	10-14	7-10

4

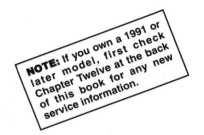
NOTE: If you own a 1991 or later model, first check Chapter Twelve at the back of this book for any new service information.

CLUTCH AND TRANSMISSION

The clutch in the Honda Rebel 250 and Twinstar is a wet multi-plate type which operates immersed in the engine oil. It is mounted on the right-hand end of the transmission main shaft. The inner clutch hub is splined to the main shaft and the outer housing can rotate freely on the main shaft. The outer housing is geared to the crankshaft.

The clutch on the Rebel 250 is basically the same as the one used on all other models but is equipped with some additional parts to smooth out clutch operation and performance.

The clutch release mechanism is mounted within the right-hand crankcase cover and is operated by the clutch cable and hand lever mounted on the handlebar.

Refer to **Figure 1** for Rebel 250 models or **Figure 2** for all other models for all clutch components.

Clutch specifications are listed in **Table 1** at the end of this chapter.

Removal

1. Place the bike on the centerstand.
2. Drain the engine oil as described under *Changing Engine Oil* in Chapter Three.
3. Remove the right-hand exhaust system as described in Chapter Six.
4. On models so equipped, remove the kickstarter pedal (**Figure 3**).
5. Loosen the locknut and adjusting nut (**Figure 4**) and remove the clutch cable from the actuating lever on the crankcase cover.
6. Remove the screws (**Figure 5**) securing the right-hand crankcase cover and remove the cover and gasket.
7. Don't lose the locating dowels. It is not necessary to remove them if they are securely in place.
8. Remove the clutch lifter rod and retainer (**Figure 6**).
9. Using a crisscross pattern, remove the clutch bolts (**Figure 7**) securing the lifter plate.
10. Remove the lifter plate and clutch springs.
11A. On Rebel 250 models, perform the following:
   a. Shift the transmission into 5th gear.
   b. Have an assistant apply the rear brake.
   c. Remove the clutch locknut and lockwasher.
11B. On all other models, remove the 20 mm circlip (**Figure 8**).
12. Remove the clutch center, friction discs and clutch plates as an assembly (**Figure 9**).
13A. On Rebel 250 models, remove the splined washer, clutch outer housing, outer housing guide and thrust washer (**Figure 10**).

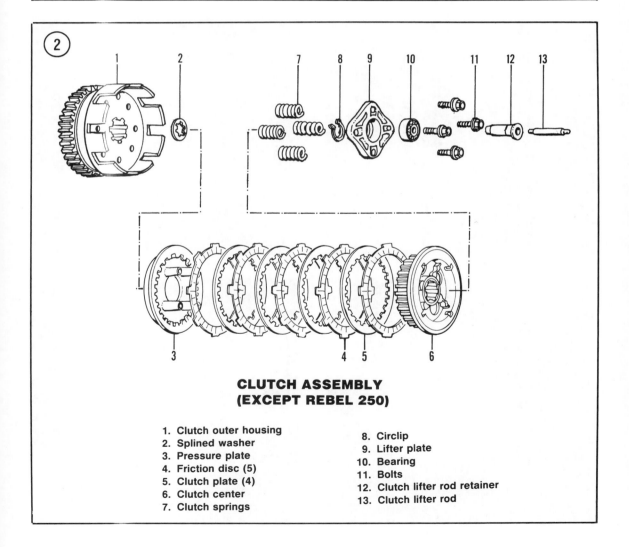

CLUTCH ASSEMBLY (REBEL 250)

1. Thrust washer
2. Clutch outer housing guide
3. Clutch outer housing
4. Splined washer
5. Pressure plate
6. Friction disc
7. Clutch plate
8. Judder spring
9. Judder spring seat
10. Clutch center
11. Lockwasher
12. Clutch spring
13. Locknut
14. Lifter plate
15. Bolt
16. Bearing
17. Lifter rod

5

**CLUTCH ASSEMBLY
(EXCEPT REBEL 250)**

1. Clutch outer housing
2. Splined washer
3. Pressure plate
4. Friction disc (5)
5. Clutch plate (4)
6. Clutch center
7. Clutch springs
8. Circlip
9. Lifter plate
10. Bearing
11. Bolts
12. Clutch lifter rod retainer
13. Clutch lifter rod

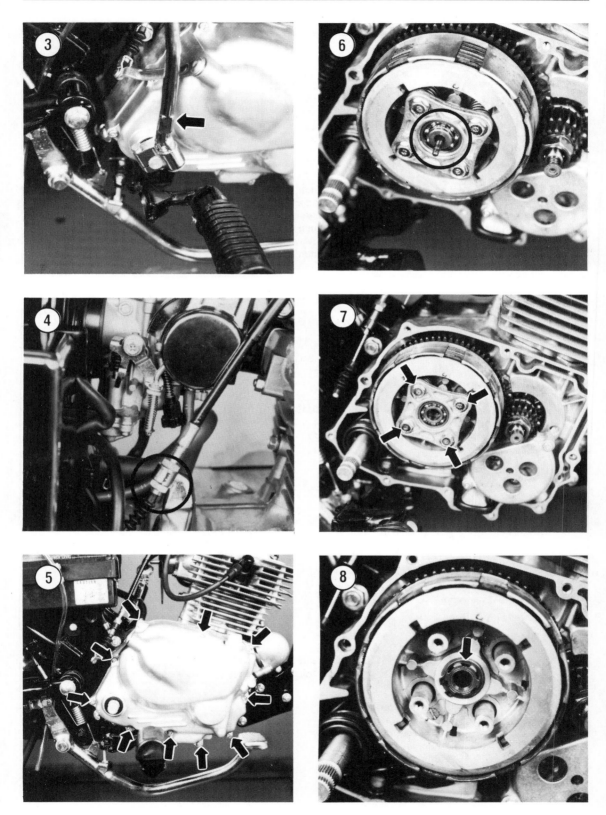

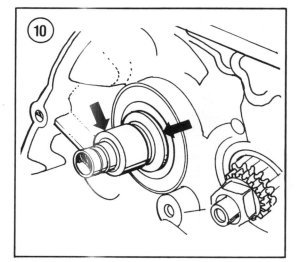

13B. On all other models, remove the splined washer (A, **Figure 11**) and clutch outer housing (B, **Figure 11**).

14. On Rebel 250 models, remove the judder spring and the judder spring seat from the clutch center.

Inspection

Refer to **Table 1** for clutch specifications.

1. Clean all clutch parts in petroleum-based solvent such as kerosene and thoroughly dry with compressed air.

2. Measure the free length of each clutch spring as shown in **Figure 12**. Compare to the specifications listed in **Table 1**. Replace any springs that have sagged to the service limit or less.

3. Measure the thickness of each friction disc at several places around the disc as shown in **Figure 13**. Compare to the specifications listed in **Table 1**. Replace any disc that is worn to the service limit or less.

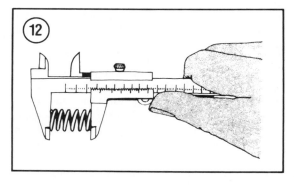

4. Check the clutch plates for warpage on a surface plate such as a piece of plate glass (**Figure 14**). Compare to the specifications listed in **Table 1**. Replace any plate that is warped to the service limit or more.

> *NOTE*
> *If any of the friction discs, clutch plates or clutch springs require replacement, you should replace all of them as a set to retain maximum clutch performance.*

5. Inspect the slots in the clutch outer housing (A, **Figure 15**) for cracks, nicks or galling where they come in contact with the friction disc tabs. If any severe damage is evident, the housing must be replaced.

6. Inspect the gear teeth (B, **Figure 15**) on the outer housing for damage. Remove any small nicks with an oilstone. If damage is severe, the housing must be replaced. Also check the teeth on the driven gear of the crankshaft; if damaged, the driven gear may also need replacing.

7. Inspect the splines (A, **Figure 16**) of the clutch center and the inner splines (B, **Figure 16**) on the pressure plate.

8. Check the bearing in the lifter guide (**Figure 17**). Make sure the bearing rotates smoothly with no signs of wear or damage. Replace if necessary.

9. On Rebel 250 models, perform the following:

   a. Measure the inside diameter of the clutch outer housing. Compare to the specifications listed in **Table 1**. Replace if worn to the service limit or more.

   b. Measure the inside and outside diameter of the clutch outer housing guide. Compare to the specifications listed in **Table 1**. Replace if worn to the service limit or beyond.

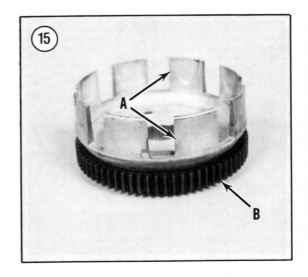

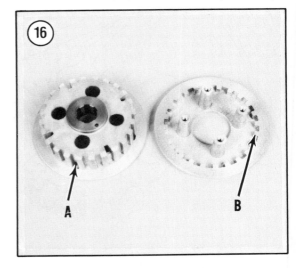

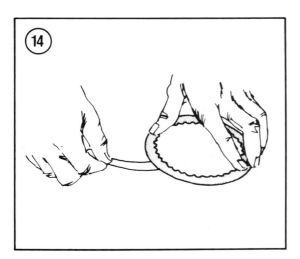

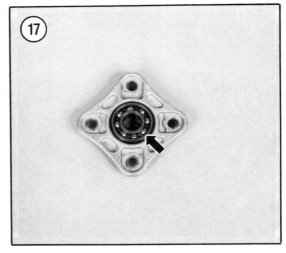

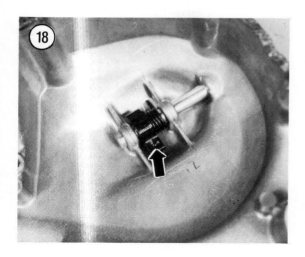

10. Check the movement of the clutch lifter arm assembly in the right-hand crankcase cover (**Figure 18**). If the arm binds or the return spring is weak or broken, replace the spring.

11. Inspect the clutch drive gears as described under *Oil Pump and Clutch Drive Gear* in Chapter Four.

Installation

1. If removed, install the clutch drive gear (**Figure 19**).

2. On Rebel 250 models, install the thrust washer and the clutch outer housing guide (**Figure 10**).

3. Install the clutch outer housing (B, **Figure 11**).

4. Install the splined washer with the rounded edge facing toward the outside.

> *CAUTION*
> *If either or both friction discs and clutch plates have been replaced with new ones, apply new engine oil to all surfaces to avoid having the clutch lock up when used for the first time.*

5A. On Rebel 250 models, perform the following:

  a. Onto the clutch center, install the judder spring seat and the judder spring as shown in **Figure 20**.

  b. Install a clutch plate, then a friction disc and alternate in this order until all discs and plates are installed. The last item installed is a friction disc.

  c. Align the friction disc tabs as this will make installation easier.

  d. Install the clutch pressure plate.

5

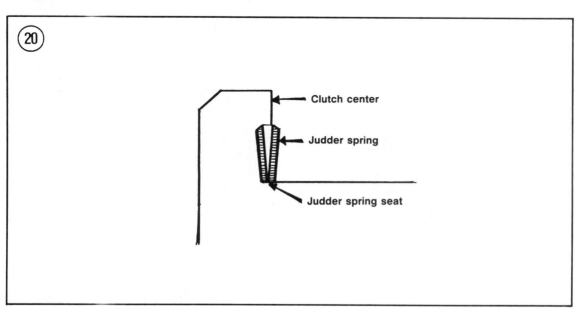

5B. On all other models, perform the following:
  a. Onto the clutch center, install a friction disc, then a clutch plate and alternate in this order until all discs and plates are installed (**Figure 21**).

  b. Align the friction disc tabs as this will make installation easier.

  c. Install the clutch pressure plate (**Figure 22**).

6. Install the clutch center, friction disc, clutch plates and pressure plate as an assembly into the clutch outer housing. Slightly rotate the clutch outer housing back and forth when installing this assembly.

7A. On Rebel 250 models, perform the following:
  a. Install the lockwasher with the dished side and the word OUTSIDE facing out.

  b. Install the clutch locknut and tighten to 36-40 N•m (36-40 ft.-lb.). To keep the clutch housing from turning, use the same tool set-up used in Step 11A, *Removal*.

7B. On all other models, install the circlip (**Figure 23**). Make sure the circlip is correctly seated in the grooves in the transmission shaft.

8. Install the clutch springs (**Figure 24**), lifter plate and bolts. Securely tighten the bolts in a crisscross pattern in 2 or 3 stages.

9. Install the lifter rod (A, **Figure 25**).

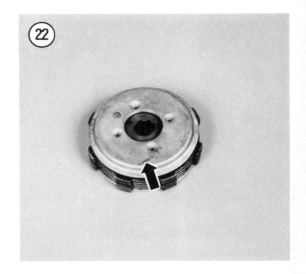

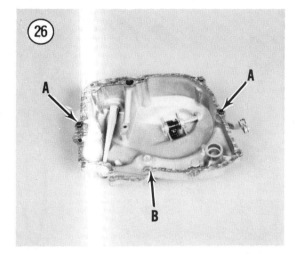

10. This is a good time to remove and clean the oil pump screen. Perform Steps 6-9 of *Oil Filter Screen Cleaning* in Chapter Three.

11. If removed, install the 2 locating dowels (A, **Figure 26**) and a new gasket (B, **Figure 26**).

NOTE
Apply a light coat of gasket sealer to the gasket surface of the crankcase cover. Use Three Bond 1104 or Gasgacinch Gasket Sealer or equivalent.

NOTE
Before installing the crankcase cover, make sure the oil presure pad and spring (B, Figure 25) are in place on the right-hand end of the crankshaft.

12. Install the crankcase cover and tighten the bolts evenly and securely.

13. On models so equipped, install the kickstarter pedal.

14. Install the right-hand exhaust system as described in Chapter Six.

15. Attach the clutch cable to the lifter arm and adjust the clutch cable as described in Chapter Three.

16. Fill the crankcase with the recommended type and quantity of engine oil. Refer to Chapter Three.

17. Road test the bike and check for leaks.

CLUTCH CABLE

Replacement

In time the clutch cable will stretch to the point where it is no longer useful and will have to be replaced.

1. Remove the right- and left-hand side covers and seat (**Figure 27**).

2. Remove the fuel tank as described in Chapter Six.

3. Loosen the locknut and adjusting barrel (**Figure 28**) at the clutch hand lever and remove the cable from the lever.

4. Loosen the locknut and adjusting nut (**Figure 4**) at the clutch lifter arm on the right-hand crankcase cover. Unhook the cable from the lifter arm.

NOTE
Before removing the cable, make a drawing of the cable routing through the frame. It is very easy to forget how it was, once it has been removed. Replace the cable exactly as it was, avoiding any sharp turns.

5A. On Rebel 250 models, unhook the clutch cable from the clip (**Figure 29**) on the engine upper mounting bracket.

5B. On all other models, unhook the wire strap (A,
Figure 30) and unhook the cable from the front clip
(B, **Figure 30**).

6. Pull the cable out from behind the headlight
and remove it. Replace with a new cable.

7. Install by reversing these removal steps, noting
the following.

8. Adjust the clutch as described in Chapter Three.

SHIFTING MECHANISM

The shifting mechanism is located in the
right-hand side of the crankcase. Removal and
installation can be performed with the engine in
the frame.

Removal/Installation

1. Remove the clutch assembly as described in
this chapter.

2. Remove the oil pump as described in Chapter
Four.

3. Remove the kickstarter assembly as described
in Chapter Four.

4. Remove the gearshift lever (**Figure 31**).

5. Unhook the shift pawl spring (A, **Figure 32**) and
remove the bolt (B, **Figure 32**) securing the shift
pawl. Remove the shift pawl.

6. Remove the bolt (**Figure 33**) securing the
stopper plate and remove the stopper plate and the
shift drum pins.

7. Withdraw the gearshift spindle assembly
(**Figure 34**).

8. Install by reversing these removal steps, noting
the following.

9. Make sure the gearshift spindle assembly return
spring is properly engaged onto the stopper plate
bolt.

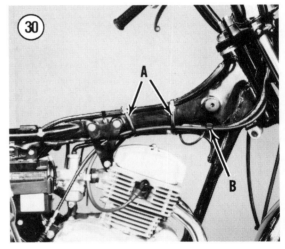

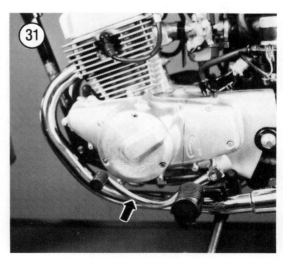

DRIVE SPROCKET
(CHAIN-DRIVEN MODELS)

Removal/Installation

1. Remove the left-hand side of the exhaust system as described in Chapter Six.

2. Remove the gearshift lever (A, **Figure 35**).

3. Remove the screws (B, **Figure 35**) securing the left-hand rear crankcase cover and remove the cover.

4. Remove the bolts securing the drive sprocket attachment plate. Rotate the attachment plate to clear the transmission shaft splines and remove the plate.

> *NOTE*
> *To keep the sprocket from turning, have an assistant apply the rear brake on to hold the drive chain taut.*

5. Remove the cotter pin, nut and washer from the rear brake torque link attachment point (**Figure 36**).

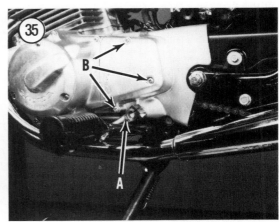

6. On models so equipped, remove the cotter pin on the rear axle.

7. Loosen the drive chain adjuster locknuts and back off the adjuster bolts or nuts (**Figure 37**).

8. Push the rear wheel forward to allow slack in the drive chain.

9. Remove the drive sprocket and drive chain from the transmission shaft.

10. Install by reversing these removal steps, noting the following.

11. If the drive chain master link was removed, install a new link clip with the closed end facing in the direction of chain travel (**Figure 38**).

12. Always install new cotter pins and bend the ends over completely.

13. Adjust the drive chain as described in Chapter Three.

Inspection

Inspect the teeth on the drive sprocket. If the teeth are visibly worn (**Figure 39**), replace the drive sprocket.

Inspect the drive chain as described in Chapter Three.

TRANSMISSION

The Rebel 250 is equipped with a 5-speed tranmission. All other models are equipped with a 4-speed unit. All transmissions are of the constant mesh type and share the same oil that is used in the engine crankcase. The engine must be removed and the crankcase disassembled to gain access to the transmission components.

Removal/Installation

1. Perform Steps 1-7 of *Crankcase Disassembly* in Chapter Four.

2. Remove the shift drum assembly as described in this chapter.

3. Remove the main shaft assembly (A, **Figure 40**) and the countershaft assembly (B, **Figure 40**).

NOTE
Before installation, coat all bearing surfaces with new engine or assembly oil.

4. Apply a coat of grease to the lower thrust washers to hold them in place on the shaft assemblies during installation.

5. Install the main shaft and countershaft assemblies by meshing them together in their

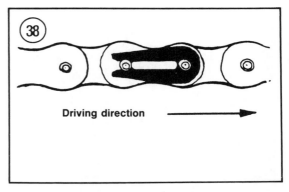

Driving direction →

proper relationship to each other. Install them into the left-hand crankcase. After both assemblies are installed, tap on the end of both shafts with a plastic or rubber mallet to make sure they are completely seated.

6. Install the shift drum assembly and forks as described in this chapter.

7. After both assemblies are installed, rotate both shafts by hand. Make sure there is no binding. Also shift through all gears to make sure the shift forks are operating properly and, if disassembled, that the transmission gears are properly installed on their respective shafts.

8. Perform Steps 7-17 of *Crankcase Assembly* in Chapter Four. Make sure the crankcase gasket surfaces are completely clean. Apply a light coat of non-hardening gasket sealer to one side of the gasket.

4-Speed Transmission
Main Shaft Disassembly/
Inspection/Assembly

Refer to **Figure 41** for this procedure.

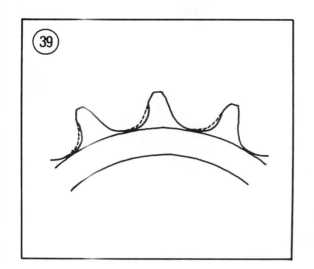

5

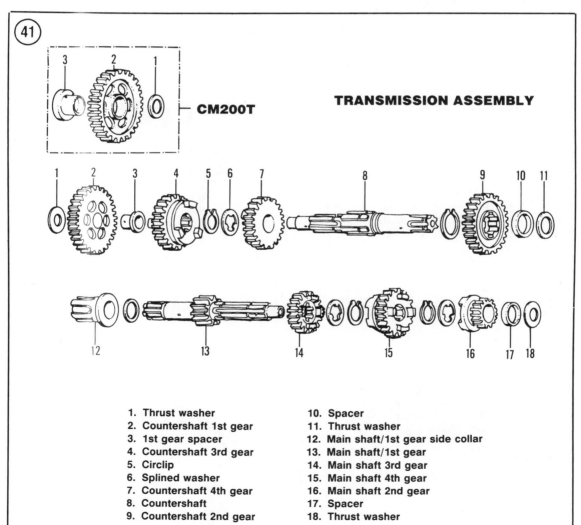

CM200T

TRANSMISSION ASSEMBLY

1. Thrust washer
2. Countershaft 1st gear
3. 1st gear spacer
4. Countershaft 3rd gear
5. Circlip
6. Splined washer
7. Countershaft 4th gear
8. Countershaft
9. Countershaft 2nd gear
10. Spacer
11. Thrust washer
12. Main shaft/1st gear side collar
13. Main shaft/1st gear
14. Main shaft 3rd gear
15. Main shaft 4th gear
16. Main shaft 2nd gear
17. Spacer
18. Thrust washer

1. Slide off the 1st gear side collar and the thrust washer (**Figure 42**).
2. Remove the thrust washer and spacer (**Figure 43**).
3. Slide off the 2nd gear, splined washer, circlip and 4th gear (**Figure 44**).
4. Remove the circlip and slide off the thrust washer and the 3th gear (**Figure 45**).
5. Clean all parts in solvent and thoroughly dry.
6. Check each gear for excessive wear, burrs, pitting or chipped or missing teeth. Make sure the gear lugs are in good condition (**Figure 46**).

NOTE
Defective gears should be replaced. It is a good idea to replace the mating gear on the countershaft even though it may not show as much wear or damage.

NOTE
The 1st gear is part of the main shaft. If the gear is defective, the shaft must be replaced.

7. Make sure that all gears and bushings slide smoothly on the main shaft splines.

NOTE
It is a good idea to replace the circips every other time the transmission is disassembled to ensure proper gear alignment.

8. Inspect the bearings (A, **Figure 47** and **Figure 48**) in the crankcase. Make sure they rotate smoothly (**Figure 49**) with no signs of wear or damage. Replace if necessary as described under *Bearing Replacment* in Chapter Four.
9. Slide on the 3rd gear and the splined washer.
10. Install the circlip and slide on the 4th gear.

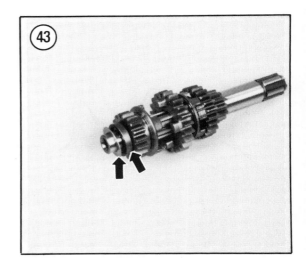

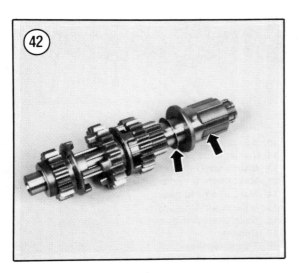

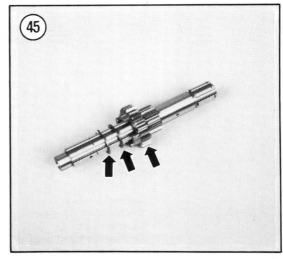

11. Install the circlip and slide on the splined washer.

12. Slide on the 2nd gear, the spacer and the thrust washer.

13. Onto the other end of the shaft, slide on the thrust washer and the 1st gear side collar.

14. Make sure all circlips are seated correctly in the main shaft grooves. Refer to **Figure 50** for correct placement of the gears.

15. Make sure each gear engages properly with the adjoining gears where applicable.

4-Speed Transmission
Countershaft Disassembly/
Inspection/Assembly

Refer to **Figure 41** for this procedure.

1. Slide off the thrust washer, spacer and the 2nd gear (**Figure 51**).

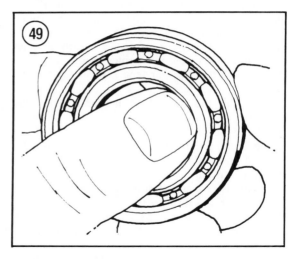

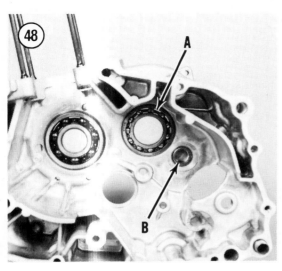

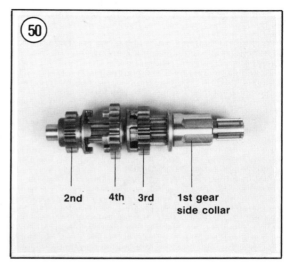

2A. On Model CM185T, remove the thrust washer, 1st gear, 1st gear spacer and 3rd gear.

2B. On Model CM200T, slide off the 1st gear spacer (**Figure 52**). Remove the 1st gear, thrust washer and 3rd gear (**Figure 53**).

3. Remove the circlip and slide off the splined washer. Then slide off the 4th gear (**Figure 54**).

4. Clean all parts in solvent and thoroughly dry.

5. Check each gear for excessive wear, burrs, pitting or chipped or missing teeth. Make sure the gear lugs are in good condition (**Figure 55**).

NOTE
Defective gears should be replaced. It is a good idea to replace the mating gear on the main shaft even though it may not show signs of wear or damage.

6. Make sure all gears and the gear bushing slide smoothly on the countershaft splines.

7. Inspect the bearings (B, **Figure 47** and **Figure 48**) in the crankcase. Make sure they rotate smoothly (**Figure 49**) with no signs of wear or damage. Replace if necessary as described under *Bearing Replacement* in Chapter Four.

8. Slide on the 4th gear (engagement lug side on last).

9. Slide on the splined washer and install the circlip.

10. Slide the 3rd gear into place.

11. Position the 1st gear spacer with the shoulder side on first.

12. Slide on the 1st gear and the thrust washer.

13. Onto the other end of the shaft, install the 2nd gear, spacer and thrust washer.

14. Make sure all circlips are seated correctly in the main shaft grooves. Refer to **Figure 56** for correct placement of all gears.

15. Make sure each gear engages properly with the adjoining gears where applicable.

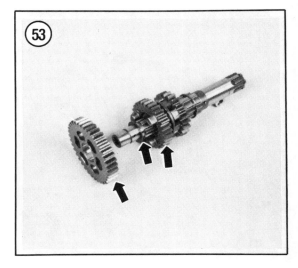

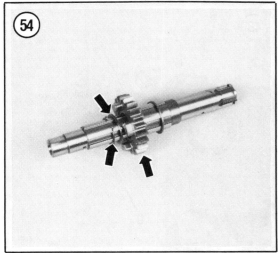

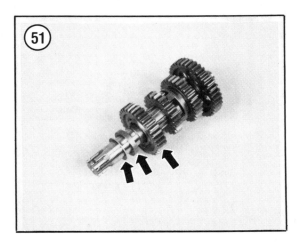

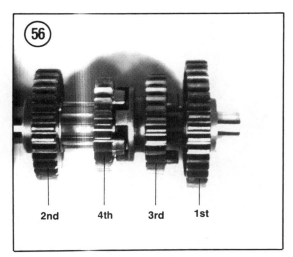

2nd   4th   3rd   1st

**5-Speed Transmission
Main Shaft Disassembly/
Inspection/Assembly**

Refer to **Figure 57** for this procedure.
1. Slide off the thrust washer and the 2nd gear.
2. Slide off the 5th gear and the splined washer.
3. Remove the circlip and slide off the 4th gear.
4. Remove the circlip and splined washer; then slide off the 3rd gear.
5. Clean all parts in solvent and thoroughly dry.
6. Check each gear for excessive wear, burrs, pitting or chipped or missing teeth. Make sure the gear lugs are in good condition (**Figure 46**).

NOTE
Defective gears should be replaced. It is a good idea to replace the mating gear on the countershaft even though it may not show as much wear or damage.

NOTE
The 1st gear is part of the main shaft. If the gear is defective, the shaft must be replaced.

7. Make sure that all gears and bushings slide smoothly on the main shaft splines.

NOTE
It is a good idea to replace the circlips every other time the transmission is disassembled to ensure proper gear alignment.

8. Slide on the 3rd gear and the splined washer.
9. Install the circlip and slide on the 4th gear.
10. Install the circlip and slide on the splined washer.

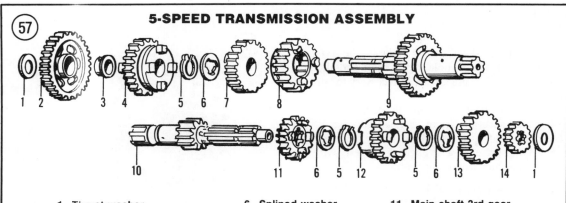

5-SPEED TRANSMISSION ASSEMBLY

1. Thrust washer
2. Countershaft 1st gear
3. Countershaft 1st gear bushing
4. Countershaft 3rd gear
5. Circlip
6. Splined washer
7. Countershaft 4th gear
8. Countershaft 5th gear
9. Countershaft/2nd gear
10. Main shaft/1st gear
11. Main shaft 3rd gear
12. Main shaft 4th gear
13. Main shaft 5th gear
14. Main shaft 2nd gear

11. Slide on the 5th gear (flush side on last).

12. Slide on the 2nd gear and the thrust washer.

13. Make sure all circlips are seated correctly in the main shaft grooves.

14. Make sure each gear engages properly with the adjoining gears where applicable.

5-Speed Transmission Countershaft Disassembly/Inspection/Assembly

Refer to **Figure 57** for this procedure.

1. Slide off the thrust washer, 1st gear and the 1st gear bushing.

2. Slide off the 3rd gear.

3. Remove the circlip and slide off the splined washer.

4. Slide off the 4th gear and the 5th gear.

5. Clean all gears in solvent and thoroughly dry.

6. Check each gear for excessive wear, burrs, pitting or chipped or missing teeth. Make sure the gear lugs are in good condition (**Figure 55**).

> *NOTE*
> *Defective gears should be replaced. It is a good idea to replace the mating gear on the main shaft even though it may not show signs of wear or damage.*

> *NOTE*
> *The 2nd gear is part of the countershaft. If the gear is defective, the shaft must be replaced.*

7. Make sure all gears and the gear bushing slide smoothly on the countershaft splines.

8. Slide on the 5th gear (engagement lug side on first).

9. Slide the 4th gear into place (flush side on first).

10. Slide on the splined washer and install the circlip.

11. Slide on the 3rd gear.

12. Position the 1st gear bushing with the shoulder side on first. Align the oil hole in the 1st gear bushing with the oil hole in the shaft and slide on the bushing. This alignment is necessary for proper oil flow.

13. Slide on the 1st gear and the thrust washer.

14. Make sure all circlips are seated correctly in the main shaft grooves.

15. Make sure each gear engages properly with the adjoining gears where applicable.

GEARSHIFT DRUM AND FORKS

Removal

1. Perform Steps 1-7 of *Crankcase Disassembly* in Chapter Four.

2. Withdraw the shift fork shaft (**Figure 58**).

3. Remove the shift drum (**Figure 59**).
4. Remove the shift forks (**Figure 60**).
5. Wash all parts in solvent and thoroughly dry.

Inspection

Refer to **Table 2** for shift fork and shaft specifications.

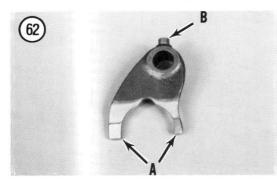

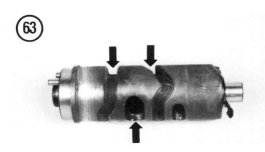

1. Inspect each shift fork for signs of wear or cracking. Make sure the forks slide smoothly on the shaft and that the shaft is not bent (**Figure 61**). Replace any worn forks.

NOTE
*Check for any arc-shaped wear or burn marks on the shift forks (A, **Figure 62**). If this is apparent, the shift fork has come in contact with the gear, indicating that the fingers are worn beyond use and the fork must be replaced.*

2. Roll the shift fork shafts on a flat surface such as a piece of plate glass and check for bends. If the fork shaft is bent, it must be replaced.
3. Check the grooves in the shift drum (**Figure 63**) for wear or roughness. If any of the groove profiles have excessive wear or damage, replace the shift drum.
4. Inspect the neutral indicator rotor (**Figure 64**). If it is bent or deformed, replace the rotor.
5. Check the cam pin followers (B, **Figure 62**) in each shift fork for wear or burrs. It should fit snug but not too tight. Check the end that rides in the shift drum for wear or burrs. Replace as necessary.
6. Measure the inside diameter of the shift forks (A, **Figure 65**) with an inside micrometer (**Figure 66**). Replace any worn beyond the limit in **Table 2**.
7. Measure the outside diameter of the shift fork shaft (B, **Figure 65**) with a micrometer. Replace if worn beyond the limit in **Table 2**.
8. Measure the width of the gearshift fingers with a micrometer (**Figure 67**). Replace any worn beyond the limit in **Table 2**.

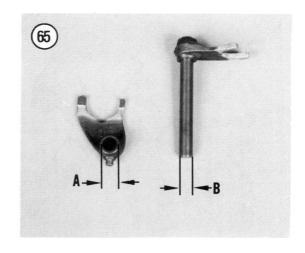

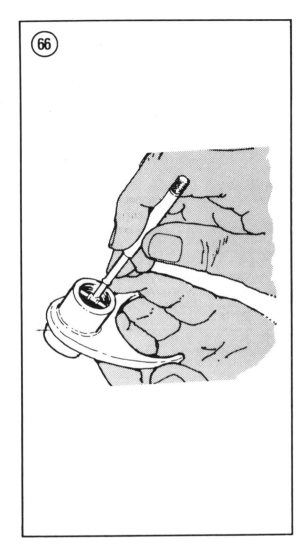

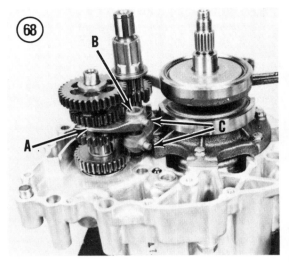

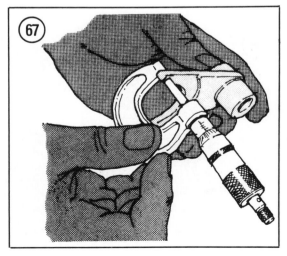

Installation

1. Coat all bearing and sliding surfaces with new engine oil or assembly oil.

2. Install the 2 shift forks into the grooves (A, **Figure 68**) in the transmission shaft assemblies.

NOTE
*Be sure to install the shift forks as shown in B, **Figure 68** and that the shift drum cam pins align (C, **Figure 68**).*

3. Install the shift drum; align the neutral switch indicator rotor with the switch in the crankcase. Properly mesh the shift fork guide pins into the grooves in the shift drum (**Figure 69**).

4. Install the shift fork shaft (**Figure 70**). Make sure it seats completely.

5. Perform Steps 7-16 of *Crankcase Assembly* in Chapter Four. Make sure the crankcase gasket surfaces are completely clean. Apply a light coat of non-hardening gasket sealer to one side of the gasket.

5

Table 1 CLUTCH SPECIFICATIONS

Item	Standard	Wear limit
Friction disc thickness	3.0 mm (0.1181 in.)	2.6 mm (0.1024 in.)
Clutch plate warpage	—	0.2 mm (0.0079 in.)
Clutch spring free length	36.2 mm (1.452 in.)	33.1 mm (1.3031 in.)
Outer housing ID	26.000-26.021 mm (1.0236-1.0244 in.)	26.04 mm (1.0252 in.)
Outer guide OD	25.959-25.980 mm (1.022-1.023 in.)	25.9 mm (1.02 in.)
Outer guide ID	20.000-20.021 mm (0.7874-0.7882 in.)	25.05 mm (0.986 in.)

Table 2 GEARSHIFT FORK AND SHAFT SPECIFICATIONS

Item	Specification	Wear limit
Shift fork inner diameter	12.000-12.018 mm (0.4724-0.4731 in.)	12.05 mm (0.4744 in.)
Shifr fork finger thickness	5.00-5.07 mm (0.1969-0.1966 in.)	4.70 mm (0.1850 in.)
Shift fork shaft outer diameter	11.976-11.994 mm (0.4515-0.4722 in.)	11.96 mm (0.4709 in.)

NOTE: If you own a 1991 or later model, first check Chapter Twelve at the back of this book for any new service information.

FUEL AND EXHAUST

The fuel system consists of the fuel tank, shutoff valve and a single carburetor. All 185-200 models are equipped with a slide valve carburetor while 250 models have the constant velocity or CV type carburetor. There are 2 different CV carburetors used among the various models. The air filter is an oiled polyurethane type and the service procedures are covered in Chapter Three.

The carburetors on all U.S. models are engineered to meet stringent EPA (Environmental Protection Agency) regulations. The carburetor is flow tested and preset at the factory for maximum performance and efficiency within EPA regulations. Altering preset carburetor jet needle and pilot screw adjustments is forbidden by law. Failure to comply with EPA regulations may result in heavy fines.

The exhaust sytem consists of 2 exhaust pipes and 2 mufflers.

This chapter includes service procedures for all parts of the fuel, emission and exhaust systems. Carburetor specifications are listed in **Table 1**.

CARBURETOR OPERATION

Understanding the function of each of the carburetor components and their relation to one another is a valuable aid for pinpointing carburetor trouble.

The carburetor's purpose is to supply and atomize fuel and mix it in correct proportions with air that is drawn in through the air intake. At the primary throttle opening (idle), a small amount of fuel is siphoned through the pilot jet by the incoming air. As the throttle is opened further, the air stream begins to siphon fuel through the main jet and needle jet. The tapered needle increases the effective flow capacity of the needle jet as it is lifted, in that it occupies progressively less of the area of the jet.

At full throttle the carburetor venturi is fully open and the needle is lifted far enough to permit the main jet to flow at full capacity.

The choke circuit on Rebel 250 models is a "bystarter" system in which the choke lever opens a valve rather than closing a butterfly in the venturi area as on many carburetors. In the open position, the slow jet discharges a stream of fuel into the carburetor venturi, enriching the mixture when the engine is cold.

CARBURETOR SERVICE

Carburetor service (removal and cleaning) should be performed when poor engine performance or hesitation is observed. If, after servicing the carburetor and making the adjustments described in this chapter, the

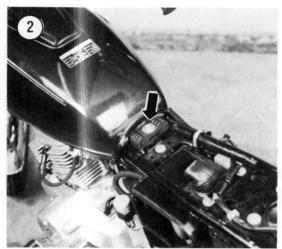

motorcycle does not perform correctly (and assuming that other factors affecting performance are correct, such as ignition timing and condition, etc.), the motorcycle should be checked by a dealer or a qualified performance tuning specialist.

CARBURETOR
(CM185T AND CM200T MODELS)

Removal/Installation

1. Remove the right- and left-hand side covers.
2. Disconnect the battery negative lead.
3. Turn the fuel shutoff valve to the OFF position (**Figure 1**) and disconnect the fuel line from the carburetor.
4. Unhook the rubber retainer or remove the bolt (**Figure 2**) from the rear of the fuel tank, pull the fuel tank to the rear and remove the fuel tank.
5. Loosen the screw (A, **Figure 3**) securing the choke cable to the carburetor and unhook the cable from the choke plate (B, **Figure 3**).
6. Loosen the clamping screw (A, **Figure 4**) and remove the nuts (B, **Figure 4**) securing the carburetor to the intake manifold.

NOTE
Prior to removing the top cap, thoroughly clean the area around it so no dirt will fall into the carburetor.

7. Unscrew the carburetor top cap (C, **Figure 4**) and carefully pull out the slide and needle assembly.
8. Pull the carburetor assembly toward the rear and remove the carburetor.
9. The carburetor heat shield can be left in place. Stuff a clean shop cloth into the intake opening in the engine to prevent the entry of foreign matter.
10. Remove the slide and needle assembly from the throttle cable. Depress the slide spring; push the throttle cable down and then up along the slot in the slide. Withdraw the cable end through the opening in the top of the slide slot.
11. Take the carburetor assembly to the work bench for disassembly and inspection.
12. Install by reversing these removal steps, noting the following.
13. Align the groove in the slide with the throttle stop screw.
14. Adjust the throttle cable as described in Chapter Three.
15. Adjust the idle speed as described in Chapter Three.

Disassembly/Cleaning/Inspection

Refer to **Figure 5** for this procedure and **Table 1** for carburetor specifications.

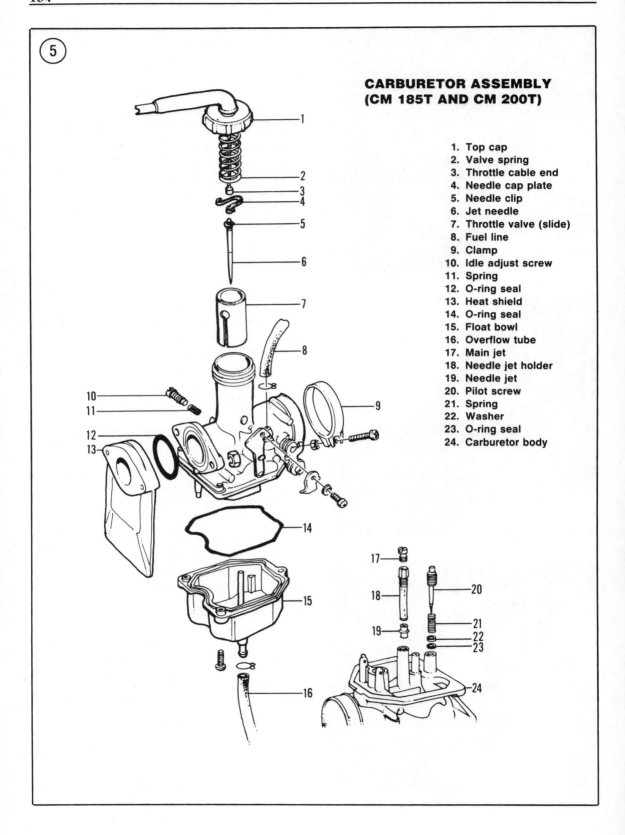

⑤

**CARBURETOR ASSEMBLY
(CM 185T AND CM 200T)**

1. Top cap
2. Valve spring
3. Throttle cable end
4. Needle cap plate
5. Needle clip
6. Jet needle
7. Throttle valve (slide)
8. Fuel line
9. Clamp
10. Idle adjust screw
11. Spring
12. O-ring seal
13. Heat shield
14. O-ring seal
15. Float bowl
16. Overflow tube
17. Main jet
18. Needle jet holder
19. Needle jet
20. Pilot screw
21. Spring
22. Washer
23. O-ring seal
24. Carburetor body

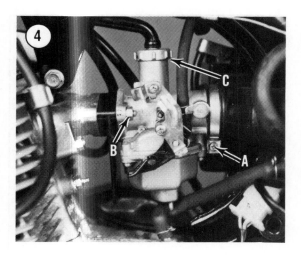

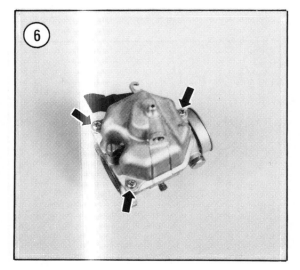

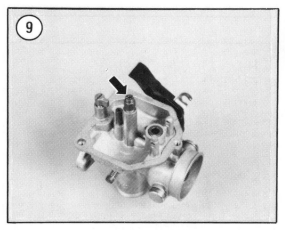

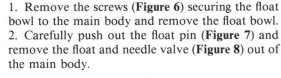

1. Remove the screws (**Figure 6**) securing the float bowl to the main body and remove the float bowl.
2. Carefully push out the float pin (**Figure 7**) and remove the float and needle valve (**Figure 8**) out of the main body.

NOTE
Don't lose the float valve as it will slide off the float when removed.

3. Unscrew the main jet (**Figure 9**), needle jet holder (**Figure 10**) and the needle jet.

NOTE
Turn the carburetor assembly over and let the needle jet fall out into your hand.

NOTE
Before removing the pilot screw, record the number of turns necessary until the screw lightly seats. Record the number of turns for each individual carburetor as the screws must be reinstalled into the exact same setting.

4. Remove the pilot screw and spring (A, **Figure 11**).

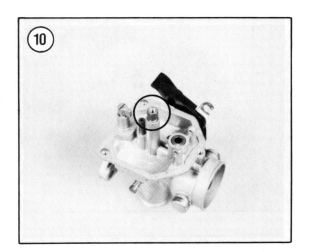

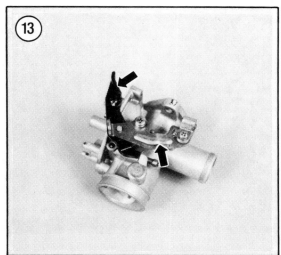

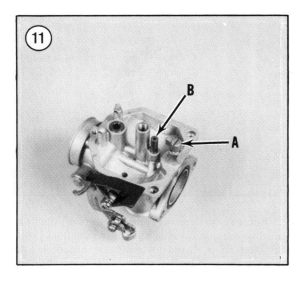

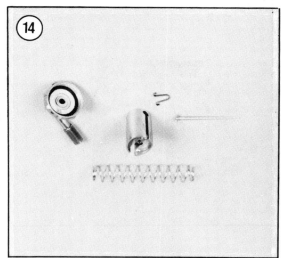

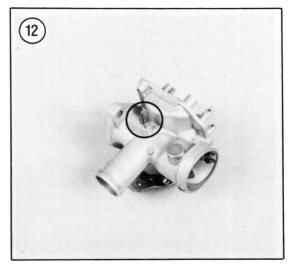

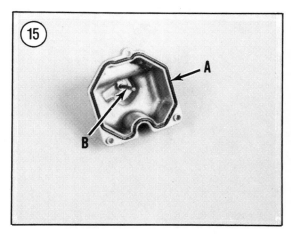

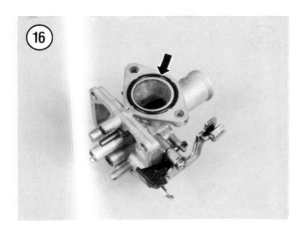

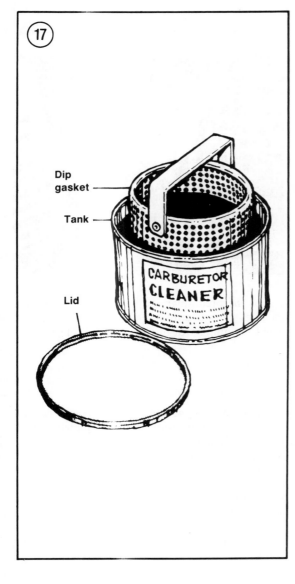

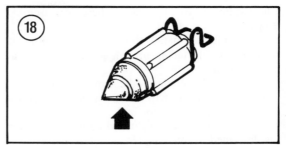

6

NOTE
Further disassembly is neither necessary nor recommended. If throttle shafts or butterflies are damaged, take the carburetor body to a dealer for replacement.

5A. On 1982 CM200T models, remove the slow air jet (B, **Figure 11**).

5B. On all other models, the slow air jet (B, **Figure 11**) cannot be removed as it is pressed into place.

6. Unscrew the idle adjust screw and spring (**Figure 12**).

7. On CM200T models, remove the screws securing the choke cable bracket and plastic choke actuating arm (**Figure 13**). Remove the bracket and arm.

8. Remove the needle cap and remove the jet needle from the throttle valve (slide) (**Figure 14**).

9. Remove the gasket from the float bowl (A, **Figure 15**).

10. Remove the O-ring seal (**Figure 16**) from the carburetor body.

11. Clean all parts, except rubber or plastic parts, in a good grade of carburetor cleaner. This solution is available at most automotive or motorcycle supply stores in a small, resealable tank with a dip basket (**Figure 17**). If it is tightly sealed when not in use, the solution will last for several cleanings. Follow the manufacturer's instructions for correct soak time (usually about 1/2 hour).

12. Remove the parts from the cleaner and blow dry with compressed air. Blow out the jets with compressed air. Do *not* use a piece of wire to clean them as minor gouges in a jet can alter flow rate and upset the fuel/air mixture.

13. Be sure to clean out the overflow tube from both ends (B, **Figure 15**).

14. Replace all O-rings and gaskets upon assembly. O-ring seals tend to become hardened after prolonged use and exposure to heat and therefore lose their ability to seal properly. Replace as necessary.

15. Inspect the end of the float valve (**Figure 18**) for wear or damage; replace if necessary.

16. Assemble by reversing these disassembly steps.

17. Be sure to install the needle jet with the chamfered side facing up (**Figure 19**) toward the needle jet holder.

18. The needle jet should be screwed in tight, but be careful not to strip the threads on it or the threads in the carburetor body.

19. Inspect the float height and adjust if necessary as described in this chapter.

20. Install the needle cap plate into the lowest position in the slide. Make sure it seats completely.

21. Make sure any small O-rings removed are correctly installed and not forgotten.

> *CAUTION*
> *The pilot screw seat will be damaged if the screw is tightened against the seat.*

22. When installing the pilot screw, be sure to screw the pilot screw into the exact same position (same number of turns) as recorded during disassembly.

23. On CM200T models, if new pilot screw is installed, turn it out the number of turns indicated in **Table 1**, from the *lightly seated* position, then install a new limiter cap as described in this chapter.

24. After the carburetor is completely assembled, invert it several times and listen for movement of the float to make sure it moves freely.

25. After assembly and installation are completed, adjust the carburetor as described in this chapter and Chapter Three.

**New Pilot Screw Adjustment
and Limiter Cap Installation
(Model CM200T)**

The pilot jet is pre-set at the factory and adjustment is not necessary unless the carburetor has been overhauled or someone has misadjusted it.

In order to comply with U.S. emission control standards, a limiter cap is attached to the end of the pilot screw. This is to prevent the owner from readjusting the pilot screw from the factory setting. The limiter cap will allow a maximum of 7/8 of a turn of the pilot screw *to a leaner mixture only*.

> *CAUTION*
> *Do not try to remove the limiter cap from the pilot screw, as it is bonded in place. It will break off and damage the pilot screw if removal is attempted.*

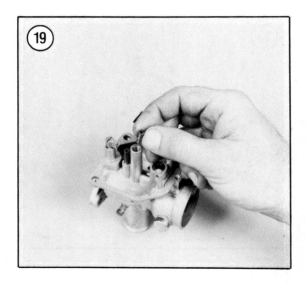

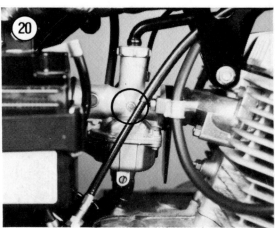

1. For the preliminary adjustment, carefully turn the pilot screw in until it seats *lightly* and then back it out the number of turns listed in **Table 1**.

> *CAUTION*
> *The pilot screw seat can be damaged if the pilot screw is tightened too hard against the seat.*

2. Start the engine and let it reach normal operating temperature. Approximately 5-10 minutes of stop-and-go riding is usually sufficient. Shut the engine off.

3. Connect a portable tachometer following the manufacturer's instructions.

4. Start the engine and turn the idle speed adjust screw (**Figure 20**) in or out to obtain the idle speed listed in **Table 1**.

5. Turn the pilot screw in slowly until the engine stops.

6. Back the pilot screw *out* one full turn and restart the engine.

7. Turn the idle speed adjust screw in or out again to obtain the idle speed listed in **Table 1**.

8. Turn the engine off and disconnect the portable tachometer.

9. Open and close the throttle a couple of times and check for variations in idle speed. Readjust if necessary.

WARNING
With the engine idling, move the handlebar from side to side. If idle speed increases during this movement, the throttle cable needs adjustment or it may be incorrectly routed through the frame. Correct this problem immediately. Do not ride the bike in this unsafe condition.

10. Install the limiter caps as follows:
   a. Apply Loctite No. 601, or equivalent, to the new limiter cap.

b. Position the limiter cap against the stop on the float bowl (**Figure 21**) so that the pilot screw can only turn *clockwise*, not counterclockwise.

c. Install the limiter cap on the pilot screw. Make sure the pilot screw does not move while installing the limiter cap.

CARBURETOR (CM250C AND REBEL 250 MODELS)

On Rebel 250 models, the choke circuit is a "bystarter" system in which the choke lever opens a valve rather than closing a butterfly in the venturi area as on many carburetors. In the open position, the slow jet discharges a stream of fuel into the carburetor venturi, enriching the mixture when the engine is cold.

Removal/Installation

NOTE
This procedure will be much easier with one person on each side of the bike.

1. Place wood block(s) under the frame to support the bike securely.

2. Remove the right- and left-hand side covers and the seat.

3. Disconnect the battery negative lead.

4. Remove the fuel tank as described in this chapter.

5. At the hand throttle, loosen the throttle cable locknut and turn the adjusting barrel (**Figure 22**) all the way in. This provides the necessary slack for ease of cable removal at the carburetor assembly.

6. At the carburetor, remove the screws securing the throttle cable cover (**Figure 23**) and remove the cover.

7. Loosen the throttle cable locknuts and adjusting nut and disconnect both throttle cables from the throttle wheel. Tie the loose ends of the cables to the frame out of the way.

8A. On CM250C models, loosen the choke cable clamp screw and disconnect the choke cable from the choke linkage on the carburetor.

8B. On Rebel 250 models, slide up the rubber boot (**Figure 24**) and unscrew the choke valve from the carburetor body (**Figure 25**). Move the choke cable out of the way. Tie the loose end of the cable to the frame out of the way.

9. On models so equipped, disconnect the hoses (**Figure 26**) from the carburetor that go to the PCV valve.

10. Loosen the clamping screw on the air filter connecting tube at the carburetor (A, **Figure 27**).

Slide the clamping band off the tube and away from the carburetor assembly.

11. Loosen the clamping screws on the intake tube on the cylinder head (B, **Figure 27**). Slide the clamping band off the tube and away from the carburetor assembly.

12. Pull the carburetor assembly toward the rear until the assembly is clear of the intake tube on the cylinder head.

13. Slowly and carefully pull the carburetor assembly out toward the right-hand side. Be careful not to damage any of the carburetor components. This is a lot easier if you have one person on each side of the bike.

14. Remove the carburetor assembly from the frame.

15. Install by reversing these removal steps, noting the following.

16. Prior to installing the carburetor assembly, coat the inside surface of all intake tubes and air filter connecting tubes with Armor All or rubber lube. This will make it easier to install the carburetor throat into the rubber tubes.

17. Be sure the throttle cables and choke cable are correctly positioned in the frame—not twisted or kinked and without any sharp bends. Tighten the locknuts securely.

18. Attach the "pull" throttle cable into the rear bracket and into the rear slot (A, **Figure 28**) in the throttle wheel.

19. Attach the "push" throttle cable into the front bracket and into the front slot (B, **Figure 28**) in the throttle wheel.

20. Attach the choke cable to its bracket.

21. Adjust the throttle cable as described in Chapter Three.

22. Adjust the choke as described in this chapter.

Disassembly/Cleaning/Inspection/Assembly

Refer to **Figure 29** (Rebel 250 models) or **Figure 30** (CM250C models) for this procedure.

1. Remove the screws (**Figure 31**) securing the carburetor top cover to the main body and remove the cover.

2. Remove the vacuum cylinder spring and vacuum cylinder assembly (**Figure 32**).

3A. On CM250C models, remove the jet needle, jet needle stopper screw and full open stopper from the vacuum cylinder.

3B. On Rebel 250 models, put an 8 mm socket or Phillips screwdriver down into the vacuum cylinder cavity. Place the socket or Phillips screwdriver on the needle holder and turn the holder 60° in either direction to unlock it from the tangs within the vacuum cylinder. Remove the

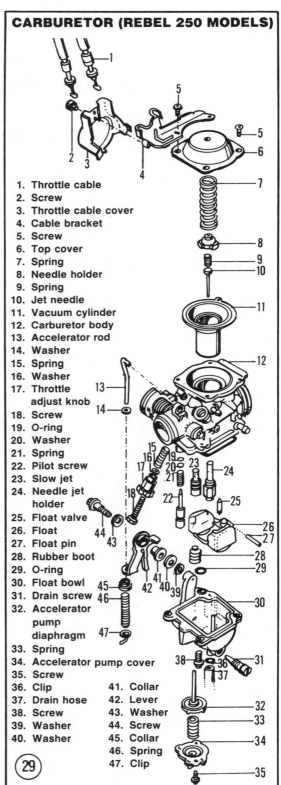

CARBURETOR (REBEL 250 MODELS)

1. Throttle cable
2. Screw
3. Throttle cable cover
4. Cable bracket
5. Screw
6. Top cover
7. Spring
8. Needle holder
9. Spring
10. Jet needle
11. Vacuum cylinder
12. Carburetor body
13. Accelerator rod
14. Washer
15. Spring
16. Washer
17. Throttle adjust knob
18. Screw
19. O-ring
20. Washer
21. Spring
22. Pilot screw
23. Slow jet
24. Needle jet holder
25. Float valve
26. Float
27. Float pin
28. Rubber boot
29. O-ring
30. Float bowl
31. Drain screw
32. Accelerator pump diaphragm
33. Spring
34. Accelerator pump cover
35. Screw
36. Clip
37. Drain hose
38. Screw
39. Washer
40. Washer
41. Collar
42. Lever
43. Washer
44. Screw
45. Collar
46. Spring
47. Clip

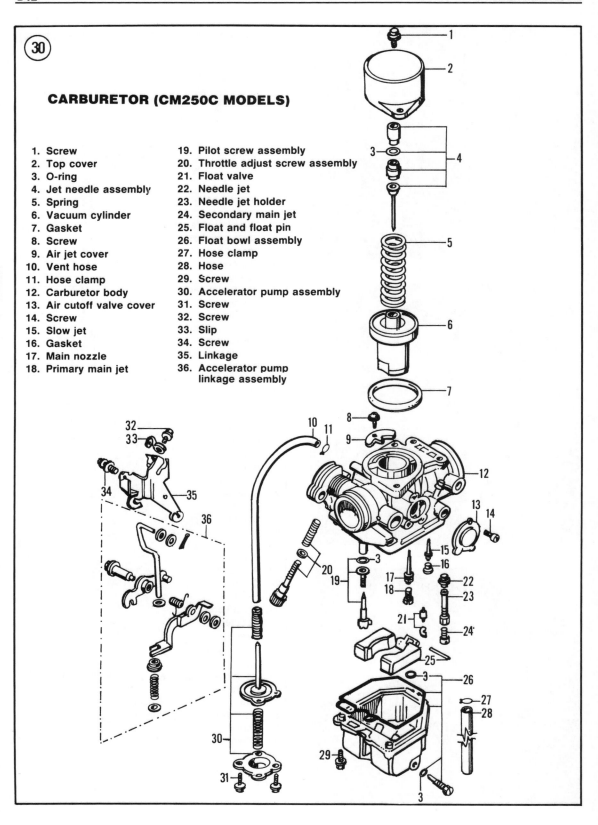

③⓪

CARBURETOR (CM250C MODELS)

1. Screw
2. Top cover
3. O-ring
4. Jet needle assembly
5. Spring
6. Vacuum cylinder
7. Gasket
8. Screw
9. Air jet cover
10. Vent hose
11. Hose clamp
12. Carburetor body
13. Air cutoff valve cover
14. Screw
15. Slow jet
16. Gasket
17. Main nozzle
18. Primary main jet
19. Pilot screw assembly
20. Throttle adjust screw assembly
21. Float valve
22. Needle jet
23. Needle jet holder
24. Secondary main jet
25. Float and float pin
26. Float bowl assembly
27. Hose clamp
28. Hose
29. Screw
30. Accelerator pump assembly
31. Screw
32. Screw
33. Slip
34. Screw
35. Linkage
36. Accelerator pump
    linkage assembly

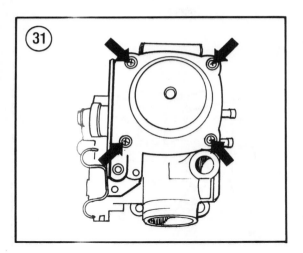

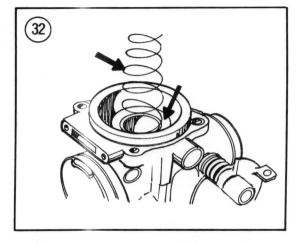

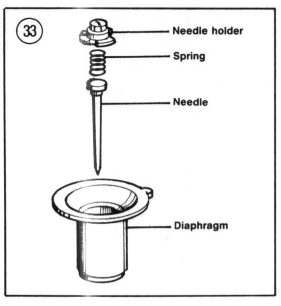

Needle holder

Spring

Needle

Diaphragm

needle holder, jet needle spring and the jet needle (**Figure 33**).

4. Remove the screws (**Figure 34**) securing the float bowl to the main body and remove the float bowl.

5. Remove the gasket from the float bowl.

6A. On CM250C models, perform the following:

   a. On 1983 models, remove the screws securing the accelerator pump cover and remove the cover (**Figure 35**).

   b. On 1983 models, carefully pull the accelerator pump diaphragm and rod (A, **Figure 36**) out from the housing. Don't lose the rubber boot (B, **Figure 36**) on the rod.

   c. Carefully push out the float pin (A, **Figure 37**).

   d. Lift the float (B, **Figure 37**) and needle valve out of the main body.

   e. Remove the slow jet plug (C, **Figure 37**) and slow jet.

   f. Remove the primary main jet (D, **Figure 37**).

g. Remove the secondary main jet (E, **Figure 37**).

h. Remove the needle jet holder (F, **Figure 37**) and the needle jet.

NOTE
Before removing the pilot screw, record the number of turns necessary until the screw lightly seats. Record the number of turns as the screw must be reinstalled into the exact same setting.

i. If necessary, remove the pilot screw assembly (G, **Figure 37**).

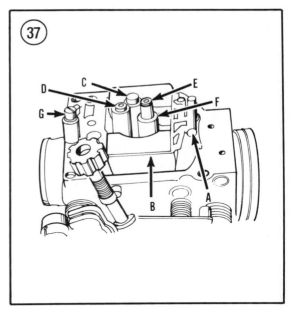

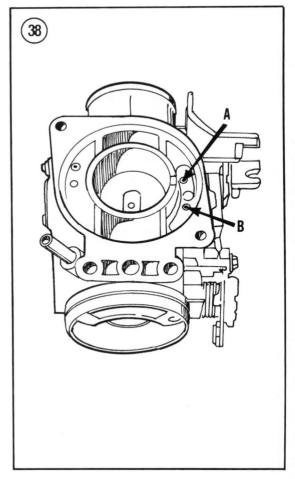

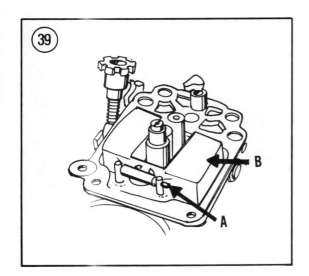

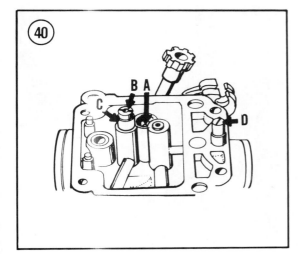

j. Remove the screw securing the air jet cover and remove the cover.

k. Using compressed air, clean out the primary main jet (A, **Figure 38**) and the secondary main jet (B, **Figure 38**) in the vacuum cylinder portion of the carburetor body.

6B. On Rebel 250 models, perform the following:

a. Remove the screws securing the accelerator pump cover and remove the cover (**Figure 35**).

b. Carefully pull the accelerator pump diaphragm and rod (A, **Figure 36**) out from the housing. Don't lose the rubber boot (B, **Figure 36**) on the rod.

c. Carefully push out the float pin (A, **Figure 39**).

d. Lift the float (B, **Figure 39**) and needle valve out of the main body.

e. Remove the slow jet (A, **Figure 40**).

f. Remove the main jet (B, **Figure 40**).

g. Remove the needle jet holder (C, **Figure 40**).

NOTE
Prior to removing the pilot screw, record the number of turns necessary until the screw lightly seats. Record the number of turns for each individual carburetor as the screws must be reinstalled into the exact same setting.

h. If necessary, remove the pilot screw assembly (D, **Figure 40**).

7. Remove the drain screw and O-ring in the float bowl. If necessary, clean out the drain tube outlet and reinstall the drain screw.

NOTE
Further disassembly is neither necessary nor recommended. If throttle shafts or butterflies are damaged, take the carburetor body to a dealer for replacement.

8. Clean all parts, except rubber or plastic parts, in a good grade of carburetor cleaner. This solution is available at most automotive or motorcycle supply stores in a small, resealable tank with a dip basket. If it is tightly sealed when not in use, the solution will last for several cleanings. Follow the manufacturer's instructions for correct soak time (usually about 1/2 hour).

9. Remove the parts from the cleaner and blow dry with compressed air. Blow out the jets with compressed air. Do *not* use a piece of wire to clean them as minor gouges in a jet can alter flow rate and upset the fuel/air mixture.

10. Inspect the end of the float valve needle (**Figure 18**) and seat for wear or damage; replace either or both parts if necessary.

11. Replace all O-rings and gaskets upon assembly. O-ring seals tend to become hardened after prolonged use and exposure to heat and therefore lose their ability to seal properly. Replace as necessary.

12. Assemble by reversing the disassembly steps, noting the following.

13. If removed, screw the pilot screw into the exact same position (same number of turns) as recorded during disassembly. If a new pilot screw was installed, do not install the limiter cap at this time.

NOTE
If a new pilot screw was installed, turn it out the number of turns indicated in **Table 1**, *from the* **lightly seated** *position.*

14. Install the vacuum cylinder into the carburetor body. Align the tab on the diaphragm with the hole in the carburetor body.

15. After assembly and installation are completed, adjust the carburetor as described in this chapter and Chapter Three.

**New Pilot Screw Adjustment
and Limiter Cap Installation
(Rebel 250 Models)**

*NOTE
Honda does not provide service
information for the CM250C models.*

This procedure is required only if a new pilot screw has been installed.

*CAUTION
The pilot screw seat can be damaged if
the pilot screw is tightened too hard
against it.*

1. Turn the pilot screw (**Figure 41**) in until it *lighty seats* then back it out the specified number of turns indicated in **Table 1**.

2. Warm up the engine to normal operating temperature. Stop-and-go riding for approximately 10 minutes is sufficient.

3. Turn the engine off and connect a portable tachometer following manufacturer's instructions.

4. Start the engine and adjust the idle speed with the idle adjust screw (**Figure 42**). Refer to **Table 1** for recommended idle speed.

5. Turn the pilot screw slowly in or out to obtain the highest engine speed.

6. Readjust the idle speed, referring to **Table 1**.

7. Turn the pilot screw *in* gradually until the engine speed drops by 100 rpm.

8. Turn the pilot screw one turn *out* from the position obtained in Step 7.

9. Readjust idle speed. Refer to **Table 1**.

10. Turn the engine off and disconnect the portable tachometer.

11. Apply Loctite No. 601 (or equivalent) to the limiter cap and install the cap against the stop on the float bowl so that the screw can only turn *clockwise*, not *counterclockwise*.

*NOTE
This prevents any adjustment that
would enrich the mixture. With the
limiter in place the pilot screw can be
turned about 7/8 of a turn only toward
a leaner mixture.*

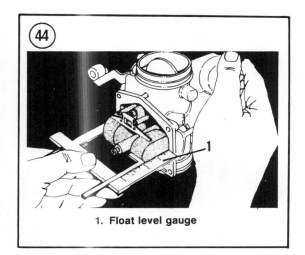

1. Float level gauge

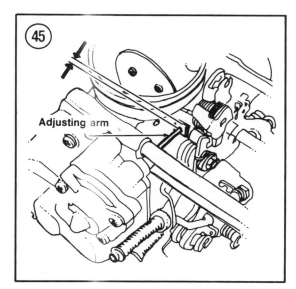

Adjusting arm

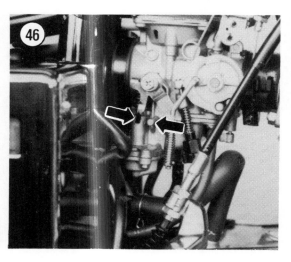

CARBURETOR ADJUSTMENTS

Float Adjustment

The carburetor assembly must be removed and partially disassembled for this adjustment.

1. Remove the carburetor as described in this chapter.

2. Remove the float bowl from the carburetor. Refer to **Figure 34** for Rebel 250 models or **Figure 43** for all other models.

3. Measure the height of the float above the carburetor body. Use a float gauge (**Figure 44**). The correct float height is listed in **Table 1**.

4. Adjust the float height by carefully bending the tang on the float arm.

NOTE
Both float sections within the carburetor must be at the same height.

5. If the float level is set too high, the result will be a rich fuel/air mixture. If set too low, the result will be a lean fuel/air mixture.

6. Reassemble and install the carburetor.

Accelerator Pump Adjustment (Models so Equipped)

The carburetor assembly must be removed for this adjustment.

1. Remove the carburetor as described in this chapter.

2. Loosen the throttle adjust screw so the throttle valve is completely closed.

3. Measure the clearance between the accelerator pump rod and the adjusting arm (**Figure 45**) with the throttle valve closed. The correct clearance is as follows:

    a. 1983 CM250C: 0-0.0016 in. (0-0.04 mm).

    b. Rebel 250: 0 in. (0 mm).

4. Adjust by bending the adjustment arm.

NOTE
***Figure 46** is shown with the carburetor installed.*

5. Measure the distance between the adjusting arm and the stopper (**Figure 46**) on the carburetor body. The correct clearance is as follows:

    a. 1983 CM250C: 0.12-0.13 in. (3.1-3.3 mm).

    b. Rebel 250: 0.26 in. (6.5 mm).

Choke Adjustment
(Rebel 250 Models)

The choke system on these models uses a fuel enrichening circuit that is controlled by a choke valve. The choke valve opens the enriching circuit by means of the choke cable and lever mounted on the left-hand side of the handlebar.

1. At the carburetor, slide the rubber boot (**Figure 24**) on the choke cable back off the choke valve.

2. Unscrew the choke valve (**Figure 25**) from the carburetor body.

3. Push the choke lever on the handlebar (**Figure 47**) all the way down to its fully closed position.

4. The distance between the end of the threads on the choke valve holder and the valve should be 0.41 in. (10.5 mm) as shown in **Figure 48**.

5. If the clearance is incorrect, loosen the locknut (A, **Figure 49**) and turn the choke cable elbow (B, **Figure 49**) until the correct amount of clearance is obtained.

6. Tighten the locknut on the choke cable.

7. Screw the choke valve into the carburetor body by hand until tight. Then tighten an additional 1/4 turn with a wrench.

8. Slide the rubber boot back into position.

Pilot Screw Adjustment
(CM185T Models)

> *NOTE*
> *The pilot screw is pre-set at the factory and adjustment is not necessary unless the carburetor has been overhauled or someone has misadjusted it.*

If adjustment is necessary, perform Steps 1-7 of *New Pilot Screw Adjustment and Limiter Cap Installation—Model CM200T* in this chapter. Step 8 does not pertain to this model as it does not require a limiter cap.

High Altitude Adjustment

Make sure the pilot jet is adjusted properly before performing this procedure.

If the bike is going to be ridden for any sustained period of time at high elevations (6,500 ft./2,000 m) the carburetor must be readjusted to improve performance and decrease exhaust emissions.

1. Start the engine and let it reach normal operating temperature. Stop-and-go riding for approximately 10 minutes is sufficient. Turn off the engine.

2. Connect a portable tachometer following the manufacturer's instructions.

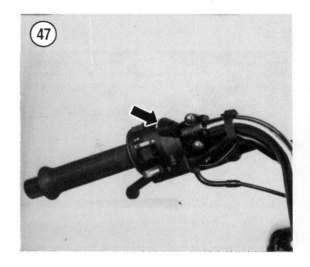

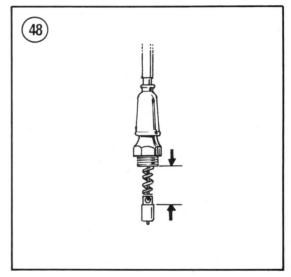

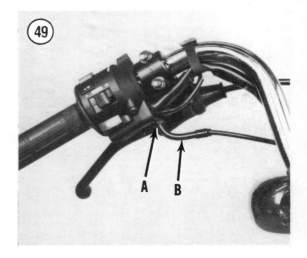

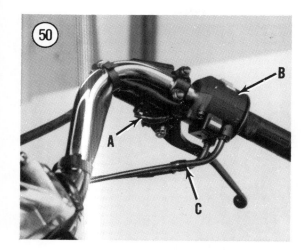

3. Turn the pilot screw (**Figure 41**) *clockwise* from the factory pre-set position.
   a. Rebel 250: 1/2 turn.
   b. All other models: 1/4 turn.
4. Restart the engine and turn the large idle screw (**Figure 42**) to achieve the idle speed listed in **Table 1**.
5. Turn the engine off and disconnect the portable tachometer.
6. When the bike is returned to lower elevations (near sea level), the pilot screw must be returned to its original position and the idle speed readjusted to idle speed listed in **Table 1**.

THROTTLE CABLE REPLACEMENT

1. Remove both side covers and the seat.
2. Remove the fuel tank as described in this chapter.
3. Disconnect the front brake light switch electrical connectors (A, **Figure 50**) from the switch.

4. Remove the screws securing the right-hand switch/throttle housing halves together (B, **Figure 50**).
5. Remove the housing from the handlebar and disengage the throttle cables (C, **Figure 50**) from the throttle grip.
6A. On single-cable models, perform the following:

> *NOTE*
> *Before removing the top cap, thoroughly clean the area around it so no dirt will fall into the carburetor.*

   a. Unscrew the top cap from the carburetor and carefully pull the throttle slide assembly out of the carburetor.
   b. Disconnect the throttle cable from the throttle slide.
   c. Pull the throttle cable out of the top cap.
6B. On dual-cable models, perform the following:
   a. On Rebel 250 models, remove the screws securing the throttle cable cover (**Figure 23**) and remove the cover.
   b. Loosen the cable locknut (A, **Figure 51**) and adjuster nuts (B, **Figure 51**).
   c. Disconnect the throttle cables from the throttle wheel.

> *NOTE*
> *The piece of string attached in the next step will be used to pull the new throttle cables back through the frame so they will be routed in exactly the same position as the old ones.*

7. Tie a piece of heavy string or cord (approximately 7 ft./2 m long) to the carburetor end of the throttle cable(s). Wrap this end with masking or duct tape. Do not use an excessive amount of tape as it must be pulled through the frame loop during removal. Tie the other end of the string to the frame or air box.
8. At the throttle grip end of the cable(s), carefully pull the cable(s) (and attached string) out through the frame, past the electrical harness and from behind the headlight housing. Make sure the attached string follows the same path as the cable(s) through the frame.
9. Remove the tape and untie the string from the old cables.
10. Lubricate the new cable(s) as described in Chapter Three.

6

11. Tie the string to the new throttle cable(s) and wrap it with tape.

12. Carefully pull the string back through the frame routing the new cable(s) through the same path as the old cable(s).

13. Remove the tape and untie the string from the cable(s) and the frame.

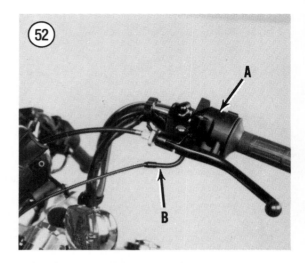

CAUTION
*On models with dual cables, the throttle cables are the push/pull type and must be installed as described and shown in Step 14 and Step 15. Do **not** interchange the 2 cables.*

14A. On single-cable models, perform the following:
  a. Install the throttle cable through the top cap.
  b. Connect the throttle cable onto the throttle slide.
  c. Carefully slide the throttle slide assembly into the carburetoor and screw on the top cap.
14B. On dual-cable models, perform the following:
  a. Attach the throttle "pull" cable to the rear bracket and into the rear hole in the throttle wheel (A, **Figure 28**). The other end is attached to the front receptacle of the throttle/switch housing.
  b. Attach the throttle "push" cable to the front bracket and into the front hole in the throttle wheel (B, **Figure 28**). The other end is attached to the rear receptacle of the throttle/switch housing.
15. Install the throttle/switch housing and tighten the screws securely.
16. Attach the front brake light switch connectors.
17. Operate the throttle grip and make sure the carburetor throttle linkage is operating correctly, with no binding. If operation is incorrect or there is binding, carefully check that the cables are attached correctly and there are no tight bends in the cables.
18. Install the carburetor assembly, fuel tank and seat.
19. Adjust the throttle cable(s) as described in Chapter Three.
20. Test ride the bike slowly at first and make sure the throttle is operating correctly.

CHOKE CABLE REPLACEMENT (REBEL 250 MODELS)

1. Remove both side covers and the seat.
2. Remove the fuel tank as described in this chapter.
3. At the carburetor, slide the rubber boot (**Figure 24**) on the choke cable back off the choke valve.
4. Unscrew the choke valve (**Figure 25**) from the carburetor body.
5. Remove the clutch switch wires at the clutch lever.
6. Remove the screws securing the left-hand switch assembly (A, **Figure 52**) and remove the switch assembly from the handlebar.
7. Remove the choke cable (B, **Figure 52**) from the left-hand switch assembly.

NOTE
The piece of string attached in the next step will be used to pull the new choke cable back through the frame so it will be routed in the same position as the old cable.

8. Tie a piece of heavy string or cord (approximately 7 ft./2 m long) to the carburetor end of the choke cable. Wrap this end with masking or duct tape. Do not use an excessive amount of tape as it must be pulled through the frame loop during removal. Tie the other end of the string to the frame or air box.
9. At the choke lever end of the cable, carefully pull the cable (and attached string) out through the frame and from behind the headlight housing. Make sure the attached string follows the same path that the cable does through the frame.

10. Remove the tape and untie the string from the old cable.

11. Lubricate the new cable as described in Chapter Three.

12. Tie the string to the new choke cable and wrap it with tape.

13. Carefully pull the string back through the frame routing the new cable through the same path as the old cable.

14. Remove the tape and untie the string from the cable and the frame.

15. Install the choke cable onto the choke lever assembly.

16. Install the choke valve into the carburetor body and and slide the rubber boot back into place.

17. Install the left-hand switch assembly halves onto the handlebar and install the screws securing the halves together.

18. Attach the clutch switch wires to the clutch lever.

19. Operate the choke lever and make sure the carburetor choke is operating correctly, with no binding. If operation is incorrect or there is binding, carefully check that the cable is attached correctly and there are no tight bends in the cable.

20. Adjust the choke cable as described in this chapter.

21. Install the side covers and the seat.

CHOKE CABLE REPLACEMENT (ALL MODELS EXCEPT REBEL 250)

1. Remove both side covers and the seat.

2. Remove the fuel tank as described in this chapter.

3. Loosen the choke cable clamp screw (A, **Figure 3**) securing the choke cable to the carburetor.

4. Unhook the choke cable from the choke plate (B, **Figure 3**).

5. Unscrew the locknut securing the choke cable to the mounting bracket at the base of the handlebar.

6. Remove the choke cable assembly from the plate.

NOTE
The piece of string attached in the next step will be used to pull the new choke cable back through the frame so it will be routed in the same position as the old cable.

7. Tie a piece of heavy string or cord (approximately 7 ft./2 m long) to the carburetor end of the choke cable. Wrap this end with masking or duct tape. Do not use an excessive amount of tape as it must be pulled through the frame loop during removal. Tie the other end of the string to the frame or air box.

8. At the choke knob end of the cable, carefully pull the cable (and attached string) out through the frame and from behind the headlight housing. Make sure the attached string follows the same path that the cable does through the frame.

9. Remove the tape and untie the string from the old cable.

10. Lubricate the new cable as described in Chapter Three.

11. Tie the string to the new choke cable and wrap it with tape.

12. Carefully pull the string back through the frame routing the new cable through the same path as the old cable.

13. Remove the tape and untie the string from the cable and the frame.

14. Install the choke cable onto the choke lever assembly.

15. Attach the choke cable to the carburetor choke linkage and tighten the clamping screw.

16. Install the choke knob into the mounting bracket at the base of the handlebar and tighten the locknut.

17. Operate the choke lever and make sure the carburetor choke linkage is operating correctly, with no binding. If operation is incorrect or there is binding, carefully check that the cable is attached correctly and there are no tight bends in the cable.

18. Install the fuel tank, side covers and the seat.

FUEL TANK

Removal/Installation

1. Place wood block(s) under the engine to support the bike securely.

2A. On Rebel 250 models, perform the following:

a. Remove both side covers.

b. Remove the bolt (**Figure 53**) on each side securing the passenger seat. Pull the passenger seat toward the rear and remove it.

c. Remove the bolts (**Figure 54**) securing the main seat and the seat belt. Pull the main seat toward the rear and remove it.

2B. On all other models, perform the following:

a. Remove both side covers (A, **Figure 55**).

b. From underneath the rear fender, remove the nuts securing the seat (B, **Figure 55**). Pull the seat toward the rear and remove it.

3. Disconnect the battery negative lead (**Figure 56**).

4. Turn the fuel shutoff valve to the OFF position (A, **Figure 57**) and disconnect the fuel line to the carburetor (B, **Figure 57**). Insert golf tee (**Figure 58**) into the end of the fuel line to prevent any residual fuel from draining out.

5A. On Rebel 250 models, perform the following:

a. Remove the bolt (**Figure 59**) on each side securing the fuel tank at the front.

b. Remove the bolt (**Figure 60**) at the rear and pull the fuel tank toward the rear and remove it.

5B. On all other models, perform the following:

a. Unhook the rubber retainer or remove the bolt (**Figure 61**) at the rear of the tank.

b. Pull the fuel tank toward the rear and remove it.

6. Install by reversing these removal steps. Check for fuel leaks.

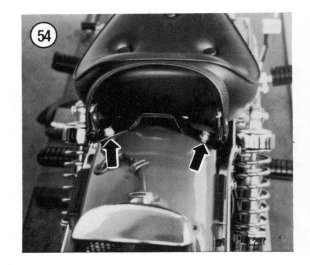

CRANKCASE BREATHER SYSTEM (U.S. ONLY)

To comply with air pollution standards, the Honda twin is equipped with a crankcase breather system (**Figure 62**). The system draws blowby gases from the crankcase and recirculates them into the fuel/air mixture and thus into the engine to be burned.

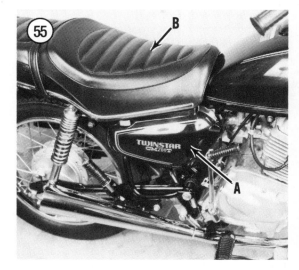

Inspection/Cleaning

Make sure all hose clamps are tight from the engine to the separator (**Figure 63**). Check all hoses for deterioration and replace as necessary.

Remove the clamp and plug (**Figure 64**) from the drain hose and drain out all residue. This cleaning procedure should be done more frequently if a considerable amount of riding is done at full throttle or in the rain.

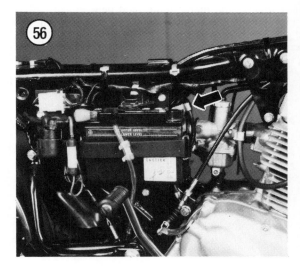

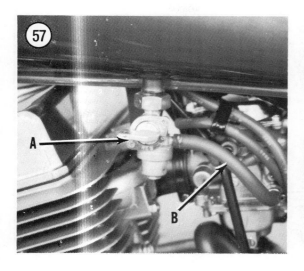

6

NOTE
Be sure to install the drain plug and clamp.

EVAPOATIVE EMISSION CONTROL SYSTEM 1983-ON CALIFORNIA MODELS ONLY

Fuel vapor from the fuel tank is routed into a charcoal canister. Refer to **Figure 65** for CM250C models or **Figure 66** for Rebel 250 models. This vapor is stored when the engine is not running. When the engine is running, these vapors are drawn through a purge control valve and into the carburetor to be burned.

Make sure all hose clamps are tight. Check all hoses for deterioration and replace as necessary (**Figure 67**).

Before disconnecting any hose, label the hose and its fittings with masking tape so the hose can be reconnected properly. The system uses many hoses which can easily be misconnected.

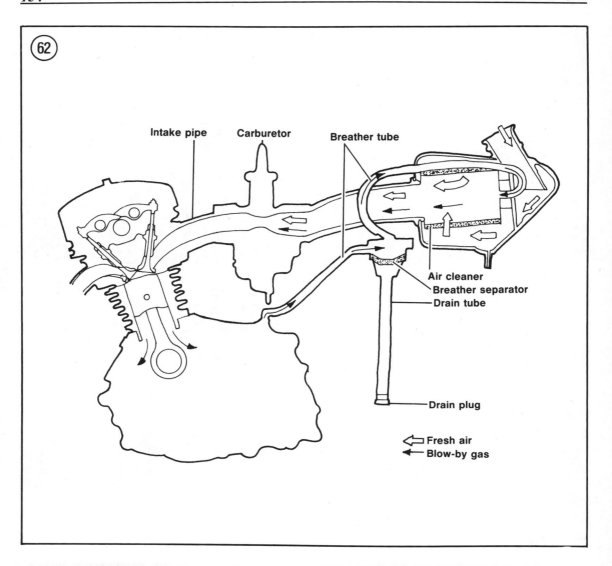

Intake pipe   Carburetor   Breather tube

Air cleaner
Breather separator
Drain tube

Drain plug

⇦ Fresh air
◄─ Blow-by gas

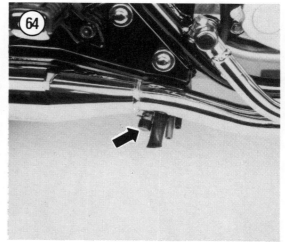

EVAPORATION SYSTEM (CM250C)

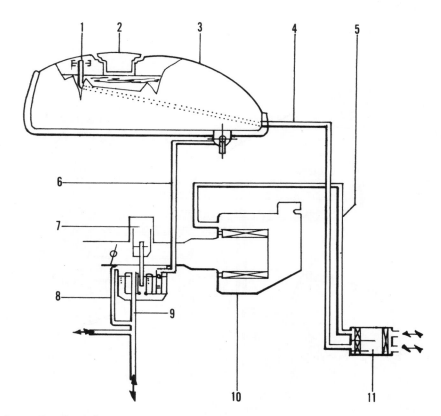

← Opening to the atmosphere

1. Fuel/vapor separator
2. Fuel filler cap
3. Fuel tank
4. Vapor charge line
5. Vapor purge line
6. Fuel line
7. Carburetor
8. Air vent line
9. Fuel reservoir vent line
10. Air filter
11. Charcoal canister

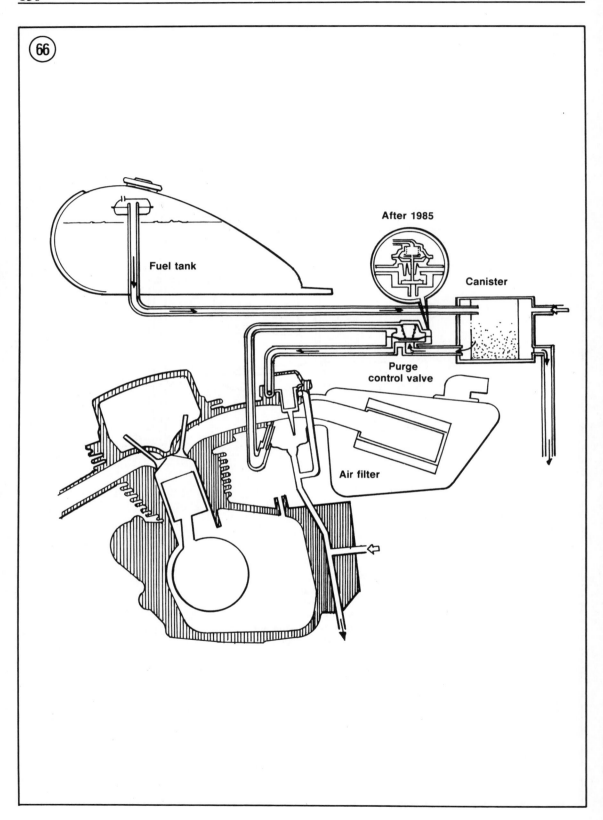

66

After 1985

Fuel tank

Canister

Purge
control valve

Air filter

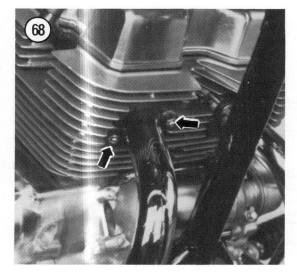

EXHAUST SYSTEM

The exhaust system consists of 2 exhaust pipes, an equalizer tube and 2 mufflers.

Removal/Installation

NOTE
This procedure is best done with the aid of a helper. One person can work on each side of the bike.

1. Place wood block(s) under the bike to support it securely.

2. Remove the nuts and lockwashers (**Figure 68**) securing the exhaust pipe flanges to the cylinder head.

3. Slide the flanges down.

4. If only removing one side of the exhaust system, loosen the bolt (**Figure 69**) clamping the equalizing tube between the mufflers.

5A. On Rebel 250 models, remove the bolts (**Figure 70**) securing the mufflers to the frame on each side. Don't lose the collar within each rubber grommet on the mounting bracket.

5B. On all other models, remove the bolts (**Figure 71**) securing the mufflers to the frame. One of the bolts also secures the rear footpeg.

6. Pull the front portion of the exhaust system forward to clear the exhaust port threaded studs and remove from the engine and the frame.

7. Inspect the gaskets at all joints; replace as necessary.

8. Be sure to install a new gasket in each exhaust port in both cylinder heads.

9. If the mufflers were separated, apply a light coat of multipurpose grease to the inside surface of the gasket in the equalizing tube. This will make insertion of the two tubes easier.

10. Install the assembly into position and install all bolts and nuts only finger-tight until the exhaust flange nuts and lockwashers are installed and securely tightened. This will minimize any exhaust leak at the cylinder head.

11. Tighten all bolts and nuts securely.

12. After installation is complete, make sure there are no exhaust leaks.

Table 1 CARBURETOR SPECIFICATIONS

	CM185T	CM200T
Carburetor model No.	PD98A	PB23A
Main jet number	No. 105	No. 105
Slow jet	—	—
Jet needle clip setting	Nonadjustable	Nonadjustable
Float level	14.5 mm (0.57 in.)	12 mm (0.49 in.)
Idle speed	1200 ± 100 rpm	1200 ± 100 rpm
Pilot screw initial setting	2 turns out	2 turns out
	250C	**Rebel 250**
Carburetor model No.		
1982	VB15A	—
1983	VB17A	—
1985-on		
49-state	—	VE08A
California	—	VE18A
Main jet number		
Primary	No. 68	—
Secondary	No. 138	—
	—	No. 135 (1985)
	—	No. 128 (1986)
Slow jet	No. 35	No. 35
Jet needle clip setting	Nonadjustable	Nonadjustable
Float level	15.5 mm (0.61 mm)	18.5 mm (0.73 in.)
Idle speed	1200 ± 100 rpm	1300 ± 100 rpm
Pilot screw initial setting		
1982	1 5/8 turns out	—
1983	2 3/4 turns out	—
1985-on	—	2 1/4 turns out

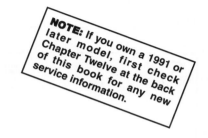

CHAPTER SEVEN

ELECTRICAL SYSTEM

The electrical system consists of the following:
a. Charging system.
b. Ignition system.
c. Lighting system.
d. Switches.
e. Electrical components.
f. Wiring.

Table 1 and **Table 2** are located at the end of this chapter.

Wiring diagrams are the end of this book.

For complete spark plug and battery information, refer to Chapter Three.

CHARGING SYSTEM

The charging system consists of the battery, alternator and a voltage regulator/rectifier. The 1978-1980 models are equipped with a 6-volt electrical system while all models since 1981 are equipped with a 12-volt electrical system. The charging systems used among the various models are shown in Figures 1-4.

Alternating current generated by the alternator is rectified to direct current. The voltage regulator (CM185T models are equipped only with a rectifier) maintains the voltage to the battery and additional electrical loads (lights, ignition, etc.) at a constant voltage regardless of variations in engine speed and load.

Output Test (Rebel 250)

Whenever charging system trouble is suspected, make sure the battery is fully charged and in good condition before going any further. Clean and test the battery as described in Chapter Three.

Prior to starting this test, start the bike and let it reach normal operating temperature then shut off the engine.

Refer to **Figure 5** for this procedure.
1. Remove the seat, the right-hand side cover and the electrical cover (**Figure 6**).
2. Remove the fuse holder cover (**Figure 7**).

NOTE
Do not disconnect the battery cables; they are to remain in the circuit.

3. Connect a 0-20-volt voltmeter to both battery terminals.
4. Connect a 0-10-amp ammeter in line with the main fuse connectors as follows:
   a. Connect the positive (+) test lead of the ammeter to the wire harness side of the fuse holder.

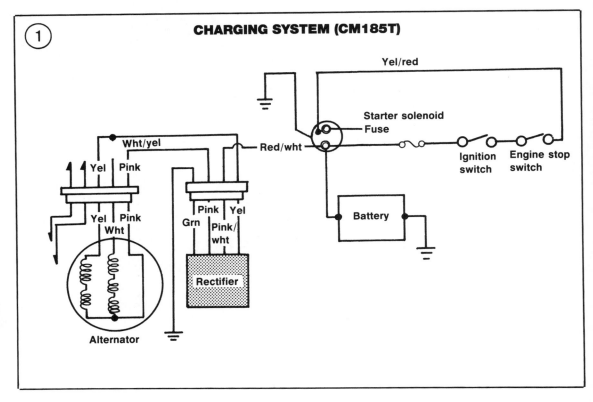

CHARGING SYSTEM (CM185T)

①

Yel/red

Starter solenoid
Fuse

Wht/yel

Red/wht

Yel   Pink

Ignition
switch

Engine stop
switch

Yel   Pink
Wht

Pink   Yel
Grn   Pink/
wht

Battery

Rectifier

Alternator

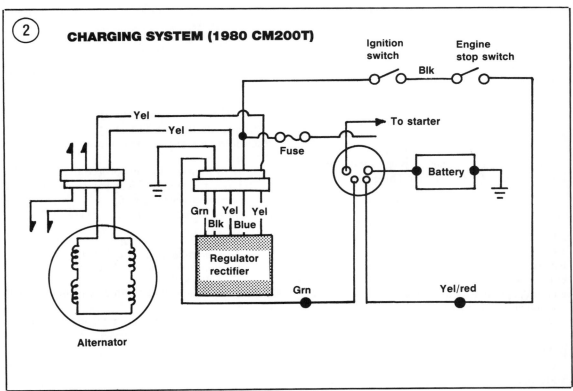

CHARGING SYSTEM (1980 CM200T)

②

Ignition
switch

Engine
stop switch

Blk

Yel

Yel

To starter

Fuse

Battery

Grn   Yel   Yel
Blk   Blue

Regulator
rectifier

Grn

Yel/red

Alternator

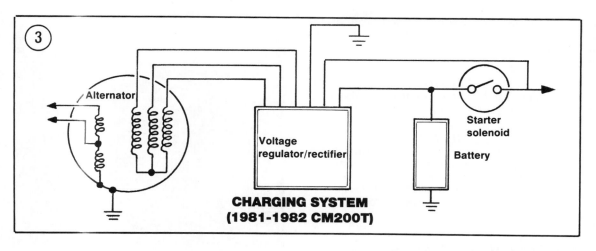

CHARGING SYSTEM (1981-1982 CM200T)

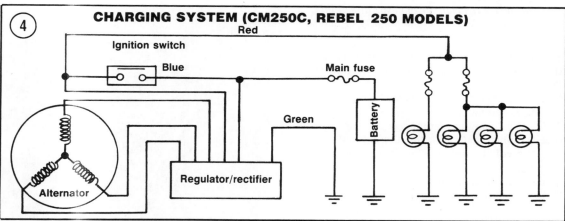

CHARGING SYSTEM (CM250C, REBEL 250 MODELS)

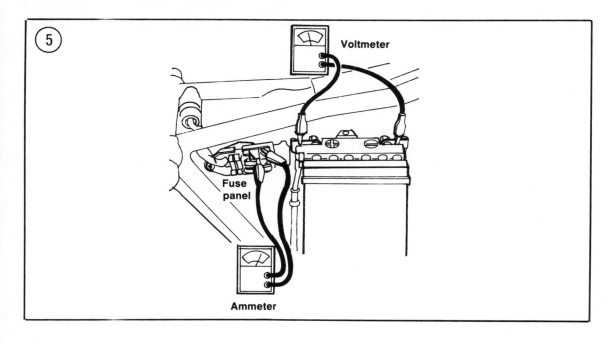

b. Connect the negative (-) test lead of the ammeter to the starter solenoid side of the fuse.

> *CAUTION*
> *In order to protect the ammeter, always run the test with the fuse in the circuit.*

> *CAUTION*
> *Do not try to test the charging system by connecting an ammeter between the positive (+) battery terminal and the starter cable. The ammeter will burn out when the electric starter is operated.*

> *NOTE*
> *During the test, if the needle of the ammeter reads in the opposite direction on the scale, reverse the polarity of the test leads.*

5. Start the engine and gradually increase engine speed and check the readings of the voltmeter and the ammeter.
6. The ammeter should read 0 amps and the voltmeter should read 14-15 volts.
7. If the charging amperage is not within specifications, first check the alternator stator and then the voltage regulator/rectifier as described in this chapter.
8. Disconnect the ammeter and the voltmeter.
9. Install all items removed.

Output Test
(All Models Except Rebel 250)

Whenever charging system trouble is suspected, make sure the battery is fully charged and in good condition before going any further. Clean and test the battery as described in Chapter Three.

Before starting this test, start the bike and let it reach normal operating temperature, then shut off the engine.
1. Remove the right-hand side cover and the seat.
2. Disconnect the battery positive (red) cable from the starter solenoid.

> *NOTE*
> *Do not disconnect the battery negative cable; it is to remain in the circuit.*

3. Connect a 0-20-volt voltmeter and 0-10-amp ammeter as shown in **Figure 8**. Connect the ammeter in series to the positive battery terminal. Connect the positive voltmeter terminal to the positive battery terminal and negative voltmeter terminal to ground.

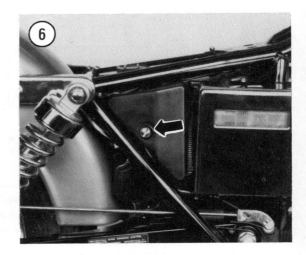

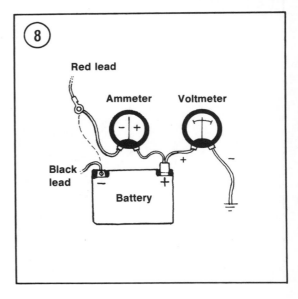

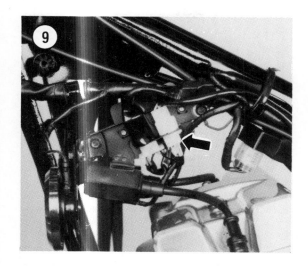

NOTE
During the test, if the needle of the ammeter reads in the opposite direction on the scale, reverse the polarity of the test leads.

4A. On 6-volt electrical systems, perform the following:

a. Start the engine and let it idle.

b. Gradually increase engine speed to 5,000 rpm. The minimum charging current should be 3.3 amps and the voltmeter should read 7.0 volts.

c. Increase engine speed to 10,000 rpm. The maximum current should be 6.0 amps and the voltage should read 8.3 volts.

d. If the charging amperage is not within specifications, first check the alternator stator and then the voltage regulator/rectifier as described in this chapter.

4B. On 12-volt electrical systems, Honda does not provide specifications for this type of test. Test the alternator stator and then the voltage regulator/rectifier as described in this chapter.

5. Disconnect the ammeter and voltmeter.

6. Reconnect the battery positive cable to the battery.

7. Install the seat and the right-hand side cover.

ALTERNATOR

An alternator is a form of electrical generator in which a magnetized field called a rotor revolves within a set of stationary coils called a stator. As the rotor revolves, alternating current is induced in the stator. The current is then rectified to direct current and used to operate the electrical accessories on the motorcycle and to charge the battery. The rotor is permanently magnetized.

Alternator rotor and stator removal and installation are covered in Chapter Four.

Rotor Testing

The altenator rotor is permanently magnetized and cannot be tested except by replacement with a rotor known to be good. A rotor can lose magnetism from old age or a sharp blow. If defective, the rotor must be replaced; it cannot be remagnetized.

Stator Testing

1. Remove the left-hand side cover or the fuel tank (Rebel 250 models) as described in Chapter Six.

2A. On Rebel 250 models, disconnect the alternator electrical connector (**Figure 9**).

2B. On all other models, disconnect the alternator electrical connector (**Figure 10**).

3. Use an ohmmeter set at R×1 and check continuity between the following terminals in the connector:

   a. CM185T: Check between the following terminals: pink-white, white-yellow and yellow-pink. There should be continuity (low resistance). Check between the following terminals and ground: pink, white and yellow. There should be no continuity (infinite resistance).

   b. 1980 CM200T: Check between the 2 yellow terminals. There should be continuity (low resistance).

   c. 1981-1982 CM200T, CM250C and Rebel 250: Check between each of the 3 yellow terminals. There should be continuity (low resistance).

7

If the results are other than specified, the stator must be replaced.

4. Use an ohmmeter set at R × 1 and check continuity between the terminals tested in Step 3 and to ground. There should be no continuity (infinite resistance). Replace the stator if any terminal shows continuity to ground. This would indicate a short within a winding.

5. On 1981-1982 CM200T models, perform the following:

    a. Use an ohmmeter set at R × 1 and check continuity between the blue and white terminals (**Figure 11**). The specified resistance between these terminals is 73-99 ohms.

    b. Use an ohmmeter set at R × 10 and check continuity between the white terminal and ground (**Figure 11**). The specified resistance is 259-351 ohms.

    c. Replace the stator if it fails to meet any of these resistance values.

NOTE
Before replacing the stator with a new one, check the electrical wires to and within the terminal connector for any opens or poor connections.

6. If the stator must be replaced, remove the alternator as described under *Alternator Removal/Installation* in Chapter Four. Follow the alternator removal procedure only to the point where the left-hand crankcase cover is removed, since the stator assembly is attached to this cover.

7. Remove the screws (A, **Figure 12**) securing the stator coil assembly and bracket. Carefully remove the rubber grommet (B, **Figure 12**) from the crankcase cover and remove the stator assembly.

8. When installing the stator assembly, route the electrical cable exactly as shown in **Figure 12**.

RECTIFIER (CM185T) AND REGULATOR/RECTIFIER (CM200T)

Removal/Installation

1. Remove the right-hand side cover and disconnect the battery negative lead (**Figure 13**).
2. Remove the left-hand side cover (Model CM185T).
3. Remove the bolt(s) (**Figure 14**) securing the rectifier or regulator/rectifier.
4. Disconnect the electrical connector and remove the rectifier or regulator/rectifier.
5. Install by reversing these removal steps.

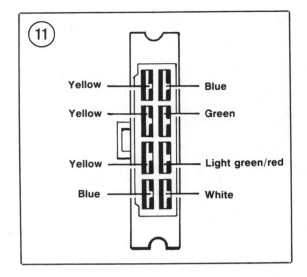

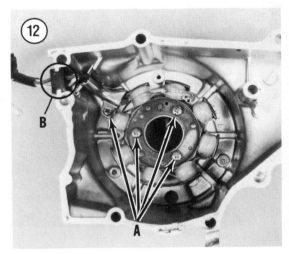

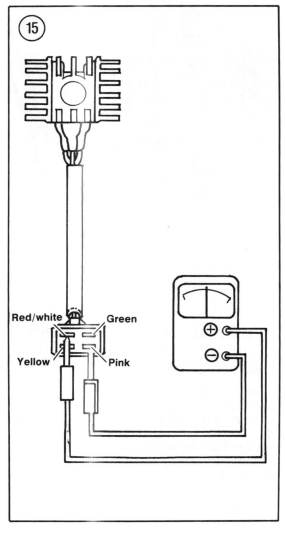

Rectifier Testing (CM185T)

The rectifier converts alternating current produced by the alternator into direct current, which is used to operate the electrical accessories and to charge the battery.

1. Disconnect the battery negative cable from the battery (**Figure 13**).
2. Remove the left-hand side cover.
3. Disconnect the rectifier 4-pin electrical connector. See **Figure 15**.
4. Use an ohmmeter set at either R×10 or R×100 and measure, and record, the resistance between each of the following pairs of terminals (**Figure 15**):
   a. Red/white to pink, yellow, green.
   b. Pink to green.
   c. Yellow to green.
5. Reverse the ohmmeter leads, then repeat Step 4. Each of the measurements must be high with the ohmmeter connected one way and low with the ohmmeter leads reversed. Honda does not provide resistance specifications, but the measurements in one direction should be at least 10 times higher than the measurements in the other direction.

Voltage Regulator/Rectifier Testing (1980 CM200T)

1. Remove the right-hand side cover and disconnect the battery negative cable from the battery (**Figure 13**).
2. Remove the seat.
3. Disconnect the voltage regulator/rectifier electrical connector (**Figure 16**).
4. Use an ohmmeter set at R×10 and measure, and record, the resistance between each of the following pairs of terminals:

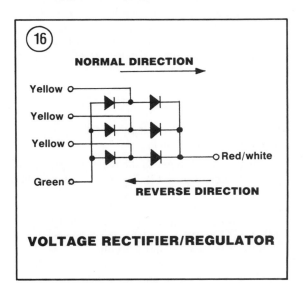

7

a. Yellow to yellow.
b. Yellow to green.
c. Yellow to red/white.
d. Green to red/white.

5. Reverse the ohmmeter leads, then repeat Step 4. Each of the measurements must be high with the ohmmeter connected one way and low with the ohmmeter leads reversed. Honda does not provide resistance specifications, but the measurements in one direction should be at least 10 times higher than the measurements in the other direction.

6. Even if only one of the elements is defective, the entire unit must be replaced; it cannot be serviced.

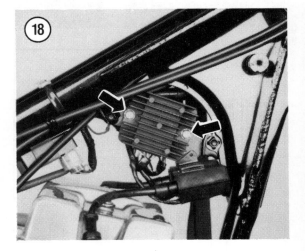

VOLTAGE REGULATOR TEST

Voltage Regulator/Rectifier Testing (1981-1982 CM200T)

1. Remove the right-hand side cover.

2. Disconnect the 2 electrical connectors from the harness. Each connector contains 3 wires.

3. Make the following measurements using an ohmmeter and referring to **Figure 16**.

   a. Connect either ohmmeter lead to the green rectifier lead. Connect the other lead to each of the yellow leads in turn. These 3 measurements must be the same, either all very high resistance (2,000 ohms minimum) or very low resistance (5-40 ohms). If one or more differ, the voltage regulator/rectifier is defective and must be replaced.

   b. Reverse the ohmmeter leads and repeat Step 3a. This time, the 3 readings must also be the same, but just the opposite from the measurements in Step 3a. For example, if all readings in Step 3a were low, all readings in this step must be high and vice versa.

4. If the voltage regulator/rectifier fails to pass any of these tests the unit is defective and must be replaced.

Voltage Regulator Performance Test (CM185T and CM200T)

1. Connect a voltmeter to the battery negative and positive leads (**Figure 17**). Leave the battery cables attached.

2. Start the engine and let it idle.

3. Increase engine speed to about 2,500 rpm.

4A. On 1978-1980 models, the voltage should stabilize between 7.0 and 8.3 volts.

4B. On 1981-1983 models, the voltage should stabilize between 14.0 and 15.0 volts.

5. At this point, the voltage regulator/rectifier should prevent any further increase in voltage.

6. If this does not happen and voltage increases above specifications, the voltage regulator/rectifier is faulty and must be replaced.

VOLTAGE REGULATOR/RECTIFIER (CM250C, REBEL 250)

Removal/Installation

1. Remove both side covers and the seat.

2. Disconnect the battery negative lead.

3. Remove the fuel tank as described in Chapter Six.

4A. On CM250C models, disconnect the electrical connector containing 6 wires.

4B. On Rebel 250 models, disconnect the 2 electrical connectors each containing 3 wires.

5. Remove the bolts (**Figure 18**) securing the voltage regulator/rectifier to the frame.

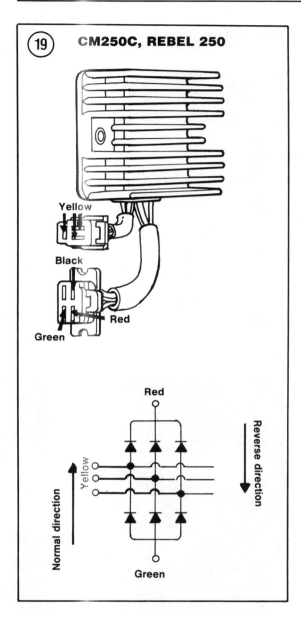

(19) **CM250C, REBEL 250**

Yellow
Black
Green
Red

Red

Yellow

Normal direction

Reverse direction

Green

4. Make the following measurements using a positive ground ohmmeter.
5. Connect the positive (+) ohmmeter lead to the yellow lead and the negative (-) ohmmeter lead to the green lead. There should be continuity (low resistance).
6. Reverse the ohmmeter leads and repeat Step 5. This time there should be no continuity (infinite resistance).
7. Connect the positive (+) ohmmeter lead to the red lead and the negative (-) ohmmeter lead to the yellow lead. There should be continuity (low resistance).
8. Reverse the ohmmeter leads and repeat Step 7. This time there should be no continuity (infinite resistance).
9. If the voltage regulator/rectifier fails to pass any of these tests the unit is defective and must be replaced.

Voltage Regulator Performance Test

Honda does not provide service information for these models.

IGNITION SYSTEM (CONTACT BREAKER POINT)

Refer to **Figure 20** for the contact breaker point ignition system.

When the breaker points are closed, current flows from the battery through the primary windings of the ignition coil, thereby building a magnetic field around the coil. The engine-driven breaker point cam rotates and the breaker point assembly is adjusted so the breaker points open as the piston reaches the firing position.

NOTE
The spark plugs are wired in series to the same ignition coil. Both spark plugs fire at the same time even though only one cylinder is at top dead center on the compression stroke. The other spark plug fires on the exhaust stroke, causing no damage or loss in performance.

As the breaker points open, the magnetic field collapses. When this occurs, a very high voltage is induced (up to approximately 15,000 volts) in the secondary winding of the ignition coil. This high voltage is sufficient to jump the gap at the spark plug causing the spark plug to fire.

The condenser assists the coil in developing high voltage and also serves to protect the breaker points. Inductance of the ignition coil primary

6. Carefully pull the voltage regulator/rectifier and the 2 electrical connectors and wires out from the frame.
7. Install by reversing these removal steps. Make sure all electrical connections are tight.

Testing

Refer to **Figure 19** for this procedure.
1. Remove the seat and both side covers.
2. Remove the fuel tank as described in Chapter Six.
3. Disconnect the 2 electrical connectors from the harness. Each connector contains 3 wires.

7

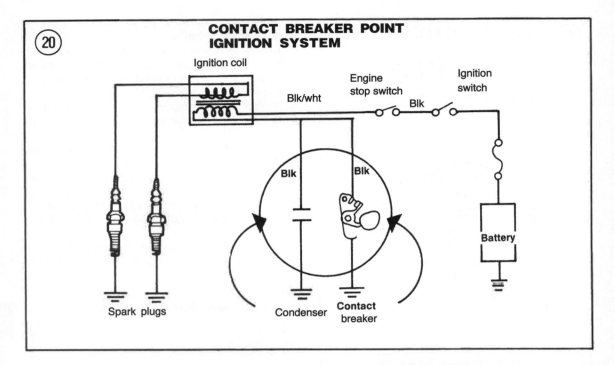

windings tends to keep a surge of current flowing through the circuit even after the breaker points have started to open. The condenser stores this surge and thus prevents arcing at the breaker points.

Condenser

The condenser is a sealed unit that requires no routine maintenance. Make sure all electrical connections are free of corrosion and are tight.

NOTE
The condenser on the CM185T is located under the seat and on CM200T models the condenser is attached to the contact breaker point base plate (A, Figure 21).

Two tests can be made on the condenser. One is to measure the condenser capacity with a condenser tester. The specified capacity is 0.24 microfarads. The other test is insulation resistance, which should not be less than 5 megohms, measured between the condenser pigtail and the case.

If the test equipment is not available, a quick test may be made by connecting the condenser case to the negative terminal of a 6-volt battery and the positive lead (pigtail) to the battery positive terminal. Allow the condenser to charge for a few seconds, then quickly disconnect the battery and touch the condenser pigtail to the condenser case

(Figure 22). If you observe a spark as the pigtail touches the case, you may assume that the condenser is good.

Service

Two major service procedures are required for the breaker point ignition system: breaker point service and ignition timing. Both procedures are vitally important to proper engine operation and reliability. Refer to Chapter Three for contact breaker point service and ignition timing procedures.

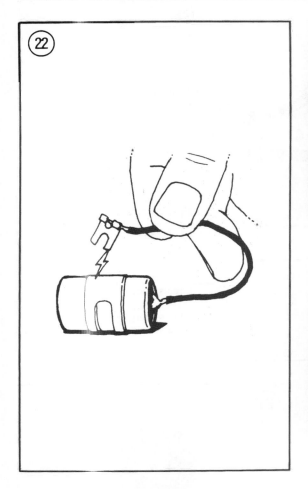

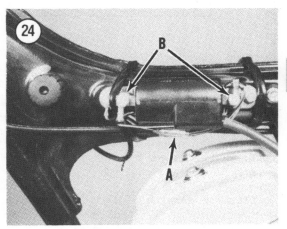

Breaker Point Removal/Installation

1. Remove the right-hand side cover and disconnect the battery negative lead **(Figure 13).**

2. Remove the screws securing the ignition cover and remove the cover and gasket.

3. Disconnect the condenser and electrical connector (B. **Figure 21)** on the breaker point assembly.

4. Remove the screws (C, **Figure 21)** securing the breaker point assembly and remove the assembly.

5. Install a new breaker point assembly by reversing these removal steps, noting the following.

6. Adjust the breaker point gap and ignition timing as described in Chapter Three.

IGNITION COIL (CONTACT BREAKER POINT IGNITION)

Removal/Installation

1. Remove the seat and both side covers.

2. Remove the fuel tank as described in Chapter Six.

3. Remove the spark plug lead **(Figure 23)** from each spark plug.

4. Disconnect the primary leads from the ignition coil (A, **Figure 24).**

5. Remove the bolts (B, **Figure 24)** securing the ignition coil to the frame and remove the coil.

6. Install by reversing these removal steps, noting the following.

7. Make sure all electrical connections are free of corrosion and are tight.

Testing

Refer to **Figure 25** for this procedure.

The ignition coil is a transformer which develops the high voltage required to jump the spark plug gap. The only maintenance required is to keep the electrical connections clean and tight. Occasionally, check that the coil is mounted securely.

If the coil condition is doubtful, there are several checks that can be made. Disconnect the ignition coil electrical wires before testing.

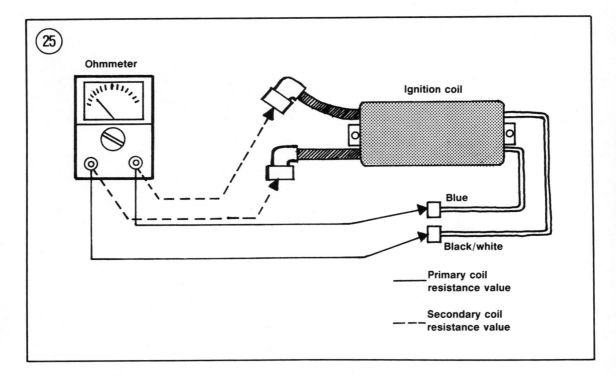

1. Use an ohmmeter set at R×1 and check for continuity between the blue and the black/white primary leads. There should be continuity (low resistance).

2. Use an ohmmeter set at R×100 and check for continuity between the spark plug wires. There should be continuity (low resistance).

3. Visually inspect the exterior of the ignition coil. If there are signs of external damage or cracks, the coil should be replaced.

4. If the ignition coil fails to pass any of these tests the coil should be replaced.

IGNITION ADVANCE MECHANISM (CONTACT BREAKER POINT IGNITION)

The ignition advance mechanism advances ignition timing (fires the spark plug sooner) as engine speed increases. If timing does not advance properly and smoothly, it will be incorrect at high engine speed. The advance mechanism must be periodically inspected to make sure it operates smoothly.

1. Remove the ignition advance mechanism as described in Chapter Four.

2. Inspect the pivot points (A, **Figure 26**) of each weight. It must pivot freely to maintain proper ignition advance. Apply lightweight grease to the pivot point pins.

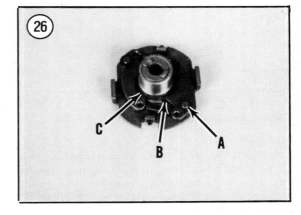

3. Inspect the pivot cam (B, **Figure 26**) operation on the shaft. It must rotate smoothly.

4. Inspect the surface of both cams (C, **Figure 26**). If worn, scratched or pitted, the advance assembly must be replaced.

IGNITION SYSTEM (ELECTRONIC IGNITION)

All models since 1981 are equipped with a fully transistorized electronic ignition system consisting of an ignition coil(s), a CDI unit, an ignition pulse generator and 2 spark plugs. Refer to **Figure 27** (1981-1982 CM200T models) or **Figure 28** (CM250C and Rebel 250 models).

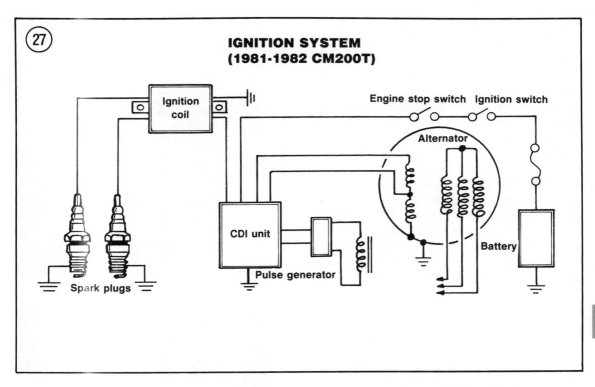

(27)

IGNITION SYSTEM
(1981-1982 CM200T)

Ignition coil

Engine stop switch Ignition switch

Alternator

CDI unit

Battery

Spark plugs

Pulse generator

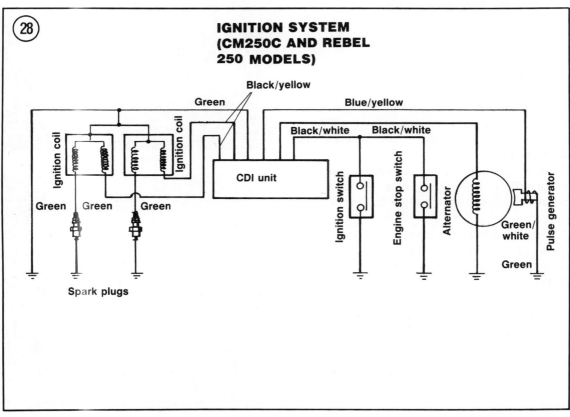

(28)

IGNITION SYSTEM
(CM250C AND REBEL
250 MODELS)

Black/yellow

Green

Blue/yellow

Ignition coil

Ignition coil

Black/white   Black/white

CDI unit

Ignition switch

Engine stop switch

Alternator

Pulse generator

Green   Green   Green

Green/white

Green

Spark plugs

All of these models are equipped with a solid state capacitor discharge ignition (CDI) system that uses no breaker points. This system provides a longer life for components and delivers a more efficient spark throughout the entire speed range of the engine. Ignition timing is fixed with no means of adjustment. If ignition is incorrect it is due to a faulty unit within the ignition system.

Direct current charges the capacitor. As the piston approaches the firing position, a pulse from the pulse generator coil triggers the silicon controlled rectifier. The rectifier in turn allows the capacitor to discharge quickly into the primary circuit of the ignition coil, where the voltage is stepped up in the secondary circuit to a value sufficient to fire the spark plugs. The distribution of the pulses from the pulse generator is controlled by the rotation of the crankshaft and is driven by the left-hand end of the crankshaft.

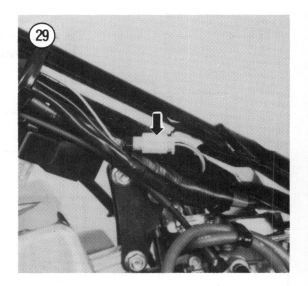

NOTE
Both spark plugs fire at the same time but only one of the cylinders will be at TDC on the compression stroke. The other cylinder is on the exhaust stroke and the spark in the cylinder has no effect on it.

CDI Precautions

Certain measures must be taken to protect the capacitor discharge system.

1. Never connect the battery backwards. If the connected battery polarity is wrong, damage will occur to the voltage regulator/rectifier, the alternator and the spark units.

2. Do not disconnect the battery when the engine is running. The resulting voltage surge will damage the voltage regulator/rectifier and possbily burn out the lights.

3. Keep the connections between the various units clean and tight. Be sure that the wiring connectors are pushed together firmly to help keep out moisture.

4. Do not substitute another type of ignition coil.

5. Each component is mounted within a rubber vibration isolator. Always be sure that the isolator is in place when installing any units of the system.

CDI Troubleshooting

Problems with the capacitor discharge system usually cause a weak spark or no spark at all.

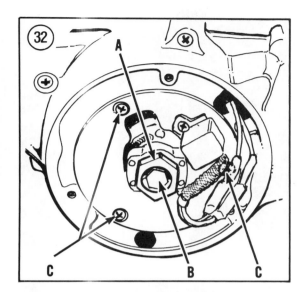

1. Check all connections to make sure they are tight and free of corrosion.
2. Check the ignition coil as described in this chapter.
3. Check the pickup coils in the ignition pulse generator with an ohmmeter:
   a. Remove the left-hand side cover.
   b. On Rebel 250 models, remove the fuel tank as described in Chapter Six.
   c. Disconnect the 2-pin ignition pulse generator electrical connector (**Figure 29**).
   d. Connect the ohmmeter leads between the 2 leads in the connector.
   e. The resistance (at 68° F/20° C) should be as follows:
      a. CM250C: 30-200 ohms.
      b. Rebel 250: 90-100 ohms.

If the pickup coil does not meet these specifications the ignition pulse generator assembly must be replaced as described in this chapter. It cannot be serviced.
4. If the ignition coil and ignition pulse generator assembly check out okay, the CDI unit is at fault and must be replaced.

IGNITION PULSE GENERATOR

Removal/Installation (CM200T)
1. Remove the right-hand side cover and disconnect the battery negative lead (**Figure 13**).
2. Remove the screws (**Figure 30**) securing the ignition cover and remove the cover and gasket.
3. Remove the screws securing the rear left-hand crankcase cover and remove the cover (A, **Figure 31**).
4. Remove the clamping bolt on the gearshift pedal and remove the gearshift pedal (B, **Figure 31**).
5. Remove the left-hand side of the exhaust system (C, **Figure 31**) as described in Chapter Six.
6. Hold onto the outer 17 mm indexing nut (A, **Figure 32**) and remove the inner bolt (B, **Figure 32**) securing the ignition pulse generator rotor. Remove the rotor.
7. Remove the screws (C, **Figure 32**) securing the base plate, disconnect the pulse generator electrical connectors and remove the pulse generator base plate assembly.
8. Install by reversing these removal steps.

Removal/Installation (CM250C and Rebel 250)
1. Remove the right-hand side cover and disconnect the battery negative lead (**Figure 13**).
2. Remove the clamping bolt on the gearshift pedal and remove the gearshift pedal (A, **Figure 33**).
3. Remove the screws securing the drive sprocket cover and remove the cover (B, **Figure 33**).
4. Remove the screws securing the left-hand crankcase cover and remove the cover (C, **Figure 33**) and gasket.
5. Remove the screws securing the pulse generator to the left-hand crankcase cover. Note the location of the metal plate next to the pulse generator. This plate must be reinstalled in the same location, as it keeps the electrical wires in place and out of the path of the pulse generator rotor.
6. Carefully remove the rubber grommet and electrical wires from the left-hand crankcase cover and remove the assembly from the cover.

7

7. Install by reversing these removal steps, noting the following.

8. Make sure the screws securing the pulse generator are tight and that the wires are routed correctly in the frame.

9. Be sure to install the metal plate in its same location as noted in Step 5.

CDI UNIT

Removal/Installation (CM200T)

1. Remove the right-hand side cover and disconnect the battery negative lead.

2. Pull the CDI unit up and out of the rubber insulator located at the rear of the battery.

3. Disconnect the 2 electrical connectors from the backside of the CDI unit.

4. Install by reversing these removal steps. Make sure all electrical connections are tight and free of corrosion.

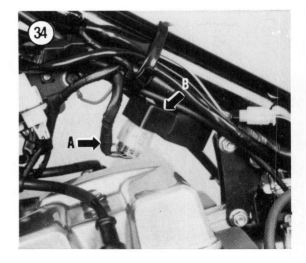

Removal/Installation (CM250C and Rebel 250)

1. Remove the left-hand side cover and disconnect the battery negative lead.

2. Remove the fuel tank as described in Chapter Six.

3. Disconnect the electrical connectors going to the CDI unit (A, **Figure 34**).

4. Pull the CDI unit (B, **Figure 34**) out of the rubber insulator located on the frame.

5. Install by reversing these removal steps. Make sure all electrical connections are tight and free of corrosion.

IGNITION COIL
(ELECTRONIC IGNITION)

Removal/Installation (Rebel 250)

1. Remove both side covers and the seat.

2. Remove the fuel tank as described in Chapter Six.

3. Disconnect the battery negative lead.

4. Disconnect the spark plug lead (**Figure 35**) from each spark plug.

5. Remove each ignition coil (**Figure 36**) from the rubber isolator on the frame and remove both coils.

6. Disconnect the primary wire connectors (**Figure 37**) from each coil.

7. Install by reversing these removal steps; note the following.

8. Make sure all electrical connections are tight and free of corrosion.

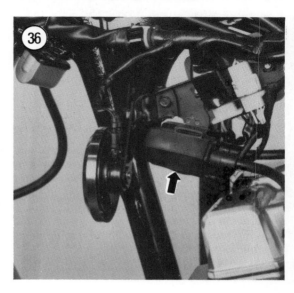

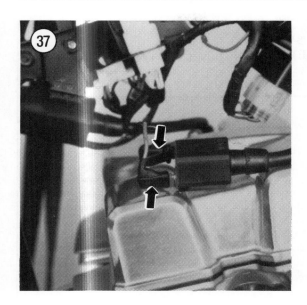

Dynamic Test

Disconnect the high voltage lead from the spark plug. Remove the spark plug from the cylinder head. Connect a new or known good spark plug to the high voltage lead and place the spark plug base on a good ground like the engine cylinder head (**Figure 38**). Position the spark plug so you can see the electrodes.

> *WARNING*
> *If it is necessary to hold the high voltage lead, do so with an insulated pair of pliers. The high voltage generated could produce serious or fatal shocks.*

Push the starter button to turn the engine over a couple of times. If a fat blue spark occurs the coil is in good condition; if not it must be replaced. Make sure that you are using a known good spark plug for this test. If the spark plug used is defective the test results will be incorrect.

Reinstall the spark plug in the cylinder head.

Continuity Test

1. Use an ohmmeter set at R×10 and measure between the 2 primary connector lugs on the coil. The specified resistance is 0.17-0.19 ohms.
2. Use an ohmmeter set at R×1,000 and measure between the secondary lead (spark plug leads) with the spark plug cap removed. The specified resistance is 3,700-4,500 ohms.
3. If either coil fails to pass either of these tests the coil(s) should be replaced.

STARTING SYSTEM

The starting system consists of a starter motor, starter solenoid and a starter button.

The layout for the Rebel 250 models is shown in **Figure 39** and all other models are shown in **Figure**

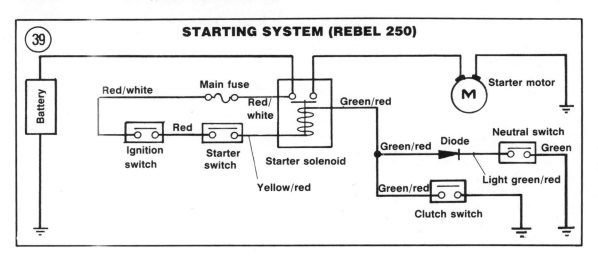

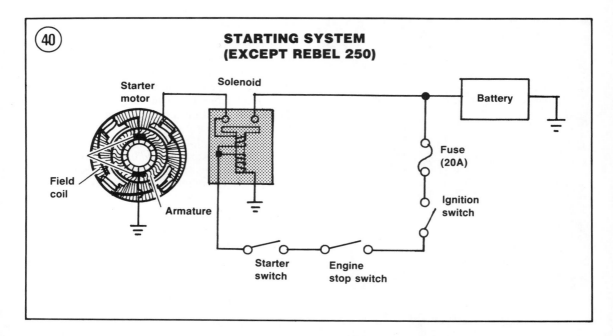

STARTING SYSTEM (EXCEPT REBEL 250)

40. When the starter button is pressed, it engages the solenoid switch that closes the circuit. The electricity flows from the battery to the starter motor.

> *CAUTION*
> *Do not operate the starter for more than 5 seconds at a time. Let it rest approximately 10 seconds, then use it again.*

Table 1 lists possible starter problems, probable causes and the most common remedies.

STARTER

Removal

1. Remove the alternator as described in Chapter Four.
2. Disconnect the electric starter cable from the starter (**Figure 41**).
3. Remove the bolt (A, **Figure 42**) securing the starter sprocket setting plate and remove the setting plate.
4. Remove the starter sprocket, starter motor sprocket and the starter chain as an assembly (B, **Figure 42**).
5. Remove the bolts (**Figure 43**) securing the starter to the crankcase.
6. Pull the starter to the left and remove the starter from the left-hand spacer.

> *NOTE*
> *Don't lose the O-ring on the starter motor.*

Installation

1. Make sure the locating dowels (**Figure 44**) are in place and install a new gasket on the left-hand spacer.
2. Make sure the large O-ring is in place and install the starter motor. Install and tighten the bolts securely.

> *NOTE*
> *Install the sprockets as shown in **Figure 45**.*

3. Install the starter chain, starter sprocket and starter motor sprocket as an assembly (B, **Figure 42**).

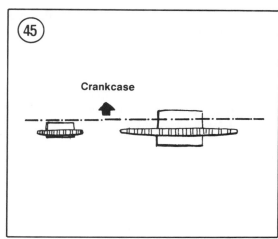

Crankcase

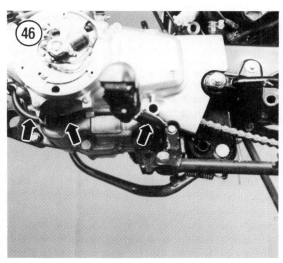

4. Install the starter sprocket setting plate and bolt (A, **Figure 42**). Tighten the bolt securely.

> *NOTE*
> *After installation, rotate the crankshaft **counterclockwise** 2-3 revolutions and check for smooth operation of the chain and sprockets.*

5. Connect the electrical wire to the starter motor and route the wire as shown in **Figure 46**.
6. Install the alternator as described in Chapter Four.

Disassembly/Inspection/Assembly

Starter motor overhaul is best left to an expert. This procedure shows how to detect a defective starter.

1. Remove the case screws and separate the case and covers.

NOTE
Write down the number of shims used on the shaft next to the commutator. Be sure to install the same number when reassembling the starter.

2. Clean all grease, dirt and carbon from the armature, case and end covers.

CAUTION
Do not immerse brushes or the wire windings in solvent as the insulation may be damaged. Wipe the windings with a cloth lightly moistened with solvent and dry thoroughly.

3. Remove the screws (**Figure 47**) securing the carbon brushes and remove the brushes. Measure the length of each brush (**Figure 48**) with a vernier caliper. If the length is 7.0 mm (0.28 in.) or less for any one of the brushes, the brush terminal assembly must be replaced. Replace both brushes as a set even though only one may be worn to this dimension.
4. Inspect the commutator (**Figure 49**). The mica in a good commutator is below the surface of the copper bars. On a worn commutator the mica and copper bars may be worn to the same level. If necessary, have the commutator serviced by a dealer or motorcycle or automotive electrical repair shop.
5. Inspect the commutator copper bars for discoloration. If a pair of bars are discolored, grounded armature coils are indicated.
6. Use an ohmmeter and check for continuity between the commutator bars (**Figure 50**); there should be continuity (low resistance) between pairs of bars. Also check continuity between the commutator bars and the shaft (**Figure 51**); there should be no continuity (infinite resistance). If the unit fails either of these tests the armature is faulty and must be replaced.
7. Use an ohmmeter and inspect the field coil by checking continuity between the starter cable terminal and the starter case; there should be no continuity (infinite resistance). Also check continuity between the starter cable terminal and each brush wire. There should be continuity (low resistance). If the unit fails either of these tests the case/field coil assembly must be replaced.

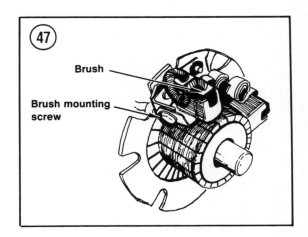

Brush
Brush mounting screw

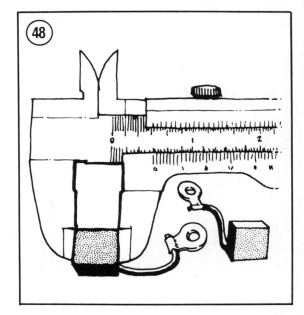

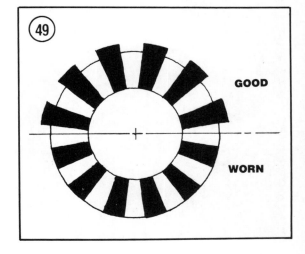

GOOD

WORN

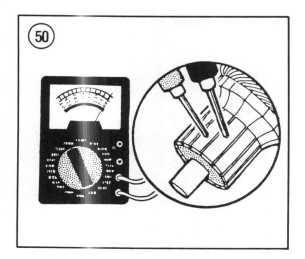

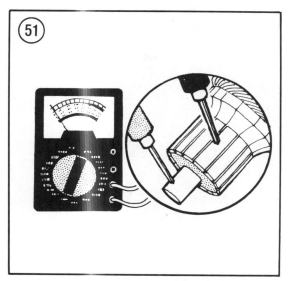

8. Assemble the case; make sure the punch marks on both the case and end covers align.

9. Install and tighten the case screws.

10. Inspect the gear and O-ring seal. If the gear is chipped or worn the armature must be replaced. Replace the O-ring if it has hardened or is starting to deteriorate.

STARTER SOLENOID

Removal/Installation

1. Turn the ignition switch to the OFF position.
2. Remove right-hand side cover and the seat.
3. Disconnect the battery negative lead.
4. Slide off the rubber protective boots and disconnect the electrical wires (**Figure 52**) from the top terminals of the solenoid.
5. Remove the solenoid from the frame. On all models except the Rebel 250 the main fuse holder is attached to the starter solenoid and will come out also.
6. Install by reversing these removal steps.

CLUTCH DIODE
(CM250C, REBEL 250)

Removal/Testing/Installation

NOTE
The 250 models are the only models equipped with a clutch diode.

1. Remove both side covers and the seat.
2. Remove the fuel tank as described in Chapter Six.
3. Disconnect the cluch diode from the wire harness (**Figure 53**).

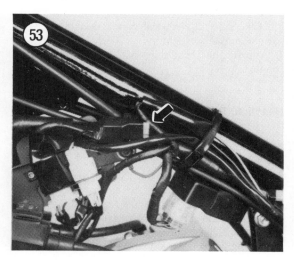

4. Use an ohmmeter and check for continuity between the 2 terminals on the clutch diode. There should be continuity (low resistance) in the normal direction and no continuity (infinite resistance) in the reverse direction. Replace the diode if it fails this test.

5. Install by reversing these removal steps.

LIGHTING SYSTEM

The lighting system consists of a headlight, taillight, brake light, turn signals, warning lights and speedometer illumination light. The 1978-1980 models have a 6-volt electrical system while the 1981-on models have a 12-volt system.

Table 2 lists replacement bulbs for these components.

Always use the correct wattage bulb as indicated in this section. The use of a higher wattage bulb will give a dim light and a lower wattage bulb will burn out prematurely.

Headlight Replacement
(Rebel 250)

1. Remove the screws securing the connection box cover and remove the cover (**Figure 54**).
2. Remove the screw and nut (A, **Figure 55**) at the base of the headlight trim bezel and remove the headlight trim bezel (B, **Figure 55**).
3. Within the connection box, disconnect the individual electrical connectors (white, green and blue) going to the headlight.
4. Carefully pull the electrical wires (**Figure 56**) out of the backside of the headlight housing and remove the sealed beam unit.
5. Install by reversing these removal steps, noting the following.
6. Make sure all electrical connections are free of corrosion and are tight.
7. Adjust the headlight as described in this chapter.

Headlight Replacement
(All Models Except Rebel 250)

1. Remove the screw (**Figure 57**) on each side of the headlight housing.
2. Pull the trim bezel and headlight out of the housing and disconnect the electrical connector from the backside of the sealed beam unit.
3. Remove the screws securing the inner ring.
4. Remove the adjusting screw and remove the inner ring and the sealed beam unit.

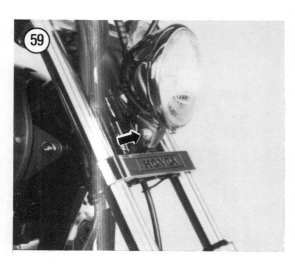

5. Install by reversing these removal steps, noting the following.

6. Adjust the headlight as described in this chapter.

Headlight Adjustment
(Rebel 250)

Adjust the headlight horizontally and vertically according to Department of Motor Vehicles regulations in your area.

> *WARNING*
> *An improperly adjusted headlight is dangerous. It may blind oncoming drivers or fail to light the roadway a safe distance ahead of you.*

To adjust the headlight horizontally, loosen the nut (**Figure 58**) securing the headlight mounting assembly to the lower fork bridge. Position the headlight correctly. Retighten the nut.

To adjust the headlight vertically, loosen the bolts (**Figure 59**) on each side of the headlight mounting assembly. Position the headlight correctly. Retighten the bolts.

Headlight Adjustment
(All Models Except Rebel 250)

Adjust the headlight vertically according to Department of Motor Vehicles regulations in your area.

To adjust the headlight horizontally, turn the adjust screw (A, **Figure 60**). Screwing it in turns the light toward the right-hand side of the rider and loosening it will direct the light to the left-hand side.

7

To adjust the headlight vertically, loosen the bolts (B, **Figure 60**) on each side of the headlight assembly. Position the headlight correctly. Retighten the bolts securely.

Taillight Replacement

1. Remove the screws securing the lens and remove the lens. Refer to **Figure 61** for Rebel 250 models or **Figure 62** for all other models.
2. Wash the inside and outside of the lens with a mild detergent and wipe dry. Wipe off the reflective base surrounding the bulbs with a soft cloth.
3. Inspect the lens gasket and replace if it is damaged or deteriorated.
4. Replace the bulb and install the lens; do not overtighten the screws as the lens may crack.

License Plate Light
Replacement (Rebel 250)

1. Remove the nuts (**Figure 63**) behind the license plate light bracket.
2. Remove the license plate light cover and lens (**Figure 64**).
3. Push in on the bulb and turn clockwise until the bulb disengages from the socket assembly.
4. Wash out the inside and outside of the lens with a mild detergent and wipe dry.
5. Inspect the lens gasket and replace if it is damaged or deteriorated.
6. Replace the bulb and install the lens and lens cover; do not overtighten the nuts as the lens may crack.

Turn Signal Light Replacement
(All Models)

1. Remove the screws securing the lens and remove the lens (**Figure 65**).
2. Wash out the inside and outside of the lens with a mild detergent and wipe dry.
3. Inspect the lens gasket and replace if it is damaged or deteriorated.
4. Replace the bulb and install the lens; do not overtighten the screws as the lens may crack.

Meter Illumination Light Replacement

CM185T

1. Disconnect the speedometer cable from the housing.
2. Remove the nut securing the speedometer case.
3. Lift up on the case and gently pull the defective lamp holder/lamp out of the case. Remove the defective bulb and replace it.
4. Install by reversing these removal steps.

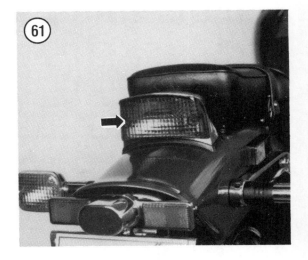

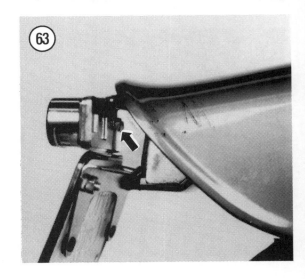

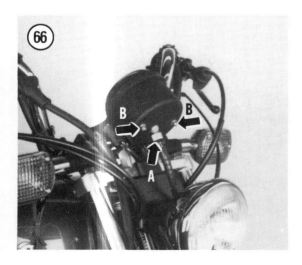

CM200T

1. Remove the headlight assembly.
2. Disconnect the speedometer cable from the housing.
3. Gently pull the defective lamp holder/lamp out of the case. Remove the defective bulb and replace it.
4. Install by reversing these removal steps.

CM250C

1. Remove the nuts securing the instrument to the mounting bracket.
2. Disconnect the speedometer cable from the housing.
3. Remove the instrument from the trim ring and cushion.

> *CAUTION*
> *In the next step do not allow the instruments to remain upside down any longer than necessary as the needle damping fluid will leak out onto the instrument face and lens.*

4. Turn the instrument cluster over and gently pull the defective lamp holder/lamp out of the case. Remove the defective bulb and replace it.
5. Install by reversing these removal steps.

Rebel 250

1. Disconnect the speedometer cable (A, **Figure 66**) from the housing.
2. Remove the nuts (B, **Figure 66**) securing the rear cover to the instrument and remove the cover.
3. Gently pull the defective lamp holder/lamp out of the case. Remove the defective bulb and replace it.
4. Install by reversing these removal steps.

Indicator Light Replacement (Rebel 250)

1. Unscrew the lens (**Figure 67**) from the top of the indicator light.
2. Gently pull the defective lamp holder/lamp (**Figure 68**) out of the lower portion of the light assembly.
3. Remove the defective bulb and replace it.
4. Install by reversing these removal steps.

Indicator Light Replacement (All Models Except Rebel 250)

Follow the procedure for *Speedometer Illumination Light Replacement* in this chapter.

SWITCHES

Front Brake Light Switch
Testing/Replacement

1. Disconnect the electrical wires to the brake light switch. Refer to **Figure 69** for drum brake models or **Figure 70** for disc brake models.
2. Use an ohmmeter and check for continuity between the 2 terminals on the brake light switch. There should be no continuity (infinite resistance) with the brake lever released. With the brake lever applied there should be continuity (low resistance). If the switch fails either of these tests the switch must be replaced.
3A. On drum brake models, remove the switch from the brake lever assembly.
3B. On disc brake models, remove the screw securing the brake switch and remove the brake switch from the brake master cylinder.
4. Install a new switch by reversing these removal steps. Make sure all electrical connections are free of corrosion and are tight.

Rear Brake Light Switch
Testing/Replacement

1. Disconnect the 2-pin electrical connector to the rear brake light switch (**Figure 71**).
2. Use an ohmmeter and check for continuity between the 2 terminals on the brake light switch. There should be no continuity (infinite resistance) with the brake pedal released. With the brake pedal down or applied there should be continuity (low resistance). If the switch fails either of these tests the switch must be replaced.

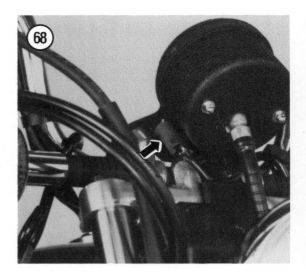

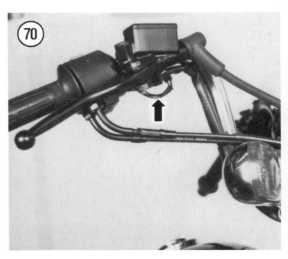

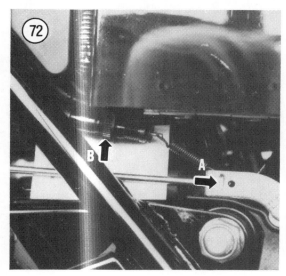

3. Unhook the return spring (A, **Figure 72**) and unscrew the locknut (B, **Figure 72**) securing the rear brake light switch to the frame. Remove the switch from the frame.

4. Install a new switch by reversing these removal steps, noting the following.

5. Make sure all electrical connections are free of corrosion and are tight.

6. Adjust the switch as described in this chapter.

Rear Brake Light Switch Adjustment

NOTE
The brake pedal height and free play must be adjusted before adjusting the switch. Refer to Chapter Three.

1. Turn the ignition switch to the ON position.

2. Depress the brake pedal. The light should come on just as the brake begins to work.

3. To make the light come on earlier, hold the switch body (B, **Figure 72**) and turn the adjusting nut until proper adjustment is obtained.

NOTE
Some riders prefer the light to come on a little early. This way, they can tap the pedal without braking to warn drivers who are following too closely.

ELECTRICAL COMPONENTS

This section contains information on all electrical components except switches which are covered separately in this chapter.

Turn Signal
Relay Replacement

1. On Rebel 250 models, perform the following:
    a. Remove both side covers and the seat.
    b. Remove the electrical panel cover (**Figure 73**).
    c. Remove the turn signal relay from behind the fuse panel (**Figure 74**).

2. On all other models, perform the following:
    a. Remove both side covers.
    b. Pull the turn signal relay (**Figure 75**) out of the rubber mount.

3. Transfer the electrical wires to the new relay and install the relay in the rubber mount. Install all parts removed.

Horn Removal/Installation

1. Disconnect the electrical connectors from the horns. Refer to **Figure 76 or A, Figure 77**.

2. Remove the bolt securing the horn to the frame (B, **Figure 77**) and remove the horn.

3. Install by reversing these removal steps. Make sure the electrical connections are tight and free of corrosion.

Horn Testing

Remove the horn as described in this chapter. Connect a 6-volt battery (1978-1980 models) or 12-volt battery (1981-on models) to the horn. If the horn is good, it will sound. If not, replace it.

Fuses

The number of fuses varies with the different models. All 185-200 models are equipped with one main fuse located next to the battery (**Figure 78**). All 250 models have 3 fuses that are also located next to the battery in a fuse panel (**Figure 79**). Always carry spare fuses.

Whenever a fuse blows, find out the reason for the failure before replacing the fuse. Usually the trouble is a short circuit in the wiring. This may be caused by worn-through insulation or a disconnected wire shorted to ground.

> *CAUTION*
> *Never substitute aluminum foil or wire for a fuse. Never use a higher amperage fuse than specified. An overload could cause a fire and complete loss of the motorcycle.*

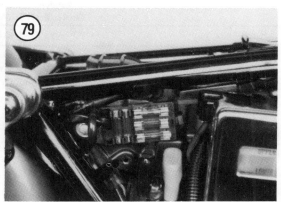

Table 1 STARTER TROUBLESHOOTING

Symptom	Probable cause	Remedy
Starter does not work	Low battery	Recharge battery
	Worn brushes	Replace brushes
	Defective relay	Repair or replace
	Defective switch	Repair or replace
	Defective wiring or connection	Repair wire or clean connection
	Internal short circuit	Repair or replace defective component
Starter action is weak	Low battery	Recharge battery
	Pitted relay contacts	Clean or replace
	Worn brushes	Replace brushes
	Defective connection	Clean and tighten
	Short circuit in commutator	Replace armature
Starter runs continuously	Stuck relay	Replace relay
Starter turns; does not turn engine	Defective starter clutch	Replace starter clutch

7

Table 2 REPLACEMENT BULBS

Item	1978-1980	1981-2000	2001-on
Headlight	6V 25/35W (1978-1979) 6V 36.5/35W (1980)	12V 50/35W	12V 60/55W
Tail/brakelight	6V 5.3/25W	12V 8/27W	12V 8/27W
Turn signals			
Front and rear	6V 17W	12V 23/23W	12V 23/23W
Instrument lights	6V 3W	12V 3.4W	12V 3.4W
Indicator lights	6V 1.7W	12V 3.4W	12V 3.4W
License plate lights	—	12V 8W	12V 8W

CHAPTER EIGHT

FRONT SUSPENSION AND STEERING

8

This chapter describes repair and maintenance procedures for the front wheel, fork and steering components.

Front suspension torque specifications are covered in Table 1 at the end of this chapter.

FRONT WHEEL
(DRUM BRAKE MODELS)

Removal

1. Place wood block(s) under the engine to support it securely with the front wheel off the ground.

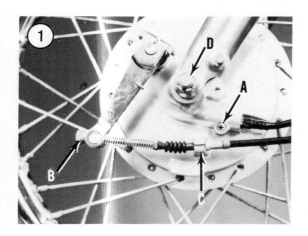

2. Remove the speedometer cable set screw (A, **Figure 1**). Pull the speedometer cable free from the hub.

3. Completely unscrew the brake cable adjusting nut (B, **Figure 1**) and disconnect the brake cable from the pivot pin on the brake arm.

4. Install the pivot pin and adjusting nut onto the brake cable to avoid misplacing them.

5. Disconnect the brake cable from the receptacle on the brake panel (C, **Figure 1**).

6. Remove the cotter pin and axle nut (D, **Figure 1**). Discard the cotter pin; never reuse an old cotter pin as it may break and fall out.

7. Hold onto the front wheel and withdraw the front axle from the right-hand side.

8. Pull the wheel down to clear the brake panel groove and remove it.

Installation

1. Make sure the axle bearing surfaces of the fork sliders and axle are free from burrs and nicks.

NOTE
The following step is necessary for proper and safe brake operation.

2. Position the wheel into place. Align the groove in the brake panel with the raised tab on the front fork (**Figure 2**).

3. Insert the front axle into the right-hand side, install the axle nut and tighten to the torque specification listed in **Table 1**.

4. Install a new cotter pin and bend the ends over completely.

5. Install the front brake cable pivot pin and brake cable into the brake arm. Install the adjusting nut.

6. Slowly rotate the wheel and install the speedometer cable into the hub. Install the cable set screw.

7. After the wheel is completely installed, rotate it several times and apply the brakes a couple of times to make sure that it rotates freely and that the brake is operating correctly.

8. Adjust the front brake lever as described in Chapter Three.

FRONT WHEEL (DISC BRAKE MODELS)

Removal

1. Place wood block(s) under the engine or frame to support it securely with the front wheel off the ground.

2. Remove the speedometer cable set screw (A, **Figure 3**). Pull the speedometer cable (B, **Figure 3**) free from the speedometer gear box. Don't lose the O-ring on the end of the cable.

3. Loosen the nuts (A, **Figure 4**) securing the axle holder.

4. Unscrew the front axle (B, **Figure 4**) from the left-hand fork leg.

5. Pull the wheel down and out of the forks and brake caliper. Don't lose the axle spacer (**Figure 5**) on the right-hand side.

> *CAUTION*
> *Do not set the wheel down on the disc surface as it may get scratched or warped. Set the sidewalls on 2 wood blocks (**Figure 6**).*

> *NOTE*
> *Insert a piece of vinyl tubing or wood in the caliper in place of the brake disc. That way if the brake lever is inadvertently squeezed, the piston will not be forced out of the cylinder. If this does happen, the caliper may have to be disassembled to reseat the piston and the system will have to be bled. By using the wood, bleeding the brake is not necessary when installing the wheel.*

Installation

1. Make sure the axle bearing surfaces of the fork sliders and axle are free from burrs and nicks.

2. Remove the vinyl tubing or piece of wood from the brake caliper.

3. Position the wheel and carefully insert the brake disc between the brake pads of the caliper assembly.

4. Position the speedometer housing tang against the back side of lug on the fork leg (**Figure 7**).

5. Make sure the axle spacer is in place (**Figure 5**).

6. Insert the front axle from the right-hand side and screw it into the left-hand fork leg.

7. Tighten the front axle to the torque specification listed in **Table 1**.

8. If removed, position the axle holder with the arrow facing forward and install the holder.

9. Tighten the front axle holder nut first and then the rear. Tighten to the torque specification listed in **Table 1**. After the nuts are tightened there should be a gap at the rear (**Figure 8**) with none at the front.

10. Make sure the O-ring seal is in place on the end of the speedometer cable. Slowly rotate the wheel and install the speedometer cable into the speedometer housing. Install the cable set screw.

11. After the wheel is completely installed, rotate it several times and apply the brakes a couple of times to make sure that it rotates freely and that the brake pads are against the disc correctly.

INSPECTION (ALL MODELS)

Measure the axial and radial runout of the wheel with a dial indicator as shown in **Figure 9**. The maximum axial and radial runout is 2.0 mm (0.08 in.). If the runout exceeds this dimension, check the wheel bearing condition.

If the wheel bearings are okay, tighten or replace bent or loose spokes. Refer to *Spoke Adjustment* in this chapter.

8

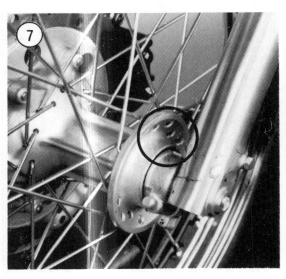

Check axle runout as described under *Front Hub Inspection* in this chapter.

FRONT HUB

Inspection

Inspect each wheel bearing before removing it from the wheel hub.

> *CAUTION*
> *Do not remove the wheel bearings for inspection purposes as they will be damaged during the removal process. Remove wheel bearings only if they are to be replaced.*

1. Perform Steps 1-3 of *Disassembly* in this chapter.
2. Turn each bearing by hand. Make sure bearings turn smoothly.
3. On non-sealed bearings, check the balls for evidence of wear, pitting or excessive heat (bluish tint). Replace the bearings if necessary; always replace as a complete set. When replacing the bearings, be sure to take your old bearings along to ensure a perfect matchup.

> *NOTE*
> *Fully sealed bearings are available from many bearing specialty shops. Fully sealed bearings provide better protection from dirt and moisture that may get into the hub.*

4. Check the axle for wear and straightness. Use V-blocks and a dial indicator as shown in **Figure 10**. If the runout is 0.2 mm (0.008 in.) or greater, the axle should be replaced.

Disassembly

Refer to **Figure 11** for drum brake models or **Figure 12** for disc brake models for this procedure.

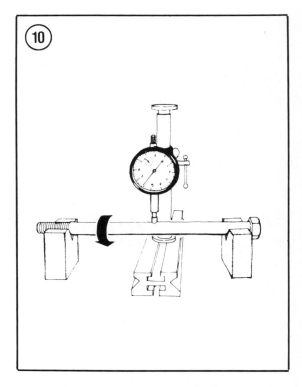

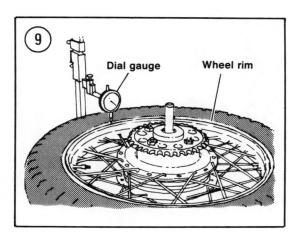

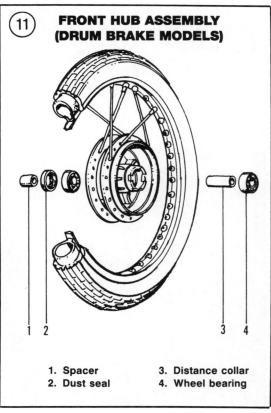

FRONT HUB ASSEMBLY (DRUM BRAKE MODELS)

1. Spacer
2. Dust seal
3. Distance collar
4. Wheel bearing

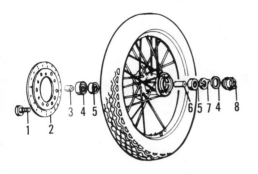

⑫ FRONT HUB ASSEMBLY (DISC BRAKE MODELS)

1. Bolt
2. Brake disc
3. Spacer
4. Dust seal
5. Wheel bearing
6. Distance collar
7. Speedometer drive dog
8. Speedometer housing

1. Remove the front wheel as described in this chapter.

2. On drum brake models, pull the brake panel assembly straight up and out of the brake drum.

3. Remove the spacer (**Figure 13**) and grease seal (**Figure 14**) from the right-hand side.

4. On disc brake models, remove the speedometer housing (**Figure 15**), the grease seal (A, **Figure 16**) and speedometer drive dog (B, **Figure 16**) from the left-hand side.

5. Before proceeding further, inspect the wheel bearings as described in this chapter. If the bearings require replacement, proceed as follows.

6. On disc brake models, remove the bolts (**Figure 17**) securing the brake disc and remove the disc.

7A. A special Honda tool set-up can be used to remove the wheel bearings as follows:

    a. Install the 15 mm bearing remover (Honda part No. 07746-0050400) into the right-hand bearing.

    b. Turn the wheel over (left-hand side up) on the workbench so the bearing remover is touching the workbench surface.

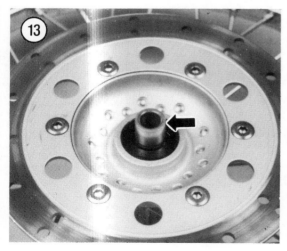

c. From the left-hand side of the hub, install the bearing remover shaft (Honda part No. 07746-0050100) into the bearing remover. Using a hammer, tap the expander into the bearing remover with a hammer.

d. Stand the wheel up to a vertical position.

e. Tap on the end of the expander and drive the right-hand bearing out of the hub. Remove the bearing and the distance collar.

f. Repeat for the left-hand bearing.

7B. If special tools are not used, perform the following:

a. To remove the right- and left-hand bearings and distance collar, insert a soft aluminum or brass drift into one side of the hub.

b. Push the distance collar over to one side and place the drift on the inner race of the lower bearing.

c. Tap the bearing out of the hub with a hammer, working around the perimeter of the inner race.

d. Repeat for the other bearing.

8. Clean the inside and the outside of the hub with solvent. Dry with compressed air.

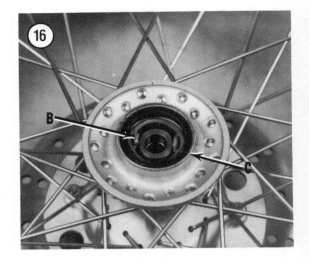

Assembly

1. On non-sealed bearings, pack the bearings with a good quality bearing grease. Work the grease in between the balls thoroughly; turn the bearing by hand a couple of times to make sure the grease is distributed evenly inside the bearing.

2. Blow any dirt or foreign matter out of the hub before installing the bearings.

> *CAUTION*
> *Install non-sealed bearings with the single sealed side facing outward. Tap the bearings squarely into place and tap on the outer race only. Use a socket (**Figure 18**) that matches the outer race diameter. Do not tap on the inner race or the bearing might be damaged. Be sure that the bearings are completely seated.*

3. Install the right-hand bearing and press the distance collar into place.

4. Install the left-hand bearing.

5. On disc brake models, install the brake disc and bolts. Tighten the bolts to the torque specification listed in **Table 1**.

6. Install the grease seal on the right-hand side.

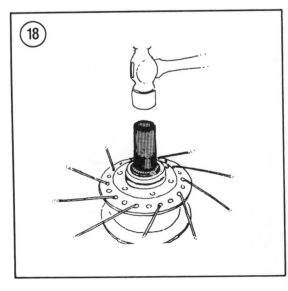

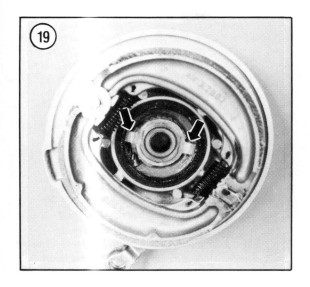

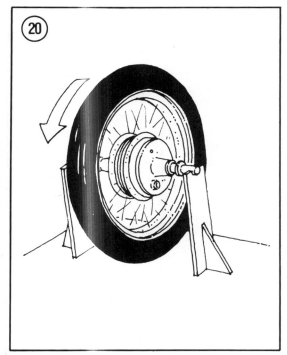

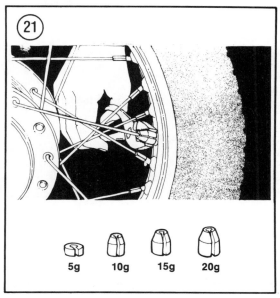

5g   10g   15g   20g

WHEELS

Wheel Balance

An unbalanced wheel is unsafe. Depending on the degree of unbalance and the speed of the motorcycle, the rider may experience anything from a mild vibration to a violent shimmy which may even result in loss of control.

On spoke wheels, the weights are attached to the spokes on the light side of the wheel.

Before you attempt to balance the wheel, check to be sure that the wheel bearings are in good condition and properly lubricated and that the brakes do not drag. The wheel must rotate freely.

> *NOTE*
> *When balancing the rear wheel do so with the final drive sprocket (or pulley) assembly attached, as it rotates with the rear wheel and affects the balance. The front brake panel does not rotate with the front wheel so it should be removed from the front wheel.*

1. Remove the wheel as described in this chapter or Chapter Nine.
2. Mount the wheel on a fixture such as the one shown in **Figure 20** so it can rotate freely.
3. Give the wheel a spin and let it coast to a stop. Mark the tire at the lowest point.
4. Spin the wheel several more times. If the wheel keeps coming to rest at the same point, it is out of balance.
5. Attach a weight to the upper (or light) side of the wheel at the spoke (**Figure 21**). Weights come

7A. On drum brake models, install the brake panel assembly into the brake drum. Align the tabs on the speedometer drive unit (**Figure 19**) with the notches in the front hub.

7B. On disc brake models, align the tangs of the speedometer drive gear with the drive dog in the hub and install the speedometer gear box.

8. Install the spacer on the right-hand side.

9. Install the front wheel as described in this chapter.

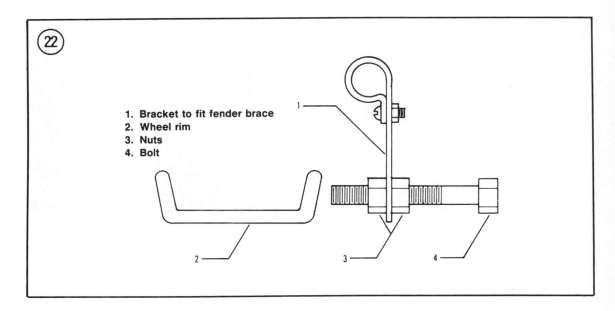

1. Bracket to fit fender brace
2. Wheel rim
3. Nuts
4. Bolt

in 4 sizes: 5, 10, 15 and 20 grams. They are crimped onto the spoke with ordinary gas pliers.

6. Experiment with different weights until the wheel, when spun, comes to rest at a different position each time.

Spoke Adjustment

Spokes loosen with use and should be checked periodically. If all appear to be loose, tighten all spokes on one side of the hub, then tighten all spokes on the other side of the hub. One half to one turn should be sufficient; do not overtighten.

After tightening the spokes; check rim runout to be sure you haven't pulled the rim out of shape.

One way to check rim runout is to mount a dial indicator onto the front fork so that it bears against one side of the rim.

If you don't have a dial indicator, improvise a device like the one shown in **Figure 22**. Adjust the position of the bolt until it just clears the rim. Rotate the wheel and note whether the clearance increases or decreases. Mark the tire with chalk or crayon at areas that produce significantly larger or smaller clearance. Clearance must not change by more than 2.0 mm (0.08 in.).

To pull the rim out, tighten the spokes which terminate on the same side of the hub and loosen spokes which terminate on the opposite side of the hub (**Figure 23**). In most cases, only a slight amount of adjustment is necessary to true a rim. After adjustment is complete, rotate the wheel and make sure another area has not been pulled out of true. Continue adjustment and checking until runout does not exceed 2.0 mm (0.08 in.).

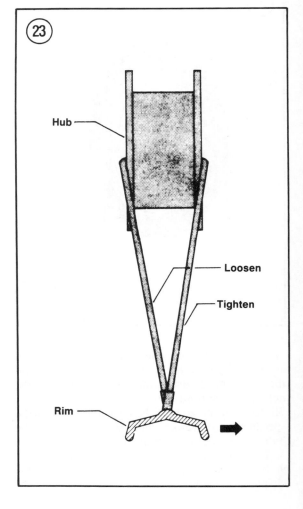

Hub

Loosen

Tighten

Rim

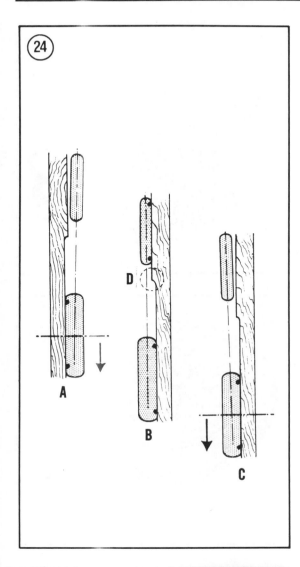

Wheel Alignment

Refer to **Figure 24** for this procedure.

1. Measure the tires at their widest point.

2. Subtract the small dimension from the larger dimension.

3. Make an alignment tool out of wood, approximately 7 feet long, with an offset equal to one-half of the dimension obtained in Step 2. Refer to (D).

4. If the wheels are not aligned as in (A) and (C), the rear wheel must be shifted to correct the alignment.

5. On models so equipped, remove the cotter pin.

6. Loosen the rear axle nut. Loosen the drive chain adjuster locknuts and turn the adjuster bolts or nuts (**Figure 25**) until the wheels align.   On belt drive models, screw the adjuster in or out until the wheels align.

> *NOTE*
> *After this procedure is completed, make sure the drive chain slack or drive belt tension is correct. Refer to Chapter Three.*

7. Tighten the adjuster locknuts and axle nut. Tighten the axle nut to the following torque specifications:
   a. Rebel 250: 50-70 N•m (36-50 ft.-lb.).
   b. All other models: 40-50 N•m (29-36 ft.-lb.).
   On models so equipped, install a new cotter pin and bend the ends over completely.

TIRE CHANGING

Removal

1. Remove the valve core to deflate the tire.

2. Press the entire bead on both sides of the tire into the center of the rim.

3. Lubricate the beads with soapy water.

> *NOTE*
> *Insert scraps of leather between the tire irons and the rim to protect the rim from damage.*

4. Insert the tire iron under the bead next to the valve (**Figure 26**). Force the bead on the opposite side of the tire into the center of the rim and pry the bead over the rim with the tire iron.

5. Insert a second tire iron next to the first to hold the bead over the rim. Then work around the tire with the first tire iron, prying the bead over the rim. Be careful not to pinch the inner tube with the tire irons.

6. Remove the valve from the hole in the rim and remove the inner tube from the tire.

NOTE
Step 7 is required only if it is necessary to completely remove the tire from the rim, as in tire replacement.

7. Stand the tire upright. Insert the tire iron between the second bead and the side of the rim that the first bead was pried over (**Figure 27**). Force the bead on the opposite side from the tire iron into the center of the rim. Pry the second bead off the rim, working around as with the first.

Installation

1. Carefully inspect the tire for any damage, especially inside.

2. A new tire may have balancing rubbers inside. These are not patches and should not be disturbed. A colored spot near the bead indicates a lighter point on the tire. This spot should be placed next to the valve stem or on models so equipped, midway betwen the 2 rim locks.

3. Check that the spoke ends not protrude through the nipples into the center of the rim. If they do they will puncture the inner tube. File off any protruding spoke ends.

4. Make sure the rubber rim tape is in place with the rough side toward the rim.

5. Install the tube valve core into the tube valve. Place the tube into the tire and inflate it just enough to round it out. Too much air will make installing the tire difficult and too little will increase the chances of pinching the tube with tire irons.

6. Lubricate both beads of the tire with soapy water. Pull the tube partly out of the tire at the valve. Squeeze the beads together to hold the tube and insert the valve into the hole in the rim (**Figure 28**). The lower bead should go into the center of the rim with the upper bead outide it.

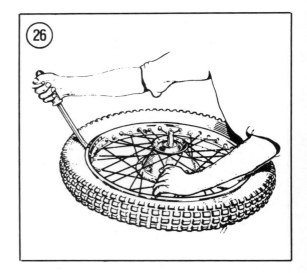

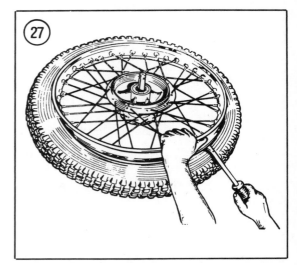

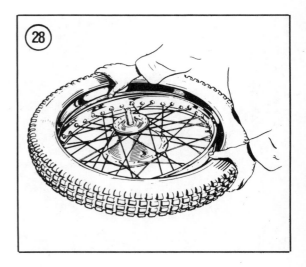

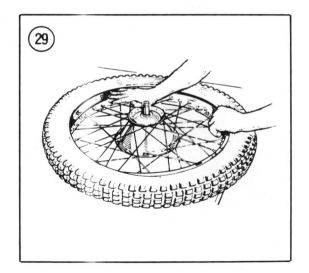

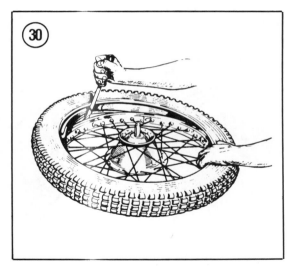

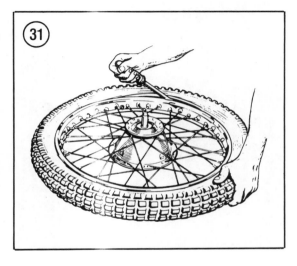

7. Place the lower bead of the tire into the center of the rim on each side of the valve stem. Work around the tire in both directions (**Figure 29**). Use a tire iron for the last few inches of bead (**Figure 30**).

8. Press the upper bead into the rim opposite the valve stem. Pry the bead into the rim on both sides of the initial point with a tire iron, working around the rim to the valve (**Figure 31**).

9. Wiggle the valve stem to be sure the tube is not trapped under the tire bead. Set the valve squarely in the rim hole before screwing on the valve stem nut.

10. Check the bead on both sides of the tire for even fit around the rim.

11. Bounce the wheel several times, rotating it each time. This will force the tire beads against the rim flanges. After the tire beads are in contact with the rim evenly, inflate the tire to seat the beads.

12. Inflate the tire to more than the recommended inflation pressure for the initial seating of the rim flanges. Once the beads are seated correctly, deflate the tire to the correct pressure described in Chapter Three.

13. Balance the wheel as described in this chapter.

TIRE REPAIRS

Patching an inner tube on the road is very difficult. A can of pressurized tire sealant may inflate the tire and seal the hole, although this is only a temporary fix.

Another solution is to carry a spare inner tube that could be installed and inflated.

If you do patch the inner tube, do not run for any length of time as the patch may rub off resulting in another flat. Install a new inner tube as soon as possible.

HANDLEBAR

Removal

1. Remove the right-hand side cover.
2. Disconnect the battery negative lead.
3. Remove the right-hand rear view mirror.
4. Disconnect the brake light switch electrical connector (A, **Figure 32**).

5. Remove the screws securing the right-hand handlebar switch assembly (B, **Figure 32**) and remove the electrical wires from the clips (C, **Figure 32**) on the handlebar.

> *CAUTION*
> *On disc brake models, cover the frame with a heavy cloth or plastic tarp to protect it from accidental spilling of brake fluid. Wash any spilled brake fluid off any painted or plated surface immediately, as it will destroy the finish. Use soapy water and rinse thoroughly.*

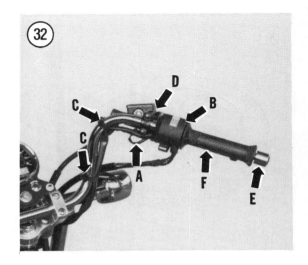

6. On disc brake models, remove the bolts (D, **Figure 32**) securing the brake master cylinder and lay it over the frame. Keep the reservoir in the upright position to minimize loss of brake fluid and to keep air from entering into the brake system. It is not necessary to remove the hydraulic brake line.

7. On models so equipped, remove the screw securing the grip end piece (E, **Figure 32**) and remove the end piece.

> *NOTE*
> *On drum brake models, the front brake lever is part of the throttle assembly and comes off as an assembly.*

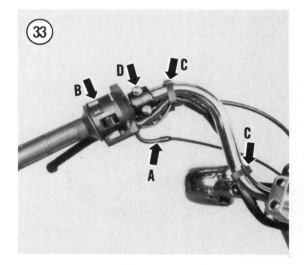

8. Remove the throttle assembly (F, **Figure 32**) and carefully lay the throttle assembly and cable(s) over the fender or back over the frame. Be careful that the cable(s) do not get crimped or damaged.

9. Remove the left-hand rear view mirror.

10. On models so equipped, disconnect the choke cable from the choke lever (A, **Figure 33**).

11. Remove the screws securing the left-hand handlebar switch assembly (B, **Figure 33**) and remove the electrical wires from the clips (C, **Figure 33**) on the handlebar.

12. Remove the bolts (D, **Figure 33**) securing the left-hand switch and clutch lever assembly and remove the assembly.

13. On models so equipped, remove the chrome caps from the Allen bolts.

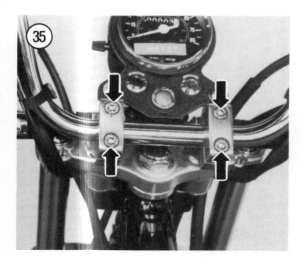

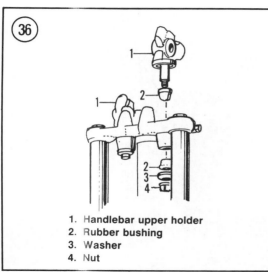

1. Handlebar upper holder
2. Rubber bushing
3. Washer
4. Nut

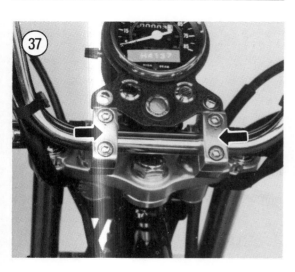

14. Remove the hex bolts (**Figure 34**) or Allen bolts (**Figure 35**) securing the handlebar upper holders in place. Remove the handlebar upper holders. Remove the handlebar.

15. To maintain a good grip on the handlebar and to prevent it from slipping down, clean the knurled section of the handlebar with a wire brush. It should be kept rough so it will be held securely by the holders. The holders should also be kept clean and free of any metal that may have been gouged loose by handlebar slippage.

Installation

> *NOTE*
> *On Rebel 250 models, if the handlebar lower holders were removed be sure to install the rubber bushings (**Figure 36**) when installing the handlebar lower holders onto the upper fork bridge.*

1. Position the handlebar on the upper fork bridge so the punch mark on the handlebar is aligned with the top surface of the handlebar lower holders or the raised portion of the upper fork bridge.

2. On models so marked, position the handlebar holder with the punch mark (**Figure 37**) toward the front. Install the handlebar holders and install the hex or Allen bolts. Tighten the forward bolts first and then the rear bolts. Tighten all bolts to the torque specification listed in **Table 1**.

3. After installation is complete, recheck the alignment of the handlebar punch mark.

4. Apply a light coat of multipurpose grease to the throttle grip area on the handlebar before installing the throttle grip assembly.

> *NOTE*
> *When installing all assemblies, align the punch mark on the handlebar with the slit on the mounting bracket (**Figure 38**).*

> *NOTE*
> *On models so equipped, align the locating pin on the right-hand switch assembly with the hole in the handlebar.*

5. Install the throttle grip assembly, the grip end piece (models so equipped) and the right-hand switch assembly.

6. On disc brake models, install the brake master cylinder onto the handlebar. Install the clamp with the UP arrow (**Figure 39**) facing up and align the clamp mating surface with the punch mark on the handlebar (**Figure 40**). Tighten the upper bolt first and then the lower bolt.

> *WARNING*
> *After installation is completed, make sure the brake lever does not come in contact with the throttle grip assembly when it is pulled on fully. On drum brake models, if it does, adjust the front brake as described in Chapter Three. On disc brake models, if it does, the brake fluid may be low in the reservoir; refill as necessary. Refer to **Front Disc Brakes** in Chapter Ten. Do not operate the motorcycle until this dangerous condition has been corrected.*

7. On models so equipped, attach the choke cable to the choke lever.

> *NOTE*
> *On models so equipped, align the locating pin on the left-hand switch assembly with the hole in the handlebar.*

8. Install the left-hand handlebar switch and clutch lever assembly. Install the clamp with the UP arrow (**Figure 41**) facing up and align the clamp mating surface with the punch mark on the handlebar. Tighten the upper bolt first and then the lower bolt.

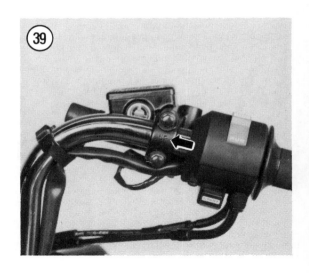

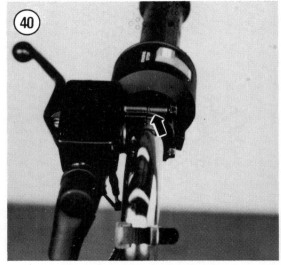

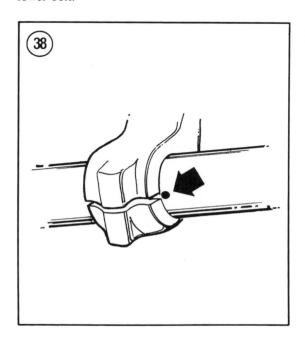

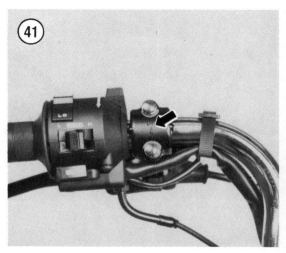

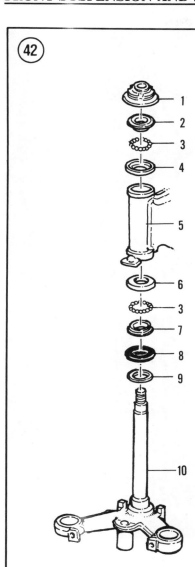

1. Adjust nut
2. Upper ball race
3. 21 steel balls
4. Upper ball race
5. Steering head
6. Bottom ball race
7. Lower ball race
8. Dust seal
9. Dust seal washer
10. Steering stem

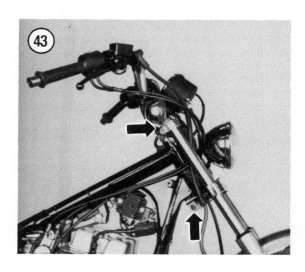

9. Connect the battery negative lead to the battery.

10. Install the right-hand side cover and rear view mirrors.

11. Adjust the throttle operation as described in Chapter Three.

STEERING HEAD AND STEM

Steering Stem
Disassembly

Refer to **Figure 42** for this procedure.

1. Remove the front wheel as described in this chapter.

2. Remove the handlebar assembly as described in this chapter.

3. Remove the headlight assembly as described in Chapter Seven.

4. Remove the bolts securing the headlight case and remove the case.

5. Remove the bolts securing the headlight/turn signal bracket assembly and remove the assembly.

6. Remove the bolts securing the front fender and remove the fender.

7. Loosen the upper and lower fork bridge bolts (**Figure 43**) and slide both fork tubes out.

NOTE
*On CM200T models, remove the plastic trim plate (**Figure 44**).*

8. Remove the steering stem nut and washer (**Figure 45**) and remove the upper fork bridge.

9. Remove the steering stem adjust nut. To loosen the adjust nut, use a large drift and hammer or use the easily improvised tool shown in **Figure 46**.

10. Have an assistant hold a large pan under the steering stem to catch any loose balls that may fall out while you carefully lower the steering stem (**Figure 47**).

11. Lower the steering stem assembly down and out of the steering head.

12. Remove the upper cone race.

13. Remove the ball bearings from the upper and lower race. There are 42 ball bearings total (21 in the upper race and 21 in the lower race).

Inspection

1. Clean the bearing races in the steering head and the bearings with solvent.

2. Check the welds around the steering head for cracks and fractures. If any are found, have them repaired by a competent frame shop or welding service.

3. Check the balls for pitting, scratches or discoloration indicating wear or corrosion. Replace them in sets if any are bad.

4. Check the upper and lower ball races for pitting, galling and corrosion. If any of these conditions exist, replace the races as described in this chapter.

5. Check the steering stem for cracks and check its races for damage or wear. If the race is damaged, the bearings should be replaced as a complete bearing set. Take the old races and bearings to your dealer to ensure accurate replacement.

Steering Head Bearing Races

The headset and steering stem bearing races are pressed into place. Because they are easily bent, do not remove them unless they are worn and require replacement.

Headset Bearing Race
Removal/Installation

NOTE
The top and bottom bearing races are the same size.

To remove the headset race, insert a hardwood stick or soft punch into the head tube (**Figure 48**)

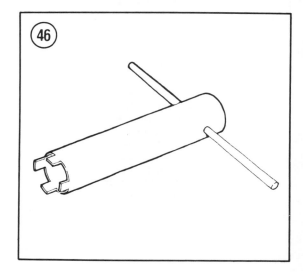

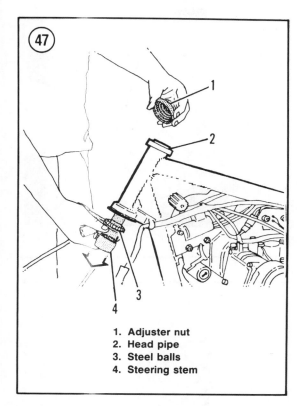

1. Adjuster nut
2. Head pipe
3. Steel balls
4. Steering stem

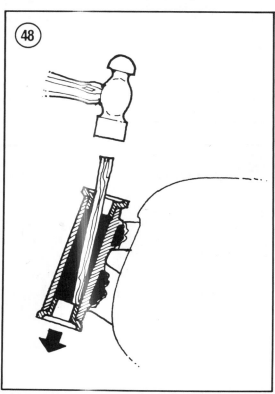

and carefully tap the race out from the inside. After it is started, tap around the race so that neither the race nor the head tube is damaged.

To install the headset race, tap it in slowly with a block of wood, a suitable size socket or piece of pipe (**Figure 49**). Make sure that the race is squarely seated in the headset race bore before tapping it into place. Tap the race in until it is flush with the steering head surface.

Steering Stem Bearing Race
and Grease Seal
Removal/Installation

Refer to **Figure 42** for this procedure.
1. To remove the steering stem race, try twisting and pulling it up by hand. If it will not come off, carefully pry it up with a screwdriver; work around in a circle, prying a little at a time.
2. Remove the lower bearing lower race, dust seal and dust seal washer.

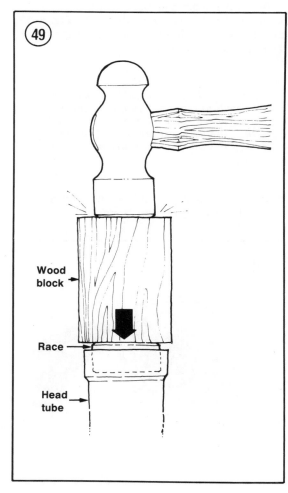

Wood block

Race

Head tube

8

3. Install the dust seal washer and dust seal. Slide the lower bearing lower race over the steering stem with the bearing surface pointing up.

4. Tap the lower race down with a piece of hardwood; work around in a circle so the race will not be bent. Make sure it is seated squarely and is all the way down.

Steering Stem Assembly

Refer to **Figure 42** for this procedure.

1. Make sure the steering head and stem races are properly seated.

2. Apply a coat of cold grease to the upper bearing race cone and fit 21 ball bearings around it (**Figure 50**).

3. Apply a coat of cold grease to the lower bearing race cone and fit 21 ball bearings around it (**Figure 51**).

4. Install the steering stem into the head tube and hold it firmly in place.

5. Install the upper ball race.

6. Install the steering stem adjust nut (**Figure 52**) and tighten it until it is snug against the upper race, then back it off 1/8 turn.

> *NOTE*
> *The adjusting nut should be just tight enough to remove both horizontal and vertical play, yet loose enough so that the assembly will turn to both lock positions under its own weight after an assist.*

7. Install the upper fork bridge and steering stem nut—only finger tight at this time.

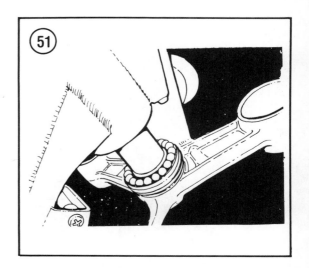

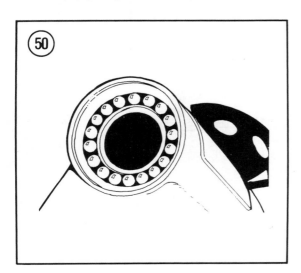

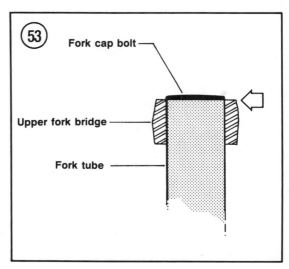

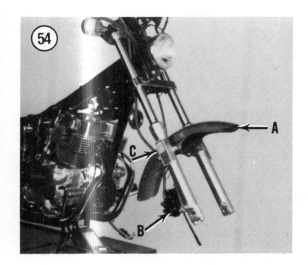

NOTE
Steps 8-10 must be performed in this order to assure proper upper and lower fork bridge-to-fork alignment.

8. Slide the fork tubes into position and tighten the lower fork bridge bolts to the torque specification listed in **Table 1**.

NOTE
*The top of the fork tube must be flush with the top of the upper fork bridge surface (**Figure 53**).*

9. Tighten the steering stem nut to the torque specification listed in **Table 1**.
10. Tighten .the upper fork bridge bolts to the torque specification listed in **Table 1**.
11. Continue assembly by reversing Steps 1-7, *Steering Stem Disassembly.*

Steering Stem Adjustment

If play develops in the steering system, it may only require adjustment. However, don't take a chance on it. Disassemble the stem and look for possible damage. Then reassemble and adjust as described in Step 6 of the *Steering Head Assembly* procedure.

FRONT FORK

The front suspension uses a spring controlled, hydraulically damped, telescopic fork. Before suspecting major trouble, drain the front fork oil and refill with the proper type and quantity; refer to Chapter Three. If you still have trouble, such as poor damping, a tendency to bottom or top out or leakage around the rubber seals, follow the service procedures in this section.

To simplify fork service and to prevent the mixing of parts, the fork legs should be removed, serviced and installed individually.

Removal/Installation

1. Remove the front wheel as described in this chapter.
2. Remove the bolts securing the front fender (A, **Figure 54**) and remove the fender.
3. Loosen, but do not remove, the fork top cap bolts (**Figure 55**).
4. On disc brake models, remove the brake caliper assembly (B, **Figure 54**) and brake hose (C, **Figure 54**) from the fork leg.
5. On CM200T models, remove the plastic trim panel (**Figure 56**).

CHAPTER EIGHT

6A. On Rebel 250 models, loosen the upper and lower fork bridge bolts (**Figure 57**).
6B. On all other models, loosen the upper and lower fork bridge bolts (**Figure 58**).
7. Remove the fork tube (**Figure 59**). It may be necessary to slightly rotate the fork tube while pulling it down and out.
8. Install by reversing these removal steps, noting the following.
9. The top of the fork tube must be flush with the top of the upper fork bridge surface (**Figure 53**).
10. Tighten the upper and lower fork bridge bolts to the torque specification listed in **Table 1**.
11. On disc brake models, install the brake caliper assembly as described in Chapter Ten.

Disassembly
(Rebel 250 Models)

Refer to **Figure 60** for this procedure.
1. Clamp the slider in a vise with soft jaws.
2. Loosen the Allen bolt on the bottom of the slider.

> *NOTE*
> *This screw has been secured with Loctite and is often very difficult to remove because the damper rod will turn inside the slider. It sometimes can be removed with an air impact driver. If you are unable to remove it, take the fork tube assemblies to a dealer and have the screws removed.*

3. Remove the Allen bolt and gasket from the slider.
4. Hold the upper fork tube in a vise with soft jaws and loosen the fork top cap bolt.

> *WARNING*
> *Be careful when removing the fork top cap bolt as the spring is under pressure. Protect your eyes accordingly.*

5. Remove the fork top cap bolt and fork spring from the fork tube.
6. Remove the fork from the vise, pour the fork oil out and discard it. Pump the fork several times by hand to expel most of the remaining oil.
7. Remove the dust seal from the slider.

> *NOTE*
> *On this type of fork, force is needed to remove the fork tube from the slider.*

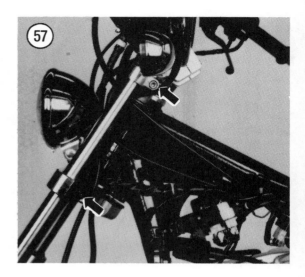

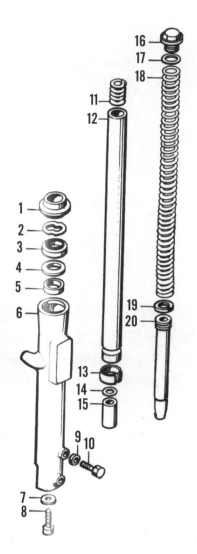

60 **FRONT FORK ASSEMBLY (REBEL 250 MODELS)**

1. Dust seal
2. Set ring
3. Oil seal
4. Backup ring
5. Fork tube bushing
6. Fork slider
7. Seal
8. Allen bolt
9. Seal
10. Drain screw
11. Rebound spring
12. Fork slider
13. Flork slider busing
14. Circlip
15. Oil lock piece
16. Fork cap bolt
17. O-ring
18. Spring
19. Piston ring
20. Damper rod

8. Remove the set ring.

9. Install the fork slider in a vise with soft jaws.

10. There is an interference fit between the bushing in the fork slider and the bushing on the fork tube. In order to remove the fork tube from the slider, pull hard on the fork tube using quick in-and-out strokes. Doing this will withdraw the bushing, backup ring and oil seal from the slider.

NOTE
It may be necessary to slightly heat the area on the slider around the oil seal prior to removal. Use a rag soaked in hot water; do not apply a flame directly to the fork slider.

11. Withdraw the fork tube from the slider.

NOTE
Do not remove the fork tube bushing unless it is going to be replaced. Inspect it as described in this chapter.

12. Remove the oil lock piece (**Figure 61**) and the circlip from the damper rod. Remove the damper rod.

13. Turn the fork tube upside down and slide off the oil seal, backup ring and slider bushing (**Figure 62**) from the fork tube.

NOTE
Do not discard the slider bushing at this time. It will be used during the installation procedure.

14. Inspect the components as described in this chapter.

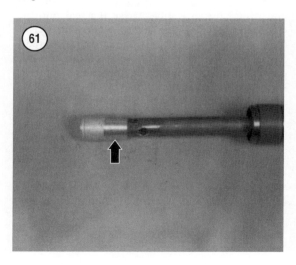

61

**Assembly
(Rebel 250 Models)**

1. Coat all parts with fresh DEXRON automatic transmission fluid or fork oil prior to installation.
2. If removed, install a new fork tube bushing (**Figure 63**).
3. Install the rebound spring onto the damper rod and insert this assembly into the fork tube (**Figure 64**).
4. Temporarily install the fork spring and fork top cap bolt to hold the damper rod in place.
5. Install the circlip and oil lock piece onto the damper rod (**Figure 61**).
6. Install the upper fork assembly into the slider (**Figure 65**).
7. Make sure the gasket (**Figure 66**) is on the Allen head screw.
8. Apply Loctite Lock N' Seal to the threads of the Allen bolt before installation. Install it in the fork slider and tighten to the torque specification listed in **Table 1**.
9. Slide the fork slider bushing down the fork tube and rest it on the slider.
10. Slide the fork slider backup ring (flange side up) down the fork tube and rest it on top of the fork slider bushing.
11. Place the old fork slider bushing on top of the backup ring. Drive the bushing into the fork slider with Honda special tool Fork Seal Driver (part No. 07747-0010100) and attachment (part No. 07747-0010500). Drive the bushing into place until it seats completely in the recess in the slider. Remove the installation tool and the old fork slider bushing.
12. Coat the new seal with ATF (automatic transmission fluid). Position the seal with the marking facing upward (**Figure 67**) and slide it down onto the fork tube. Drive the seal into the slider with Honda special tool Fork Seal Driver (part No. 07747-0010100) and attachment (part No. 07747-0010500). Drive the oil seal in until the groove in the slider can be seen above the top surface of the oil seal.
13. Install the circlip with the sharp side facing up. Make sure the circlip is completely seated in the groove in the fork slider.
14. Install the dust seal into the slider.
15. Remove the fork top cap bolt and the fork spring.
16. Fill the fork tube with the correct quantity of DEXRON automatic transmission fluid or fork oil. Refer to Chapter Three.
17. Install the fork spring with the closer wound coils toward the bottom of the fork tube.

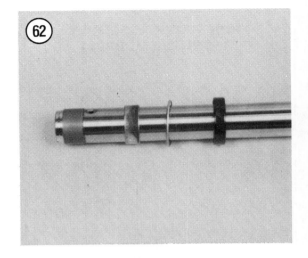

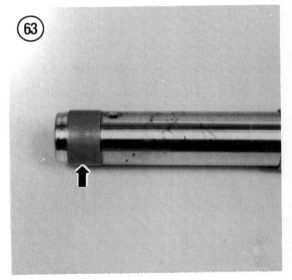

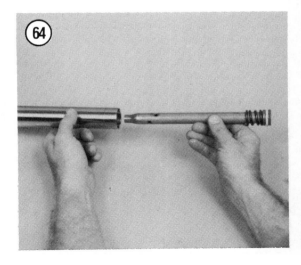

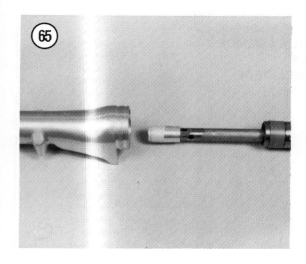

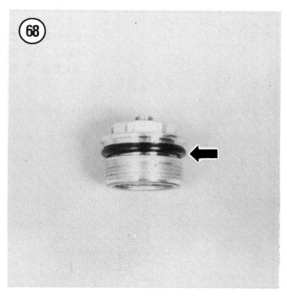

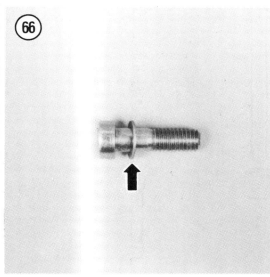

18. Inspect the O-ring seal (**Figure 68**) on the fork top cap bolt; replace if necessary.

19. Install the fork top cap bolt while pushing down on the spring. Start the bolt slowly; don't cross-thread it.

20. Place the slider in a vise with soft jaws and tighten the top fork cap bolt to the torque specification listed in **Table 1**.

21. Repeat this procedure for the other fork assembly.

22. Install the fork assemblies as described in this chapter.

Disassembly
(All Models Except Rebel 250)

Refer to **Figure 69** for this procedure.

1. Clamp the slider in a vise with soft jaws.

2. Loosen the Allen bolt on the bottom of the slider.

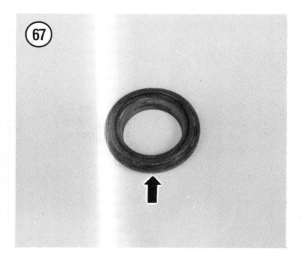

> *NOTE*
> *This screw has been secured with Loctite and is often very difficult to remove because the damper rod will turn inside the slider. It sometimes can be removed with an air impact driver. If you are unable to remove it, take the fork tubes to a dealer and have the screws removed.*

3. Remove the Allen bolt and gasket from the slider.

**FRONT FORK ASSEMBLY
(ALL MODELS
EXCEPT REBEL 250)**

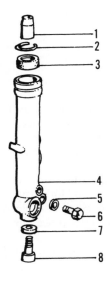

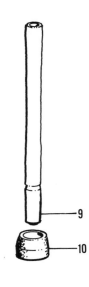

1. Oil lock piece
2. Set ring
3. Oil seal
4. Slider

5. Seal
6. Drain screw
7. Seal
8. Allen bolt

9. Fork tube
10. Dust seal
11. Fork cap bolt
12. O-ring seal

13. Fork spring
14. Piston ring
15. Damper rod

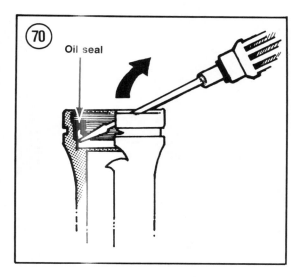

Oil seal

4. Hold the upper fork tube in a vise with soft jaws and loosen the fork top cap bolt.

WARNING
Be careful when removing the fork top cap bolt as the spring is under pressure. Protect your eyes accordingly.

5. Remove the fork top cap bolt and fork spring from the fork tube.
6. Remove the fork from the vise, pour the fork oil out and discard it. Pump the fork several times by hand to expel most of the remaining oil.
7. Remove the dust seal from the slider.
8. Pull the fork tube out of the slider.

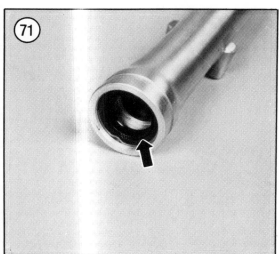

NOTE
It may be necessary to slightly heat the area on the slider around the oil seal before removal. Use a rag soaked in hot water; do not apply a flame directly to the fork slider.

9. If oil has been leaking from the top of the slider, remove the set ring from the top of the slider and remove the oil seal. Use a dull screwdriver blade and remove the oil seal (**Figure 70**). Do not damage the outer or inner surface of the slider.
10. Inspect the components as described in this chapter.

Assembly
(All Models Except Rebel 250)

1. Coat all parts with fresh DEXRON automatic transmission fluid or fork oil before installation.
2. If removed, install the oil seal and set ring (**Figure 71**). Coat all parts with fresh fork oil prior to installation. Drive the seal into the slider (**Figure 72**) with Honda special tool No. 07747-0010100 (fork seal driver body) and No. 07747-0010400 (driver attachment C), or suitable size socket. Drive the seal in until the set ring groove appears.
3. Install the damper rod into the fork tube (**Figure 73**).
4. Temporarily install the fork spring and fork top cap bolt to hold the damper rod in place.
5. Install the oil lock piece onto the damper rod (**Figure 74**).
6. Install the upper fork assembly into the slider (**Figure 75**).

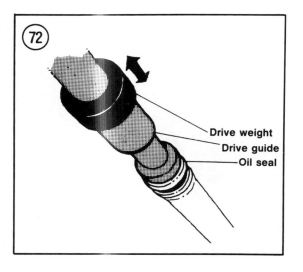

Drive weight
Drive guide
Oil seal

8

7. Make sure the gasket (**Figure 76**) is on the Allen head screw.

8. Apply Loctite Lock N' Seal to the threads of the Allen bolt prior to installation. Install it in the fork slider and tighten to the torque specification listed in **Table 1**.

9. Install the rubber boot into place on the slider (**Figure 77**).

10. Remove the fork top cap bolt and the fork spring.

11. Fill the fork tube with the correct quantity of DEXRON automatic transmission fluid or fork oil. Refer to Chapter Three.

12. Install the fork spring with the closer wound coils toward the top of the fork tube (**Figure 78**).

13. Inspect the O-ring seal on the fork top cap bolt; replace if necessary.

14. Make sure the O-ring seal (A, **Figure 79**) is in place on the fork top cap bolt.

15. Install the fork top cap bolt (B, **Figure 79**) while pushing down on the spring. Start the bolt slowly; don't cross-thread it.

16. Place the slider in a vise with soft jaws and tighten the top fork cap bolt to the torque specification listed in **Table 1**.

17. Repeat this procedure for the other fork assembly.

18. Install the fork assemblies as described in this chapter.

Inspection
(All Models)

1. Thoroughly clean all parts in solvent and dry them. Check the fork tube for signs of wear or scratches.

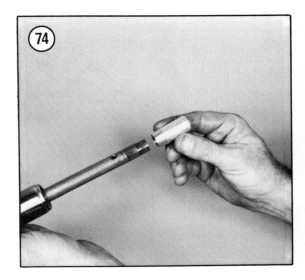

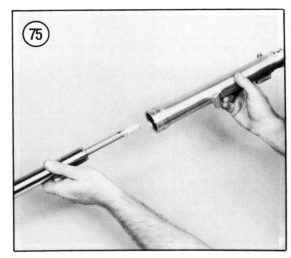

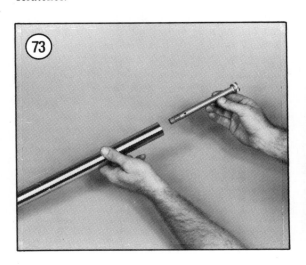

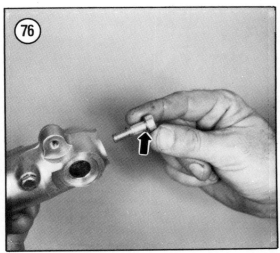

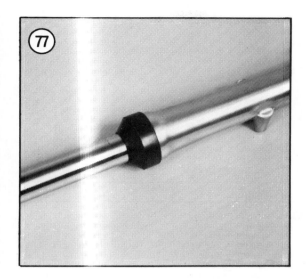

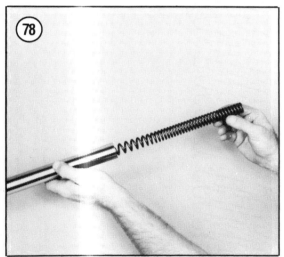

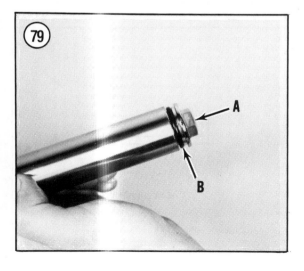

2. Check the damper rod for straightness. **Figure 80** shows one method. The rod should be replaced if the runout is 0.2 mm (0.008 in.) or greater.

3. Carefully check the damper rod and piston ring for wear or damage (**Figure 81**).

4. Check the upper fork tube for straightness. If bent or severely scratched, it should be replaced.

5. Check the lower slider for dents or exterior damage that may cause the upper fork tube to hang up during riding. Replace if necessary.

6. Measure the uncompressed length of the fork spring (not rebound spring) as shown in **Figure 82**. If the spring has sagged to the following dimension the spring must be replaced:
    a. Rebel 250: 535 mm (21.2 in.).
    b. All other models: 495 mm (19.5 in.).

8

7. On Rebel 250 models, inspect the slider and fork tube bushings. If either is scratched or scored they must be replaced. If the Teflon coating is worn off so that the copper base material is showing on approximately 3/4 of the total surface, the bushing must be replaced. Also check for distortion on the check points of the backup ring; replace as necessary. Refer to **Figure 83**.

8. Any parts that are worn or damaged should be replaced. Simply cleaning and reinstalling unserviceable components will not improve performance of the front suspension.

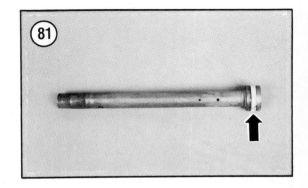

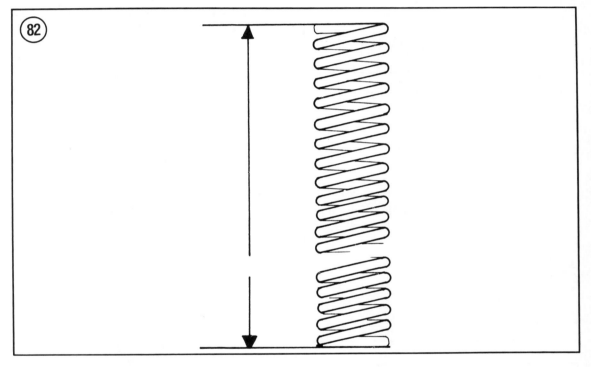

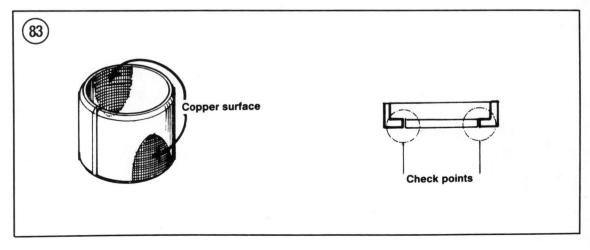

Copper surface

Check points

Table 1 FRONT SUSPENSION TORQUE SPECIFICATIONS

Item	N•m	ft.-lb.
Front axle nut		
185 models	40-50	29-36
200 models	50-70	36-50
Front axle		
250 models	55-70	40-51
Front axle holder nuts	18-25	13-18
Disc brakes		
Caliper mounting bolts	24-30	17-22
Caliper pad pin bolt	15-20	10-14
Brake system union bolts	25-35	18-22
Brake disc bolts	37-43	27-31
Handlebar holder bolts		
1978-1983	25-30	14-18
1985-on	20-30	14-22
Fork bridge bolts		
Upper		
1978-1983	25-30	18-21
1985-on	9-13	6.5-9.4
Lower		
1978-1983	18-23	13-17
1985-on	30-40	22-29
Fork cap bolt		
1978-1983	25-30	18-21
1985-on	15-30	11-22
Front fork Allen bolt	15-25	11-18
Steering stem nut		
1978-1983	60-70	44-51
1985-on	60-90	44-66

8

CHAPTER NINE

REAR SUSPENSION

This chapter includes repair and replacement procedures for the rear wheel and rear suspension components.

Refer to **Table 1** at the end of the chapter for rear suspension torque specifications.

REAR WHEEL

Removal/Installation
(Chain-driven Models)

1. Place block(s) under the engine so that the rear wheel clears the ground.
2. Remove the rear brake light switch return spring (**Figure 1**) from the brake pedal.
3. Completely unscrew the rear brake adjusting nut (**Figure 2**).
4. Depress the brake pedal and remove the brake rod from the pivot joint in the brake arm. Install the pivot joint and the adjusting nut onto the brake rod to avoid misplacing them.
5. Remove the cotter pin, nut, washer and rubber washer from the rear brake torque link (**Figure 3**). Install the rubber washer, washer and nut on the bolt in the torque link to avoid misplacing them.
6. On models so equipped, remove the cotter pin from the rear axle nut. Discard the cotter pin—never reuse a cotter pin as it may break and fall out.

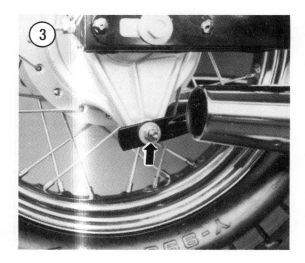

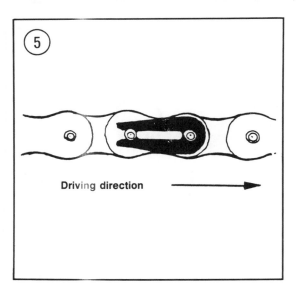

Driving direction ⟶

7. Loosen the rear axle nut (A, **Figure 4**).
8. Loosen the drive chain adjuster locknuts (B, **Figure 4**).
9. Loosen both drive chain adjusting bolts or nuts (C, **Figure 4**).
10. Push the rear wheel forward until the drive chain is loose.
11. Remove the rear axle nut and withdraw the rear axle from the right-hand side.
12. Slip the drive chain off the driven sprocket; pull the wheel to the rear and off the swing arm.
13. Install by reversing these removal steps, noting the following.
14. Make sure both drive chain adjusters are installed on the swing arm and that they are positioned with the alignment notches toward the top.
15. Install the rear axle into the right-hand side—first through the right-hand chain adjuster and spacer, next through the wheel hub, then through the left-hand chain adjuster.
16. Make sure the return spring is installed on the brake rod and reinstall the brake rod in the pivot joint. Install the adjusting nut.
17. If the drive chain master link was removed, install a new clip on the master link and install it so that the closed end of the clip is facing the direction of chain travel (**Figure 5**).
18. Tighten the rear axle nut to the torque specification listed in **Table 1**.
19. On models so equipped, install a new cotter pin and bend the ends over completely.
20. After the wheel is installed, completely rotate it and apply the brake several times to make sure it rotates freely and that the brakes work properly.
21. Adjust the rear brake free play and the drive chain as described in Chapter Three.

Removal/Installation (Belt-driven Models)

1. Place block(s) under the engine so that the rear wheel clears the ground.
2. Completely unscrew the rear brake adjusting nut.
3. Depress the brake pedal and remove the brake rod from the pivot joint in the brake arm. Install the pivot joint and the adjusting nut onto the brake rod to avoid misplacing them.
4. Remove the cotter pin, nut, washer and rubber washer from the rear brake torque link. Install the rubber washer, washer and nut onto the bolt on the torque link to avoid misplacing them.

5. Remove the upper and lower nut, lockwasher and washer securing the left-hand shock absorber and remove the shock absorber from the frame and swing arm.

6. Remove the bolts securing the drive belt cover and remove the cover.

7. Loosen the drive belt adjuster locknuts and both drive belt adjusting bolts at the rear axle.

8. Loosen the rear axle nut.

9. Push the rear wheel forward until the drive belt is loose.

10. Remove the rear axle nut and withdraw the rear axle from the right-hand side.

11. Slip the drive belt off the driven pulley; pull the wheel to the rear and off the swing arm.

12. Install by reversing these removal steps, noting the following.

13. Make sure both drive belt adjusters are installed on the swing arm and that they are positioned with the alignment notches toward the top.

14. Install the rear axle into the right-hand side—first through the right-hand belt adjuster and spacer, next through the wheel hub, then through the left-hand belt adjuster.

15. Make sure the return spring is installed on the brake rod and reinstall the brake rod in the pivot joint. Install the adjusting nut.

16. Tighten the rear axle nut to the torque specification listed in **Table 1**.

17. After the wheel is installed, completely rotate it and apply the brake several times to make sure it rotates freely and that the brakes work properly.

18. Adjust the rear brake free play and the drive belt as described in Chapter Three.

Inspection

Measure the radial and axial runout of the wheel rim with a dial indicator as shown in **Figure 6**. The maximum permissible limit for both is 2.0 mm (0.08 in.).

Tighten or replace any bent or loose spokes. Refer to *Spoke Adjustment* in Chapter Eight.

Check axle runout as described under *Rear Hub Inspection* in this chapter.

REAR HUB

Inspection

Inspect each wheel bearing prior to removing it from the wheel hub.

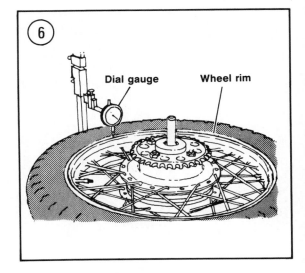

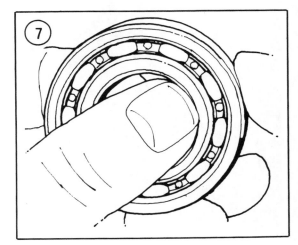

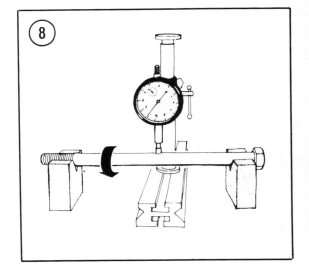

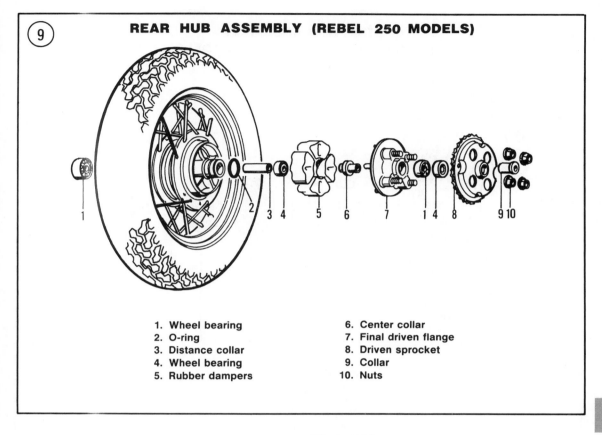

REAR HUB ASSEMBLY (REBEL 250 MODELS)

1. Wheel bearing
2. O-ring
3. Distance collar
4. Wheel bearing
5. Rubber dampers
6. Center collar
7. Final driven flange
8. Driven sprocket
9. Collar
10. Nuts

CAUTION
Do not remove the wheel bearings for inspection as they will be damaged during removal. Remove wheel bearings only if they are to be replaced.

1. Perform Step 1 and Step 2 of *Disassembly* in this chapter.
2. Turn each bearing by hand (**Figure 7**). Make sure the bearings turn smoothly.
3. On non-sealed bearings, check the balls for evidence of wear, pitting or excessive heat (bluish tint). Replace the bearings if necessary; always replace as a complete set. When replacing the bearings, be sure to take your old bearings along to ensure a perfect matchup.

NOTE
Fully sealed bearings are available from many bearing specialty shops. Fully sealed bearings provide better protection from dirt and moisture that may get into the hub.

4. Check the axle for wear and straightness. Use V-blocks and a dial indicator as shown in **Figure 8**. If the runout is 0.2 mm (0.008 in.) or greater, the axle should be replaced.

Disassembly

Refer to **Figure 9** for Rebel 250 models or **Figure 10** for all other models for this procedure.
1. Remove the rear wheel as described in this chapter.
2A. On Rebel 250 models, remove the final driven sprocket as described in this chapter. The final driven sprocket must be removed to gain access to the left-hand bearing.
2B. On all other models, if necessary, remove the final driven sprocket or driven pulley as described in this chapter.
3. Before proceeding further, inspect the wheel bearings as described in this chapter. If they must be replaced, proceed as follows.
4. Remove the spacer and grease seal (**Figure 11**) from the left-hand side.
5A. A special Honda tool set-up can be used to remove the wheel bearings as follows:
   a. Install the 15 mm bearing remover head (Honda part No. 07746-0050400) into the right-hand bearing (**Figure 12**).
   b. Turn the wheel over (left-hand side up) on the workbench so the end of the bearing remover is touching the workbench surface.

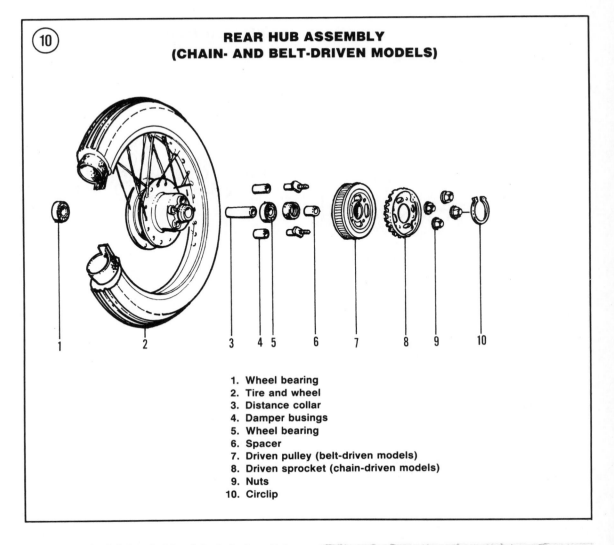

**REAR HUB ASSEMBLY
(CHAIN- AND BELT-DRIVEN MODELS)**

1. Wheel bearing
2. Tire and wheel
3. Distance collar
4. Damper busings
5. Wheel bearing
6. Spacer
7. Driven pulley (belt-driven models)
8. Driven sprocket (chain-driven models)
9. Nuts
10. Circlip

c. From the left-hand side of the hub, install the bearing remover shaft (Honda part No. 07746-050100) into the bearing remover. Using a hammer, tap the expander into the bearing remover with a hammer.

d. Stand the wheel up to a vertical position.

e. Tap on the end of the expander and drive the right-hand bearing out of the hub. Remove the bearing and the distance collar.

f. Repeat for the left-hand bearing.

5B. If special tools are not used, perform the following:

a. To remove the right- and left-hand bearings and distance collar, insert a soft aluminum or brass drift into one side of the hub.

b. Push the distance collar over to one side and place the drift on the inner race of the lower bearing.

c. Tap the bearing out of the hub with a hammer, working around the perimeter of the inner race.

d. Repeat for the other bearing.

6. Clean the inside and the outside of the hub with solvent. Dry with compressed air.

Assembly

1. On non-sealed bearings, pack the bearings with a good quality bearing grease. Work the grease in between the balls thoroughly; turn the bearing by hand a couple of times to make sure the grease is distributed evenly inside the bearing.

2. Blow any dirt or foreign matter out of the hub before installing the bearings.

3. Pack the hub with multipurpose grease.

4. Press the distance collar into the hub from the left-hand side.

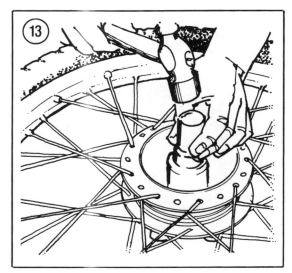

CAUTION
Install the standard bearings (they are sealed on one side only) with the sealed side facing out. Tap the bearings squarely into place and tap only on the outer race. Use a socket (Figure 13) that matches the outer race diameter. Do not tap on the inner race or the bearing will be damaged. Be sure to tap the bearings in until they seat completely.

5. Install the left-hand bearing into the hub.

6. Install the right-hand bearing into the hub.

7A. On Rebel 250 models, install the final driven sprocket as described in this chapter.

7B. On all other models, if removed, install the final driven sprocket or driven pulley as described in this chapter.

8. Install the rear wheel as described in this chapter.

FINAL DRIVEN SPROCKET AND FLANGE (REBEL 250)

Removal/Disassembly

Refer to **Figure 9** for this procedure.

1. If the driven sprocket is going to be removed from the final driven flange, loosen the nuts (**Figure 14**) securing the driven sprocket.

2. Remove the rear wheel as described in this chapter.

3. Remove the side collar from the driven sprocket.

4. Stand the wheel upright.

5. Insert the wooden handle of a hammer through the spokes from the right-hand side and place the handle against the back side of the driven sprocket teeth.

6. Carefully tap around the perimeter of the driven sprocket with the hammer handle evenly and disengage the final driven sprocket and final driven flange from the wheel hub.

7. If necessary, remove the rubber dampers and O-ring seal from the wheel hub.

8. Remove the center collar from the back side of the final driven flange.

9. Remove the oil seal from the final driven flange.

10. If bearing removal is necessary, perform the following:

   a. Set the final driven flange assembly with the sprocket side down on the workbench.

   b. Insert a soft aluminum or brass drift into the final driven flange side of the assembly.

   c. Tap the bearing out of the final driven flange with a hammer, working around the perimeter of the inner race.

11. Clean the inside and the outside of the flange with solvent. Dry with compressed air.

12. To remove the driven sprocket from the final driven flange, perform the following:

   a. Remove the nuts (loosened in Step 1) securing the driven sprocket.

   b. Remove the driven sprocket from the driven flange.

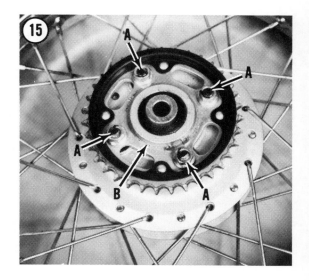

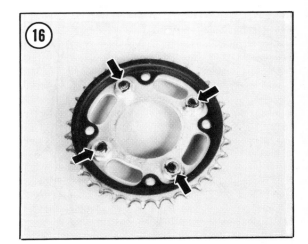

Assembly/Installation

1. If removed, install the driven sprocket onto the final driven flange, as follows:

   a. Install the driven sprocket into the final driven flange.

   b. Install the nuts securing the driven sprocket, do not tighten at this time.

2. To install the bearing, perform the following:

   a. Set the final driven flange assembly with the final driven flange side down on the workbench.

   b. Tap the bearing squarely into place and tap only on the outer race. Use a socket that matches the outer race diameter. Do not tap on the inner race or the bearing will be damaged. Be sure to tap the bearing until it seats completely.

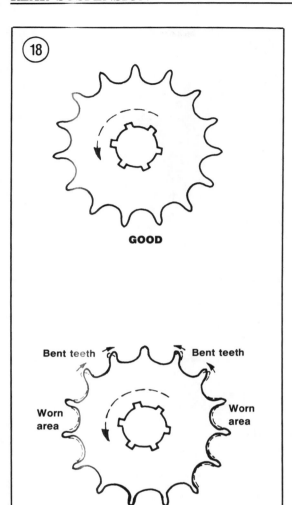

GOOD

Bent teeth   Bent teeth

Worn
area   Worn
area

WORN

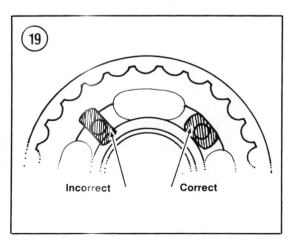

Incorrect   Correct

3. Install the oil seal into the final driven flange.
4. Install the center collar into the backside of the final driven flange.
5. Inspect the rubber dampers, replace as a set if any are starting to deteriorate or are damaged. Install the rubber dampers and O-ring seal into the wheel hub.
6. Install the final driven sprocket and final driven flange into the wheel hub. Make sure it is completely seated in the wheel hub. Tap around the perimeter with a soft faced mallet.
7. Install the side collar into the driven sprocket.
8. If removed, tighten the nuts securing the driven sprocket to the torque specification listed in **Table 1**.

FINAL DRIVEN SPROCKET (CM185T, CM200T AND 1982 CM250C)

Removal

Refer to **Figure 7** for this procedure.

1. Remove the rear wheel as described in this chapter.
2. Loosen the nuts (A, **Figure 15**) and the large circlip (B, **Figure 15**) securing the sprocket to the rear hub.
3. Pull the sprocket assembly up and out of the rear hub.
4. If necessary, remove the nuts (**Figure 16**) from the fixing bolts and remove the fixing bolts from the sprocket.
5. Remove the sprocket assembly from the rear hub.

Inspection

1. Inspect the rubber dampers (**Figure 17**). Replace as a set if any are starting to deteriorate or are damaged.
2. Inspect the teeth on the sprocket (**Figure 16**). If the teeth are visibly worn (**Figure 18**), replace the sprocket.
3. If the sprocket requires replacement, the drive chain is probably also worn and must be replaced as described in this chapter.

Installation

1. If the fixing bolts were removed, install them correctly into the groove in the backside of the sprocket. Refer to **Figure 19** and **Figure 20**. Install the nuts and tighten only finger-tight at this time.

2. Apply multipurpose grease to the left-hand side of the hub where the sprocket goes and to the inside surface of the sprocket.

3. Install the sprocket into the rear hub; carefully guide the fixing bolts into the damper rubber in the rear hub. Push the sprocket all the way until it seats.

4. Install the large circlip with the chamfered side toward the sprocket (**Figure 21**).

5. Tighten the nuts securing the sprocket to the torque specification listed in **Table 1**.

6. Install the rear wheel as described in this chapter.

DRIVE PULLEY, FINAL DRIVEN PULLEY, AND DRIVE BELT (1983 CM250C)

Drive Pulley
Removal/Installation

1. Place block(s) under the engine so that the rear wheel clears the ground.

2. Shift the transmission into 1st gear.

3. Remove the bolts securing the left-hand foot peg and remove the foot peg assembly.

4. Remove the clamping bolt securing the gearshift lever and remove the gearshift lever.

5. Remove the bolts securing the drive pulley cover and remove the cover.

6. Have an assistant hold the rear brake on and loosen the bolts (**Figure 22**) securing the drive pulley retaining plate (**Figure 22**).

7. Completely unscrew the rear brake adjusting nut.

8. Depress the brake pedal and remove the brake rod from the pivot joint in the brake arm. Install the pivot joint and the adjusting nut onto the brake rod to avoid misplacing them.

9. Remove the cotter pin, nut, washer and rubber washer from the rear brake torque link. Install the rubber washer, washer and nut onto the bolt in the torque link to avoid misplacing them.

10. Loosen the drive belt adjuster locknuts and both drive belt adjusting bolts at the rear wheel.

11. Loosen the rear axle nut.

12. Push the rear wheel forward until the drive belt is loose.

13. Remove the drive pulley bolts and retaining plate.

14. Remove the drive pulley from drive pulley and the transmission shaft.

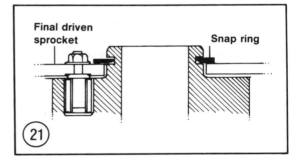

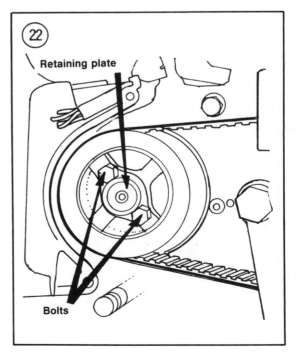

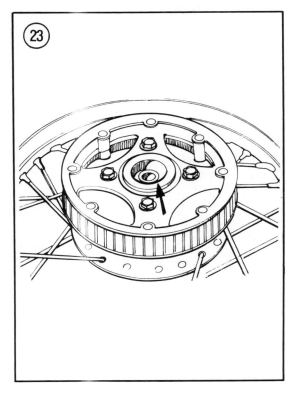

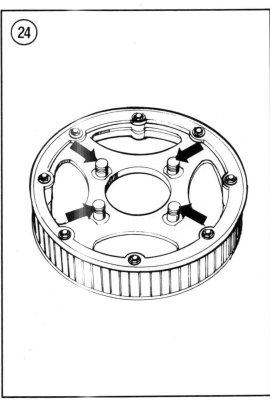

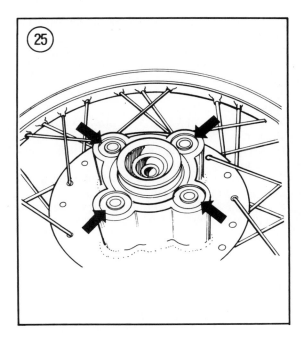

15. Inspect the drive pulley as described in this chapter.

16. Install by reversing these removal steps, noting the following.

17. Tighten the drive pulley bolts securely.

18. Adjust the rear brake and the drive belt as described in Chapter Three.

Driven Pulley
Removal/Installation

1. Remove the rear wheel as described in this chapter.

2. Remove the circlip securing the driven pulley to the rear hub (**Figure 23**).

3. Pull the driven pulley straight up and off the rear hub.

4. Inspect the driven pulley as described in this chapter.

5. Install by reversing these removal steps, noting the following.

6. Apply a light coat of grease to the driven pulley hub studs and the inside diameter of the driven pulley (**Figure 24**).

7. Do not apply any grease to the rubber dampers in the rear hub (**Figure 25**).

8. Make sure the circlip is seated correctly in the rear hub groove.

Drive Belt
Removal/Installation

1. Remove the rear wheel as described in this chapter.

2. Remove the bolts (A, **Figure 26**) securing the muffler and the rear footpeg.

3. Remove the swing arm pivot bolt (B, **Figure 26**) and remove the swing arm as described in this chapter.

4. Remove the drive belt from the frame and swing arm.

5. Inspect the drive belt as described in this chapter.

6. Install by reversing these removal steps, noting the following.

7. Be sure to install the drive belt onto the swing arm prior to installing the swing arm.

8. Tighten the swing arm pivot bolt to the torque specification listed in **Table 1**.

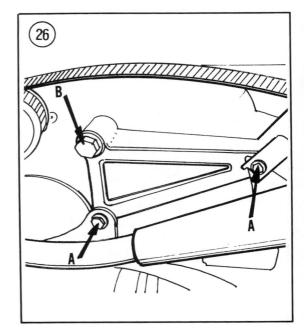

Inspection

> *CAUTION*
> *Do not use steam, kerosene or any other type of petroleum-based solvent to clean the drive belt as the belt will be damaged and must be replaced.*

1. If the belt is dirty, clean only with water and a clean cloth. Thoroughly dry with clean cloths.

2. Inspect the belt for wear or deterioration. Replace the belt if it is cracked or if there are 20 places or more where the reinforcement fabric is visible (**Figure 27**).

3. Inspect the drive and driven pulleys for wear or damage. Check for worn or damaged teeth on each pulley (**Figure 28**).

4. If either the drive pulley or driven pulley requires replacement, replace both pulleys and the drive belt as a set.

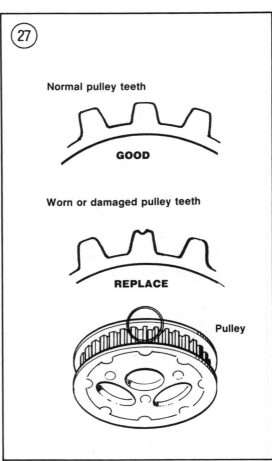

DRIVE CHAIN

Removal/Installation

1. Place wood block(s) under the engine or frame so the rear wheel clears the ground.

2. Remove the gearshift lever (A, **Figure 29**) and screws securing the rear left-hand crankcase cover (B, **Figure 29**). Remove the rear left-hand crankcase cover.

3. Remove the clip from the master link (**Figure 30**) and remove the master link.

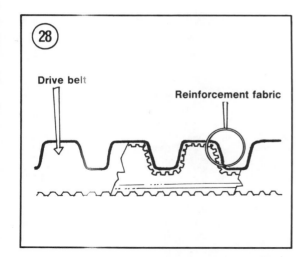

Drive belt

Reinforcement fabric

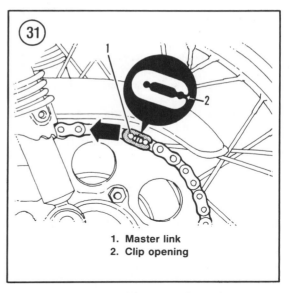

1. Master link
2. Clip opening

4. Remove the drive chain from the drive and driven sprockets.

5. For service and inspection of the drive chain, refer to *Drive Chain Cleaning, Inspection and Lubrication* in Chapter Three.

6. Install by reversing these removal steps, noting the following.

7. Install the master link clip with the closed end facing the direction of chain travel (**Figure 31**).

8. Adjust the drive chain as described in Chapter Three.

Drive Chain Slider
Inspection (Rebel 250)

Inspect the drive chain slider (**Figure 32**) on the left-hand side of the swing arm for wear or damage.

Honda does not provide a service limit dimension for replacement. If a groove is worn 1/3 of the way through the slider, replace the slider.

If replacement is necessary, perform the following:

a. Remove the swing arm as described in this chapter.

b. Remove the screws securing the slider to the swing arm and remove the slider.

c. Install a new slider and reinstall the swing arm.

SWING ARM

Under normal use and with correct periodic lubrication, the swing arm bushings will have a long service life. However, in time the bushings will wear and must be replaced. Common symptoms of excessive bushing wear are wheel hop, pulling to one side under acceleration and pulling to the other side during braking.

Removal/Installation

1. Remove the exhaust system (A, **Figure 33**) as described in Chapter Six.
2. Remove the rear wheel (B, **Figure 33**) as described in this chapter.
3. Remove both shock absorber lower mounting nuts, lockwashers and nuts (C, **Figure 33**) and move the shock absorbers up and out of the way.

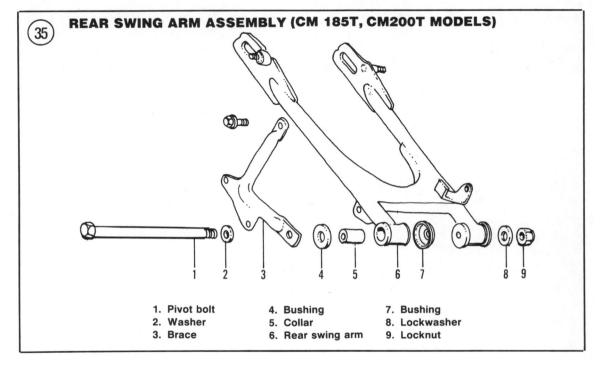

REAR SWING ARM ASSEMBLY (CM 185T, CM200T MODELS)

1. Pivot bolt
2. Washer
3. Brace
4. Bushing
5. Collar
6. Rear swing arm
7. Bushing
8. Lockwasher
9. Locknut

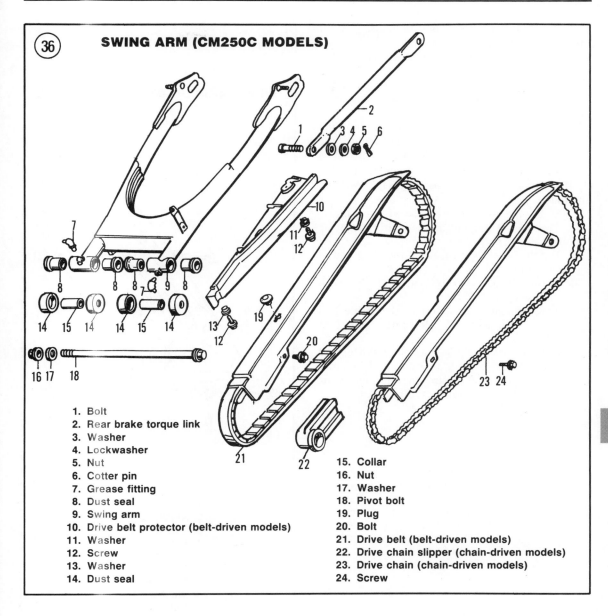

SWING ARM (CM250C MODELS)

1. Bolt
2. Rear brake torque link
3. Washer
4. Lockwasher
5. Nut
6. Cotter pin
7. Grease fitting
8. Dust seal
9. Swing arm
10. Drive belt protector (belt-driven models)
11. Washer
12. Screw
13. Washer
14. Dust seal
15. Collar
16. Nut
17. Washer
18. Pivot bolt
19. Plug
20. Bolt
21. Drive belt (belt-driven models)
22. Drive chain slipper (chain-driven models)
23. Drive chain (chain-driven models)
24. Screw

9

NOTE
It is not necessary to remove the shock absorbers.

4A. On chain-driven models, remove the drive chain cover.

4B. On belt-driven models, the drive belt cover was removed during rear wheel removal.

5. Remove the self-locking nut (**Figure 34**) and remove the swing arm pivot bolt.

6. Pull back on the swing arm and remove it from the frame.

7. Install by reversing these removal steps, noting the following.

8. Tighten the pivot bolt and nut and shock absorber lower mounting nut to the torque specifications listed in **Table 1**.

9. Adjust the drive chain or drive belt and the rear brake as described in Chapter Three.

Disassembly/Inspection/Assembly

Refer to the following exploded view drawings for this procedure:

a. **Figure 35**: CM185T and CM200T models.
b. **Figure 36**: CM250C models.
c. **Figure 37**: Rebel 250 models.

1. Remove the dust seal from each side of both pivot points on the swing arm.

2. Push the pivot collar out of each side of the swing arm.

3. Inspect the inside and outside surfaces of the pivot collars for wear or damage; replace if necessary.

4. Inspect the bushings within each end of the swing arm for wear or damage. Do not remove the bushings unless they are going to be replaced as they will be damaged during the removal steps.

5. If bushing replacement is necessary, perform the following:

   a. Secure the swing arm in vise with soft jaws.
   b. Tap the bushing out of one end of the swing arm.
   c. Tap the other bushing out of the other end of the swing arm.
   d. Wash all parts in solvent and dry with compressed air.
   e. Apply a light coat of oil to the inside and outside surfaces of all parts prior to installation.
   f. Tap the new bushing into place slowly and squarely with a piece of wood and hammer (**Figure 38**). Make sure the bushing seats completely and is not cocked in place.

CAUTION
Never reinstall a bushing that has been removed. During removal it becomes slightly damaged and is no longer true to alignment. If installed, it will damage the pivot collar and create an unsafe riding condition.

6. Apply a light coat of multipurpose grease to the pivot collars and install the collars. Install the dust seals.

SHOCK ABSORBERS

The rear shock absorbers are spring controlled and hydraulically damped.

The shock absorber damper unit is sealed and cannot be serviced. Service is limited to removal and replacement of the damper unit and/or the spring.

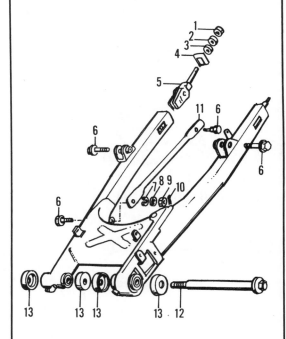

SWING ARM (REBEL 250 MODELS)

1. Locknut
2. Adjusting nut
3. Washer
4. Plate
5. Adjuster
6. Bolt
7. Lockwasher
8. Washer
9. Nut
10. Cotter pin
11. Brake torque link
12. Rear brake torque link
13. Dust seal

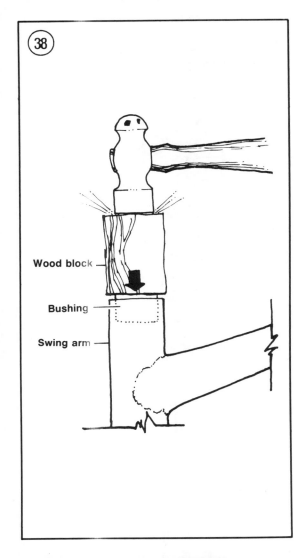

Wood block

Bushing

Swing arm

Removal/Installation

Removal and installation of the shock absorbers is easier if they are done separately. The remaining shock unit will support the rear of the bike and maintain the correct relationship between the top and bottom shock mounts on the frame and swing arm.

1. Place wood block(s) under the frame or engine to support the bike securely so the rear wheel clears the ground.
2. Remove the seat and on CM185T models, remove the exhaust system as described in Chapter Six.
3. Remove the upper nut, lockwasher and washer (A, **Figure 39**).
4. On models so equipped, remove the grab bar from the shock absorber upper mounting stud.
5. Remove the lower nut, lockwasher and washer (B, **Figure 39**).
6. Pull the shock absorber straight off the upper and lower mounting studs and remove the shock absorber.
7. Install by reversing these removal steps, noting the following.
8. Tighten the nuts to the torque specification listed in **Table 1**.
9. On models so equipped, install the grab bar on the outside surface of the shock absorber.
10. Repeat for the other side.
11. Push down on the rear of the bike and observe the shocks; make sure they are not binding.

Disassembly/Inspection/Assembly (CM185T and CM200T)

Refer to **Figure 40** for CM185T and 1980-1981 CM200T models or **Figure 41** for 1982 CM200T models for this procedure.

> *WARNING*
> *Without the proper tools, this procedure can be dangerous. The spring can fly loose, causing injury. For a small bench fee, a dealer can do the job for you.*

1. Install a compression tool as shown in **Figure 42**. Also required for this shock absorber is the spring holder (**Figure 43**). These special tools are available from a Honda dealer. They are the shock absorber compression tool (part No. 07959-3290001) and spring holder tool (part No. 07967-1150100).

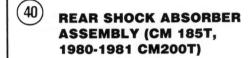

40 REAR SHOCK ABSORBER ASSEMBLY (CM 185T, 1980-1981 CM200T)

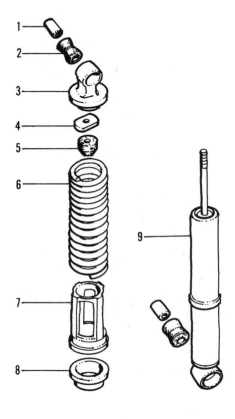

1. Bushing
2. Joint rubber
3. Upper joint
4. Locknut
5. Rubber stopper
6. Spring
7. Spring guide
8. Lower spring seat
9. Damper unit

41 REAR SHOCK ABSORBER (1982 CM200T MODELS)

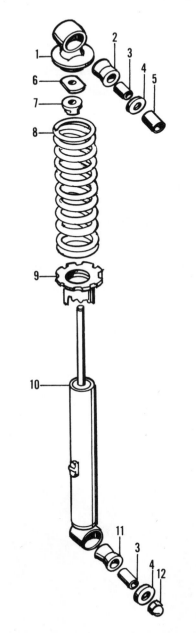

1. Upper joint
2. Rubber bushing
3. Collar
4. Washer
5. Nut
6. Locknut
7. Damper rubber
8. Spring
9. Spring adjuster
10. Damper unit
11. Rubber bushing
12. Nut

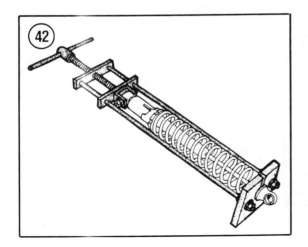

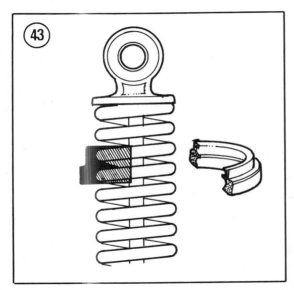

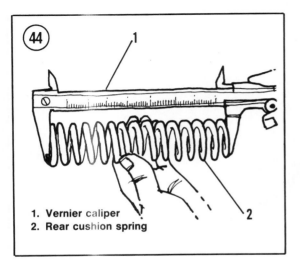

1. **Vernier caliper**
2. **Rear cushion spring**

2. Compress the spring with the compression tool and spring holder just enough to gain access to the locknut.

3. Clamp the upper joint in a vise equipped with soft jaws.

4. Loosen the locknut and unscrew the upper joint.

5. Release spring tension and remove the shock from the compression tool. Remove the spring holder.

6. Slide off the spring and spring adjuster (models so equipped).

7. Measure the free length (**Figure 44**). The spring must be replaced if it has sagged to the service limit of 175.6 mm (6.91 in.) or less.

8. Check the damper unit for leakage and make sure the damper rod is straight.

NOTE
The damper unit cannot be rebuilt; it must be replaced.

9. Assembly is the reverse of the disassembly steps. Noting the following.

NOTE
Apply Loctite Lock N' Seal to the threads before installing the upper joint. Tighten the locknut securely.

Disassembly/Inspection/Assembly (CM250C and Rebel 250)

Refer to **Figure 45** for CM250C models or **Figure 46** for Rebel 250 models for this procedure.

WARNING
Without the proper tools, this procedure can be dangerous. The spring can fly loose, causing injury. For a small bench fee, a dealer can do the job for you.

1. Install a compression tools a shown in **Figure 42**. Also required for this shock absorber is the compressor attachment. These special tools are available from a Honda dealer. They are the shock absorber compression tool (part No. 07959-3290001) and compressor attachment (part No. 07959-MB1000).

2. Compress the spring with the compression tool and compressor attachment just enough to gain access to the locknut.

3. Clamp the upper joint in a vise equipped with soft jaws.

9

REAR SHOCK ABSORBER (CM250C MODELS)

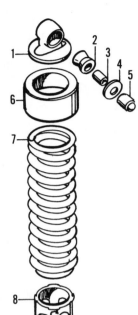

1. Upper joint
2. Rubber bushing
3. Collar
4. Washer
5. Nut
6. Upper spring seat
7. Spring
8. Spring guide
9. Spacer
10. Locknut
11. Stopper
12. Spring adjuster
13. Rubber bushing
14. Nut

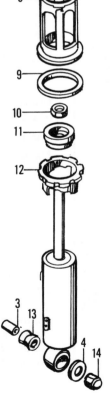

REAR SHOCK ABSORBER (REBEL 250 MODELS)

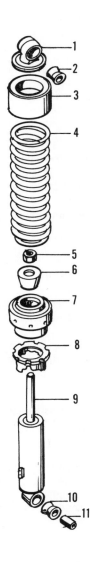

1. Upper joint
2. Rubber bushing
3. Upper spring seat
4. Spring
5. Locknut
6. Damper rubber
7. Lower spring seat
8. Spring adjuster
9. Damper unit
10. Rubber bushing
11. Bushing

9

4. Loosen the locknut and unscrew the upper joint.

5. Release spring tension and remove the shock from the compression tool and compressor attachment.

6A. On CM250C models, slide off the upper spring seat, spring, spring guide, spacer and the spring adjuster.

6B. On Rebel 250 models, slide off the upper spring seat, spring, lower spring seat and the spring adjuster.

> *NOTE*
> *Honda does not provide the service limit dimension for the spring on the CM250C models.*

7. On Rebel 250 models, measure the free length (**Figure 44**). The spring must be replaced if it has sagged to the service limit of 183 mm (7.21 in.) or less.

8. Check the dmaper unit for leakage and make sure the damper rod is straight.

> *NOTE*
> *The damper unit cannot be rebuilt; it must be replaced.*

9. Assembly is the reverse of the disassembly steps. Note the following.

10. On models so equipped, install the spring with the closer wound coils toward the top of the shock absorber unit.

> *NOTE*
> *Apply Loctite Lock N' Seal to the threads before installing the upper joint. Tighten the locknut securely.*

**Shock Absorber Spring
Pre-load Adjustment
(Models so Equipped)**

Spring pre-load adjustment can be adjusted by rotating the spring lower seat at the base of the spring (**Figure 47**). Rotate it *clockwise* to increase spring pre-load or *counterclockwise* to decrease spring pre-load. Use the spanner wrench provided in the owner's tool kit for adjustment. Both spring lower seats must be indexed on the same detent.

Table 1 REAR SUSPENSION TORQUE SPECIFICATIONS

Item	N·m	ft.-lb.
Rear axle nut		
1978-1981	40-50	26-36
1982	55-65	40-47
1985-on	80-100	58-72
Brake torque link nut	20-25	14-18
Shock absorber mounting nuts	30-40	22-29
Driven sprocket nuts		
1978-1983	55-65	40-47
1985-on	60-70	43-51
Swing arm pivot bolt nut		
1978-1983	50-60	36-43
1985-on	50-70	36-50

NOTE: If you own a 1991 or later model, first check Chapter Twelve at the back of this book for any new service information.

CHAPTER TEN

BRAKES

The brake system consists of either a drum brake or single disc on the front wheel and a drum brake on the rear.

Each drum brake is equipped with a wear indicator. Refer to **Figure 1** for front wheel or **Figure 2** for the rear wheel. The indicator(s) should be inspected frequently. When the two arrows align it is time to replace the brake linings.

Refer to **Table 1** for brake specifications and **Table 2** for torque specifications. **Table 1** and **Table 2** are at the end of this chapter.

FRONT DRUM BRAKE

Disassembly

1. Remove the front wheel as described in Chapter Eight.
2. Pull the brake assembly straight up and out of the brake drum (**Figure 3**).
3. Remove the cotter pin and washer from the brake backing plate (**Figure 4**).

NOTE
In the following step, place a clean shop cloth on the brake linings to protect them from oil and grease during removal.

10

4. Remove the brake shoes from the backing plate. Pull up on the center of each shoe as shown in **Figure 5**.

5. Remove the return springs and separate the brake shoes.

6. Mark the position of the brake arm relative to the camshaft so it will be installed in the same position.

7. Remove the bolt and nut securing the brake arm and remove the brake arm, wear indicator and dust seal. Withdraw the camshaft from the backing plate.

Inspection

1. Thoroughly clean and dry all parts except the brake linings.

2. Check the contact surface of the drum (**Figure 6**) for scoring. If there are grooves deep enough to snag your fingernail the drum should be reground.

3. Measure the inside diameter of the brake drum with vernier calipers (**Figure 7**). If the measurement is greater than the service limit listed in **Table 1** the brake drum must be replaced.

4. If the drum can be turned and still stay within the maximum service limit diameter, the linings will have to be replaced and the new ones arced to conform to the new drum contour.

5. Measure the brake linings with a vernier caliper (**Figure 8**). They should be replaced if the lining portion is worn to the service limit dimension or less. Refer to specifications listed in **Table 1**.

6. Inspect the linings for imbedded foreign material. Dirt can be removed with a stiff wire brush. Check for any traces of oil or grease; if the linings are contaminated they must be replaced.

7. Inspect the cam lobe and pivot pin area of the backing plate for wear or corrosion. Minor roughness can be removed with fine emery cloth.

8. Inspect the brake shoe return springs for wear. If they are stretched, they will not fully retract the brake shoes. Replace as necessary.

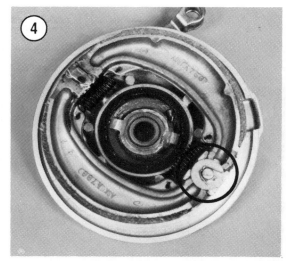

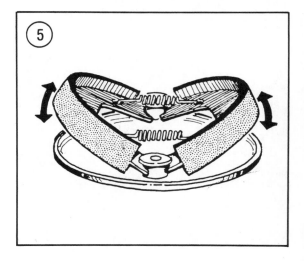

Assembly

1. Grease the camshaft with a light coat of molybdenum disulfide grease. Install the cam into the backing plate from the backside.

2. From the outside of the backing plate, install the dust seal.

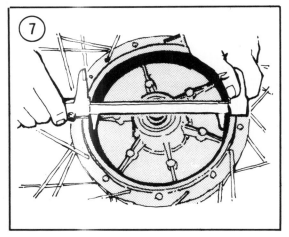

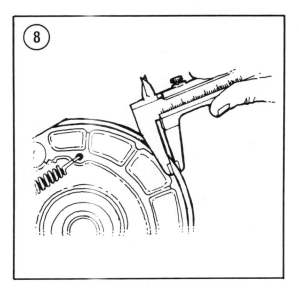

3. Align the wear indicator to the camshaft as shown in **Figure 9** and push it down all the way to the backing plate.

4. When installing the brake arm onto the camshaft, be sure to align the marks on the two parts made in *Disassembly*, Step 6. Tighten the bolt and nut securely.

5. Grease the camshaft and pivot post with a light coat of molybdenum disulfide grease; avoid getting any grease on the brake backing plate where the brake linings may come in contact with it.

NOTE
If new linings are being installed, file off the leading edge of each shoe a little so that the brake will not grab when applied.

6. Hold the brake shoes in a "V" formation with the return springs attached and snap them into place on the brake backing plate. Make sure they are firmly seated on it.

7. Install the lockwasher and a new cotter pin. Bend the ends over completely.

8. Align the speedometer tabs with the slots in the hub. Install the brake panel assembly into the brake drum.

9. Install the front wheel as described in Chapter Eight.

10. Adjust the front brake as described in Chapter Three.

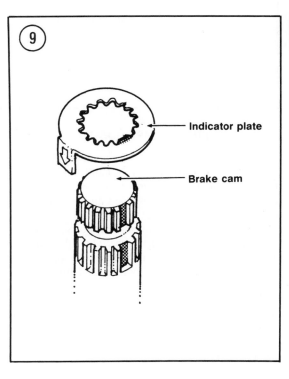

Indicator plate

Brake cam

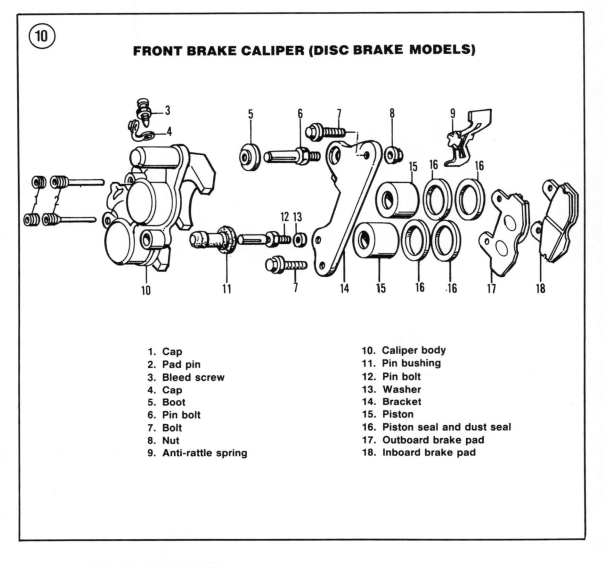

FRONT BRAKE CALIPER (DISC BRAKE MODELS)

1. Cap
2. Pad pin
3. Bleed screw
4. Cap
5. Boot
6. Pin bolt
7. Bolt
8. Nut
9. Anti-rattle spring
10. Caliper body
11. Pin bushing
12. Pin bolt
13. Washer
14. Bracket
15. Piston
16. Piston seal and dust seal
17. Outboard brake pad
18. Inboard brake pad

FRONT DISC BRAKE

The front disc brake is actuated by hydraulic fluid and is controlled by a hand lever on the master cylinder. As the brake pads wear, the brake fluid level drops in the reservoir and automatically adjusts for wear.

When working on hydraulic brake systems, it is necessary that the work area and all tools be absolutely clean. Any tiny particles of foreign matter and grit in the caliper assembly or the master cylinder can damage the components. Also, sharp tools must not be used inside the caliper or on the piston. If there is any doubt about your ability to correctly and safely carry out major service on the brake components, take the job to a dealer or brake specialist.

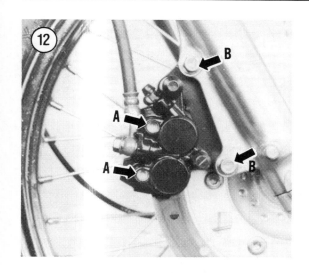

FRONT BRAKE
PAD REPLACEMENT

There is no recommended mileage interval for changing the friction pads in the disc brake. Pad wear depends greatly on riding habits and conditions. The pads should be checked for wear every 6,400 km (4,000 miles) and replaced when the wear indicator reaches the edge of the brake disc. To maintain an even brake pressure on the disc always replace both pads in the caliper at the same time.

CAUTION
Check the pads more frequently when the wear line approaches the disc. On some pads the wear line is very close to the metal backing plate. If pad wear happens to be uneven for some reason the backing plate may come in contact with the disc and cause damage.

Refer to **Figure 10** for this procedure.
1. Remove the caps from the pad pins (**Figure 11**).
2. Loosen both pad pins (A, **Figure 12**).
3. Remove the bolts (B, **Figure 12**) securing the brake caliper assembly to the front fork.
4. Carefully slide the caliper assembly off the brake disc and remove the caliper assembly.
5. Remove both pad pins and remove both brake pads.
6. Clean the pad recess and the end of the pistons (**Figure 13**) with a soft brush. Do not use solvent, a wire brush or any hard tool which would damage the cylinders or pistons.
7. Carefully remove any rust or corrosion from the disc.
8. Lightly coat the end of the pistons and the backs of the new pads (*not* the friction material) with disc brake lubricant.

NOTE
When purchasing new pads, check with your dealer to make sure the friction compound of the new pad is compatible with the disc material. Remove any roughness from the backs of the new pads with a fine-cut file; blow them clean with compressed air.

9. When new pads are installed in the caliper the master cylinder brake fluid level will rise as the caliper pistons are repositioned. Perform the following:
   a. Clean the top of the master cylinder of all dirt and foreign matter.
   b. Remove the screws securing the cap (**Figure 14**). Remove the cap and the diaphragm from

10

the master cylinder and slowly push the caliper pistons into the caliper. Constantly check the reservoir to make sure brake fluid does not overflow. Remove fluid, if necessary, prior to it overflowing.

c. The pistons should move freely. If they don't and there is evidence of them sticking in the cylinder, the caliper should be removed and serviced as described in this chapter.

10. Push the caliper pistons in all the way to allow room for the new pads.

11. Install the anti-rattle spring as shown in **Figure 15**.

12. Partially install both pad pins (**Figure 16**).

13. Install the outboard pad (**Figure 17**) and partially install the pad pins through that pad (**Figure 18**).

14. Install the inboard pad (**Figure 19**).

15. Push the pad pins all the way through both pads and into the other side of the caliper.

16. Tighten the pad pins only finger-tight at this time.

17. Carefully install the caliper assembly onto the disc, being careful not to damage the brake pads.

18. Install the bolts securing the brake caliper assembly to the front fork and tighten to the torque specifications listed in **Table 2**.

19. Tighten the pad pins to the torque specification listed in **Table 2**. Install the pad pin caps.

20. Place wood block(s) under the frame so that the front wheel is off the ground. Spin the front wheel and activate the brake lever as many times as it takes to refill the cylinder in the caliper and correctly locate the pads.

21. Refill the master cylinder reservoir, if necessary, to maintain the correct fluid level as seen through the viewing port on the side (**Figure 20**). Install the diaphragm and top cap. Tighten the screws securely.

WARNING
Use brake fluid clearly marked DOT 3 or DOT 4 from a sealed container. Other types may vaporize and cause brake failure. Always use the same brand name; do not intermix as many brands are not compatible. Do not intermix silicone based (DOT 5) brake fluid as it can cause brake component damage leading to brake system failure.

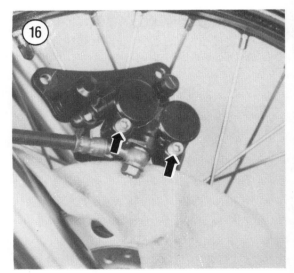

22. Bed the pads in gradually for the first 50 miles (80 km) by using only light pressure as much as possible. Immediate hard application will glaze the new friction pads and greatly reduce the effectiveness of the brake.

FRONT MASTER CYLINDER

Removal/Installation

1. Remove the rear view mirror from the master cylinder.

CAUTION
Cover the fuel tank and instrument cluster with a heavy cloth or plastic tarp to protect them from accidental brake fluid spills. Wash brake fluid off any painted or plated surfaces or plastic parts immediately, as it will destroy the finish. Use soapy water and rinse completely.

2. Pull back the rubber boot (A, **Figure 21**) and remove the union bolt (B, **Figure 21**) securing the brake hose to the master cylinder. Remove the brake hose. Tie the brake hose up and cover the end to prevent the entry of foreign matter.
3. Disconnect the front brake light switch wires (C, **Figure 21**).
4. Remove the clamping bolts (**Figure 22**) and clamp securing the master cylinder to the handlebar and remove the master cylinder.

10

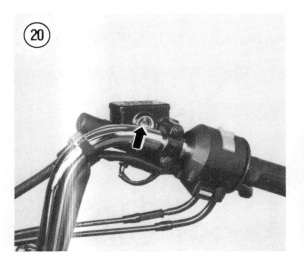

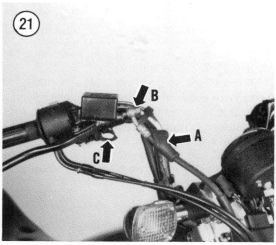

5. Install by reversing these removal steps, noting the following.

6. Install the clamp with the "UP" arrow (**Figure 23**) facing up. Align the face of the clamp with the punch mark on the handlebar (**Figure 24**). Tighten the upper bolt first, then the lower to the torque specification listed in **Table 2**.

7. Install the brake hose onto the master cylinder. Be sure to place a sealing washer on each side of the fitting and install the union bolt. Tighten the union bolt to the torque specifications listed in **Table 2**.

8. Bleed the brake as described in this chapter.

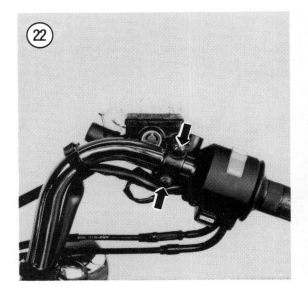

Disassembly

Refer to **Figure 25** for this procedure.

1. Remove the master cylinder as described in this chapter.

2. Remove the bolt and nut securing the brake lever and remove the lever.

3. Remove the screws securing the cover and remove the cover and diaphragm; pour out the brake fluid and discard it. *Never* reuse brake fluid.

4. Remove the rubber boot from the area where the hand lever actuates the internal piston.

5. Using circlip pliers, remove the internal circlip from the body.

6. Remove the piston assembly and the spring.

7. Remove the brake light switch if necessary.

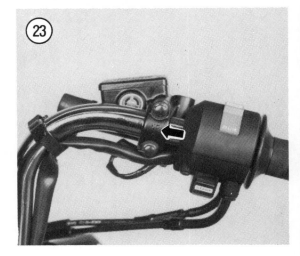

Inspection

1. Clean all parts in denatured alcohol or fresh brake fluid. Inspect the cylinder bore and piston contact surfaces for signs of wear and damage. If either part is less than perfect, replace it.

2. Check the end of the piston for wear caused by the hand lever. Replace if worn.

3. Replace the piston assembly if either the primary or secondary cup requires replacement.

4. Inspect the pivot hole in the hand lever. If worn or elongated it must be replaced.

5. Make sure the passages in the bottom of the brake fluid reservoir are clear. Check the reservoir cap and diaphragm for damage and deterioration and replace as necessary.

6. Inspect the threads in the bore for the brake line.

7. Check the hand lever pivot lugs on the master cylinder body for cracks.

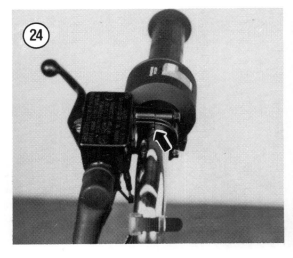

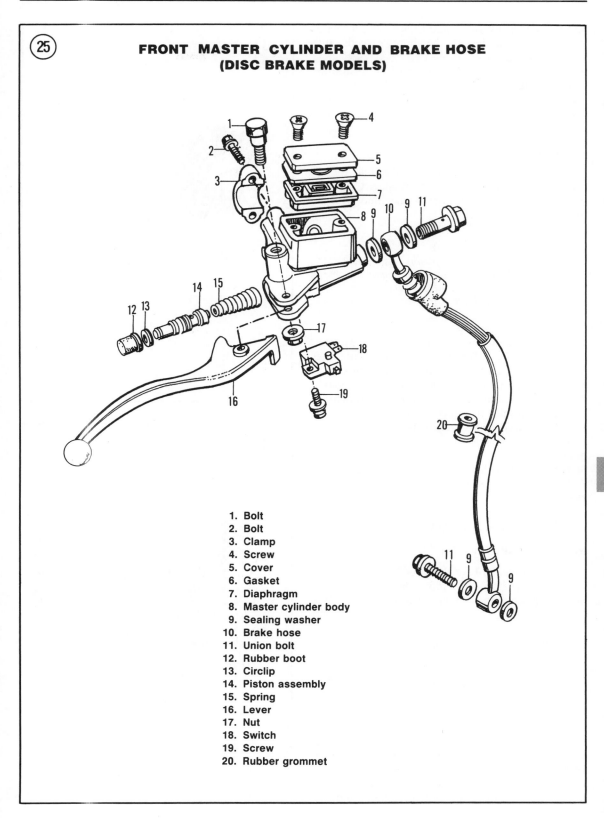

㉕ FRONT MASTER CYLINDER AND BRAKE HOSE
(DISC BRAKE MODELS)

1. Bolt
2. Bolt
3. Clamp
4. Screw
5. Cover
6. Gasket
7. Diaphragm
8. Master cylinder body
9. Sealing washer
10. Brake hose
11. Union bolt
12. Rubber boot
13. Circlip
14. Piston assembly
15. Spring
16. Lever
17. Nut
18. Switch
19. Screw
20. Rubber grommet

10

8. Measure the cylinder bore (**Figure 26**). Replace the master cylinder if the bore exceeds the specifications given in **Table 1**.

9. Measure the outside diameter of the piston as shown in **Figure 27** with a micrometer. Replace the piston assembly if it is less than the specifications given in **Table 1**.

Assembly

1. Soak the new cups in fresh brake fluid for at least 15 minutes to make them pliable. Coat the inside of the cylinder with fresh brake fluid prior to the assembly of parts.

> *CAUTION*
> *When installing the piston assembly, do not allow the cups to turn inside out as they will be damaged and allow brake fluid leakage within the cylinder bore.*

2. Install the spring and piston assembly into the cylinder together. Install the spring with the tapered end facing toward the secondary cup.

3. Install the circlip and slide in the rubber boot.

4. Install the diaphragm and cover. Do not tighten the cover screws at this time as fluid will have to be added later when the system is bled.

5. Install the brake lever onto the master cylinder body.

6. If removed, install the brake light switch.

7. Install the master cylinder as described in this chapter.

FRONT CALIPER

Removal/Installation

Refer to **Figure 10** for this procedure.

It is not necessary to remove the front wheel in order to remove the caliper assembly.

> *CAUTION*
> *Do not spill any brake fluid on the painted portion of the front wheel. Wash off any spilled brake fluid immediately, as it will destroy the finish. Use soapy water and rinse completely.*

1. Place a container under the brake line at the caliper. Remove the union bolt and sealing washers (A, **Figure 28**) securing the brake line to the caliper assembly. Remove the brake line and let the brake fluid drain out into the container.

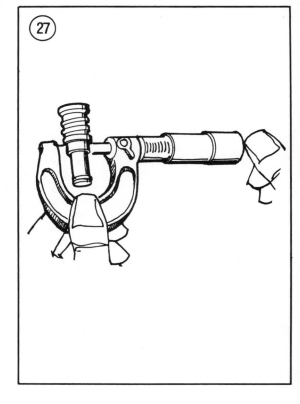

Dispose of this brake fluid—never reuse brake fluid. To prevent the entry of moisture and dirt, cap the end of the brake line and tie the loose end up to the forks.

2. Loosen the bolts (B, **Figure 28**) securing the brake caliper assembly to the front fork gradually in several steps. Push on the caliper while loosening the bolt to push the pistons back into the caliper.

3. Remove the bolts securing the brake caliper assembly to the front fork.

4. Remove the caliper assembly from the brake disc.

5. Install by reversing these removal steps, noting the following.

6. Carefully install the caliper assembly onto the disc being careful not to damage the brake pads.

7. Install the bolts securing the brake caliper assembly to the front fork and tighten to the torque specifications listed in **Table 2**.

8. If the caliper bracket was removed from the caliper, lubricate the caliper pin bolts and pin bushing on the caliper bracket with silicone grease.

9. Install the brake hose, with a sealing washer on each side of the fitting, onto the caliper. Install the union bolt and tighten to the torque specifications listed in **Table 2**.

10. Bleed the brake as described in this chapter.

WARNING
Do not ride the motorcycle until you are sure that the brakes are operating properly.

Rebuilding

If the caliper leaks, the caliper should be rebuilt. If the pistons stick in the cylinders, indicating severe wear or galling, the entire unit should be replaced. Rebuilding a leaky caliper requires special tools and experience.

Caliper service should be entrusted to a dealer, motorcycle repair shop or brake specialist. Considerable money can be saved by removing the caliper yourself and taking it in for repair.

FRONT BRAKE HOSE REPLACEMENT

There is no factory-recommended replacement interval but it is a good idea to replace all brake hoses every four years or when they show signs of cracking or damage.

Refer to **Figure 25** for this procedure.

CAUTION
Cover the front wheel, fender and fuel tank with a heavy cloth or plastic tarp to protect it from accidental spilling of brake fluid. Wash off any brake fluid from any painted or plated surface or plastic parts immediately, as it will destroy the finish. Use soapy water and rinse completely.

1. Place a container under the brake hose at the caliper. Remove the union bolt and sealing washers (A, **Figure 29**) securing the brake hose fitting to the caliper assembly.

2. Remove brake hose from the clip on the fender stay (B, **Figure 29**) and lower fork bridge (C, **Figure 29**).

3. Remove the brake hose and let the brake fluid drain out into the container. To prevent the entry of moisture and dirt, plug the brake hose inlet in the caliper.

WARNING
Dispose of this brake fluid—never reuse brake fluid. Contaminated brake fluid can cause brake failure.

10

4. Pull back the rubber boot (A, **Figure 21**) and remove the union bolt and sealing washers (B, **Figure 21**) securing the brake hose to the master cylinder. Remove the hose and sealing washers.

5. Remove the brake hose.

6. Install a new hose, sealing washers and union bolts in the reverse order of removal. Be sure to install new sealing washers in the correct positions; refer to **Figure 25**.

7. Tighten all union bolts to torque specifications listed in **Table 2**.

8. Refill the master cylinder reservoir, if necessary, to maintain the correct fluid level as seen through the viewing port on the side (**Figure 20**). Install the diaphragm and top cap. Tighten the screws securely.

> *WARNING*
> *Use brake fluid clearly marked DOT 3 or DOT 4 from a sealed container. Other types may vaporize and cause brake failure. Always use the same brand name; do not intermix as many brands are not compatible. Do not intermix silicone-based (DOT 5) brake fluid as it can cause brake component damage leading to brake system failure.*

> *WARNING*
> *Do not ride the motorcycle until you are sure that the brakes are operating properly.*

FRONT BRAKE DISC

Removal/Installation

1. Remove the front wheel as described in Chapter Eight.

> *NOTE*
> *Place a piece of wood or vinyl tube in the caliper in place of the disc. This way, if the brake lever is inadvertently squeezed the pistons will not be forced out of the cylinders. If this does happen, the caliper might have to be disassembled to reseat the pistons and the system will have to be bled. By using the wood or vinyl tube, bleeding the system is not necessary when installing the wheel.*

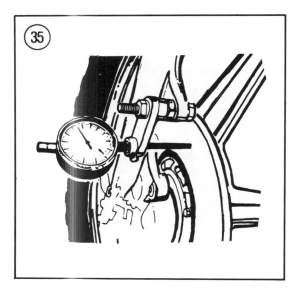

CAUTION
*Do not set the wheel down on the disc surface, as it may get scratched or warped. Set the wheel on 2 blocks of wood (**Figure 30**).*

2. Remove the speedometer housing (**Figure 31**) from the left-hand side and the spacer (**Figure 32**) from the right-hand side.
3. Remove the Allen bolts (**Figure 33**) securing the brake disc to the hub and remove the disc.
4. Install by reversing these removal steps, noting the following.
5. Tighten the disc mounting Allen bolts to the torque specifications listed in **Table 2**.

Inspection

It is not necessary to remove the disc from the wheel to inspect it. Small marks on the disc are not important, but radial scratches deep enough to snag a fingernail reduce braking effectiveness and increase brake pad wear. If these grooves are found, the disc should be replaced.
1. Measure the thickness of the disc at several locations around the disc with a micrometer or vernier caliper (**Figure 34**). The disc must be replaced if the thickness in any area is less than that specified in **Table 1**.
2. Make sure the disc bolts are tight prior to running this check. Check the disc runout with a dial indicator as shown in **Figure 35**.
3. Slowly rotate the wheel and watch the dial indicator. If the runout exceeds that listed in **Table 1** the disc must be replaced.
4. Clean the disc of any rust or corrosion and wipe clean with lacquer thinner. Never use a petroleum solvent that may leave an oil residue on the disc.

BLEEDING THE SYSTEM

This procedure is not necessary unless the brakes feel spongy, there has been a leak in the system, a component has been replaced or the brake fluid has been replaced.
1. Remove the dust cap from the brake bleed valve.
2. Connect a length of clear tubing to the bleed valve (**Figure 36**) on the caliper (**Figure 37**).
3. Place the other end of the tube into a clean container.
4. Fill the container with enough fresh brake fluid to keep the end submerged. The tube should be

long enough so that a loop can be made higher than the bleed valve to prevent air from being drawn into the caliper during bleeding.

> *CAUTION*
> *Cover the fuel tank and instrument cluster with a heavy cloth or plastic tarp to protect it from the accidental spilling of brake fluid. Wash off any brake fluid from any painted or plated surface or plastic parts immediately, as it will destroy the finish. Use soapy water and rinse completely.*

5. Clean the cover of the master cylinder of all dirt and foreign matter. Remove the screws securing the top cover and remove the cover and diaphragm. Fill the reservoir almost to the top lip; insert the diaphragm and the cover loosely. Leave the cover in place during this procedure to prevent the entry of dirt.

> *WARNING*
> *Use brake fluid clearly marked DOT 3 or DOT 4 from a sealed container. Other types may vaporize and cause brake failure. Always use the same brand name; do not intermix as many brands are not compatible. Do not intermix silicone-based (DOT 5) brake fluid as it can cause brake component damage leading to brake system failure.*

6. Slowly apply the brake lever several times. Hold the lever in the applied position.
7. Open the bleed valve about one-half turn. Allow the lever to travel to its limit. When this limit is reached, tighten the bleed screw.
8. As the fluid enters the system, the level will drop in the reservoir. Maintain the level at about 3/8 inch from the top of the reservoir to prevent air from being drawn into the system.
9. Continue to pump the lever and fill the reservoir until the fluid emerging from the hose is completely free of bubbles.

> *NOTE*
> *Do not allow the reservoir to empty during the bleeding operation or more air will enter the system. If this occurs, the entire procedure must be repeated.*

10. Hold the lever in, tighten the bleed valve, remove the bleed tube and install the bleed valve dust cap.

11. Refill the master cylinder reservoir, if necessary, to maintain the correct fluid level as seen through the viewing port on the side (**Figure 20**). Install the diaphragm and top cap. Tighten the screws securely.
12. Install the reservoir cover and tighten the screws.
13. Test the feel of the brake lever. It should be firm and should offer the same resistance each time it's operated. If it feels spongy, it is likely that there still is air in the system and it must be bled again. When all air has been bled from the system and the fluid level is correct in the reservoir, double-check for leaks and tighten all the fittings and connections.

> *WARNING*
> *Before riding the motorcycle, make certain that the brakes are operating correctly by operating the lever several times.*

6. Remove the bolt and nut securing the brake arm and remove the brake arm, wear indicator and dust seal. Withdraw the camshaft from the backing plate.

Inspection

1. Thoroughly clean and dry all parts except the brake linings.
2. Check the contact surface of the drum (**Figure 39**) for scoring. If there are grooves deep enough to snag your fingernail the drum should be reground.
3. Measure the inside diameter of the brake drum with vernier calipers (**Figure 7**). If the measurement is greater than the service limit listed in **Table 1** the brake drum must be replaced.
4. If the drum can be turned and still stay within the maximum service limit diameter, the linings will have to be replaced and the new ones arced to conform to the new drum contour.
5. Measure the brake linings with a vernier caliper (**Figure 8**). They should be replaced if the lining portion is worn to the service limit dimension or less. Refer to specifications listed in **Table 1**.
6. Inspect the linings for embedded foreign material. Dirt can be removed with a stiff wire brush. Check for any traces of oil or grease; if they are contaminated they must be replaced.
7. Inspect the cam lobe and pivot pin area of the backing plate for wear or corrosion. Minor roughness can be removed with fine emery cloth.
8. Inspect the brake shoe return springs for wear. If they are stretched, they will not fully retract the brake shoes. Replace as necessary.

10

REAR DRUM BRAKE

Disassembly

1. Remove the rear wheel as described in Chapter Nine.
2. Pull the brake assembly straight up and out of the brake drum.
3. Remove the cotter pin and washer from the brake backing plate (**Figure 38**).

> *NOTE*
> *Place a clean shop rag on the linings to protect them from oil and grease during removal.*

4. Remove the brake shoes from the backing plate. Pull up on the center of each shoe as shown in **Figure 5**.
5. Remove the return springs and separate the brake shoes.

Assembly

1. Grease the camshaft with a light coat of molybdenum disulfide grease. Install the cam into the backing plate from the backside.
2. From the outside of the backing plate, install the dust seal.
3. Align the wear indicator to the camshaft as shown in **Figure 9** and push it down all the way to the backing plate.
4. When installing the brake arm onto the camshaft, be sure to align the punch marks on the two parts (**Figure 40**). Tighten the bolt and nut securely.

5. Grease the camshaft and pivot post with a light coat of molybdenum disulfide grease; avoid getting any grease on the brake backing plate where the brake linings may come in contact with it.

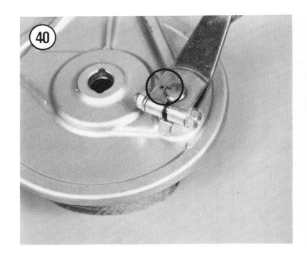

> *NOTE*
> *If new linings are being installed, file off the leading edge of each shoe a little so that the brake will not grab when applied.*

6. Hold the brake shoes in a "V" formation with the return springs attached and snap them into place on the brake backing plate. Make sure they are firmly seated on it.
7. Install the lockwasher and a new cotter pin. Bend the ends over completely.
8. Install the brake panel assembly into the brake drum.
9. Install the rear wheel as described in Chapter Eight.
10. Adjust the rear brake as described in Chapter Three.

FRONT BRAKE CABLE
(DRUM BRAKE MODELS)

Front brake adjustment should be checked at the interval listed in Chapter Three as the cable stretches with use and increases brake lever free play. Free play is the distance that the brake lever travels between the released position and the point when the brake shoes come in contact with the brake drum.

If the brake adjustment described in Chapter Three can no longer be achieved, the brake cable must be replaced.

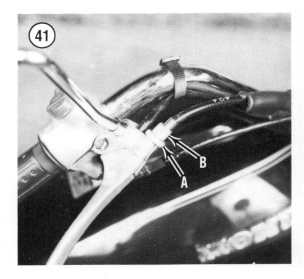

Replacement

1. At the brake lever, loosen the locknut (A, **Figure 41**) and turn the adjuster (B, **Figure 41**) all the way into the cable sheath.
2. At the brake panel assembly, unscrew the adjusting nut (**Figure 42**) completely from the brake arm pin. Withdraw the pin from the brake lever and disconnect the cable from the backing plate.
3. Pull the hand lever all the way back to the grip. Remove the cable nipple holder and remove the cable from the lever.

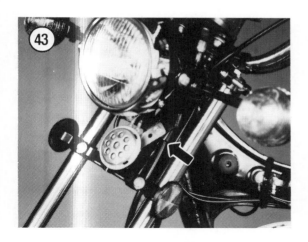

NOTE
Prior to removing the brake cable, make a drawing (or take a Polaroid picture) of the cable routing through the frame. It is very easy to forget how it was, once the cable has been removed. Replace the cable exactly as it was, avoiding any sharp turns.

4. Remove the cable from the clip on the throttle cable and cable guide on the front fork (**Figure 43**) and front fender.

5. Remove the brake cable from the frame.

6. Install by reversing these removal steps, noting the following.

7. Adjust the front brake as described in Chapter Three.

REAR BRAKE PEDAL

Removal/Installation

1. Place a support block under the engine or frame to hold the bike securely.

2. Completely unscrew the rear brake adjusting nut (A, **Figure 44**).

3. Depress the brake pedal and remove the brake rod (B, **Figure 44**) from the pivot joint in the brake arm (C, **Figure 44**). Remove the pivot joint from the brake arm and install the pivot joint and the adjusting nut onto the brake rod to avoid misplacing them.

4A. On Rebel 250 models, perform the following:

   a. Disconnect the brake switch spring (**Figure 45**) from the brake arm.

   b. Using needle nose Vise Grips pliers, disconnect the brake pedal return spring (A, **Figure 46**) from the brake pivot shaft.

   c. Remove the cotter pin from the backside of the pivot pin (B, **Figure 46**) and remove the brake rod from the pivot shaft.

   d. Remove the clamping bolt (C, **Figure 46**) securing the brake pedal to the pivot shaft and remove the brake pedal (D, **Figure 46**).

   e. Remove the pivot shaft from the frame.

4B. On all other models, perform the following:

   a. Disconnect the brake light switch spring (A, **Figure 47**).

   b. Using Vise Grips pliers, disconnect the brake pedal return spring (B, **Figure 47**) from the brake pedal arm.

   c. Remove the cotter pin and washer (**Figure 48**) from the pivot shaft.

10

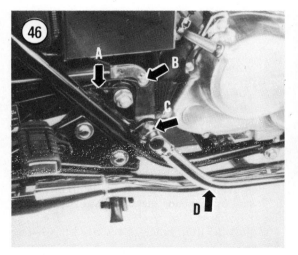

d. Slide the brake pedal from the pivot shaft and remove the brake pedal.

e. Remove the pivot shaft from the frame.

5. Install by reversing these removal steps, noting the following.

6. Apply a light coat of multipurpose grease to all pivot areas prior to installation.

7. Install new cotter pin(s)—never reuse an old one as it may break and fall out.

8. Adjust the rear brake as described in Chapter Three.

Table 1 BRAKE SPECIFICATIONS

Item	Specification	Wear limit
Brake drum ID		
Front drum	140.0 mm (5.512 in.)	141.0 mm (5.5512 in.)
Rear drum	130.0 mm (5.12 in.)	131.0 mm (5.15 in.)
Brake shoe thickness	4.0 mm (0.1517 in.)	2.0 mm (0.0787 in.)
Master cylinder		
Cylinder bore ID	12.7 mm (0.5 in.)	12.744 mm (0.5022 in.)
Piston OD	12.7 mm (0.5 in.)	12.64 mm (0.498 in.)
Front caliper		
Cylinder bore ID	25.4 mm (1.0 in.)	25.450 mm (1.002 in.)
Piston OD	25.368 mm (0.9987 in.)	25.300 mm (0.9961 in.)
Front brake disc thickness	4.0 mm (0.16 in.)	3.5 mm (0.14 in.)
Disc runout	-	0.3 mm (0.012 in.)

Table 2 BRAKE TORQUE SPECIFICATIONS

Item	N·m	ft.-lb.
Caliper mounting bolts	24-30	17-22
Brake pad pin bolt	15-20	10-14
Brake system union bolts	25-35	18-22
Brake disc bolts	37-43	27-31
Master cylinder clamp bolts	10-14	7-10

10

CHAPTER ELEVEN

FRAME AND REPAINTING

This chapter includes service procedures for the kickstand, centerstand and footpegs.

This chapter also describes procedures for completely stripping the frame. Recommendations are provided for repainting the stripped frame.

KICKSTAND (SIDESTAND)

Removal/Installation

1. Place a wood block(s) under the frame to support the bike securely.

2. Raise the kickstand and disconnect the return spring (A, **Figure 1**) from the pin on the frame with Vise Grips.

3. Remove the cotter pin (or nut) and unbolt the kickstand from the frame (B, **Figure 1**).

4. Install by reversing these removal steps. Apply a light coat of multipurpose grease to the pivot surfaces of the frame tab and the kickstand yoke before installation.

CENTERSTAND
(MODELS SO EQUIPPED)

Removal/Installation

1. Place a wood block(s) under the frame to hold the bike securely in place.

2. Raise the centerstand and use Vise Grips pliers to unhook the return spring for the centerstand.

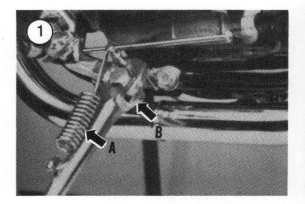

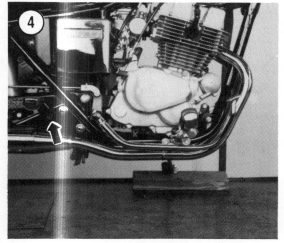

3. Remove the cotter pin from the pivot shaft.

4. Withdraw the pivot shaft from the left-hand side of the frame.

5. Remove the centerstand from the frame.

6. Install by reversing these removal steps, noting the following.

7. Apply multipurpose grease to the pivot shaft and to the pivot area of the frame and centerstand where the pivot shaft rides.

FOOTPEGS

Front Footpeg Replacement

On Rebel 250 models, remove the bolts (**Figure 2**) securing the front footpeg to the frame and remove the front footpeg assembly.

On all other models, remove the cotter pin and washer (**Figure 3**), pull out the pin and remove the front foot peg.

On models so equipped, when installing the footpeg assembly be sure to install a new cotter pin—never reuse an old one as it may break and fall out.

Rear Footpeg Replacement

On Rebel 250 models, remove the bolt (**Figure 4**) securing the rear footpeg to the muffler mounting bracket and remove the rear footpeg assembly.

On all other models, remove the bolt (**Figure 5**) securing the rear footpeg to the muffler mounting bracket and remove the rear footpeg assembly. This bolt also holds the mufflers in place.

When installing the footpegs, make sure the alignment tabs are correctly positioned. Tighten the bolts to the following torque specifiction:

  a. Rebel 250: 35-40 N•m (22-29 ft.-lb.).

  b. All other models: 20-25 N•m (14-18 ft.-lb.).

FRAME

The frame does not require routine maintenance. However, it should be inspected immediately after any accident or spill.

Component Removal/Installation

1. Remove the seat, side cover panels and fuel tank.

2. Remove the engine as described in Chapter Four.

3. Remove the front wheel, steering head and front forks as described in Chapter Eight.

4. Remove the rear wheel, shock absorber and swing arm as described in Chapter Nine.

11

5. Remove the battery as described in Chapter Three.

6. Remove the electrical components and wiring harness.

7. Remove the kickstand and footpegs as described in this chapter.

8. Remove the centerstand as described in this chapter.

9. Remove the steering head races from the steering head tube as described in Chapter Eight.

10. Inspect the frame for bends, cracks or other damage, especially around welded joints and areas that are rusted.

11. Assemble by reversing these removal steps.

Stripping and Painting

Remove all components from the frame. Thoroughly strip off all old paint. The best way is to have it sandblasted down to bare metal. If this is not possible, you can use a liquid paint remover and steel wool and a fine, hard wire brush.

CAUTION
*On some models, the fenders, side covers, frame covers and air box are molded plastic (**Figure 6**). If you wish to change the color of the parts, consult an automotive paint supplier for the proper procedure. Do not use any liquid paint remover on these components as it will damage the surface. The color is an integral part of some of these components and cannot be removed.*

When the frame is down to bare metal, have it inspected for hairline and internal cracks. Magnaflux is the most common and complete process.

Make sure that the primer is compatible with the type of paint you are going to use for the finish color. Spray on one or two coats of primer as smoothly as possible. Let it dry thoroughly and use a fine grade of wet sandpaper (400-600 grit) to remove any flaws. Carefully wipe the surface clean and then spray a couple of coats of the final color. Use either lacquer or enamel base paint and follow the manufacturer's instructions.

A shop specializing in painting will probably do the best job. However, you can do a surprisingly good job with a good grade of spray paint. Spend a few extra dollars and get a good grade of paint as it will make a difference in how good it looks and how long it will stand up. It's a good idea to shake the can and make sure the ball inside the can is loose when you purchase the can of paint. Shake the can as long as is stated on the can. Then immerse the can

upright in a pot or bucket of *warm* water (not hot—not over 120° F).

WARNING
*Higher temperatures could cause the can to burst. **Do not** place the can in direct contact with any flame or heat source.*

Leave the can in the water for several minutes. When thoroughly warmed, shake the can again and spray the frame. Be sure to get into all the crevices where there may be rust problems. Several light mist coats are better than one heavy coat. Spray painting is best done in temperatures of 70-80° F (21-26° C); any temperature above or below this will give you problems.

After the final coat has dried completely, at least 48 hours, any overspray or orange peel may be removed with a *light* application of Dupont rubbing compound (red color) and finished with Dupont polishing compound (white color). Be careful not to rub too hard or you will go through the finish.

Finish off with a couple coats of good wax before reassembling all the components.

It's a good idea to keep the frame touched up with fresh paint if any minor rust spots or scratches appear.

An alternative to painting is powder coating. The process involves spraying electrically charged particles of pigment and resin on the object to be coated, which is negatively charged. The charged powder particles adhere to the electrically grounded object until heated and fused into a smooth coating in a curing oven. Powder coated surfaces are more resistant to chipping, scratching, fading and wearing than other finishes. A variety of colors and textures are available. Powder coating also has advantages over paint, as no environmentally hazardous solvents are used.

CHAPTER TWELVE

1991 AND LATER SERVICE INFORMATION

> This chapter contains all procedures and specifications unique to the Honda 250 cc Rebel and Nighthawk models produced since 1991. If a specific procedure, or specification, is not included in this supplement, unless otherwise specified, refer to the 250 cc models of the main body of this book.
>
> The headings in this supplement correspond to those in the chapters of the main body of this book.

CHAPTER THREE

LUBRICATION, MAINTENANCE AND TUNE-UP

ROUTINE CHECKS

Battery

All models since 1991 are equipped with a maintenance free battery. The electrolyte level cannot be checked on this type of sealed battery.

BATTERY

Removal and Installation

On all models covered in this supplement, the negative side is grounded. When removing the battery, disconnect the negative (–) cable first, then the positive (+) cable. This minimizes the chance of a tool shorting to ground when disconnecting the battery positive cable.

1A. On Rebel 250 models, perform the following:
 a. Remove the right-hand side panel.
 b. Remove the battery hold-down band.
 c. Disconnect the battery negative (–) lead then the positive (+) lead from the battery.

1B. On Nighthawk 250 models, perform the following:
 a. Remove the seat and rear fairing as described in the Chapter Eleven section of this supplement.
 b. Disconnect the battery negative (–) lead then the positive (+) lead from the battery.
 c. Remove the bolt and nut securing the battery holder to the frame. Remove the battery holder.

2. Slide the battery and tray out and remove from the bike's frame.

3. Remove the battery from the tray.

4. Install by reversing these removal steps, noting the following:
 a. Position the battery with the negative (–) terminal facing toward the front of the bike.
 b. Make sure the terminals and cable connectors are free of corrosion and are clean. Tighten the bolts securely.

Inspection and Testing (Maintenance Free Battery)

The battery electrolyte level cannot be serviced. *Never* attempt to remove the sealing bar cap from the top of the battery. This bar cap was removed for initial filling of electrolyte prior to delivery of the bike or battery and is not to be removed thereafter. The battery does not require periodic electrolyte inspection or water refilling.

> *WARNING*
> *Even though the battery is a sealed type, protect your eyes, skin and clothing. Electrolyte is corrosive and can cause severe chemical skin burns and permanent injury. The battery case may be cracked and leaking electrolyte. If any electrolyte is spilled or splashed on clothing or skin, immediately neutralize with a solution of baking soda and water, then flush with an abundance of clean water. Electrolyte splashed into the eyes is extremely harmful. Always wear safety glasses while working with a battery. If you get electrolyte in your eyes, call a physician immediately and force your eyes open and flood them*

with cool, clean water for approximately 15 minutes.

1. Remove the battery as described in this section of the supplement. Do not clean the battery while it is mounted in the frame.

2. Inspect the battery tray for contamination or damage. Clean with a solution of baking soda and water.

3. Set the battery on a stack of newspapers or shop cloths to protect the surface of the workbench.

4. Check the entire battery case for cracks or other damage. If the battery case is warped, discolored or has a raised top, the battery has been suffering from overcharging or overheating.

5. Check the battery terminal bolts, spacers and nuts for corrosion or damage. Clean parts thoroughly with a solution of baking soda and water. Replace severely corroded or damaged parts.

6. If corroded, clean the top of the battery with a stiff bristle brush using a baking soda and water solution.

7. Check the battery cable clamps for corrosion and damage. If corrosion is minor, clean the battery cable clamps with a stiff wire brush. Replace severely worn or damaged cables.

8. Connect a digital voltmeter between the battery negative and positive leads. Note the following:

   a. If the battery voltage is 13.0-13.2 volts (at 20° C [68° F]), or greater, the battery is fully charged

   b. If the battery voltage is 12.3 volts (at 20° C [68° F]), or less, the battery is undercharged and requires charging.

9. If the battery is undercharged, recharge it as described in this section of the supplement.

Charging
(Maintenance Free Battery)

On the maintenance free battery, if recharging is required, a digital voltmeter and a special type of charger with a built-in ammeter must be used. Honda recommends the Cristie Battery Charger which has a built-in battery tester along with a timer. It is recommended that the battery be recharged by a Honda dealership to avoid damage to a good battery that only requires recharging. The following procedure is included if you choose to recharge this type of battery.

If a battery not in use loses its charge within a week after charging, the battery is defective. A good battery should only self-discharge approximately 1 percent each day.

CAUTION
*Always remove the battery from the bike before connecting charging equipment. **Always** disconnect the battery cables from the battery. During the charging procedure the charger may destroy the diodes within the voltage regulator/rectifier if the cables are left connected.*

WARNING
During charging, highly explosive hydrogen gas is released from the battery. Charge the battery only in a well-ventilated area and away from open flames (including pilot lights on some gas home appliances). Do not allow any smoking in the area. Never check the charge of the battery by arcing across the terminals. The resulting spark can ignite the hydrogen gas.

1. Remove the battery from the bike as described in this chapter.

2. Set the battery on a stack of newspapers or shop cloths to protect the surface of the workbench.

3. Connect the positive (+) charger lead to the positive (+) battery terminal and the negative (–) charger lead to the negative (–) battery terminal.

4. Set the charger at 12 volts. If the output of the charger is variable, it is best to select the low setting.

5. The charging time depends on the discharged condition of the battery. Use the suggested charging amperage and length of time charge on the battery label. Normally, a battery should be charged at a slow charge rate of 1/10th its given capacity.

6. Turn the charger ON.

7. After the battery has been charged for the predetermined time, turn the charger off, disconnect the leads and measure the battery voltage. Refer to the following:

   a. If the battery voltage is 13.0-13.2 volts (at 20° C [68° F]) or greater, the battery is fully charged

   b. If the battery voltage is 12.3 volts (at 20° C [68° F]) or less, the battery requires additional charging time.

8. If the battery voltage remains stable for one hour, the battery is charged.

12

New Battery Installation

When replacing the old battery, make sure it is charged completely prior to installing it in the bike. Failure to do so will reduce the life of the battery. Using a new battery without an initial charge will cause permanent battery damage. That is, the battery will never be able to hold more than an 80% charge. Charging a new battery after it has been used will not bring its charge to 100%. When purchasing a new battery from a dealership or parts store, verify its charge status. If' necessary, have them perform the initial or booster charge prior to picking up the battery.

NOTE
Recycle your old battery. *When you replace the old battery, turn in the old battery at that time. The lead plates and the plastic case can be recycled. Most motorcycle dealerships will accept your old battery in trade when you purchase a new one, Never place an old battery in your household trash since it is illegal, in most states, to place any acid or lead (heavy metal) contents in landfills. There is also the danger of the battery being crushed in the trash truck and spraying acid on the truck or landfill operator.*

PERIODIC MAINTENANCE

Air Filter Element Cleaning

Replace the air filter element every 12,000 miles (19,200 km). Honda does not recommend cleaning this type of dry air filter element. It must be replaced at the indicated mileage interval, or if it is damaged or starts to deteriorate.

The air filter removes dust and abrasive particles before the air enters the carburetor and engine. Without the air filter, very fine particles could enter into the engine and cause rapid wear of the piston rings, cylinder bores and bearings. They also might clog small passages in the carburetor. Never run the bike without the element installed.

Proper air filter servicing can ensure long service from your engine.

1A. On Rebel 250 models, remove the left-hand side panel.

1B. On Nighthawk 250 models, remove the seat and rear fairing as described in the Chapter Eleven section of this supplement.

2. Remove the screws securing the air filter element cover and remove the cover.

3. Disconnect the breather tube from the air filter element.

4. Pull out and remove the element set spring.

5. Remove the air filter element from the air box and discard it.

6. Install by reversing these removal steps. Make sure the element is correctly seated into the air box so there is no air leak.

TUNE-UP

The tune-up procedures are the same as on previous years with the exception of the recommended spark plug numbers and idle speed. The new specifications are listed in **Table 1**.

Table 1 TUNE-UP SPECIFICATIONS

Spark plug type	
Standard heat range	ND U20FSR-U or NGK CR6HSA
Cold weather*	ND U16FSR-U or NGK CR5HSA
Extended high-speed riding	ND U22FSR-U or NGK CR7HSA
Idle speed	
Rebel 250	1,400 ± 100 rpm
Nighthawk 250	1,500 ± 100 rpm
Ignition timing mark (1996-on Rebel 250)	F @ 1,400 rpm
Cylinder compression (1996-on Rebel 250)	1,100 kPa (159 psi) @ 600 rpm
Capacities	
1996-on Rebel 250	
Engine oil	
Oil change	1.5 liters (1.6 US qt., 1.3 Imp qt.)
Disassembly	1.8 liters (1.9 US qt., 1.6 Imp qt.)
Fork oil (per leg)	234 cc (7.9 oz.)
Fuel	10.0 liters (2.64 U.S. gal., 2.20 Imp gal.)
Torque specifications	
1996-on Rebel 250	
Cylinder head bolts	12 Nm (106 in.-lb.)
Cylinder head/camshaft holder nut	23 Nm (17 ft.-lb.)

*Cold weather climate – below 5 C (41 F)

12

CHAPTER FOUR

ENGINE

ENGINE

Removal/Installation

Removal and installation of the engine on the Nighthawk 250 is the same as on 1978-1983 models as described in Chapter Four in the main body of this book.

Piston Ring
Removal/Installation

Piston ring removal is the same as on previous models. Installation is the same with the exception of the ring cross section shape. The second ring is square on the inner and outer surface. The top ring is chamfered on the top inner surface and square on the outer surface.

Install the rings with the N mark facing UP.

SPECIFICATIONS

All engine specifications are the same as on previous 250 cc models with the exception of those listed in Table 2.

Table 2 ENGINE SPECIFICATIONS

Item	Specification	Wear limit
Oil pump (Rebel 250)		
Inner rotor tip-to-outer rotor clearance	0.15 mm (0.006 in.)	0.20 mm (0.08 in.)
Outer rotor-to-body clearance	0.15-0.21 mm (0.006-0.008 in.)	0.25 mm (0.010 in.)
End of rotor-to-body side clearance	0.05-0.13 mm (0.02-0.005 in.)	0.14 mm (0.006 in.)
Oil pump (Nighthawk 250)		
Inner rotor tip-to-outer rotor clearance	0.15 mm (0.006 in.)	0.20 mm (0.08 in.)
Outer rotor-to-body clearance	0.5-0.18 mm (0.06-0.008 in.)	0.20 mm (0.008 in.)
End of rotor-to-body side clearance	0.03-0.11 mm (0.01-0.004 in.)	0.14 mm (0.006 in.)
1996-on Rebel 250		
Cylinder head bolts	12 Nm (106 in.-lb.)	
Cylinder head/camshaft holder nut	23 Nm (17 ft.-lb.)	
Bore	53.000-53.010 mm (2.0866-2.0870 in.)	53.10 mm (2.091 in.)
Out of round	-	0.05 mm (0.002 in.)
Taper	-	0.05 mm (0.002 in.)
Warp across top	-	0.05 mm (0.002 in.)
Piston-to-cylinder clearance	0.010-0.040 mm (0.0004-0.0016 in.)	0.10 mm (0.004 in.)
Piston ring end gap		
Top ring	0.15-0.30 mm (0.006-0.012 in.)	0.45 mm (0.018 in.)
2nd ring	0.30-0.45 mm (0.012-0.018 in.)	0.60 mm (0.024 in.)
Oil (side rail)	0.2-0.7 mm (0.01-0.03 in.)	0.90 (0.035 in.)
Camshaft (1996-on Rebel 250)		
Cam lobe height		
Intake	27.383-27.543 mm (1.0781-1.0844 in.)	27.2 mm (1.07 in.)
Exhaust	27.209-27.369 mm (1.0712-1.0775 in.)	27.0 mm (1.06 in.)
Valve seat width (1996-on Rebel 250)		
Intake and exhaust	1.0-1.1 mm (0.039-0.043 in.)	1.8 mm (0.07 in.)

CHAPTER FIVE

CLUTCH AND TRANSMISSION

CLUTCH

Installation (Rebel 250)

Clutch installation procedures are the same as previous models with the exception of the clutch nut torque specification. Tighten the clutch nut to 74 N•m (54 ft.-lb).

Table 3 CLUTCH AND TRANSMISSION SPECIFICATIONS

Item	Specification	Wear limit
Friction disc thickness (1996-on Rebel 250 models)	2.92-3.08 mm (0.115-0.121 in.)	2.6 mm (0.10 in.)
Clutch spring free length (1996-on Rebel 250 models)	37.8 mm (1.49 in.)	36.0 mm (1.42 in.)
Shift fork finger thickness (1996-on Rebel 250 models)	4.93-5.00 mm (0.194-0.197 in.)	4.80 mm (0.189 in.)

12

CHAPTER SIX

FUEL AND EXHAUST

All carburetor procedures are the same design as previous models with the exception of the model numbers and various specifications changes.

Refer to Table 4 for carburetor model numbers and specifications.

FUEL TANK

Removal/Installation (Nighthawk 250)

Refer to the fuel tank procedure referring to models other than Rebel 250 models in Chapter Six in the main body of this book.

Table 4 CARBURETOR SPECIFICATIONS

Item	Rebel 250	Nighthawk 250
Carburetor model number		
49-state	VE35C	VE35A
California	VE36B	VE36A
Canada	VE35D	-
Main jet number		
All models except 1996-on Rebel 250	No. 110	No. 110
1996 on Rebel 250	No. 108	-
Slow jet number		
All models except 1996-on Rebel 250	No. 35	No. 35
All models except 1996- on Rebel 250	No. 38	-
Jet needle clip setting	Nonadjustable	Nonadjustable
Float level	18.5 mm (0.73 in.)	18.5 mm (0.73 in.)
Idle speed	1,400 100 rpm	1,500 100 rpm
Pilot screw		
Initial setting	2 ¾ turns out 1 ½ turns out	

CHAPTER SEVEN

ELECTRICAL SYSTEM

CHARGING SYSTEM (NIGHTHAWK 250)

Voltage Regulator/Rectifier Removal/Installation

1. Remove the seat.

2. Disconnect the battery negative lead.

3. Disconnect the 6-pin electrical connector (containing 3 yellow, 1 green, 1 red/white wires) from the voltage regulator/rectifier.

4. Connect a voltmeter to the battery charge line on the harness side of the connector as follows:

   a. Positive (+) test probe to the red/white terminal.

   b. Negative (−) test probe to ground.

   c. There should be battery voltage present.

5. Connect an ohmmeter to each of the yellow terminals on the harness side. There should be 0.2-0.6 ohm for each set of yellow terminals. The resistance reading should be the same for all 3 yellow terminals.

6. If the voltage regulator/rectifier fails any of these tests the unit is faulty and must be replaced.

Voltage Regulator/Rectifier Removal/Installation

1. Remove the seat.

2. Disconnect the battery negative lead.

3. Disconnect the 6-pin electrical connector (containing 3 yellow, 1 green, 1 red/white wires) from the voltage regulator/rectifier.

4. Remove the bolts securing the voltage regulator/rectifier to the frame mounting bracket and remove the unit.

5. Install by reversing these removal steps. Make sure the electrical connector is free of corrosion and is tight.

IGNITION SYSTEM

All models since 1991 are equipped with a transistorized electronic ignition system consisting of 2 ignition coils, an ignition control module (ICM), an ignition pulse generator, a neutral switch and diode, a clutch switch, a clutch/sidestand switch diode and 2 spark plugs as shown in **Figure 1**.

The ICM is the new name of the CDI unit used on previous years, and all precautions relate to this unit as well as the CDI unit. Refer to the CDI precautions in Chapter Seven in the main body of this book prior to performing any service procedures relating to the ignition system.

NOTE
Honda does not provide any resistance specifications for the ignition coils for these models.

STARTING SYSTEM

All models since 1991 are equipped with starting systems consisting of a starter motor, starter solenoid (starter relay switch), clutch switch and diode, neutral switch, sidestand switch, a clutch/sidestand diode and a start button as shown in **Figure 2**.

The starter will only work when the sidestand is in the raised position and the transmission is in neutral or the clutch lever is pulled in.

STARTER SOLENOID (STARTER RELAY SWITCH)

The main fuse (20A) is contained within the electrical connector on top of the starter relay switch. Removal and installation of the starter relay switch is the same as on previous models.

12

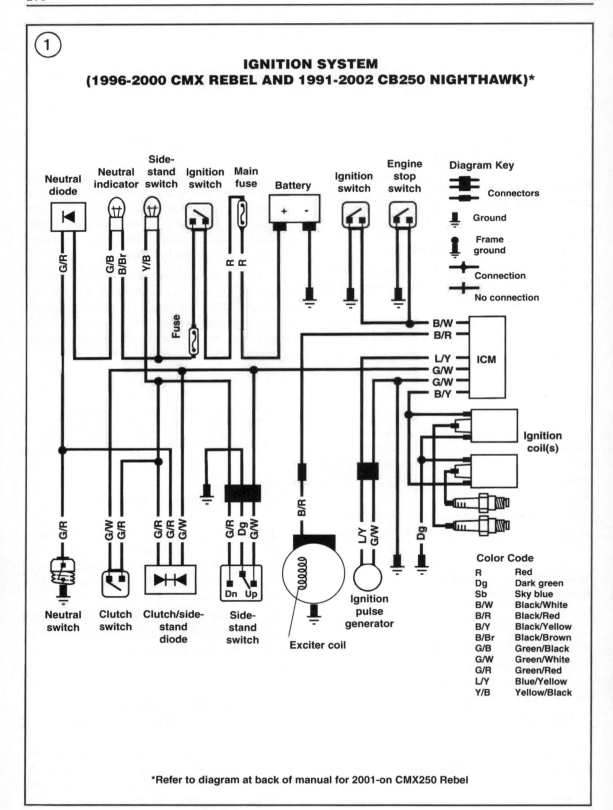

**IGNITION SYSTEM
(1996-2000 CMX REBEL AND 1991-2002 CB250 NIGHTHAWK)***

*Refer to diagram at back of manual for 2001-on CMX250 Rebel

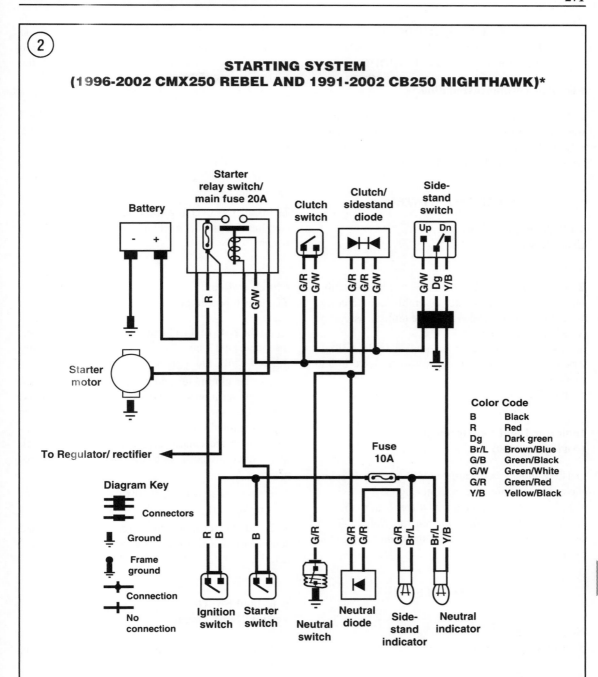

(2)

STARTING SYSTEM
(1996-2002 CMX250 REBEL AND 1991-2002 CB250 NIGHTHAWK)*

Battery

Starter relay switch/ main fuse 20A

Clutch switch

Clutch/ sidestand diode

Side-stand switch

Up   Dn

R   G/W   G/R G/W   G/R G/R G/W   G/W Dg Y/B

Starter motor

To Regulator/ rectifier

Fuse 10A

Color Code

B	Black
R	Red
Dg	Dark green
Br/L	Brown/Blue
G/B	Green/Black
G/W	Green/White
G/R	Green/Red
Y/B	Yellow/Black

Diagram Key

Connectors

Ground

Frame ground

Connection

No connection

R B   B   G/R   G/R G/R   G/R Br/L   Br/L Y/B

Ignition switch

Starter switch

Neutral switch

Neutral diode

Side-stand indicator

Neutral indicator

*Refer to diagram at back of manual for 2003-on CMX250 Rebel.

12

CLUTCH DIODE
(CLUTCH/SIDESTAND DIODE AND
NEUTRAL SWITCH DIODE)

Removal Testing/Installation

The removal, testing and installation procedures for both diodes are the same as described under *Clutch Diode (CM250C, Rebel 250)* in Chapter Seven in the main body of this book.

LIGHTING SYSTEM

Taillight Replacement
(Nighthawk 250)

1. Remove the seat.
2. Reach into the backside of the taillight assembly and rotate the bulb/socket assembly counterclockwise. Remove the socket from the taillight assembly.
3. Replace the bulb.
4. Insert the bulb/socket assembly into the taillight assembly and rotate it clockwise to lock it into position.
5. Install the seat.

Indicator Light Replacement
(Nighthawk 250)

These models are equipped with a separate round meter that contains the indicator lights.

Indicator light replacement is identical to the *Meter Illumination Light Replacement (Rebel 250)* as described in Chapter Seven in the main body of this book.

SWITCHES

Neutral Switch
Testing/Replacement

1. Remove the fuel tank as described in Chapter Six in the main body of this book.
2. Disconnect the neutral switch electrical connector (light green/red) from the diode located directly above the cylinder head cover on the left-hand side.
3. Shift the transmission into the neutral position.
4. Use an ohmmeter and check for continuity between the switch side of the light green/red connector and ground. There should be continuity (low

resistance) with the transmission in neutral and no continuity (infinite resistance) with the transmission in gear. If the switch fails either of these tests, the switch must be replaced.
5. Remove the starter, starter gears and chain and the crankcase left-hand spacer as described under *Starter Removal* in Chapter Seven in the main body of this book.
6. Remove the mounting bolt and plate securing the neutral switch. Remove the switch from the left-hand crankcase.
7. Install by reversing these removal steps. Make sure the electrical connector is free of corrosion and is tight.

Clutch Switch
Testing/Replacement

1. At the base of the clutch lever mounting bracket, disconnect the 2-pin electrical connector (containing 1 green/white and 1 green/red) wire.
2. Use an ohmmeter and check for continuity between the terminals on the switch. There should be continuity (low resistance) with the clutch lever applied (pulled in) and no continuity (infinite resistance) with the clutch lever released. If the switch fails either of these tests, the switch must be replaced.
3. Remove the switch from the clutch lever mounting bracket.
4. Install by reversing these removal steps. Make sure the electrical connector is free of corrosion and is tight.

Sidestand Switch
Testing/Replacement

1. Remove the fuel tank as described in Chapter Six in the main body of this book.
2. Disconnect the sidestand switch 3-pin electrical connector (containing 1 green/red, 1 yellow/black and 1 green wire) from the wiring harness directly above the rear of the cylinder head cover on the left-hand side.
3. Shift the transmission into the neutral position.
4. Use an ohmmeter and check for continuity as follows:

a. *Sidestand down*-There should be continuity (low resistance) between the yellow/black and the green wires.

b. *Sidestand up*-There should be continuity (low resistance) between the green/white and the green wires.

If the switch fails either of these tests, the switch must be replaced.

5. Remove the mounting bolt and the sidestand switch from the pivot point of the sidestand. Discard the bolt as a new bolt must be used during installation.

6. Install by reversing these removal steps while noting the following:

a. Align the pin with the hole in the sidestand and the switch groove with the return spring holding pin.

b. Install a new mounting bolt and tighten securely.

c. Make sure the electrical connector is free of corrosion and is tight.

ELECTRICAL COMPONENTS

Main Fuse

The main fuse (20A) is contained within the electrical connector on top of the starter relay switch.

CHAPTER EIGHT

FRONT SUSPENSION AND STEERING

FRONT WHEEL
(REBEL 250)

NOTE
The front brake disc is now located on the left-hand side of the wheel instead of the right-hand side as on prior models.

Removal/Installation

1. Place wooden blocks under the engine or frame to support the bike with the front wheel off the ground.

2. Remove the speedometer cable set screw. Pull the speedometer cable free from the speedometer drive gear assembly.

3. On the right-hand fork slider, loosen the front axle pinch bolt. It is not necessary to remove the bolt, just loosen it.

4. Unscrew the front axle from the left-hand fork slider

5. Support the front wheel, then remove the front axle from the forks and wheel.

6. Pull the wheel down and out of the forks.

NOTE
Insert a piece of vinyl tubing or wood in the caliper in place of the brake disc. Then, if the brake lever is inadvertently squeezed, the pistons will not be forced out of the cylinder. If this does happen, the caliper must be disassembled to reseat the pistons and the system will have to be bled.

7. Remove the axle spacer from right-hand side of the hub and the speedometer gear box from the left-hand side. Reinstall all parts onto the front axle to avoid misplacing them.

CAUTION
Do not set the wheel down on either disc surface as it may get scratched or warped. Set the sidewalls on 2 wooden blocks.

Installation

1. Make sure all axle contact surfaces on the right-hand fork slider are free of dirt and small burrs.

12

2.   Apply a light coat of grease to the axle, bearings and the grease seals within the speedometer gear box.

3.   Move the front wheel into position.

4.   Install the axle spacer into the right-hand side of the hub and the speedometer gear box into the left-hand side.

5.   Position the wheel into place being careful not to damage the leading edges of the brake pads with the disc.

6.   Carefully insert the front axle from the right-hand side and slide it through the right-hand fork slider, wheel hub, then screw it into the left-hand fork slider.

7.   Position the speedometer gear box with the cable inlet pointing toward the rear to accept the speedometer cable.

8.   After the front wheel and axle are installed, make sure the right-hand axle spacer and the speedometer drive gear assembly are correctly located in back of the stopper on the fork slider.

9.   Tighten the front axle to 62 N•m (46 ft.-lb.) and tighten the pinch bolt securely.

10.   Install the speedometer cable into the gear box and tighten the set screw securely.

11.   After the wheel is completely installed, roll the bike back and forth several times, apply the brakes a couple of times to make sure the wheel rotates freely and that the brake pads are against the disc correctly.

Table 5 FRONT SUSPENSION TORQUE SPECIFICATIONS (1996-on Rebel 250)

Item	N m	ft.-lb.
Front axle bolt	62	46
Fork bridge pinch bolt, upper	11	97 in.-lb.
Fork bridge pinch bolt, lower	34	25
Fork cap bolt	22	16
Front fork Allen bolt	20	15
Steering stem nut	74	54
Steering stem adjusting nut	3	26.5 in.-lb.

CHAPTER NINE
REAR SUSPENSION

Table 6 REAR SUSPENSION TORQUE SPECIFICATIONS (1996-on Rebel 250)

Item	N m		ft.-lb.
Rear axle nut	88	65	
Rear wheel spoke	4	35.4 in.-lb.	
Tire valve nut	3	26.5 in.-lb.	
Driven sprocket nut	64	37	
Shock absorber mounts			
Upper bolt	26	20	
Lower bolt	42	31	
Swing arm pivot bolt/nut	88	65	
Drive chain slider screw	3	26.5 in.-lb.	
Drive chain adjuster nut	10	89 in.-lb.	

CHAPTER TEN
BRAKES

FRONT BRAKE PAD REPLACEMENT (REBEL 250)

The front brake pad replacement procedure is the same as on previous years except that the brake disc and caliper assembly are now mounted on the left-hand side of the wheel.

FRONT CALIPER (REBEL 250)

Removal/Installation

The front brake caliper removal and installation procedures are the same as on previous years except that the brake caliper assembly is now mounted on the left-hand fork slider.

13

13

N

O

P

R

S

T

13

WIRING DIAGRAMS

1978-1979 CM185T

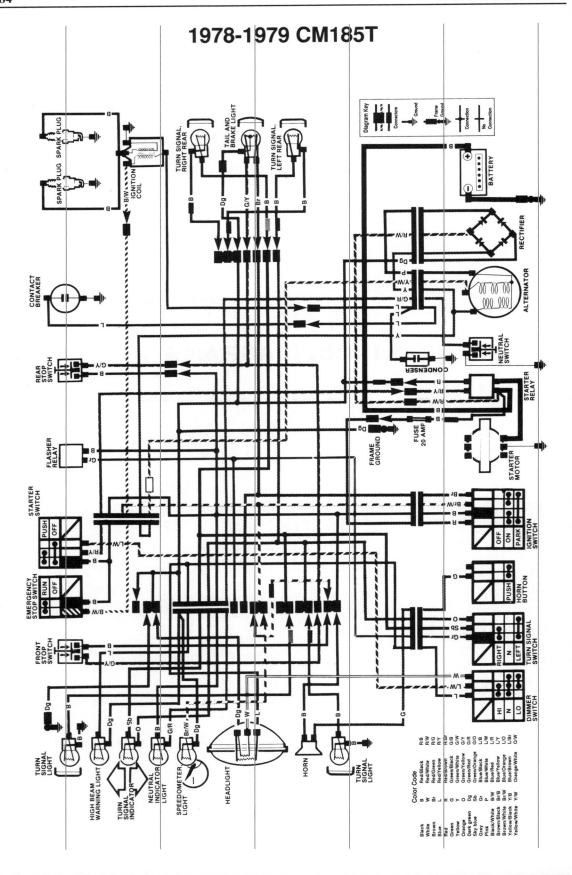

1980 CM200T

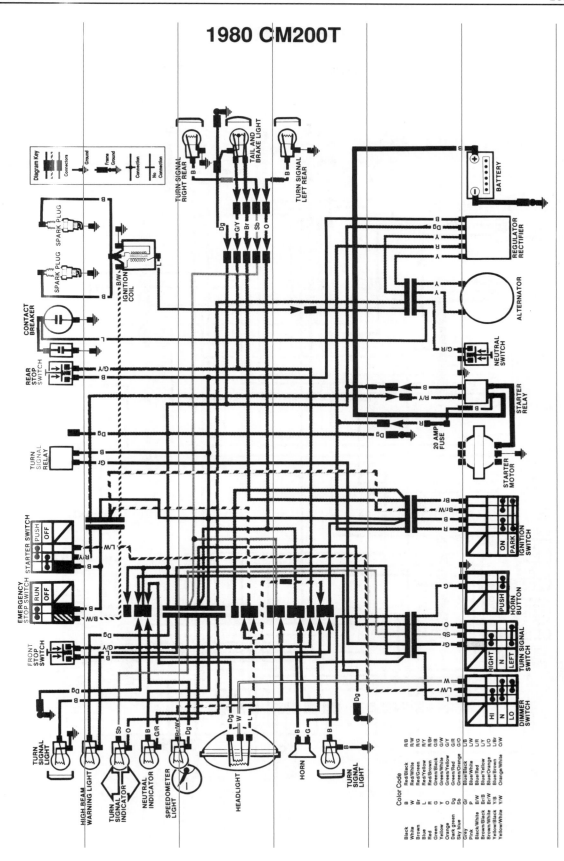

1981 CM200T

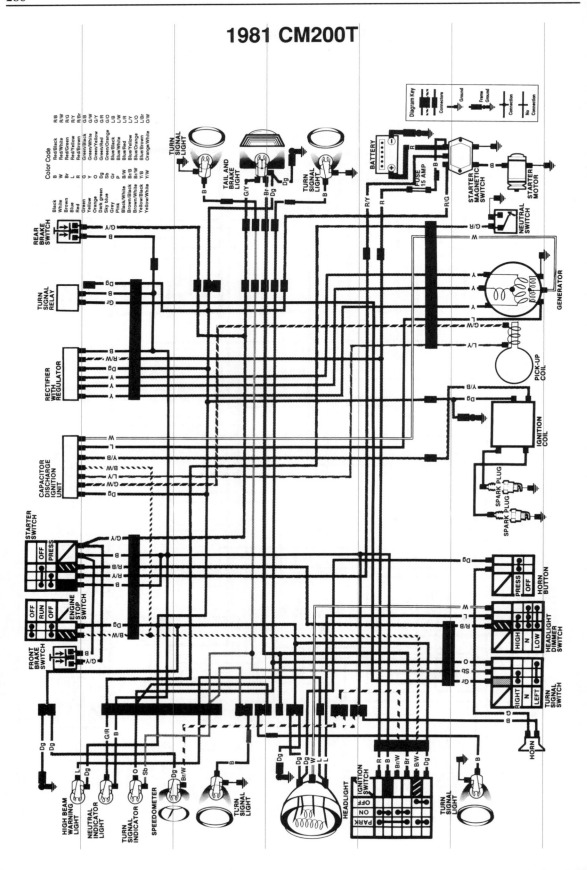

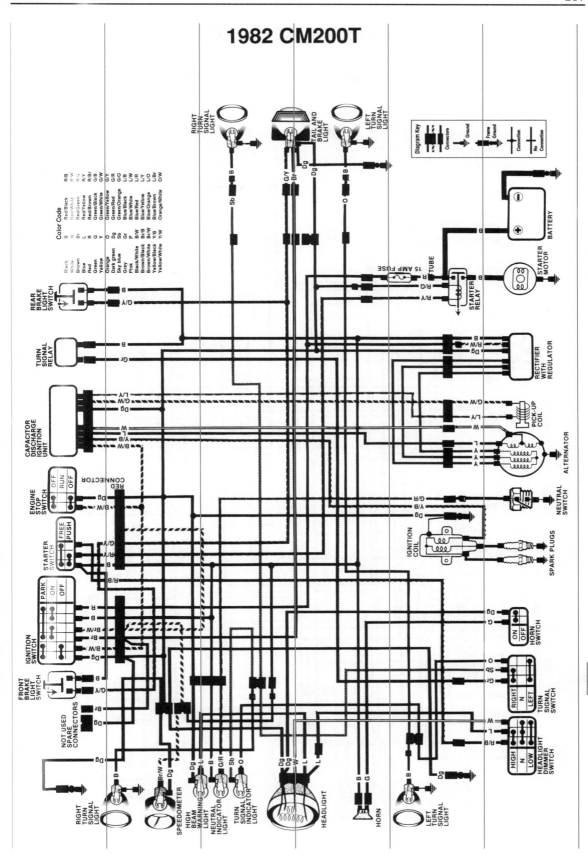

1982 CM200T

1982-1983 CM250C

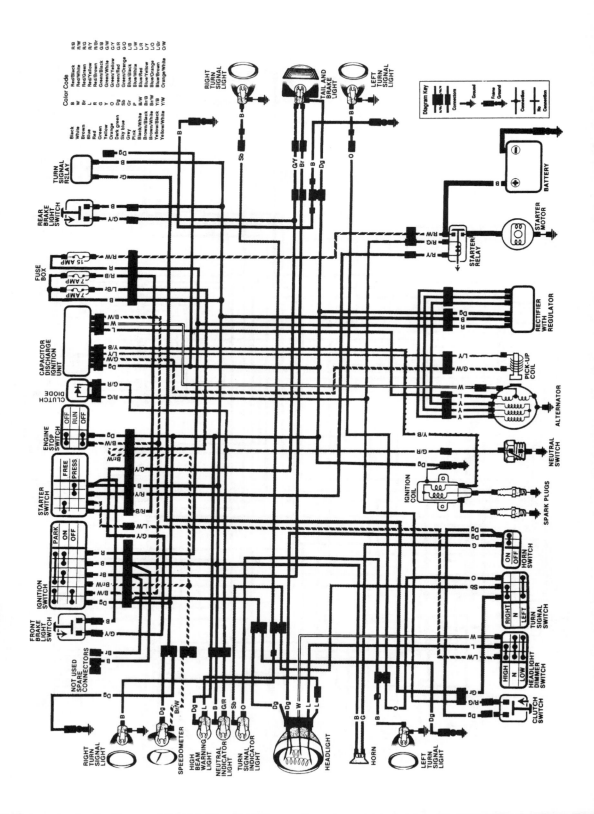

1985-1987 CMX250C AND 1986 CMX250CD

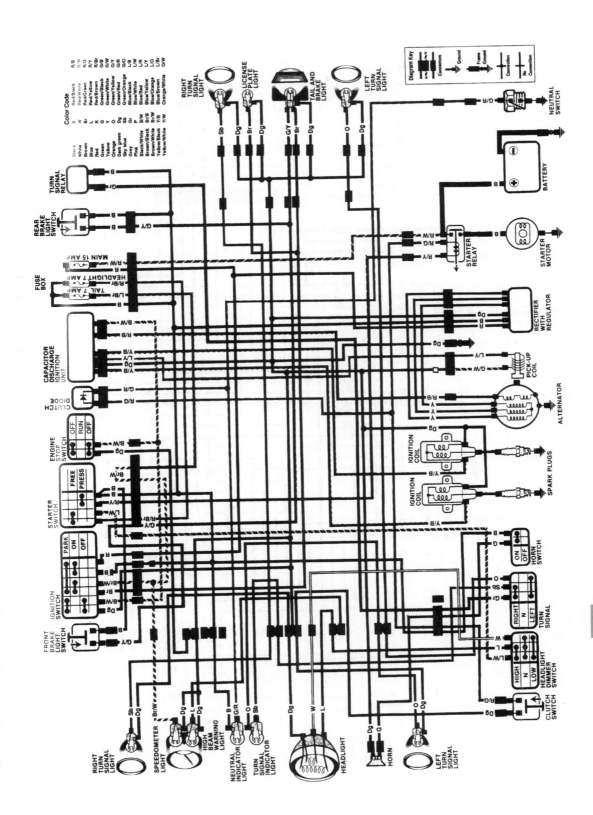

1991-2002 CB250

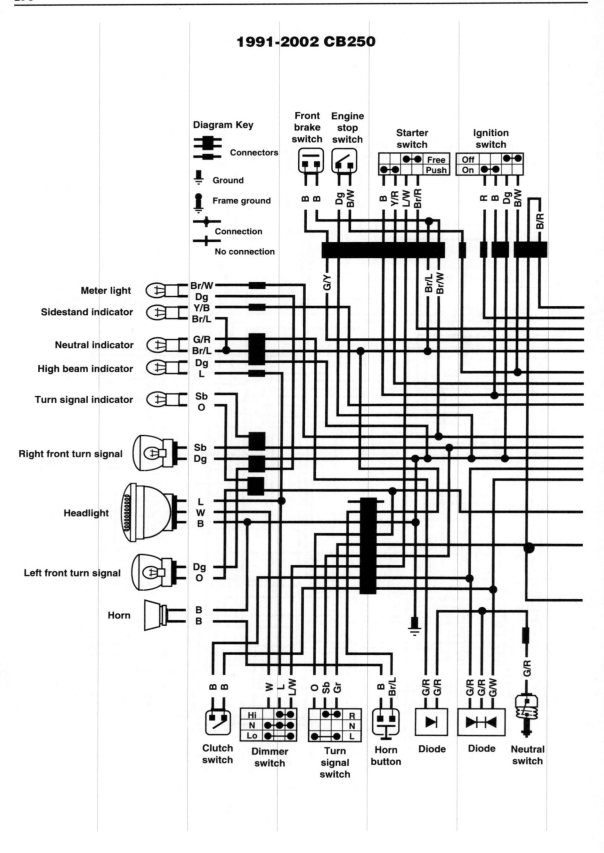

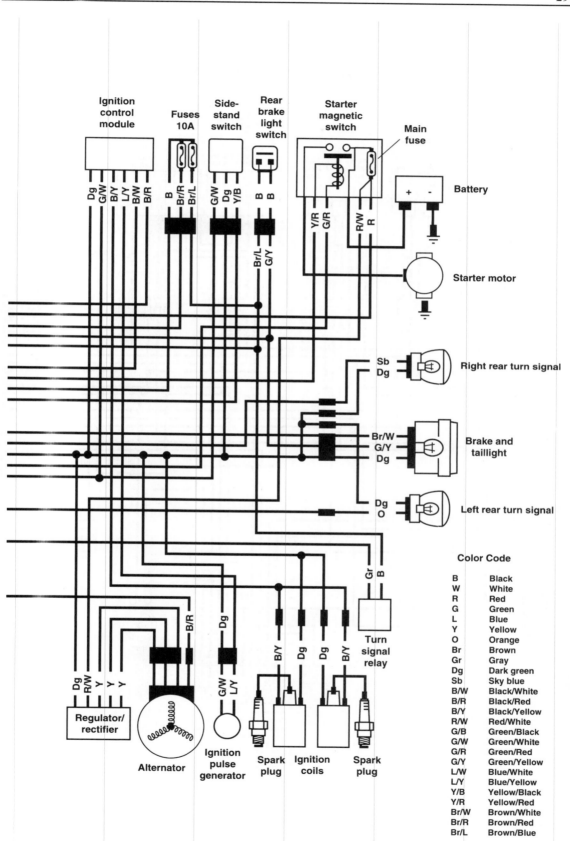

Ignition control module

Fuses 10A

Side-stand switch

Rear brake light switch

Starter magnetic switch

Main fuse

Battery

Starter motor

Right rear turn signal

Brake and taillight

Left rear turn signal

Turn signal relay

Regulator/rectifier

Alternator

Ignition pulse generator

Spark plug

Ignition coils

Spark plug

Color Code

B	Black
W	White
R	Red
G	Green
L	Blue
Y	Yellow
O	Orange
Br	Brown
Gr	Gray
Dg	Dark green
Sb	Sky blue
B/W	Black/White
B/R	Black/Red
B/Y	Black/Yellow
R/W	Red/White
G/B	Green/Black
G/W	Green/White
G/R	Green/Red
G/Y	Green/Yellow
L/W	Blue/White
L/Y	Blue/Yellow
Y/B	Yellow/Black
Y/R	Yellow/Red
Br/W	Brown/White
Br/R	Brown/Red
Br/L	Brown/Blue

14

1996-2016 CMX250C

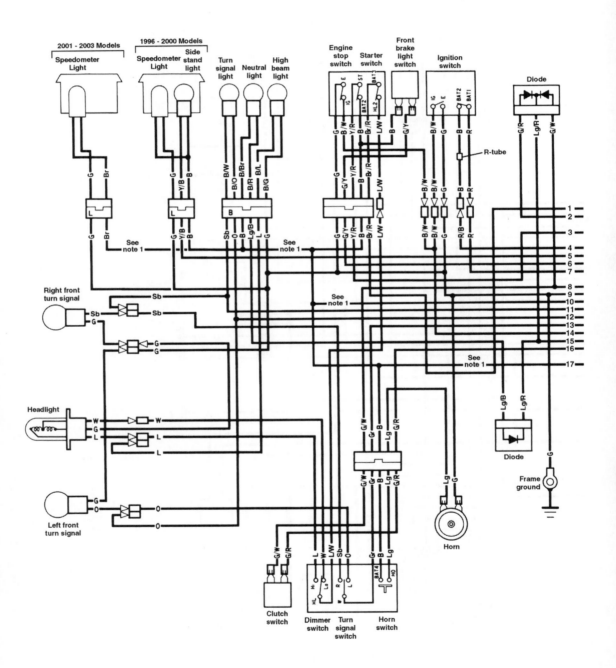

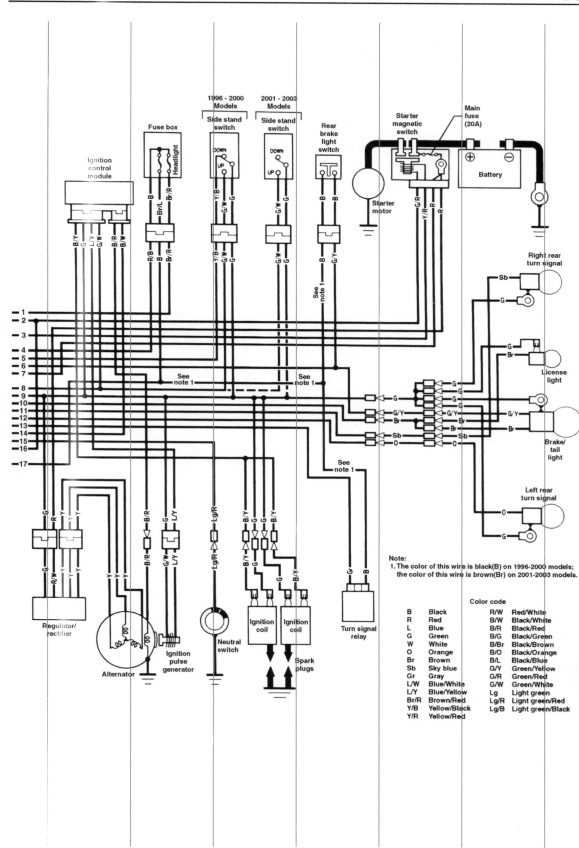

Note:
1. The color of this wire is black(B) on 1996-2000 models; the color of this wire is brown(Br) on 2001-2003 models.

Color code			
B	Black	R/W	Red/White
R	Red	B/W	Black/White
L	Blue	B/R	Black/Red
G	Green	B/G	Black/Green
W	White	B/Br	Black/Brown
O	Orange	B/O	Black/Orange
Br	Brown	B/L	Black/Blue
Sb	Sky blue	G/Y	Green/Yellow
Gr	Gray	G/R	Green/Red
L/W	Blue/White	G/W	Green/White
L/Y	Blue/Yellow	Lg	Light green
Br/R	Brown/Red	Lg/R	Light green/Red
Y/B	Yellow/Black	Lg/B	Light green/Black
Y/R	Yellow/Red		

14

NOTES

NOTES

NOTES

MAINTENANCE LOG

Date	Miles	Type of Service

BMW

M308	500 & 600cc Twins, 55-69
M309	F650, 1994-2000
M500-3	BMW K-Series, 85-97
M501	K1200RS, GT & LT, 98-05
M502-3	BMW R50/5-R100GS PD, 70-96
M503-3	R850, R1100, R1150 and R1200C, 93-05

HARLEY-DAVIDSON

M419	Sportsters, 59-85
M429-5	XL/XLH Sportster, 86-03
M427-1	XL Sportster, 04-06
M418	Panheads, 48-65
M420	Shovelheads,66-84
M421-3	FLS/FXS Evolution,84-99
M423-2	FLS/FXS Twin Cam, 00-05
M422-3	FLH/FLT/FXR Evolution, 84-98
M430-4	FLH/FLT Twin Cam, 99-05
M424-2	FXD Evolution, 91-98
M425-3	FXD Twin Cam, 99-05
M426	VRSC Series, 02-07

HONDA

ATVs

M316	Odyssey FL250, 77-84
M311	ATC, TRX & Fourtrax 70-125, 70-87
M433	Fourtrax 90, 93-00
M326	ATC185 & 200, 80-86
M347	ATC200X & Fourtrax 200SX, 86-88
M455	ATC250 & Fourtrax 200/ 250, 84-87
M342	ATC250R, 81-84
M348	TRX250R/Fourtrax 250R & ATC250R, 85-89
M456-3	TRX250X 87-92; TRX300EX 93-04
M215	TRX250EX, 01-05
M446-3	TRX250 Recon & Recon ES, 97-07
M346-3	TRX300/Fourtrax 300 & TRX300FW/Fourtrax 4x4, 88-00
M200-2	TRX350 Rancher, 00-06
M459-3	TRX400 Foreman 95-03
M454-3	TRX400EX 99-05
M205	TRX450 Foreman, 98-04
M210	TRX500 Rubicon, 01-04

Singles

M310-13	50-110cc OHC Singles, 65-99
M319-2	XR50R, CRF50F, XR70R & CRF70F, 97-05
M315	100-350cc OHC, 69-82
M317	125-250cc Elsinore, 73-80
M442	CR60-125R Pro-Link, 81-88
M431-2	CR80R, 89-95, CR125R, 89-91
M435	CR80R, 96-02
M457-2	CR125R & CR250R, 92-97
M464	CR125R, 1998-2002
M443	CR250R-500R Pro-Link, 81-87
M432-3	CR250R, 88-91 & CR500R, 88-01
M437	CR250R, 97-01
M352	CRF250R, CRF250X, CRF450R & CRF450X, 02-05
M312-13	XL/XR75-100, 75-03
M318-4	XL/XR/TLR 125-200, 79-03
M328-4	XL/XR250, 78-00; XL/XR350R 83-85; XR200R, 84-85; XR250L, 91-96
M320-2	XR400R, 96-04
M339-8	XL/XR 500-600, 79-90
M221	XR600R & XR650L, 91-07
M225	XR650R, 00-07

Twins

M321	125-200cc Twins, 65-78
M322	250-350cc Twins, 64-74
M323	250-360cc Twins, 74-77
M324-5	Twinstar, Rebel 250 & Nighthawk 250, 78-03
M334	400-450cc Twins, 78-87
M333	450 & 500cc Twins, 65-76
M335	CX & GL500/650, 78-83
M344	VT500, 83-88
M313	VT700 & 750, 83-87
M314-3	VT750 Shadow Chain Drive, 98-06
M440	VT1100C Shadow, 85-96
M460-4	VT1100 Series, 95-07
M230	VTX1800 Series, 02-08

Fours

M332	CB350-550, SOHC, 71-78
M345	CB550 & 650, 83-85
M336	CB650,79-82
M341	CB750 SOHC, 69-78
M337	CB750 DOHC, 79-82
M436	CB750 Nighthawk, 91-93 & 95-99
M325	CB900, 1000 & 1100, 80-83
M439	600 Hurricane, 87-90
M441-2	CBR600F2 & F3, 91-98
M445-2	CBR600F4, 99-06
M220	CBR600RR, 03-06
M434-2	CBR900RR Fireblade, 93-99
M329	500cc V-Fours, 64-86
M438	VFR800 Interceptor, 98-00
M349	700-1000 Interceptor, 83-85
M458-2	VFR700F-750F, 86-97
M327	700-1100cc V-Fours, 82-88
M340	GL1000 & 1100, 75-83
M504	GL1200, 84-87
M508	ST1100/Pan European, 90-02

Sixes

M505	GL1500 Gold Wing, 88-92
M506-2	GL1500 Gold Wing, 93-00
M507-2	GL1800 Gold Wing, 01-05
M462-2	GL1500C Valkyrie, 97-03

KAWASAKI

ATVs

M465-2	Bayou KLF220 & KLF250, 88-03
M466-4	Bayou KLF300, 86-04
M467	Bayou KLF400, 93-99
M470	Lakota KEF300, 95-99
M385-2	Mojave KSF250, 87-04

Singles

M350-9	80-350cc Rotary Valve, 66-01
M444-2	KX60, 83-02; KX80 83-90
M448	KX80/85/100, 89-03
M351	KDX200, 83-88
M447-3	KX125 & KX250, 82-91 KX500, 83-04
M472-2	KX125, 92-00
M473-2	KX250, 92-00
M474-3	KLR650, 87-07

Twins

M355	KZ400, KZ/Z440, EN450 & EN500, 74-95
M360-3	EX500, GPZ500S, Ninja 500 R, 87-02
M356-5	Vulcan 700 & 750, 85-06
M354-3	Vulcan 800 & Vulcan 800 Classic, 95-05
M357-2	Vulcan 1500, 87-99
M471-3	Vulcan 1500 Series, 96-08

Fours

M449	KZ500/550 & ZX550, 79-85
M450	KZ, Z & ZX750, 80-85
M358	KZ650, 77-83
M359-3	Z & KZ 900-1000cc, 73-81
M451-3	KZ, ZX & ZN 1000 &1100cc, 81-02
M452-3	ZX500 & Ninja ZX600, 85-97
M468-2	Ninja ZX-6, 90-04
M469	Ninja ZX-7, 91-98
M453-3	Ninja ZX900, ZX1000 & ZX1100, 84-01
M409	Concours, 86-04

POLARIS

ATVs

M496	3-, 4- and 6-Wheel Models w/250-425cc Engines, 85-95
M362-2	Magnum and Big Boss, 96-99
M363	Scrambler 500 4X4, 97-00
M365-3	Sportsman/Xplorer, 96-08

SUZUKI

ATVs

M381	ALT/LT 125 & 185, 83-87
M475	LT230 & LT250, 85-90
M380-2	LT250R Quad Racer, 85-92
M270	LT-Z400, 03-07
M343	LTF500F Quadrunner, 98-00
M483-2	King Quad/ Quad Runner 250, 87-98

Singles

M371	RM50-400 Twin Shock, 75-81
M369	125-400cc 64-81
M379	RM125-500 Single Shock, 81-88
M476	DR250-350, 90-94
M477-2	DR-Z400, 00-08
M384-4	LS650 Savage/S40, 86-07
M386	RM80-250, 89-95
M400	RM125, 96-00
M401	RM250, 96-02

Twins

M372	GS400-450 Chain Drive, 77-87
M481-5	VS700-800 Intruder, 85-07
M260	Volusia/Boulevard C50, 01-06
M482-3	VS1400 Intruder, 87-07
M261	1500 Intruder/C90, 98-07
M484-3	GS500E Twins, 89-02
M361	SV650, 1999-2002

Triple

M368	GT380, GT550 & GT750, 72-77

Fours

M373	GS550, 77-86
M364	GS650, 81-83
M370	GS750, 77-82
M376	GS850-1100 Shaft Drive, 79-84
M378	GS1100 Chain Drive, 80-81
M383-3	Katana 600, 88-96 GSX-R750-1100, 86-87
M331	GSX-R600, 97-00
M264	GSX-R600, 01-05
M478-2	GSX-R750, 88-92 GSX750F Katana, 89-96
M485	GSX-R750, 96-99
M377	GSX-R1000, 01-04
M266	GSX-R1000, 05-06
M265	GSX1300R Hayabusa, 99-07
M338	Bandit 600, 95-00
M353	GSF1200 Bandit, 96-03

YAMAHA

ATVs

M499-2	YFM80, 85-88 & 92-08
M394	YTM200, 250 & YFM200, 83-86
M488-5	Blaster, 88-05
M489-2	Timberwolf, 89-00
M487-5	Warrior, 87-04
M486-6	Banshee, 87-06
M490-3	Moto-4 & Big Bear, 87-04
M493	Kodiak, 93-98
M280-2	Raptor 660R, 01-05
M285	Grizzly 660, 02-07

Singles

M492-2	PW50 & PW80, BW80 Big Wheel 80, 81-02
M410	80-175 Piston Port, 68-76
M415	250-400 Piston Port, 68-76
M412	DT & MX 100-400, 77-83
M414	IT125-490, 76-86
M393	YZ50-80 Monoshock, 78-90
M413	YZ100-490 Monoshock, 76-84
M390	YZ125-250, 85-87 YZ490, 85-90
M391	YZ125-250, 88-93 & WR250Z, 91-93
M497-2	YZ125, 94-01
M498	YZ250, 94-98 WR250Z, 94-97
M406	YZ250F & WR250F, 01-03
M491-2	YZ400F, YZ426F, WR400F WR426F, 98-02
M417	XT125-250, 80-84
M480-3	XT/TT 350, 85-00
M405	XT/TT 500, 76-81
M416	XT/TT 600, 83-89

Twins

M403	XS1, XS2, XS650 & TX650, 70-82
M395-10	XV535-1100 Virago, 81-03
M495-5	V-Star 650, 98-07
M281-3	V-Star 1100, 99-07
M282	Road Star, 99-05

Triple

M404	XS750 & XS850, 77-81

Fours

M387	XJ550, XJ600 & FJ600, 81-92
M494	XJ600 Seca II/Diversion, 92-98
M388	YX600 Radian & FZ600, 86-90
M396	FZR600, 89-93
M392	FZ700-750 & Fazer, 85-87
M411	XS1100, 78-81
M397	FJ1100 & 1200, 84-93
M375	V-Max, 85-03
M374	Royal Star, 96-03
M461	YZF-R6, 99-04
M398	YZF-R1, 98-03
M399	FZ1, 01-05

VINTAGE MOTORCYCLES

Clymer® Collection Series

M330	Vintage British Street Bikes, BSA, 500–600cc Unit Twins; Norton, 750 & 850cc Commandos; Triumph, 500-750cc Twins
M300	Vintage Dirt Bikes, V. 1 Bultaco, 125-370cc Singles; Montesa, 123-360cc Singles; Ossa, 125-250cc Singles
M305	Vintage Japanese Street Bikes Honda, 250 & 305cc Twins; Kawasaki, 250-750cc Triples; Kawasaki, 900 & 1000cc Fours